THE UPPER ROOM

Disciplines

2014

UPPER
ROOM BOOKS®
NASHVILLE

An Outline for Small-Group Use of Disciplines

Here is a simple plan for a one-hour, weekly group meeting based on reading *Disciplines*. One person may act as convener every week, or the role can rotate among group members. You may want to light a white Christ candle each week to signal the beginning of your time together.

Opening

Convener: Let us come into the presence of God.
Others: Lord Jesus Christ, thank you for being with us. Let us hear your word to us as we speak to one another.

Scripture

Convener reads the scripture suggested for that day in *Disciplines*. After a one- or two-minute silence, convener asks: What did you hear God saying to you in this passage? What response does this call for? (Group members respond in turn or as led.)

Reflection

• What scripture passage(s) and meditation(s) from this week was (were) particularly meaningful for you? Why? (Group members respond in turn or as led.)
• What actions were you nudged to take in response to the week's meditations? (Group members respond in turn or as led.)
• Where were you challenged in your discipleship this week? How did you respond to the challenge? (Group members respond in turn or as led.)

Praying Together

Convener says: Based on today's discussion, what people and situations do you want us to pray for now and in the coming week? Convener or other volunteer then prays about the concerns named.

Departing

Convener says: Let us go in peace to serve God and our neighbors in all that we do.

Adapted from *The Upper Room* daily devotional guide, January–February 2001. © 2000 The Upper Room. Used by permission.

CONTENTS

FOREWORD

The old leather book on my grandmother's nightstand fascinated me. Worn thin at the edges and along the creases of the spine, tan hide showed through what had once been a soft black cover embossed with shiny gold lines and letters. Before I was old enough to know it was a Bible, I knew it was a book that my grandmother treasured. I knew it was a book that she picked up every night and read in the dim lamplight of her bedroom. I knew this because she let me sleep in her room when I was a little girl, and I watched her as I snuggled to sleep under a quilt on my little cot set up at the foot of her bed.

I never thought to ask my grandmother about that nightly practice of reading scripture before bedtime. I do not know who taught her to do so or why she had settled on reading at night instead of reading in the morning. My imagination fills in some of the answers to these questions now, but what I value most is the cherished image in my memory of my grandmother in that soft light—Bible in her lap and glasses on her nose as she turned to God's word at the close of the day.

Since those childhood years, I too have found a rhythm of reading and living with scripture. Morning has become my preferred devotional time, perhaps in part because this was when my mother could be found each day in her favorite reading chair as morning light streamed across the pages of her Bible. But others have influenced my spiritual life and practice—teachers, friends, pastors, artists, and authors. All have helped guide me into the hope-sustaining word of God.

I include the contributors to *Disciplines* in this circle of influence on my spiritual life. The daily and weekly insights and reflections by the authors, poets, pastors, and spiritual guides provide food for thought and nourishment for spirit. Each year the varied voices and traditions represented through the pages of this faithful resource always press me to expand my perspective and heart around how God's word is alive in the world—a world for which God created us and for which God calls us to care. Whether I spend time alone with God in the early morning of a day or in an afternoon conversation with others to plan for worship, the writers of *Disciplines* serve as companions in faith and faithfulness for me.

So as you and I prepare to join with the contributors of this volume of *Disciplines*, let us do so with a holy anticipation that in these pages we will encounter a diverse community of thoughtful Christian writers and theologians who guide us toward a deeper relationship with the God who is always with us, night and day. May we each explore, excavate, and expand the possible blessings that come through the spiritual discipline of reading and reflecting on scripture.

And finally, may we each look for a time and space, a posture and attitude, from which we learn to attend to God's life-giving light breaking through to us from the grace-filled word of God.

—PAMELA C. HAWKINS

Editor's Note

Each week opens with a Scripture Overview and Questions and Thoughts for Reflection—for both group and personal use. The overview explores the ties among the several scripture passages for each week. Then, four questions or thoughts for reflection help stir our minds toward greater understanding of God's word.

Time and Eternity

JANUARY 1-5, 2014 • MELISSA TIDWELL

SCRIPTURE OVERVIEW: These scriptures chosen to mark the new year give us a panorama of perspectives, from Ecclesiastes as a poetic musing on how life is measured out in seasons, to the vision in Revelation of what we commonly consider the end of time itself. Psalm 8 asks what the role is for humans in God's magnificent creation, and Matthew 25 gives us a sobering criterion for how that role might be judged. At the core of all these scriptures is a strong sense of God's presence, loving steadfastness in which we can rest.

QUESTIONS AND THOUGHTS FOR REFLECTION

- Read Ecclesiastes 3:1-13. With what season mentioned in this passage do you most identify your life right now? A time for sowing or for reaping? a time for silence or speech? How have you discerned changes in seasons of your life?
- Read Revelation 21:1-6. What scripture passages do you turn to for comfort and reassurance? How is their meaning like or different from this passage in Revelation?
- Read Psalm 8. What do you understand the word *dominion* to mean in this passage? Where do you exercise dominion in your role at home, at work, or in the community?
- Read Matthew 2:1-12. What questions is your spiritual journey leading you to ask and live out? Where have those questions been answered through dreams or answers to prayer? through relationships? through events?

Former editor, *Alive Now* magazine; currently a student at Columbia Theological, Decatur, Georgia

NEW YEAR'S DAY

A new year offers the gift of time. How will the next twelve months unfold? We may experience times of accomplishment and times of failure. A medical concern, a family sorrow, or a crisis may arise. And there will be occasions for rejoicing—a new child in the family, a new work responsibility, or an old friend who surfaces on Facebook. All our seasons, all our days, bring us measures of hope and happiness, challenge and change.

The writer of Ecclesiastes, known as the Preacher, speaks with poetic power about the gifts and demands of time. The lyrical evocation of this well-loved passage stands in contrast to the other well-known passage of this book, which sighs with a world-weary fatalism that asserts that most of our human efforts amount to nothing more than chasing after wind. Work and joy are the two poles that determine mortal existence, and they are both deemed to be good but fleeting. And while this response to experience may seem cynical or even faithless, a close reading shows that the Preacher's ultimate belief rests in God's sovereignty. God, beyond worry or toil or even time itself, has given us time so that we might begin to comprehend how God stands both in and beyond time, always the same and always new.

As this year begins, you might consider how to approach the coming year as an opportunity for spiritual growth. Can you learn to be mindfully present in the moment, receptive to grace, willing to learn and to continue the powerful process of transformation? What seeds that were planted long ago might bear fruit? What blessing of God's gifts might you be ready to live into? As the days unfold, may you be strengthened by the sense of God's presence in all things that measure our days.

Let us gratefully receive our days as your gift, God of all our years, and return that gift to you in work and joy, prayer and action, wisdom and faith. Amen.

Human life is brief and when compared to God, we are tiny and weak. Yet God knows us, cares for us, and has given us responsibility to care for one another and for the earth. Between these two realities we make daily choices that build a life.

Psalm 8 alternates words of praise for God's majesty with words that describe humans as crowned with glory and honor. God's work of creation mirrors God's power. Compared to this power, humans are pretty puny. And yet, God has chosen us for a special role, placed us just a little lower than the angels, and given us dominion over the earth.

The language of dominion—the idea that God has given humans the earth as a realm to rule—is a double-edged sword. It certainly gives us a significant role to play, a purpose, a chance to exercise our gifts in concert with God's design. On the other edge, dominion can become an ugly justification for waste, greed, and brutish behavior.

If we let either edge control us entirely, we can do damage to ourselves and others. We can grow arrogant and destructive if we become enamored of our power. Or we can check out entirely, wallow in our weakness, and fail to do our part. Both are distortions. Our spiritual life is the regulator that keeps us in balance, that makes dominion a task of stewardship, that makes relationship the source of accountability and renewal.

Psalm 8 begins and ends with the same line, a celebration of God's power. It reminds us that God has the first and the last word in the work of creation. God invites us to participate in a joyful call and a sobering charge, in which we can find a life's work and an eternal purpose.

Majestic is your name in all the earth, God our sovereign. May our lives be hymns of praise that reflect your good gifts. Amen.

When I read this passage, I find myself trying to maneuver a way around the hard words of this teaching. *How many times do you have to recognize Jesus among the poor?* I wonder. *Can you still be a sheep if you just did it once? Or a few times?* I become like the lawyer who asks Jesus what a person has to do to inherit eternal life. When Jesus tells him to love God and neighbor, the lawyer asks, "But who is my neighbor?"

Some commentators support the lawyer in me by suggesting that the judgment in this passage is not of Christians but of the other nations of the world, those without faith. But I think that analysis attempts to fudge on the larger point of this passage. These verses convey a message about how we want to be found living when Jesus returns. So we take this teaching at face value as a call from Jesus to act with compassion toward those in need of our care. Each opportunity we have to offer food to the hungry provides an occasion to align ourselves with Christ's total solidarity with the poor, the prisoner, the homeless, the sick. Each missed opportunity underscores our rejection of Christ.

Our shock and dismay at the idea of rejecting Jesus brings us to another level on which we might consider this passage. The truth is, we can't help every homeless person we meet, can't visit all the sick and imprisoned—even if we make it our full-time job. So we are, by one standard, goats. And maybe it's helpful to understand that we can't enter the kingdom as righteous based only on our own striving. We need grace and depend on God for that grace just as the hungry depend on us for food. So we live in gratitude for the grace we have received, and our efforts to the poor come not only from a sense of obligation but from a sense of thanksgiving.

Bread of heaven, feed us and strengthen in us the will to feed others. Let us see your face in the face of the hungry, and serve you with generosity and gladness. Amen.

The book of Revelation has acquired a reputation at the hands of unscrupulous interpreters who have used it to make people fearful, to predict political upheaval, or to forecast doom. The word *apocalyptic* gets thrown around as a descriptor of a final cataclysmic upheaval. But *apocalypse* comes from the Greek word meaning "revelation." When all is revealed, when we see clearly where God has been at work all along and toward what purpose, we well might tremble at what will be revealed. But we need not fear.

Recently, in a theological conversation, I referred to God's *providence*. My conversation partner asked me to define that term. On my first attempt, I fumbled with some abstract mishmash about God's power through creation working toward the ultimate purpose of bringing about the good. Then I remembered the powerful quote from Martin Luther King Jr., who said, "The arc of the moral universe is long, but it bends towards justice."

Revelation unfolds a series of coded images as responses to the political and social realities of the time of its writing. But at the core of the symbolic and impressionistic imagery of this book is a vision of God's providence, of history coming to the end of one era with the promise of a new heaven and a new earth, a promise that pain will be no more. Even death will have no power as God dwells among us. The arc of time is long, and we have no way of knowing exactly where to place ourselves on its curving progress. But we can know that it bends towards justice, and that God—the Alpha and Omega—is making all things new.

Holy One, you are the God of the mountains and the trumpet blast, of power and strength. And yet you have promised to come tenderly to wipe away every tear. Help us trust in both your mercy and your might and to look to the future with hope that your reality will be revealed. Amen.

SUNDAY, JANUARY 5 ~ *Read Matthew 2:1-12*

EPIPHANY SUNDAY

The word *theophany* refers to a human encounter with the divine. Moses' encounter with the burning bush is the example that may come first to mind.

The magi have a mysterious star, the arduous journey, their discovery of the infant Jesus, all of which is also a theophany. But the Western Christian tradition that developed around this story has tended to describe it as an *epiphany*, from the Greek word meaning "manifestation." In current usage, the word *epiphany* has come to mean "insight" or "realization." The magi represent our seeking and finding, the continual unfolding of God's presence for us and call to us.

The difference between a theophany and an epiphany might come in the form of the divine in the revelation. In much of the Bible, these sorts of experiences are marked off by fire, earthquake, by visions and voices; the Epiphany story is not entirely different. But in classic theophanies, the God that is revealed in the experience remains a voice or a vision, a powerful transcendent force that is not of this world. What is revealed in the house over which the star comes to rest is not a disembodied voice but a physical manifestation, the Word become flesh in Jesus.

In our spiritual journeys, we frequently set out with a huge question in mind, a grand vision in which we want to know one big thing—the will of God or the meaning of a star. And what we frequently find made manifest is something else in answer, something real and embodied: human beings to love and serve who give us insights into the real nature of this journey and the different road we must take to get home.

God of stars and wanderers, guide us as we seek insight and purpose, to see your face revealed and your kingdom realized. Amen.

God Has No Favorites

JANUARY 6-12, 2014 • MARY A. AVRAM

SCRIPTURE OVERVIEW: Many will read the Isaiah text and identify the servant with Jesus, the one God enables to do the work of justice and transformation. The psalm announces the glory of God, a king powerful over the turbulence of nature and whose voice is a transcendent revelation. Matthew's story of Jesus' baptism joins the themes of servant and king. The baptism inaugurates Jesus' ministry in which he proclaims God's righteousness. Peter's speech in Acts reminds us that Jesus' baptism carries with it the promise of baptism in the Spirit.

QUESTIONS AND THOUGHTS FOR REFLECTION

- Read Psalm 29 several times both silently and aloud. What emotions does the psalm raise in you? What in the psalm causes you to feel as you do? How might you use these emotions to the praise and glory of God?
- Read Isaiah 42:1-9. What do these verses reveal to you about the character of God? Prayerfully think about a time in your life when the support and tender care of God were there for you whether or not you knew it at the time.
- Read Matthew 3:13-17. How might you and your faith community give greater witness to God's love for everyone and affirm that Jesus is Lord of all?
- Read Acts 10:34-43. What is your understanding of the term *personal experience*? Where and how have you "seen" God? What personal testimony about God can you give to others?

Retired spiritual director, School of Theology, University of the South, Sewanee, Tennessee; spiritual guide, The Academy for Spiritual Formation and the Three-Year Covenant Community; elder, St. Simons Island Presbyterian Church, St. Simons Island, Georgia

MONDAY, JANUARY 6 ~ *Read Psalm 29*

The book of Psalms is the prayer book of the Bible and today's psalm is noted as a hymn of David. Some Bible versions refer to this psalm as The Voice of God in a Great Storm, for it calls us to remember that Yahweh is Lord of all—and Yahweh speaks! In verses 3-9, all the verses but two begin with the words: *The voice of the LORD.* This God of glory and power now manifests in acts of strength. The voice of the Lord is heard in thunder and flames of fire. This voice controls the waters and "strips the forest bare." The voice of the Lord is heard and seen in all creation. Watch! Listen!

On the night of Jesus' birth, the heavens broke open and angel-song from throngs of the heavenly host rang forth on earth, "Glory to God in the highest heaven, and on earth peace among those whom [God] favors" (Luke 2:14). It is to this magnitude of praising and glorifying God that David, the sweet singer of psalms, called the people of God then and calls us now. Glory and praise are due the Lord, and we worship the Lord in the splendor of the Lord's holiness, not in the reflected shards of glory we call our own.

We worship a God who is Lord of the storms, and, therefore, Lord of life. This God exercises power over life's turbulent aspects. This strong and blessed God offers the attributes of strength and blessing to the people. Our response is, "Glory!" Our lives offer daily opportunities to give praise and glory to God. Three choices lie before us: ignore the opportunity, take the praise and glory for ourselves, offer the praise and glory to God with open hands and grateful heart. How will you choose?

Thine, Lord, is the kingdom, the power, and the glory forever. Amen.

God Has No Favorites

These four verses open the first of four poems in Isaiah called the Servant Songs. These songs raise questions about the identity of "my servant" because the prophet uses the term in reference to the nation of Israel *and* an individual. While Christians often ascribe these words of prophetic utterance to the Spirit-filling work of Jesus Christ, the "servant" of God is one who does the transforming work of God in the world.

Three times in these four verses God speaks about justice. In faithfulness the servant of the Lord will bring forth justice to the nations. The islands and coastlands, the faraway places, await the hope of God's teaching. We are reminded again that Yahweh is God of all.

Powered by God's Spirit, the servant brings the gentle justice of God. The servant will honor the weak but faithfully establish justice in the earth, staying steadily on course. The imagery in verse 3 stirs my heart, and I confess that at times in my life I have felt like a "bruised reed" that can no longer stand by itself or a "dimly burning wick" that is about to go out and leave only darkness. In these times when my only prayer is "help!" I try to remember Isaiah 42:3 and envision the support of the servant who walks alongside me. The servant cups my weak flame until it gets a good start and burns well. My prayer of "help!" becomes transformed into "thank you!" Our God fosters loving care for weak vessels.

Holy and Gracious One, thank you for life and for your presence in the midst of all of life—no matter what. Amen.

God, the Lord, is speaking!—Creator of the heavens and the earth, who gives breath and spirit to those who walk upon it. Pay attention! Hear the calling! Hear, Israel, what the Lord God has done *for* you and will do *through* you. You have been given as a covenant to the people. To the nations you are light, to the blind you bring sight, to the prisoners of darkness you bring liberation.

Look and see! The first prophecies have come to pass. These, now, are new things that God the Lord is foretelling. They will "spring forth" says God. God dispatches a servant to fulfill old promises: "the former things have come to pass."

Be aware that God, the Lord of all, brings new things into being! As Christians, we who affirm the servant who completed the former promises acknowledge the One who comes to fulfill the "new things" of the latter days. For Christians, that servant is Jesus Christ. We recall that Jesus "on the night when he was betrayed took a loaf of bread, and when he had given thanks, he broke it and said, 'This is my body that is for you.'. . . He took the cup also, after supper, saying, 'This cup is the new covenant in my blood. Do this . . . in remembrance of me'" (1 Cor. 11:23-25).

Jesus, the light of the world. Jesus who gave sight to the blind. Jesus who raised the dead from their prisons of darkness. Jesus who fulfilled the law and the prophets. Jesus, broken bread and poured-out wine, a new covenant of grace and love for all.

Take a piece of torn bread and a small glass of grape juice. Lay them out before you. Lean back into God's presence and prayerfully envision Jesus offering them to you with his words of the new covenant in his body broken and blood shed for you and for all. Give thanks!

Jesus comes to John for baptism. He does not dispute John's claim that John needs to be baptized by him. Jesus simply replies, "Let it be so now; it is proper for us in this way to fulfill *all* righteousness" (emphasis added). John consents, and the deed is done.

Jesus comes as obedient child of God and sets the example for behavior. He and the servant of Isaiah bring justice and righteousness. In fulfilling *all* righteousness, Jesus sets before us the prototype for *our* lives, for *all* people.

Sometimes, as I walk on the beach of the island where I live, I find myself an unwitting part of a baptismal service. I don't know the people, don't know the church denomination, but I participate and acknowledge that we are brothers and sisters in Christ. "In the one Spirit we were all baptized into one body" (1 Cor. 12:13). In the beach services, the members gathered clap their hands, sing "Alleluia," and rejoice together. If I listen closely, I believe I hear the angels in heaven rejoicing too. This is a beloved moment in the life of the church and for every person involved.

Do you know when you were baptized? Where? How? Your age? Was there a celebration? Knowing these aspects will not make your baptism better, nor will it make the inward grace stronger, for this is God's work. But it could enliven you for the outward and visible sign: the transformative work of God in the world—the ushering in of *all* righteousness.

At the end of the Gospel of Matthew, Jesus commands his disciples to go out and make disciples of all nations and baptize them in the name of the Father, the Son, and the Holy Spirit. He says to them, "I am with you always, to the end of the age" (Matt. 29:20). Yes!

God, may I live daily remembering my baptism, in the name of the Father, the Son, and the Holy Spirit. Alleluia! Amen.

John baptizes Jesus, and as he comes up out of the water still dripping with the Jordan River, the heavens open and he sees the Spirit of God descending toward him like a dove.

The Spirit of God alights upon him as a heavenly voice announces from heaven, "This is my Son, the Beloved, with whom I am well pleased." The revelation to the crowd involves the action of the Father, the Son, and the Holy Spirit. The voice does not address Jesus directly; the announcement is not for Jesus' benefit but for ours.

These words from Matthew above launch Jesus into the wilderness where the Spirit leads him. The three synoptic Gospels—Matthew, Mark, and Luke—identify Jesus' baptism and the epiphany followed by his forty-day fast and temptation in the desert as the precursor to his public ministry. Jesus' "time" has come, and he begins to preach saying, "Repent, for the kingdom of heaven has come near" (Matt. 3:2; 4:17). He goes through all Judea "doing good and healing . . . , for God was with him" (Acts 10:38).

God's claim on Jesus' life is confirmed for us in God's naming him "the Beloved"; the obedience of Jesus' life confirms the manner in which Christ-followers are to live. Do you understand yourself to be God's beloved? How has that understanding shaped your living?

"This is [*fill in your name*], the Beloved, with whom I am well pleased." Who has spoken these words to you? When have you spoken them to another? May the power of this affirmation and confirmation lead you into the world in obedience.

Prayerfully reflect on your daily life and ask God to increase in you the grace of obedience in following Jesus.

Through a series of God-directed events described earlier in chapter 10, we find Simon Peter in Caesarea at the home of Cornelius, a Gentile and an officer in the Roman army. Cornelius gathers all his family, household, and friends and waits expectantly for Peter's arrival. Peter comes speaking of the good news of peace through Jesus Christ, who is Lord of *all*. Cornelius and his entire household believe and are baptized.

Historically, God's word came to and through Israel, but it was destined for the whole world and its time has come. Peter opens his sermon by speaking what he acknowledges with his mind: "I truly understand that God shows no partiality, but in every nation anyone who fears him and does what is right is acceptable to him." After the mass baptism at the home of Cornelius, Peter moves from mind affirmation to an assimilation into his emotions and thoughts. Clearly, Peter has come to a new understanding of God's will in his time. Despite his initial inability even to figure out his vision, he learns God's will and follows. "God has shown me," he states. God serves as the source of Peter's revelation.

Peter speaks to Cornelius and those gathered not as one who knows *about* Jesus but as an eyewitness to all that Jesus has done. And still God teaches Peter: Do not call anyone common or unclean for God shows no partiality; God loves everyone. Peter, the witness and eyewitness bears personal testimony of personal experience of God—a movement from head to heart.

What have you experienced and what do you know of God that you can pass on to others in words and actions? How can you express God's lack of favorites?

SUNDAY, JANUARY 12 ~ *Read Acts 10:37-43*

BAPTISM OF THE LORD SUNDAY

In these verses, which conclude Peter's first preaching of the gospel to Gentiles, God offers comfort, strength, promise, and challenge to us today. Those "chosen by God as witnesses" are charged to preach, to testify, to bear witness that Jesus of Nazareth is God's appointed and anointed One. He is judge of the living and the dead. Peter goes as a witness to Cornelius, and the events at that home make him a witness yet again.

God's will and revelation continue to unfold in Peter's life and in the lives of those to whom he witnesses. In the power of the Holy Spirit he—we—learn and live these truths "by heart." We speak of them when the opportunity is given and from the abundance of the heart that the mouth speaks (Matt. 12:34).

In our baptism we receive a new life and a new name. We share a common bloodline with all the baptized, the shed blood of our Lord and Savior, Jesus Christ. We share a common table spread with the bread and cup of Holy Communion with our Lord God and one another. We share a common calling from God to bear witness in the entirety of our lives that Jesus is Lord of all and that God loves everyone with everlasting, unmerited grace and love. We know ourselves and others to be the Beloved.

Thank you, Lord Jesus Christ, for your peace and forgiveness and for making me new in you. Thank you for the many Christ-bearing witnesses you bring into my life and heart. In your Spirit, Holy One, may I bear the light and love of Christ to others. Amen.

The Identity and Mission of God's People

JANUARY 13–19, 2014 • CARL S. HOFMANN

SCRIPTURE OVERVIEW: The theme of God's calling all believers to a life of ministry runs through all four of this week's scripture passages. We discover that God's call always requires a response! The Isaiah passage, one of the Servant Songs that point to Jesus, reminds us that God is the one who pursues and calls. The psalmist exemplifies the call to give witness when God shows up and is found to be faithful. In the opening of his first letter to the church in Corinth, Paul reminds us of his own calling and then goes on to emphasize that all are called by God and set apart for ministry. And in John's Gospel, we receive an example of testifying to God's presence in our lives and the important calling of bringing others to Jesus.

QUESTIONS AND THOUGHTS FOR REFLECTION

- Read Isaiah 49:1-7. In what ways can we today creatively shine forth Christ's light to the world?
- Read Psalm 40:1-11. Think back on a time when you felt like you were in "the desolate pit, . . . the miry bog." How did this affect the way you prayed? How did God respond to your prayer?
- Read 1 Corinthians 1:1-9. What roles, accomplishments, achievements, or degrees seem to define you? How does your identity in Christ challenge these?
- Read John 1:29-42. John pointed people to Jesus. How are you pointing people to Jesus? If you find this task hard, what steps can you take to become more at ease in this area?

Associate pastor in the area of spiritual formation and discipleship, First Presbyterian Church, Boulder, Colorado

Ilive in the Rocky Mountain Front Range of Colorado. As I drive over a mesa into work each morning, the rising sun illumines the Boulder Flatirons, the foothills, and the Continental Divide to the west. In the right light, I see the layering of these geographic features; I appreciate the depth of this stunning profile. Foreground, middle-ground, background—what majesty!

I've come to view Old Testament prophecy similarly. When the prophet receives a word from the Lord, there's usually a foreground: an immediate application in that specific time and place. The Lord comforts and challenges Israel with a word for its historic situation. It's the Flatiron formation in my vista—vivid, immediate, and compelling. In our Isaiah passage, this is God's servant, the prophet, or even Israel personified. He is—Israel is—God's messenger to the world, God's light to the nations.

But then, as we read deeper into the Bible, moving into the New Testament, we watch the fulfillment of Israel's story in Jesus Christ. This is the middle-ground, the Rocky Mountain foothills, in my analogy. In our passage, Isaiah's Servant finds ultimate identity for Christians in Jesus, the one described throughout John's Gospel as "the light of the world" (8:12).

As we press on in the biblical narrative, the story moves even further, this time to the background: Jesus Christ, the Suffering Servant of God, the Light of the World, calls his people to join him in his mission. He sends us out, declaring, "You are the light of the world" (Matt. 5:14). In Christ, we now proclaim God's salvation to the end of the earth. As breathtaking as my morning commute is, the biblical vista is even more stunning: In the right light, we see God's depth of layering, the centrality of God's work in Jesus Christ, the church's challenge to take God's mission to the world.

Lord, thank you for the sweeping story of salvation, for the light of the world Jesus Christ. Amen.

As a young man, following a scary experience with a routine eye exam, I received an unexpected diagnosis of "glaucoma suspect." Glaucoma, a silent disease, can permanently blind us. This diagnosis began my uncomfortable journey to visit optometrists, ophthalmologists, glaucoma and retinal specialists, and a close call with an emergency department. I now manage my disease through eye drops and extensive eye exams. I dread these exams. They involve bright lights, flash photography of my inner eye, and pressing my face into machines that make me dizzy and claustrophobic. Then comes the invasive poking and probing. All of this to manage my elevated eye pressure and ensure that I don't lose peripheral vision and end up going blind. Bright lights. Aggressive searching. The loss of peripheral vision. The threat of blindness.

In the book of Isaiah, in the Lord's hands the prophet is often like an unwelcome probe, uncomfortably examining Israel's spiritual vision, searching out signs of impending blindness. The light of the Lord, shone through the penetrating word delivered through Isaiah, causes a people walking in darkness to recoil, to want to run and hide. The Light searches out signs of spiritual disease, blurred vision, and blindness. The Light, uncomfortable and unwelcome at first, is God's instrument of good.

Spiritual blindness often comes on gradually; it's an insidious creeping killer that can wreck our vision permanently. The routine searching of God's word, the intrusive probing of its light—in the hands of the Great Physician—are instruments of health and healing, of hope and restoration. As God's people, we need these routine eye exams. Without them, we can lose our sight. And without them, we lose our ability to shine God's light to the nations.

God of light, search me and know me. See if there is any wicked way in me, and lead me in the way everlasting. Amen.

Well, I guess there's nothing left to do but pray." Have you ever heard this? Have you ever thought this or said this yourself? Usually, we hear these words when we or those we love are in a dire circumstance and have run out of options. It's often said in a hospital after all medical or surgical means of healing have been tried—and come up short. It's said when someone is lost in the wilderness or facing financial catastrophe. "There's nothing left to do but pray." We say this when there's no plan B, when we've hit a wall in life, or when we're stuck and we don't know what to do.

As some may know, the Chinese word for crisis combines two characters for two words: *danger* and *opportunity*. When we run out of human solutions, we feel vulnerable, afraid, and hopeless. We're in danger. At that point, God can do some of the best work imaginable, for it offers opportunity.

Psalm 40 celebrates God's rescue when all seems lost: "desolate pit," "miry bog"—these words signal grave illness, death, annihilation. There's no plan B; in other words, "There's nothing left to do but pray." Prayer, Psalm 40 shows us, is not a last-ditch effort or a wistful, wishful piety. Prayer is calling on God's ultimate power to deliver. "He inclined to me and heard my cry. He drew me up."

In our extreme need, God can work exceptional deliverance. The psalmist thanks God in the assembly of corporate worship, urging others to share in God's praise, to trust in God's faithfulness, to depend on God's steadfast love. These divine certainties form a foundation that can support us in times of grave illness, a tragic loss, a natural catastrophe.

Lord, teach me to call on you not only when I'm out of options but whenever I face need. Help me depend upon your steadfast love and faithfulness each day. Amen.

Passports, please!" the immigration officer snapped at us, without even bothering to look up. My family and I had been standing over two hours in a lengthy queue of people from around the world. To enter the United Kingdom, we needed an official sign of our identity: a passport.

A passport is a much-coveted item. It opens doors, provides protections, and gives rights and privileges to its citizen-owners. It tells border guards who we are, where we're from, and where we've been. It's our identity.

Or is it? In his epistles, Paul frequently reminds his readers of their true identities. They may be Corinthians, Galatians, or Philippians; but first and foremost, they are the church of God, those "sanctified in Christ Jesus," "called to be saints." This stamp of their true identity cannot be captured in a passport. The call of God in Jesus Christ is the ultimate naturalization process: It lifts us beyond earthly borders, human politics, anything and everything that labels us in a limited, reductionist manner. God's call gave Paul his identity and mission as an apostle of Jesus Christ. God's call on the mixed-up, motley Corinthians gave them a self-understanding that far superseded their geography or nationality.

To follow Jesus Christ, to respond to his call, and to stamp this in our awareness through our baptisms is our ultimate passport. We are Christ-followers first, citizens of the kingdom of God. Jesus defines us—telling us both who and whose we are. He binds us together with brothers and sisters in every time and every place. This challenges all nationalism and prejudice, racism, classism, and denominationalism. Our eternal identity strips away all earthly labels.

Lord, lift up our eyes to see the riches of our true identity in Jesus Christ. When we're tempted to label ourselves and others in earthly categories, show us our unity in Christ. Amen.

As a young child, I was a proud member of the "Clean Plate Club." This meant that I was entitled to dessert only if I ate everything on my dinner plate. My "just desserts" only followed *after* I finished dinner. I was taught early on through chores and allowances, homework and good grades that achievement brought accolades. We all learn this one way or another. "A full day's work for a full day's pay." Much of Western culture is based on work and rewards. If we're not careful, our identities can be forged in this alchemy: We become what we do, and we are what we earn. Before we know it, our titles, diplomas, portfolios, roles, responsibilities, salaries, homes, and possessions begin to define us. We've worked hard to earn them, but they end up owning us.

Grace throws open the shutters of this airless existence. Grace is God's free gift to those burned out on the enslavement of a works-reward existence. "Grace to you and peace from God our Father," says Paul. In other words, rich blessings, free of charge, to you who lay down your exhausted efforts and simply trust in Jesus Christ. Paul thanks God always for this grace given in Jesus, this enrichment without effort, this generous gifting, this faithful strengthening that comes from God's sheer kindness—and not our earnest, anxious striving. Grace challenges our self-sufficiency and self-reliance. Grace tells us to quit clutching onto our discipline and hard work to gain and secure our identity. Grace forces us to lay down the burden of performance and perfectionism. Grace turns our grimaces into grins, as we realize God loves us and embraces us in the work of his Son, Jesus Christ.

In what areas are you striving for reward, even God's reward? How does grace challenge or comfort you? Discuss these things with God.

It's all about you!" My personal calendar system had this slogan emblazoned on its advertising and renewal forms. Presumably, it was meant to attract customers with its promise of customization: Your daily calendar can be tailored to your preferences and your style. "It's all about you!" is fallen humankind's motto and egocentric mantra. My career; my life; my wishes; my needs, ambitions, and aspirations. It's all about me, me at the center of my existence; me as the end-all, be-all of my reality. Me, me, me.

Of course, we never state it this boldly. No, we're much more subtle. Instead, this selfish egoism seeps out as we elbow our way to the front of the line, as we interrupt others and talk above them. It's all about me.

John the Baptizer could easily have fallen into this all-too-human habit. He has a flourishing ministry: Going out of their way, people flock to hear him and hang on his every word. Yet John, by the grace of God, rises above this selfish human tendency. "He must increase, but I must decrease" (John 3:30), John later says of his cousin Jesus. In other words, "It's not about me." John's gift to his contemporaries and scripture's readers is his self-effacement.

In the famous Isenheim altarpiece of the early 1500s, Matthias Grünewald depicts John pointing at Jesus with a long, bony finger. John's main ministry comes in pointing to someone other than himself. John reminds us that true life and peace are found only in Jesus Christ. And, ironically, fullness of identity and a profound sense of self-worth also are found only in Jesus Christ. "It's not about us." That sounds harsh at first, but it is pure gospel.

Lamb of God, forgive me for my self-absorption and pride. Give me the grace of self-forgetfulness as I discover the joy of centering my life on you. Amen.

Rebecca Manley Pippert begins her classic book *Out of the Saltshaker and into the World: Evangelism as a Way of Life* with these words: "Christians and non-Christians have something in common: we're both uptight about evangelism." So true! We in the church have a vague, discomforting awareness that we need to share God's good news in Jesus Christ with others beyond our walls—but we feel too inadequate, insecure, and downright frightened to do anything about it. The first chapter of John's Gospel gives us some insight and help in this confounding challenge of sharing our faith.

John the Baptizer points to Jesus. He makes it all about Jesus and not about himself. That's the first step. We release our obsessions with ourselves—our words, our methods, our adequacy in sharing the gospel. It's not about us; it's about Jesus. Our job is to lift him up and make sure he's clearly depicted through the scripture we share, in the honesty and transparency of our lifestyle. Clarity is the point. Are we pointing clearly to him?

Next, it's about motivating people to "test drive Jesus." The two disciples, after watching John point to Jesus, decide to step out and follow him. They get on the path and move closer to Jesus. They take a few steps to get a better glimpse. As we point to Jesus and inspire other people to consider him, do we make it an "all-or-nothing" proposition? If so, we raise the bar unattainably high. What we need to do is encourage folks to take a step closer, to listen to him a bit more, to move in his general direction and see what happens. "Come and see" is what Jesus says. It's what we need to say too. I like to think of evangelism in concentric circles: Are we helping people move in closer to Jesus, to take a step forward, to come and see?

Lord, make me aware of people I can help point to you. Give me courage, and give me opportunities. Amen.

Let's Go Fishin'!

JANUARY 20–26, 2014 • TERRELL M. MCDANIEL

SCRIPTURE OVERVIEW: In these texts, light does not merely illumine; it brings a changed situation, in which people depressed by the darkness can experience the new day. The psalmist's confession of Yahweh links light with salvation. The Gospel lesson expresses deliverance in terms of the nearness of God's reign, with Jesus overcoming diseases of every sort. Light permits well-being.

In these texts light becomes personalized. The psalm speaks of God as "my light and my salvation." The text from Isaiah refers to a human agent of vindication but at the same time anticipates the coming of the Child who exercises supreme authority and brings an era of endless peace. In Matthew, Jesus acts powerfully in calling disciples and healing the sick, fulfilling the word spoken by Isaiah. Light is a mode of God's presence, especially to those who sit in the region and shadow of death

QUESTIONS AND THOUGHTS FOR REFLECTION

- Read Isaiah 9:1-4. In what ways have you seen movement from darkness into light for yourself personally and in the Christian community?
- Read Psalm 27:1, 4-9. What do you fear right now? How have you experienced God's sheltering you, hiding you, or lifting you up?
- Read 1 Corinthians 1:10-18. What are your greatest vulnerabilities to succumbing to pride or divisiveness? Think first of the areas in which you feel most righteous or competent as a Christian.
- Read Matthew 4:12-23. What does it mean to you to fish for people? How has your understanding changed over the years? What led to those changes?

Clinical and corporate psychologist, Nashville, Tennessee

The Gospel lesson notes an important part of a Christian's personal mission statement: We are to fish for people. John's ministry had emphasized repentance, but Jesus adds new dimensions: teaching, healing, and bringing about the reign of God.

As a young evangelical, I thought "fishing for people" meant getting converts. But it is so much more than that! We aren't simply to preach the good news; we're to enact it. In fishing for people, Jesus wants us to create a boat of shalom, where everyone is known, loved, served, and celebrated. This shalom is a place of healing, restoration, and fulfillment of our potential—all to celebrate God's grace and to invite more people into it. In fact, no one is to be left out! God will search out the stray soul like a lost coin (Luke 15:8-10) and will give everything—everything—to gain the treasure of one individual's presence (Matt. 13:44-45). God wants every last one in the boat. It's our job to invite them in.

But first comes repentance. Like these fishermen, we must leave behind the prejudices and expectations of our occupational and familial worlds to follow Jesus. Those people "we" never liked? Learn to love them. That stubborn trait "we" are known for? Get over it. We must leave behind all those familiar, well-learned, "normal" attitudes and ways of living that simply aren't consistent with God's kingdom. Instead, we must adopt ways that, by the standards of the world, are foolish: loving mercy, living justly, and walking humbly; promoting justice that runs like water; being poor in spirit; loving our enemies and our neighbors as ourselves.

So, would you like to be the good news for someone? Let's go fishin'!

Gracious God, I want to be a disciple. Help me become the kind of person worthy of casting your net for people. Amen.

The new fishers of people got the chance to watch the Master create shalom. But the time came for them to do things on their own. As for us, we have to learn approaches and procedures without such an awesome apprenticeship.

Good United Methodists, appreciating an efficient model, fish for people through five primary means: prayers, presence, gifts, service, and witness. Let's consider the one I believe is the most important, presence.

As a student of psychotherapy, I would learn the methods of a different therapist every semester. I would strive to pursue matters in exactly his or her way. But as I matured, my mentors began to expect me to put all of my experiences together and let them reside in the back of my mind. In the foreground of my awareness, they said, was to "be in the room" with a person—to be in the moment, offering my presence.

My mentors implored me to trust myself as an agent of healing and change with my clients. To deserve that self-trust, I had to prepare for that moment: practicing disciplines, understanding myself, and developing the humility to participate in a life-changing process controlled not by me but by Someone higher.

You, my friend, are one of the great treasures unearthed by the kingdom of God—remember? (Matt. 13:44-45). Your unique life—transformed by your submission to God's grace and honed by the spiritual practices of a disciple—can be a powerful witness to what goodness, compassion, and love can be.

You have the potential to participate in healing and changing lives; you can help pull people out of the deep and into the boat. God's boat. Dare you trust yourself to fulfill that potential?

God of miracles, I am overwhelmed by the fact that you treasure me. You choose me. You believe in me. I pray for the chance to become what you envision and to participate in the transformation of the world. Amen.

Being present and using your voice may elicit retribution. Likewise, you can easily overdo it in your assertions and end up not doing good but harm. When you pray honestly and authentically (thinking that God may not like what you have to say), when you show up at controversial rallies or protests because you will not remain silent against injustice, when you contribute to a cause not yet considered mainstream, when you serve in ministry to people some of us don't approve of, when you befriend a social outcast, or when you bear witness to a truth that most of us don't—or won't—accept, you are stepping out in faith. That can be frightening.

Addressing the potential for aggression and violence requires courage. It is the courage to live and be present in the world and to reflect God's love, sometimes despite yourself! Sometimes you display courage by maintaining dialogue with someone even though it creates tension between you; other times, courage comes in letting a topic go, at least for the time being. Sometimes you show courage by praying for someone you think is dead wrong. And sometimes, it means admitting that you, yourself, are wrong. The psalmist expresses his confidence in God as light and salvation. Even in his living he states, "Whom shall I fear?"

If you are wondering whether God has your back when you put yourself "out there" for God's purposes, this psalm is your answer. God will provide for you if you keep your humility, your eyes on the Divine intention, your voice readied in praise and joy, and your ear tuned to what God wants from you.

Sing and praise God! Do good! Do no harm! Love God! Go fishing! And if you are in tune with God, whom should you fear?

O Lord! Listen to my voice, and help me to hear your answers! You are my light, my salvation, and my fortress! I only ask that I live in your house forever! Amen.

That boat in which you ride patrols a dark and sometimes stormy sea. This passage relays the good news that the darkness is past, that there is light ahead, and that you are now in the boat—safe, dry, and welcomed. Those coming in from the deep long to know that the days of oppression lie behind them.

I once knew a woman who had lived a horrific childhood. The messages she received about herself told her that she was trash and unlovable. Because that message can affect other aspects, that message had been reinforced over her lifetime by countless events. I happened to be with her when she realized that God loved her, treasured her, and, just perhaps, found her to be a delight. She later told me that the world was divided at that moment into a hopeless past and a boundless, bright future. This woman came to experience the light of God's love because she had come to know specific people who displayed it for no apparent reason other than, as she later began to realize, that "God had shone it on them too."

By just being themselves—living in and extending God's shalom, the people around my friend were God's instruments to transform and save her life. She found herself in the presence of a community of love and affirmation that she had always hoped had existed. Their faithful presence pointed her to God's light. In turn, she soon began fishing for people too.

What light have you seen? What yoke has been lifted for you? What is the prize, the great harvest, for which you must thank God? The answer to those questions likely holds the vitality behind your prayers, presence, gifts, service, or witness—the reason that your individual presence can be so vital to God's work today. What a treasure indeed!

Thank you for loving me, gracious God. Help me to shed your light through my expressions of your love. Amen.

Paul writes to the Corinthians about their tendency to become fractured over matters that reflect pride more than unity toward the cause of Christ. Dissension arises as members align themselves with special-interest groups and key leaders. And he raises a pertinent question: "Has Christ been divided?" He wants the Corinthians to be of one mind and purpose. Specifically, Paul wants them to eschew pride and to support one another in living out the good news.

Recently, I witnessed a public brouhaha among Christians. All were well meaning, but they disagreed vehemently on a matter of morality. It's good to disagree and have constructive dialogue, but the ways they expressed their disagreement became counterproductive. Divisive pride led to rival "camps." A few wise voices tried to encourage members of both sides to behave in a Christian way, but those voices were drowned out. The groups seldom, if ever, affirmed their love or respect for each other. And there was insufficient mention of loving, accepting, and celebrating those at the center of the controversy. When outsiders saw our now dysfunctional family posing, arguing, and demonizing like everyone else in the world, they likely swam away from the boat of shalom—choosing rather to perish. As I watched this public display among Christians, I thought, *What have we wrought?* We indeed emptied the cross of its power.

I take some comfort in knowing that ours is not the first generation to mess up. In fact, it looks like an old family tradition! The redeeming grace comes in our ability to repent, start over, and try to repair the damage. We remain a sinful church in need of redemption. But when we fall overboard, there is plenty of room to get us all back in the boat.

Reflect on your own pride. Reaffirm aloud your humility that all the good in you comes not from your own devices but from Christ within you.

Brothers and sisters, allow me to testify: When you have a big mouth, it is easy to put your foot in it! This can result in embarrassment and lack of productivity in personal affairs, and it can be a source of sorrow and shame when the heart desires to live in and reflect God's reign.

I can be a prideful man. My life has been an amazing journey, not the least of which has been my realization of God's amazing grace, sent right down to me. It's awesome! It's something to be proud of, but "let the one who boasts, boast in the Lord" (1 Cor. 1:31). My pride can become a big hole in the net I am casting for people, a net that should have everything to do with God and nothing to do with me.

Sometimes when I fail, I repent on my own. Sometimes it takes a loving brother or sister, like Paul, to help me get straight. In this passage, Paul corrects the flock without putting them down. He finds a way to show his love for them even as he disapproves of their actions.

One of the hard-earned realizations I spoke of earlier this week has been that while I can have presence, that presence must point to Someone, Something greater. It seems so simple, yet so hard to learn. My most effective tool of influence is to calm down, take time to be in the moment, and say, "Tell me more about your journey." Then I can truly celebrate God's unique presence and action in other people's lives. I can share their joys and sorrows and celebrate where their story connects to God's story—from their unique point of view.

My prideful self can't fully explain this, but I'll tell you something: In those moments, I can be truly wonderful—and it has absolutely nothing to do with me.

O God, in everything I say and do, help me to reflect you. Amen.

Isaiah announces new possibilities for Israel as the formerly obscure possibilities emerge in the light of God. Isaiah notes a contrast between the former days and the latter days. Israel moves from contempt to glory, from oppression to liberation.

Friend, you and I are part of the long human journey from darkness to light, a campaign that will shatter the yoke of oppression and provide a rich harvest for all people. At our journey's end, we will dance with joy! Our mission is to live in a way that will bring more and more people in touch with the Source of light. This week, we have considered the task of simply being present—being ourselves as we transform into and reflect the image of Christ.

I was conscious of you and your travails as I wrote. That awareness held me accountable, and I imagined that you held me in love. Thinking of you made me cognizant of the mystical connection that we all share. You need not be physically present to make an impact. You influenced me! Likewise, your prayers for those who don't even realize that you are doing so create power for good in their lives. Your material donations to the church's missions affect people all over the world. The exercise of your personal gifts in your own ministry extend far beyond your sight—even beyond your vision. Your simple service and compassion to others reverberates past them into places you'll never know. And the witness that only your life can provide is essential to tell the whole story of the kingdom.

I cannot wait to hear the stories of the good done in a world that needs it more every day—of the lives that have been touched, even transformed, by contact with you. You serve as an exemplar of the love, affirmation, and welcome of Jesus Christ. For the Fisher of People, you were quite a catch!

Thank you, Lord, for the chance to serve your kingdom and for your unwavering presence in our lives. Amen.

Doing Justice

JANUARY 27–FEBRUARY 2, 2014 • CRAIG KATZENMILLER

SCRIPTURE OVERVIEW: The four texts for this Sunday join in warning the people of God not to be confused or intimidated by appearances or by how the larger society values this or that. A faithful hearing and responsiveness to the God of the Bible may not fare so well or look so good in terms of the world's standards of judgment. But what is required and blessed is a community ordered according to the covenantal commitments, shaped by God's gracious promises, and attuned to what Paul called the "foolishness" and "weakness" of God.

QUESTIONS AND THOUGHTS FOR REFLECTION

- Read Micah 6:1-8. How can I take steps to reject the private/public (sacred/secular) dichotomy, living publicly the claims I make in private? What practices can I adopt in order to take the call to poverty of spirit seriously as I seek to live into the call to "do justice"?
- Read Psalm 15. How can I make practicing the actions identified in today's psalm part of my everyday life?
- Read 1 Corinthians 1:18-31. What steps can I take to boast in myself less and less each day and instead look to the cross of Jesus as my source of boasting? What are the implications for my life if I embrace the scandal of self-emptying love, as displayed by Jesus on the cross?
- Read Matthew 5:1-12. How does the call to "rejoice and be glad" affect my understanding of working for justice?

Student currently pursuing a PhD in Liturgy and Ethics at the Julius-Maximilians-Universität, Würzburg, Germany

We enter a courtroom scene to hear God's cross-examination of the Israelites. This passage comes after a series of accusations about the economic injustices in the prophet Micah's community. Starting in chapter 6, God invites the people to speak to the unjust actions identified earlier. God asks, "O my people, what have I done to you?" The defendants are invited to defend their actions before the mountains, which have witnessed generations of divine help. However, God answers the posed question by recounting God's great deeds: God has delivered their ancestors out of slavery and has saved them from various enemies.

The brief narrative retelling of Israel's history reminds Micah's hearers of God's preferential option for the oppressed. To those who were enslaved, God offered freedom. To those who were besieged, God offered shelter. But here, in this courtroom, God accuses the people who were once delivered from oppression of themselves oppressing the poor among them. The people have no defense.

Today, we have the opportunity to place ourselves in the defendants' seats. How do we actively participate in the oppression of others? For example, what questions might we raise about the conditions of the people who make the clothes we wear and the food we eat? The journey we take this week toward doing justice starts with the invitation to introspection. Thus, we can ask what other aspects of our lives need examining and weighing on the scales of God's justice. Until we see the ways in which we collude with injustice, we cannot reorient ourselves and our communities toward justice.

God of justice, soften our hearts to see the faces of the oppressed around us, and embolden us to call for their just treatment. Be with us through the exercise of examining our conscience. Amen.

TUESDAY, JANUARY 28 ~ *Read Micah 6:6-8*

Standing accused in the courtroom, the people finally respond in verses 6 and 7, raising questions of their own. We can read their response at least two ways: First, we can hear the questions as sincere inquiry. However, based on the story up to this point, we can also imagine the people, who are now themselves acting as oppressors, standing there defiantly, saying, "I give my sacrifices. What more do you want? My firstborn?"

When we interpret the people's words in this latter way, we see a people so far from God that they know neither the story of God's saving help nor the proper response to that story. This reading seems more faithful to the narrative flow of Micah. Micah accuses the people of committing economic injustice in their community, and now, standing in court before God, the people react in a not-too-unfamiliar way. That is, the people in Micah's day, as people so often do in our day, say, "I do what's required of me." Think of the people today who go to church on Sunday and who then spend their work weeks trapping persons in cycles of economic slavery through, for example, high-interest-rate loans. Today we might say this practice reflects the private/public (or sacred/secular) dichotomy our culture creates. This dichotomy argues, "Privately, I worship God. Publicly, I do whatever's required to succeed in life. And that's okay." God's reply indicates a need to move beyond religious action to covenant living that guides our actions in worship and in the rest of the week.

So we come to the climax of this court scene. The prophet declares, "[God] has told you, O mortal, what is good." What does God require? Lives of justice, kindness, and humility before God. The people of God may choose between lives of commodity and lives of covenant.

God of justice, draw us near your heart today so that we can live lives of justice, kindness, and humility. Amen.

The psalmist writes that those who abide in God's tent live a certain way. Their lives reflect God's moral imperatives. Here again, we face the notion of private versus public life. The text does not say that those who privately offer sacrifices in exactly the correct way will "dwell on God's holy hill." No, the psalmist affirms that just acts are the requisite for a life with God. Respectively, the psalmist identifies blameless living, honest speech, friendly conduct, rejection of evil, honor of the faithful, and economic fairness. These are public acts carried out in the midst of community.

The psalmist concludes the psalm by saying that those who act in this fashion will not be moved. Those who act justly and pursue justice for others will become fixed in their cause. Whether that cause becomes the rights of persons working in inhumane conditions, of persons living in prisons, or of persons struggling to make ends meet, people who live just lives will not be moved by the storms that come as part of the struggle for justice.

A friend of mine works with persons on the street. A few years ago, when the local government in her town tried to pass laws making it illegal for homeless persons to set up tents on government property, she and her husband led the legal charge to keep the law from passing. For her, protecting "the least of these" from displacement was part of her call to live a just life. She was arrested during the course of events for her show of solidarity with those being displaced, but she continued fighting for their rights. As the psalmist said, her life of lived justice made her unmovable.

God of justice, give us courage to live lives of justice and bring us so completely into just living that we "shall never be moved" from that way of life. Amen.

Having considered lived justice so far this week, we turn now to the crux of the matter: the scandal of Christ's cross for building a just society.

That word *scandal* is important. Paul writes that the cross of Jesus doesn't make sense from the perspective of the "wisdom of the world." He writes that the wise, the scribes, and the debaters of this age don't "get it." Ironically enough, I sit down to write this meditation the day after one of the 2012 presidential debates. Presidential debates exemplify how great people of the world can miss the point. There on the stage are two persons who nearly come to blows over the right use of power—economic, legislative, military. The right use of power in presidential politics equates to wisdom. But the cross of Jesus puts this wisdom to shame.

The great scandal of the cross is that power comes not by displaying strength but through self-emptying. The foolishness of God in the cross creates space for reconciliation.

What, then, makes for a just society? The wisdom of the world says punishment. The foolishness of God says reconciliation. How scandalous, right? When people who commit injustice are brought to justice, according to the scandal of the cross, they are not punished but reconciled. The cross becomes a stumbling block to the wisdom of the world. The challenge for those of us who wish to live according to God's foolishness, which is "wiser than human wisdom," is to embrace the scandal of the cross. Only then will we bear witness to the world as to what justice looks like at its purest.

God of justice, through his self-emptying life and death, your Son showed the world its own folly. Help those of us called to live according to the cross to accept the call to empty ourselves. Amen.

In the wider context of the opening of Paul's first letter to the Corinthians, we have to remember that Paul is also talking about being united in Christ. So if the scandal of the cross exposes the world's wisdom as folly, then it is essential for those who live according to the scandal of the cross to bear witness to the unity found through Christ's self-emptying love.

When we look at how to "do justice," we look only to Christ. The ideas of the wise, the scribes, and the debaters of this age are not good enough; likewise, the visions of one Christian versus another Christian cannot be good enough. God called us in our weakness so that none of us would be able to boast in his or her own achievements. Our ideas, our strategies, our good intentions cannot achieve what the foolishness of God has already achieved, namely, reconciliation through the cross of Christ. Our work then is to boast in the scandal of Christ and his cross alone. I have a friend who has made this his life's work through teaching history. History, as a discipline, tends to rehash justice narratives that assume the wisdom of the world is true wisdom. However, my friend teaches history in a way that questions these narratives against the self-emptying scandal of the cross. He teaches his students to question what a scandalous allegiance to the cross of Christ might say about those moments of power display. He imparts to his students the ability to think outside the box about many themes but especially about justice. God's justice differs from that of the world.

God of justice, give us a sense of oneness in the call to show that the wisdom of this age is foolishness compared to the scandal of the cross. Amen.

Living into the scandal of the cross requires the embracing of concrete practice. Today's reading gives us a glimpse into several practices that make for justice; they are, loosely defined, poverty of spirit, presence, humility, activism, mercy, purity, peacemaking, and cross-bearing. If we, as Christ-followers, are to show the world what justice looks like, we live according to these practices.

Note, however, that since the Reformation persons have tended to interpret Jesus' words in the Beatitudes—and, indeed, his words throughout the Sermon on the Mount—as lofty ideals that realistically can't be obeyed all the time. But the apostolic community's witness as well as that of church history throughout its first three centuries unanimously affirm that these are not unrealistic ideals but a scandalous way of life for the church.

Taking these eight Beatitudes seriously, then, becomes critical to forming communities that do justice. Each one of the eight flows out of the one that precedes it; thus, the call for poverty of spirit becomes fundamental for understanding all the Beatitudes. This Gospel's call for poverty of spirit is one of comprehensive poverty. As we consider the scandal of Christ's cross as the wisdom of God, we acknowledge that being poor in spirit goes far beyond simple talk about economic poverty—though the witness of Jesus' life assumes the involvement of economic poverty. Poverty of spirit implies relinquishing the desire for power, for controlling outcomes. We meet the world through the self-emptying love that led Jesus to the cross. In a world that depends on the alleged "strong" and "wise" to navigate outcomes by any means necessary, the Beatitudes call us to vulnerability in love. This loving poverty then becomes the foundational practice for living justice.

God of justice, help us to live in poverty of spirit. Amen.

Today we hear the call to "rejoice and be glad." The work of justice is the joyous work of longing for God's will to "be done, on earth as it is in heaven"—for which Jesus himself prays later in this Sermon on the Mount. And as we live into that longing, we rejoice in happy thanksgiving.

Still, the life of justice will not be an easy one. This call to "rejoice and be glad" is here bookended by the stark reminder that we will face persecution from the powers-that-be—the sort of persecution that led Jesus to his cross—and the equally stark reminder that throughout history prophets of God, those who sought justice, have received harsh treatment. But we know that any suffering we experience because of our longing for justice is somehow gathered up into Jesus' suffering on the cross.

Through the cross, Jesus lives Micah's call to "do justice," "love kindness," and "walk humbly" to the fullest. Likewise, his self-emptying love shows the scandalous love of the triune God—the scandalous love that seeks mercy instead of sacrifice, reconciliation instead of punishment.

In the end, we are to "rejoice and be glad" because we have the opportunity to live into God's story of reconciliation. We know the final word is not found at the cross of Jesus. The final word—or rather the new first word—is found at the empty tomb. Jesus' resurrection vindicates God's Messiah and reveals the hope that undergirds all work for justice. We strive to "do justice" because we know that to do so is to strive for resurrection here and now. And in moments when we partner with God to glimpse resurrection now, we will "rejoice and be glad."

God of justice, give us perseverance to continue living into the story of your justice for the weak and disenfranchised. Amen.

A New Kind of Righteousness

FEBRUARY 3–9, 2014 • JERRY P. HAAS

SCRIPTURE OVERVIEW: A common theme for all of our lectionary readings this week is this: living genuinely out of a deep inner sense of connectedness to the Trinity (God, Jesus, and the Holy Spirit). By living out of this spiritual center, we match our actions with our words and avoid the judgment the prophet Isaiah casts upon the people of Israel. Psalm 112 is a hymn of praise for the blessings God brings upon those who revere and follow. In Paul's letter to the Corinthians, he urges them to move beyond their flirtation with wisdom and go to the deeper regions of the Spirit, the source of true wisdom. And, finally, Jesus, in his Sermon on the Mount, calls his listeners to move beyond the mere words of the law to the deep meaning and intent of the law.

QUESTIONS AND THOUGHTS FOR REFLECTION

- Read Isaiah 58:1-12. Does a spiritual practice such as fasting sometimes distract you from pursuing justice and mercy?
- Read Psalm 112:1-10. How can you live your life in such a way that your heart will be "firm, secure in the LORD?"
- Read 1 Corinthians 2:1-16. What does spiritual maturity as a Christ-follower involve for you?
- Read Matthew 5:13-20. As a follower of Jesus Christ, how are you growing in saltiness, as a light to others and as a more righteous person?

Spiritual director and retired United Methodist minister living in the Tucson, Arizona area

What does it mean to be righteous? How are we to live before God and with others? When the Israelites return to Judah after the Babylonian Exile, they face enormous losses and spiritual confusion. The Temple has been destroyed and God's favor seems lost as well. *What did we do wrong?* they must have wondered, and *How can we win our way back to God?* When confronted by significant loss, we all ask such questions, don't we?

One way to try to get right with God—and that's what it means to be righteous—involves engaging in ritual practices that close us off from the world, such as those in monastic orders. While at times such withdrawal is necessary, taken to extreme we end up hiding from God and the world. Notice how Sunday morning worship in some of our churches takes on a rigid quality as though stuck in a certain period of time and afraid of the Holy Spirit. *Hiding* in ritual does not draw us closer to God.

Isaiah 58 points out a radical alternative. Getting right before God involves pursuing justice, letting the oppressed go free, and sharing bread with the hungry. These actions follow the ordinance of God; this is what it means to be righteous. Religious ritual makes sense when tied to the work of redemption. God's presence is alive and real on Sunday mornings when worship celebrates and initiates works of justice and mercy.

In the Russian Orthodox Church, after the congregants have received Holy Communion, the church distributes the leftover bread to the poor—a simple gesture that signifies an important connection. Worship flows out into mission because true righteousness establishes a right relationship with God and with those in need.

O God, keep us from hiding from the world's needs as we seek to grow in our relationship with you. Amen.

While serving on the staff of The Upper Room, I often found myself in conversation with others about how to deepen the prayer life of those who seek to follow Christ today. I loved learning new and old ways to pray and wanted to share those spiritual practices with others. Christian spirituality offers a vast storehouse of possibilities. Over the years I learned many different ways to pray—with scripture (*lectio divina*), with icons, with the labyrinth, with Taizé chants, and with Korean *tongsun kido* shouts. Each offered a special gift and a fresh new encounter with the living God. Joining with others in such practices, I experienced a sense of spiritual community that gave me new hope for the church.

As I grew in my prayer practice, I realized I needed to balance my discipleship with service. So one day I volunteered for "Room in the Inn," a cooperative effort by congregations in Nashville to feed and shelter homeless persons by inviting them as guests for the night. The sign-up sheet was full, except for one of the slots for "overnight host," so I marked my name and made plans to spend the night at the church. During the evening meal, I realized that the other host was not coming, and I would be alone with a dozen homeless men. I greeted the guests and noticed a very large man who was behaving as if he were off his medication. I found his appearance frightening, so I deliberately chose to sit across from him at the evening meal and build whatever relationship I could before turning in for the night.

That night my prayer life took on a new vitality! I realized how easy it is to live in a spiritual bubble, cut off from the needs of the world. Isaiah writes, "Bring the homeless poor into your house." That's a prescription for spiritual growth as well as for engagement in mission!

O God, stir us up in your compassion to new acts of mercy and justice. Amen.

The theme of righteousness continues in this psalm of celebration. The truly happy are those who delight in God, setting a good example throughout the day. Who is truly secure? Those who conduct their affairs with justice and who give generously to the poor—these are the people who are truly at peace. When evil things happen, those who are righteous do not give in to fear because "their hearts are firm, secure in the LORD."

Does the psalmist promise too much when he suggests that "wealth and riches" will follow such a life of integrity? It certainly doesn't always happen. We know situations in which kind and generous people fail to achieve material success. Yet if people love God, work for justice, and give generously to others, are they not already rich?

In 2001 I traveled to Mozambique, an extremely poor country in southern Africa, as part of a teaching team from the General Board of Discipleship of The United Methodist Church. Our team from the United States represented far greater financial prosperity than our hosts. Yet the Mozambicans reflected a spiritual vitality that shamed us. Some walked for days to attend the meeting; we complained about the long flight and the bumpy streets. We were tired and cranky; they lifted our spirits with beautiful smiles, joyful singing, and dancing. We brought heavy suitcases; they came with little or nothing.

One of my colleagues Pat Luna stood up to speak. *What could she possibly say*, I wondered? Pat began by complimenting their joyful spirits. She pointed out that we often lack such joy in our country, in spite of our wealth. She reminded us that true wealth comes in right relationships with our families and with our neighbors. Happiness comes when we lay our whole life before God, including our pocketbooks. As she talked, we all came to see more clearly what it means to live a righteous life.

O God, help me to live more joyfully and with less fear. Amen.

THURSDAY, FEBRUARY 6 ~ *Read 1 Corinthians 2:1-5*

In his letters to the church in Corinth, Paul seeks to provide practical, theological guidance for individuals and for the congregation. While they can easily become fixated on personalities or secondary matters, he wants them to focus on the bigger questions of their identity as Christ-followers. Without quenching the enormous energy and vitality of the Corinthian believers, his goal is to channel their gifts in love and for the sake of others. In chapter 1 he proclaims the foolishness of the cross (v. 18) and in so doing he offers a new kind of righteousness, measured not by the law but by the self-giving love of Jesus Christ.

Here in chapter 2 Paul adds another dimension. Because the city of Corinth attracts followers of the mystery religions, Paul uses the language of mystery and wisdom to proclaim the good news. He refers for the first time in this letter to the work of the Spirit in the formation of faith. Logical persuasion is not enough, nor is it enough to point to Christ crucified. The Spirit shapes our faith so that it "might rest not on human wisdom but on the power of God."

What does this mean in practical terms? I think of Les, a dedicated layperson who served for years on a variety of administrative committees in the church, devoting hours to thankless jobs that involved great detail. Les followed the example of Christ, offering himself for others. But Les was not simply a "church worker." He nurtured his spiritual life by attending worship regularly, enjoying fellowship with others, and reading and praying through the devotional magazine *Alive Now.* He enjoyed nature and saw in it the mystery and wonder of God's creating power. Humble and hard-working, Les kept close to the Spirit. And he never burned out.

Guide us, O God, to follow the way of the cross without growing hard-hearted or bitter. Amen.

Paul now focuses more clearly on divine wisdom as a gift of the Holy Spirit. He directs his comments toward those who consider themselves spiritually "mature," but the average Christ-follower and the whole congregation remain in view. God's Spirit enables us to perceive the revelation of God in Jesus Christ. What was hidden for ages has now been revealed. While the Spirit has an intimate connection to Christ, the Spirit has its own role as it "searches everything, even the depths of God." The Spirit's gift of wisdom helps us know the world for what it is. It empowers the discernment of all things and opens the way for the outpouring of the "gifts of God's Spirit."

Paul distinguishes human wisdom from divine wisdom. Human wisdom is subject to "the rulers of this age." The source of divine wisdom is "truly God's." He exhibits a strong confidence in the Spirit of God, for it leads us to "the mind of Christ." As individual Christians, and as Christian communities, we have not only the example of Christ's self-giving love to guide our lives; we receive wisdom greater than our own through the Holy Spirit to discern our way. Later Paul will offer more instruction on the gifts given by the Spirit (1 Corinthians 12), but for now he speaks specifically of the gift of wisdom.

While often comforting, this wisdom given by the Holy Spirit can sometimes be disturbing! Matters of right and wrong become more complex than they appear. Take the case of Dietrich Bonhoeffer, a Lutheran pastor in Germany during World War II. After much prayer and discernment, he participated in a plot to kill Hitler and ultimately was captured and executed by the Nazi government for treason. His writings and his life challenge easy assumptions about the results of the Holy Spirit's guidance.

Ask the Spirit to disturb all your easy answers to what it means to be a Christ-follower today.

Picture Jesus' disciples gathered on the hillside. Jesus has recently called them from their fishing nets. After pronouncing the Beatitudes, he says to them, "You are the salt of the earth. . . . You are the light of the world." They probably wondered who he was talking about! They have only begun to follow him. No boot camp, no instruction manual, no on-the-job training— yet Jesus declares their worth and value to the whole world.

Today we may call someone a "salty Christian" when he or she brings experience and determination to his or her call. Salty Christians flavor the soup of Christian community. They encourage the rest of us to sit up and take notice by challenging our complacency and reminding us to hang in there when things are tough.

"Light-bearing Christians" bring hope in darkness. They help us see God in places we couldn't imagine. Greta Moffett is one example from my life. She served as Conference Lay Leader during a difficult time in my annual conference. Through countless hours of meetings involving litigation, she continued to offer perspective and humor when the situation seemed too overwhelming. She never lost sight of the church's mission and developed relationships with church leaders from around the world even in the midst of this struggle.

Sometimes the salty Christians are also the light-bearers. The two are not mutually exclusive. Make notes of the qualities of each, then make your own list of "salty Christians" and "light-bearing Christians."

How do the qualities of salt and light add to the discussion of a new kind of righteousness? Finally, consider how you can grow in your saltiness and in your light-bearing capacity.

O God, when I am tired or discouraged and find it difficult to be your disciple, help me to remember the salty, light-bearing Christians in my life and, most of all, your hope in me. Amen.

Scholars agree that Matthew's Gospel was written for members of a predominantly Jewish community, newly converted as Christ-followers. Matthew often quotes the Old Testament and portrays Jesus as the new law-giver. Righteousness is a recurrent theme. Chapter 1 refers to Joseph as a "righteous man" though he follows not a traditional understanding of righteousness but a series of dreams given to him by the Holy Spirit. In today's story, Matthew challenges us to probe into what it means to be right with God and right with humanity.

Read in this context, Matthew 5:17-20 seems surprising. Jesus makes it clear that the righteousness of his followers must differ from that of the scribes and Pharisees. This week, we've outlined the way God calls us to a new kind of righteousness—a righteousness that seeks justice and includes the poor (Isa. 58); a righteousness modeled after Jesus Christ and him crucified (1 Cor. 2); a righteousness that delights in God even in the midst of evil and disturbing times (Ps. 112). Perhaps Matthew does not want this new community to stray too far from the Torah law that has grounded them for centuries. The New Testament and the church's history record stories of communities who strayed too far in pursuit of the Spirit.

While Matthew's Gospel is tough, it provides a balance that has guided the Christian community for centuries. Matthew displays such balance by using the word *unless*. In this passage, it sounds an ominous warning: "Unless your righteousness exceeds . . . , you will never enter the kingdom of heaven." The next time the word occurs is in Matthew 18:3: "Unless you change and become like children, you will never enter the kingdom of heaven." Perhaps when we take both verses to heart, we'll come closer to knowing how Jesus wants us to live.

O God, keep me from taking myself too seriously. Instead, let me delight in you as Creator, Savior, and Friend. Amen.

Choose Love

FEBRUARY 10–16, 2014 • AMIE H. VAUGHAN

SCRIPTURE OVERVIEW: How are Christians to understand and relate to the Jewish law? The text from Deuteronomy confronts Israel with a sharp choice: follow the commandments of Yahweh or bow to the gods of the Canaanites. Choosing the law means choosing a way of life. Psalm 119 praises the Torah as God's gift bestowed on Israel to be the authentic guide as to how life should be lived. Jesus becomes the authoritative interpreter of the Torah, the one who pushes beyond external behavior to a consistency between disposition and deed. Christians are invited by the text to be different and become what Paul describes as "spiritual people."

QUESTIONS AND THOUGHTS FOR REFLECTION

- Read Deuteronomy 30:15-20. Moses puts the choice before the people in the starkest and simplest terms: life or death, blessings or curses, God or idols. What would you choose? Why? In what areas do you still choose something other than life and God?
- Read Psalm 119:1-8. Where do you find happiness? How might you rewrite these verses?
- Read Matthew 5:21-37. In what ways do you take seriously these teachings of Jesus? What did you have to change about your life to do so?
- Read 1 Corinthians 3:1-9. Who has influenced your spiritual maturity? In what ways do you want to grow more?

Recent PhD graduate in Practical Theology, the University of Aberdeen, Scotland; now living back home with mum in Mt. Juliet, Tennessee; member of Providence United Methodist Church; book lover and aspiring writer, seeking God's next step for her life

I have never been good at making decisions. I worry and fret, trying to examine every angle and determine every outcome. I put them off as long as I can, usually out of fear of making the wrong choice. As a teen, even deciding what to order at a restaurant could lead to tears. I want matters to be clear-cut and simple, but that rarely is an option; life, generally speaking, is more complicated than that. Or is it?

Moses has been leading the Israelites for forty years—ever since their deliverance from Pharaoh out of Egypt. They have seen God's amazing care and provision for them repeatedly, as well as having experienced God's power up close and personal. Despite all God has done for them, Moses knows all too well how stubborn the Israelites can be and how often they choose to complain and see only the negative of any given situation—which explains why they are only now on the verge of the Promised Land.

God has already told Moses that he won't be entering the land with the people; Moses knows that he will soon die. These verses in Deuteronomy are part of his farewell speech—his last chance to guide the flock he's been shepherding for so long, the last chance to help them. He will no longer be around to intercede with God on their behalf; they will have to sink or swim on their own now. So he lays it all out for them, in as much detail as possible. The Torah, the first five books of the Hebrew and Christian Scriptures, are filled with the instructions from God that Moses gives Israel on how to live.

But in the end, Moses keeps it simple: Love God and choose life, or love other gods and choose death.

Loving Parent, thank you for giving us choices and for sending us guides to help us choose. Amen.

Poor Moses. I can imagine his frustration; I hear it in verse 19. Although the people have driven him nuts for decades, he cares about them. I think he's worried because he knows them—their weaknesses as well as their strengths. He truly wants them to choose well; to *know* they will love God, live, and be blessed. Yet, he fears they won't choose wisely. Perhaps that's why he sounds so harsh—because he's worried.

Moses sets before the people a choice between blessings and curses, life and death. He cannot make this choice for them, but he does all he can to ensure they realize the importance of getting this decision right. God's promises are on the line, promises that have passed down from generation to generation since the time of Abraham. The Israelites have seen with their own eyes what God can do for them and what life is like when God removes divine blessing.

This decision involves more than individual assent to a set of propositions, however; it involves the whole community. Moses has set out the principles, regulations, commandments, and laws, but this choice comes down to more than simply following rules. At the very heart of the law is one command: Love the Lord your God. Moses says this twice in these few verses: Fulfill the law by loving God. Those who love God will keep God's commands and walk in God's ways. Those ways will set Israel apart from the surrounding nations. Moses warns them not to let their hearts be drawn away by anything or anyone else.

This remains the case for us today. The choice is ours, and Moses encourages us to love God and choose life!

Lord of love and life, help us to choose you, today and every day. Amen.

Choose Love   61

The Sermon on the Mount (Matt. 5:1–7:29) is probably the most familiar set of Jesus' teachings, including the Beatitudes, the Lord's Prayer, and the Golden Rule. Today's passage falls toward the beginning, following immediately on from Jesus' claim that he came to fulfill the law, not abolish it. Moses gave the people the law, so they would know how to live out the love they have for God. Unfortunately, many had focused on the legalities and forms of action presented in the law rather than the understanding that all life and action should flow from love of God. They kept the letter and lost the spirit of it. Jesus comes as the new interpreter of the law.

The Gospels relate numerous instances of Jesus' frustration with persons who were missing his point. I fear that I am often just like those folks—all too frequently I do what I know I should because it's "right" or so I don't get in trouble—not because I have the right attitude about it. I find this especially true when it comes to relating to God and others. I don't murder, steal, or commit adultery, which I find to be fairly easy to avoid. I also read my Bible, go to church, and give to those in need—but not always with the right attitude. I do it because I'm supposed to.

Jesus is addressing not just our actions but our attitudes. He goes beyond the expectation that the commandments be obeyed. People are to avoid sin, of course, but not simply to avoid punishment. He desires a lifestyle change as we choose to love God and allow that choice to influence every aspect of our relationships and actions.

Pray today for areas where your attitude may not always fit your actions.

I have to admit that I do not like these verses. Generally when I read the Sermon on the Mount, I read through them as quickly as I can—hoping that if I ignore them, they'll go away. That doesn't work. I know they're here, and I know what they say. It's my attitude that's the problem, and I am aware of that (although it doesn't make this teaching any easier to deal with).

Avoiding murder has not proved difficult for me over the years; avoiding anger, insults, and name-calling (even if only in my own heart) is nearly impossible. I'm easily annoyed; I'm good at holding a grudge; and I'm not always quick to apologize or seek reconciliation. I can think of people right now, including my sister, who are angry with me—and I am angry with them. At best, we are not speaking to one another. And here Jesus tells me those actions (and my attitude) are not so far removed from taking their life and that I'll be judged for those actions the same as if I'd committed the deed!

However, Jesus proposes a solution and gives it to us straight: be reconciled, seek out those you have wronged, come to terms quickly. If we do this, our offerings to God are acceptable. If we do not, we are liable to judgment.

It comes down, once again, to our choices and attitudes and whether or not our lives are being lived out of love for God. If we do not love others enough to apologize and choose reconciliation when we have wronged or been wronged, then we do not love God as much as we think we do. I stand convicted.

Gracious God, forgive our anger and mean-spirited attitudes toward others, and help us to seek reconciliation where it is needed. Amen.

W hat are you writing on?" In my PhD years, this question arose more than any other. It often felt like I *was* my thesis—that my thesis solely encompassed my being.

Just like those folks who made inquiries about me, we can easily objectify people—view them as objects—and relate to them only as we can use them. Women (and many men) know what it feels like to be sexually objectified, seen merely as a body—with feelings but no agency or ability to choose and act. Some respond by wanting to protect, while others want to exploit. Neither response takes into account the actual person who has thoughts, abilities, and plans of his or her own.

Here Jesus addresses the concrete problems of adultery, divorce, and swearing falsely. In each instance, Jesus goes beyond the "rule" to promote a broader interpretation. As he addresses adultery and divorce, in which many women of his time got the worse end of the deal, he requires wholesome relationships. In John's Gospel (7:53–8:11) the crowd is ready to stone the woman "caught in the act," but where is the man? Jesus sets a higher standard than the law in order to protect this woman. He also addresses the issue of objectifying people. It begins with our thoughts and how we view others; how we treat them develops from that perspective.

Our words are likewise powerful. I'd never thought about the phrase "giving one's word"; it's not just any word, but the one I alone can give. It is active, creative, a promise, a commitment, and a self-imposed obligation. Jesus says our word should be counted on, simply spoken and simply kept. It is a sign of the kind of people we choose to be—those who acknowledge the value of others, and live out our love of God by loving others.

Living Word, guide my thoughts and words to and about others so that by loving others, I may love you better. Amen.

The high school years are not an easy time for many people. They may feel judged by where and with whom they "belong." I would not want to go back and relive those days of growing up and trying to find my place.

I imagine the Corinthian church to which Paul writes resembles a typical high school. Paul started this strong and gifted church on his second missionary journey. Its congregants were largely Gentiles who needed guidance in moving from their former religious lifestyle to the higher standards of the Christian life they are now called to live. They have received the Holy Spirit but are not mature in the faith yet; they are, in fact, acting decidedly immature. Paul describes them as "infants in Christ." They are not yet "spiritual people" who are ready for solid food. Paul himself serves as a "wet nurse," feeding them with milk.

Evidence of their being infants in Christ is the quarreling and jealousy among members of the community. Cliques form within this church as people align themselves with different ministers—Paul and Apollos being mentioned specifically. Each group thinks itself better than the others; jealousy and bickering run rampant. Instead of seeking unity and spiritual maturity, they choose to fill the church with division and competition, behavior better suited to human inclinations and the world of the flesh. Paul writes to remind the Corinthians that *all* believers are servants of God, and the common purpose is to love God and live God's way. All unite in Christ for the glory of God.

Faith in Christ now requires that they live by the highest standard—loving God, first and foremost, and allowing that love to shape all their actions and relationships. Paul reminds them—and us—that choosing to love God includes loving others and seeking unity.

Holy Spirit, make us one in Christ and one with each other, as we strive to grow in grace and love. Amen.

This psalm is divided into sections, arranged in the order of the Hebrew alphabet. We lose the psalmist's intricate development of the psalm in translation. What we don't lose is the high regard with which the psalmist holds God's law, and the positive outcomes he believes come from living according to that law. The entire psalm is one of praise and thanksgiving for God's divine revelation to humankind, embodied in the law, which blesses those who keep it: Happy are they! The first three verses of this psalm note the well-being that comes with living according to God's law.

The next few verses stress the importance of the law in God's thinking: "You [God] have commanded your precepts to be kept diligently." And finally, our passage closes with the psalmist's affirmation and desire to keep God's law, a resolve to live God's way. Happy, then, is the psalmist. Deep down, everybody desires happiness, don't they? What does happiness mean here?

Happy are those who are wealthy? beautiful? famous? No. For the psalmist, happiness comes from seeking God with the whole heart, living blamelessly, and following God's way.

This week's meditations place choices before us: We choose how we will live. Through love of God, we allow that love to shape our lifestyle—individually and communally. We close this week with this reading from the prayer book of the Bible. The first half of these verses offer proverb and exhortation, giving glory to God for God's commands and encouragement to us to live in them. The second half give voice to worship and supplication, seeking God's help to live according to God's way so we can offer praise from a right heart. May this be the prayer of our hearts as well.

Thank you, God, for revealing to us the way to true happiness that lies in you alone. Help and guide us as we seek to follow your way of love. Amen.

Making It Plain

FEBRUARY 17–23, 2014 • OUIDA LEE

SCRIPTURE OVERVIEW: These texts evidence relentless concern with the moral requirements that belong to life with the God of the Bible. They assume the foundation of covenantal law in God's rescuing acts. That foundation is implicit in undergirding these several treatments of God's commands. The psalmist is aware that God's commands constitute a radical counterobedience. The text from Leviticus brings us to the core claims of covenantal law. The rule of the God of Israel leads directly to focus on the neighbor. The neighbor is not just an inconvenience or an intrusion but is the stuff of moral awareness. Paul's admonitions to the Corinthian Christians state the bold claim that Jesus Christ is the central focus of every Christian's commitment. The Gospel reading invites the community to reflect on, imagine, and devise extra measures of neighbor love that reflect the character of God.

QUESTIONS AND THOUGHTS FOR REFLECTION

- Read Leviticus 19:1-2, 9-18. How do you reflect God's holiness to others?
- Read Psalm 119:33-40. What divine promise has God confirmed in your life?
- Read 1 Corinthians 3:10-11, 16-23. What helps you remember that you are God's temple, built on the strong foundation of Jesus Christ?
- Read Matthew 5:38-48. When have you taken to heart Jesus' words to turn the other cheek? How did the situation resolve itself?

Lead pastor, Church of the Disciple, DeSoto, Texas; president of Black Clergy Women of The United Methodist Church

In a world that constantly changes, shifts, upgrades, and downsizes, we sense a merging in preparation of a world where scarcity becomes the new paradigm. The clarion call from the writer of the Old Testament text is, "Be holy." *Holy*—a word that goes unheard among the clanging noise of the gong and tinkling cymbals of our world's antics.

What does it mean to be holy? The word *holy* is a translation of the Hebrew word *qadash*, which means "to consecrate, dedicate, sanctify." The God of Israel embodies this meaning; therefore, those who worship this holy God are to reflect that characteristic in their living.

Moses, God's hand-selected leader of the people of Israel, issues this message, which the nation is to hear as a mandate. Their mission is to be a people called out and set apart as God's representatives. This people will enter a new land free from their bondage. The new land will bring new expectations. God's holiness will become evident in Israel's obedience.

These verses invite us to reflect on our daily walk of faith. How does our living reflect our obedience to a God of holiness? How do we attempt to restrict God's will and power through our inattention to holiness? We may respond, "Who's calling us to accountability? Who cares if we live in a holy way? Isn't holy something we do in church? Isn't that enough?"

Yet God's call to live lives of radical obedience comes to us. The choice is ours. That call emphasizes the critical connection between holiness and obedience. We can move beyond the sphere of the common to the place of the sacred.

Gracious God, move us beyond the compromise to a place of resolution, all through your loving-kindness. Amen.

Holiness calls for radical change. We move beyond merely stating that we are holy because God is holy by *actually living* in this countercultural way. We can easily declare our sanctity; enacting it becomes more difficult—especially in a world with such a wide chasm between the wealthy and the economically disenfranchised.

The harvest provision notes an important aspect of Israel's ethical tradition. The gleanings of fields and vineyards are to be left *deliberately* for the poor and the sojourner. This economic requirement, which costs the farmer, is an act of social justice. We may pontificate about our generosity when our "fields" are flourishing. Even then we may assert that these fields belong to us—but we're expected to leave behind grain and grapes for the wayfarer? Holiness and obedience to a holy God require that we leave gleanings for people we do not know or choose to know. How easily we allow our holier-than-thou attitudes to prohibit the holy will of God for our lives.

Obedience issues in the desire to do God's will. The request does not entail a handout to the wayside traveler; it entails leaving food in the field so that the wanderer does not have to become a beggar. God provides and invites our participation in the providing.

In an attempt to live out the gift of sharing, my congregation is growing a community garden. While members of the congregation are free to take from the garden, they intentionally leave produce on the vines for the community. The sharing comes at Jesus' invitation and reminder that it is more blessed to give than to receive.

O Lord, in a world where the poor are forgotten, help us to set aside self-defeating attitudes and learn to share. Amen.

We acknowledge that living a holy life involves more than a simple affirmation or fair treatment of the wayfarer; it is a call to transformation. No longer can we simply view the condition of others, offer a helping hand, and believe that we have done our part. God is inviting us into relationship and to love our neighbor as we love ourselves.

Today's scripture probably calls to mind those parameters we call the Ten Commandments: Do not lie. Do not steal. Do not deal falsely. These are no fly-by-night requests. The Lord commands that the change in our lives extends to others—not only to our loved ones but to our workplace colleagues and those in our neighborhoods. The change includes our actions, reactions, and inactions. Partiality and favoritism drop out of the equation; retaliation and grudge-holding are not tolerated.

Today's scripture raises concern about the well-being of the economically disadvantaged (those who are oppressed) and the physically disadvantaged (those who are subject to abuse). Our relationship to a holy God manifests in our caring relationship to and concern for others—dealing fairly with *all* people. "You shall not be partial to the poor or defer to the great."

Notice the repeated words after each prohibition: "I am the LORD." God's character is made manifest in God's people. So we have work to do—personal, confrontational, and unavoidable. Often we want to choose our "holy," but today's scripture lays out clear guidelines. God's people must desire holiness; we cannot choose our "holy."

Demanding God, your message is plain. Surrendering our will to yours will reveal our love for neighbor. No need to tell others; it will be in plain sight. Amen.

The psalmist knows that the law of the Lord has the potential to perfect his life if he follows and obeys. His words voice the requests of one who desires God's direction and a willingness to learn: "Teach me, O LORD. . . . Give me understanding. . . . Lead me, . . . Turn my heart. . . . my eyes."

"Teach me, O LORD, the way of your statutes." The psalmist yearns for more than intellectualizing; he desires a thorough understanding and personal enlightenment by God. He has many teachers, but he covets an intimacy with God for instruction and direction, daily application and a renewed lifestyle. The writer promises to "observe it to the end," an acknowledgment that this is a lifetime commitment. However, in following these statutes, he gains freedom from manipulation and control. Therefore, the desire is to refocus on the word of the Lord; only with God's help can we navigate the twists and turns of life— and as Leviticus affirms, learn to love neighbor as self.

We too are invited to take these words for our own. As we come to trust and have faith in God, our lives change. Our words and behavior toward others reflect our understanding of God's law. And by keeping God's decrees, we draw nearer to God and through grace accept the will of God for our lives. Through the binding nature of covenant, the Holy One confirms the divine promise and gives us life.

O God, as we study your word and seek a deeper intimacy with you, open our eyes of faith and trust, our ears and heart for understanding, our minds for greater wisdom. Amen.

Paul shifts his metaphor from planting to building. Though we know Paul to be a professional tent maker, he spent much of his time consumed with building foundations. As he notes, "Like a skilled master builder I laid a foundation." He goes on to state that while he laid the foundation, others have now taken up the work of building on it. Paul's work of surveying, staking, and excavating in the Corinthian community has led to the establishment of a solid foundation in Jesus Christ.

Paul, the wise master builder of the faith community, established numerous churches in the Greco-Roman world. In today's passage, he reminds the believers not only that they have a sure foundation but that they themselves are special buildings: temples, dwelling places of God's spirit. "God's temple is holy, and you are that temple."

However, some believers in Corinth want to acclaim particular individuals as their leaders. Perhaps they wish to name the churches in their honor. Paul reminds the divided believers that though many planted and watered, only God gave the increase. Despite the many master builders, there is only one foundation: Jesus Christ.

In a world of shifting sands, Christians need a sure foundation. The apostle Paul reminds us, "Do not deceive yourselves." We see many builders today, but the sure foundation of Christ does not change. This serves as a holy reminder that there is but One who loves unconditionally, forgives without penalty, and provides without priming. For we "belong to Christ, and Christ belongs to God."

Dear God, forgive our preference for worldly wisdom, our pompous pride, our self-reliance. Bring us back to your unshakable foundation. Amen.

An eye for an eye, and a tooth for a tooth.'" Here in the midst of his Sermon on the Mount, Jesus issues radical responses to our natural desire for retaliation. He explains how to interpret the law within the context of love. We read these words as part of the explanation (see Exod. 21:24-25) of the Decalogue, which was written to limit the vengeance exacted for abuse. (We do not take a leg for an eye or a foot for a tooth.) As the Old Testament taught, "Do not say, 'I will repay evil'; wait for the LORD, and he will help you" (Prov. 20:22).

In reality, both we and the Israelites have trouble waiting for God's justice. We hold grudges against those who have wronged us and feel justified in doing so. While we may not openly display our anger, the seething spirit of anger within awaits the opportunity to raise its head. Jesus addresses our natural inclinations with seemingly unnatural actions toward those who wrong us. We neither get even nor speak evil of the matter. We turn the other cheek. These startling responses call to mind our startling God, and they enable peaceful relationships that reflect our relationship with God. All will be reconciled through Christ Jesus.

Jesus teaches us to release revenge, to render good for evil. He calls us to forgiveness, to the surrender of our personal will to that of God, to let go and allow the love of God to permeate our hearts. Living into "holy" requires so much from us—we achieve it only through giving ourselves to Jesus.

We approach your seat of grace, asking for mercy and patience from you, O God. Amen.

Our transcendent God goes ahead of us, enlivening our thinking and behavior, inviting us into a relationship that leads into community. "Love your enemies." Hebrew Scriptures record no words that encourage the hating of enemies.

In his sermon from the mountainside, Jesus states his standard of righteousness and reveals that all of us have fallen short. Jesus offers a clear understanding of what God expects of each of us. Not only are we to love our enemies, but we are to pray for those who persecute us. These are matters of the heart rather than the head.

Jesus speaks these words to the faith community at a time when walls and barriers need to fall. He extends community beyond the Israelite tribes. Why? Because love is the nature of God's character, and we are "children of [our] Father in heaven." We too love God and neighbor.

Some people might suggest that when Jesus said to love our neighbor, we could hate our enemies. This view gives us the right to choose whom we identify as enemy and neighbor. Yet, Jesus asserts that love is the basis of Christian community, a community not bound by a set of rules that excludes others.

Through the words of scripture, we have come to understand that love and holiness begin with God and then flow out through our interactions with others. They reach beyond the church walls, revealed through our deeds for the least, the last, and the lost.

As we grow in Christian faith, we confess our need of companions on the journey and realize that the trek is impossible without Jesus in our midst.

Thank you, loving Savior, for healing our hurts, stretching us beyond our unforgiveness, and teaching us your love and compassion Amen.

Seek

FEBRUARY 24—MARCH 2, 2014 • TRAVIS TAMERIUS

SCRIPTURE OVERVIEW: In deep deference and careful obedience, Moses enters the zone of God's glory, which certifies Moses' authority. Psalm 99 praises the kingship of Yahweh, while bringing to mind the human agents of God's rule who facilitate Yahweh's conversation with the people. The Gospel lesson, like Exodus 24, characterizes what is not fully seen or clearly heard. Jesus is taken up into the zone of God's glory and so is filled with transcendent authority. Speech about glory points to the assignment of new authority. The epistle reading asserts the authority of the true teachers of the church, who rightly present and interpret the scriptural tradition.

QUESTIONS AND THOUGHTS FOR REFLECTION

- Read Exodus 24:12-18. When did you last experience a life-altering encounter with God?
- Read Psalm 99. What practices or disciplines do you employ to train the mind to see the invisible?
- Read 2 Peter 1:16-21. When in your life have you been startled by the unexpected presence of God's glory? Whom do you recognize as having been transformed by following the way of Christ?
- Read Matthew 17:1-9. How do you attempt to script God's work in your life? How can you open yourself to God's grace?

University chaplain; director of the Center for Ethics and Global Studies, William Woods University (Disciples of Christ), Fulton, Missouri

On April 3, 1968, Martin Luther King Jr. addressed a packed church in Memphis, Tennessee, attempting to awaken the conscience of a nation. He eloquently described the history of the struggle for civil rights in America and the difficult days that lay ahead. Nearing the end of his sermon, King reached a crescendo when he said, "I've been to the mountaintop." Those simple words were greeted with a thunderous response from the congregants. They knew the reference to Moses. They knew the ancient story of liberation. And they knew of their own restless yearning for freedom and equality. King concluded his message with hope, saying, "Mine eyes have seen the glory of the coming of the Lord." Those would be his last public words. The following day, King was shot dead outside of the Lorraine Motel.

Today's reading returns us to the Exodus story that nourished King and provided inspiration for the civil rights movement. God has summoned Moses to the mountaintop for one more glimpse of divine glory. The nation of Israel has left the oppressive, but familiar, land of Egypt and is venturing toward an unknown land of promise. In between the agony they once knew and the glory that awaits them is a wilderness experience that will test their faith. The desert will become God's pathway to the promise.

When life grew hard during Israel's forty years in the wilderness, I suspect that Moses frequently recalled his mountaintop experience on Sinai. A mountaintop gives perspective. The panoramic view provides a larger landscape for our vision.

What inspires you when you find yourself lost in a spiritual desert? What sustains you during difficult days and long nights of struggle? Call to mind where you once caught sight of God's presence. And look in faith to the future of God's glory.

God of fire and of cloud, grant us a vision of your abiding presence and give us strength for today. Amen.

When I read this passage, I am usually drawn to the aura of glory revealed in the consuming fire and the shadowy cloud cover. In this encounter with God, something happens that overwhelms the senses, commands attention, and sanctifies the space as holy ground. Reading the passage again, I'm struck by the focus on time. God tells Moses to come and wait. Moses tells the elders, "Wait here for us." Moses goes up the mountain, a cloud settles over it for six days, and Moses waits for God. After God speaks, Moses spends another forty days and nights on the mountain—long enough for the people to wonder if their leader will ever return.

Pause for a moment, and consider these words from the text: "come up to me" and "wait." Perhaps you've noticed this before in reading through the Bible. A lot of people spend a lot of time waiting for God to act. Abraham and Sarah wait twenty-five years for God to keep the promise of a child. The Israelites wander in the wilderness for forty years before a new generation enters the Promised Land. Centuries later, the people of God are stranded in Babylon for seventy years.

I imagine that you know something about waiting. Like the people of God back then, you are waiting for God to act *right now*. Like me, you hunger for transformation and eagerly anticipate God's showing up. Maybe not in a glory cloud or a devouring fire but to show up nonetheless —in your relationships, health, monthly budget, and the headlines of the local newspaper.

Draw strength from this fact: You're not alone. We're all in this together—wanting to see the glory, praying for help, waiting for an answer, and discovering God's good news when the long wait is over.

God, grant me "the assurance of things hoped for, the conviction of things not seen" (Heb. 11:1). Amen.

In Lewis Carroll's *Through the Looking-Glass,* Alice expresses her inability to believe impossible things. The Queen responds in the following fashion: "I dare say you haven't had much practice. When I was your age, I always did it for half an hour a day. Why, sometimes I've believed as many as six impossible things before breakfast."

If you're like me, what you do before breakfast is routine. From rising out of bed to pouring the first cup of coffee, the pattern is fairly predictable. The Queen in *Through the Looking-Glass* suggests we add another item to our list of things to do before breakfast: Practice believing the impossible.

Good advice. We need help in seeing that which is unseen, noticing the beautiful, and believing that God is present right now, at this time in our lives, and right here in this particular place. We need practice believing that wonderfully more is going on in the world than what we see in the mirror or read in the newspaper.

Fortunately, certain habits train the mind to see invisibilities. The Queen advises Alice to "draw a long breath" and "shut [her] eyes" in order to believe impossibilities. In the same way, devotion to prayer and meditation on scripture can open our eyes to God's presence in the life we already know.

Let me suggest that having read the psalm for today, you now pray the psalm. Stretch out your soul in the spacious landscape of the songwriter's vision and say this of your own life: God is king. The Lord is exalted. Our God is a lover of justice. The Lord God is a forgiving God.

Tomorrow before breakfast, practice seeing that which is unseen.

Lover of justice, help me to do justice, love mercy, and walk humbly with you. Amen.

In a scene reminiscent of Moses on Mount Sinai, Peter, James, and John have front-row seats to the opening night of God's glory show. They witness Jesus, their friend and teacher, in splendorous dress, his face shining like the sun, his clothes brilliantly white. And then, strangely, Moses and Elijah walk right out of the glory days of long ago and straight into the neighborhood of now. Peter, feeling out of place like someone underdressed for a five-star restaurant, breaks the awesome silence with nervous chatter. Tripping over his tongue, I can imagine, he says to Jesus, "Lord, it is good for us to be here." Attempting to make the strange more familiar, Peter then proposes that he do something useful: "I will make three dwellings here." All this sounds reasonable enough. Peter projects confidence, like he knows what in the world is going on, and he aims to prove it with a hammer and a tent peg.

Then suddenly, the Voice speaks. Interrupting Peter's good intentions, God acknowledges Jesus as the beloved son and instructs the disciples to "listen to him!"

Sometimes we need to hear those words. Right now, it is not about me saying the right words. Right now, it is not about me doing more for God. It's not about controlling the moment, scripting God's work in my life, or domesticating the Divine. It's about stopping. It's about being silent for a while and listening and paying attention to Jesus. And because of that, it's also about looking in the mirror and recognizing our own face as the face of God's "beloved," a son or daughter in whom God takes immense pleasure.

Lover of my soul, I know I miss so much of what you are doing in and through and around me. Give me ears to hear and eyes to see the glory that is in front of me. Amen.

FRIDAY, FEBRUARY 28 ~ *Read 2 Peter 1:16-21*

As I write this, twelve people are dead and over fifty people wounded after a young man opened fire in a crowded movie theater in Aurora, Colorado. The moviegoers were watching the midnight premiere of *The Dark Knight Rises* when the unthinkable occurred. In a matter of moments, a comic book myth about a dark knight rising had become a real-life tragedy about the darkness that can surround us. Is there no escape from evil—even in our places of escape?

The headlines of the newspaper and the headlines of the Bible are not all that different. In the Bible, we read numerous ugly stories about outrageous acts of violence and brutality and shocking indifference. From Genesis to Revelation, we witness the vandalism of God's creation design and the desecration of persons made in God's image. When we hear such stories, we rightly wonder, *Where is the glory?*

The author of Second Peter replies and tells us to pay attention to the good news as to a "lamp shining in a dark place." Notice the honest acknowledgment that following Jesus occurs in a dark place. It's difficult out there. We're often in trouble. It's easy to get lost, frightened, or simply overwhelmed.

And yet, in that very place, a different headline is being written. A Lamp shines in the darkness. And still more, there are *lamps* shining in the darkness. As you and I live out the good news of God and follow the way of Jesus, we bear witness to glory. The smallest acts of kindness—a gentle word, a patient ear, a helping hand—all become candles in the darkness that light the way home.

Light of the world, keep me focused on the way of Jesus and shine brightly in the darkness of my life. Light up my own life that I may bring hope and goodness to those around me. Amen.

Imagine it is the Christmas shopping season. You're at a sub-urban mall. It's hard to find a parking spot. It is frigid outside and a long walk to warmth. When you get inside the mall, you are elbow to elbow with other shoppers carting their goods around like so many pack mules. After a morning of power shopping, you feel stressed because you're trying to stretch your dollars to cover the names on your list. Your feet grow tired, and your belly grows hungry.

Now imagine sitting in the café court eating your lunch while surrounded by strangers. Think of the surprise when suddenly, one of those strangers arises from her table and begins to sing the opening lines of Handel's *Hallelujah* chorus. Though she is obviously quite talented, you also think her a bit odd. Soon after, other shoppers stand and take their parts—altos, tenors, basses, and sopranos all joining in the song of the season. You put your sandwich down, realizing this event is more than one woman's eccentricities. Something else is going on here. You have just witnessed a flash mob of glory. A majestic song performed for unsuspecting shoppers has transformed the moment. An indistinguishable café court has become an unlikely cathedral. The busyness of the day has become a pathway to God.

In today's passage, Peter calls to mind the Transfiguration when God conveyed honor and glory on Jesus with the words, "This is my Son, the Beloved." Peter recalls the voice of God directing the focus toward Jesus as the revelation of divine glory. And now, years later, the writer urges the young Christian community to keep their attention on Jesus. Frequently, God's glory is incongruous with its surroundings. It shows up in unexpected places, moments, and people. As you get ready to begin a new week in God's world, stay alert.

God, help me see that there is always more here than meets the eye and that the presence of Christ is always near. Amen.

TRANSFIGURATION SUNDAY

In the movie *The Bucket List*, a terminally ill patient makes a list of all the things he wants to do in life before he "kicks the bucket." At the top of the list, on a piece of lined, yellow paper, Carter writes, "Witness something majestic." Before he dies, he wants to catch sight of something that is arresting in its glory and beauty, something that is breathtaking to behold.

Pause for a moment. When have you witnessed something majestic? Where have you seen the radiance of God's glory? Maybe it was your first visit to the ocean, when you came within earshot of the roar of the waves crashing against the rocks or rhythmically bathing the sand every few seconds. Maybe it was from a window seat at thirty thousand feet as you looked upon the clouds or surveyed a patchwork of American farms. Or maybe it was the first time you ever laid eyes on a newborn baby. Or perhaps you were lucky enough to see a work of art that made you whisper to no one in particular, "Wow."

Glory is all around. Peter, James, and John glimpsed it in Jesus: his dazzling apparel, his conversation with the greats of the faith. But take note. Glory can wear a disguise. It can be spotted in countless, hidden acts of devotion, where the left hand doesn't know what the right hand is doing (Matt. 6:3). Glory can show up in the shabby dress of heartache and disappointment. Glory can surprise us at it shows its face in the face of a neighbor or a stranger.

Remember this: The early Christians glimpsed God's glory in a crucified man hanging on a cross. That mind-bending mystery permits us to look upon our own lives with new eyes and to see in our own loss and weakness the signature of God's presence and the promise of resurrection.

God of the Resurrection, open my heart to the possibility of a new beginning and to the grace of each day's gift. Amen.

Always We Begin Again

MARCH 3–9, 2014 • LIB CAMPBELL

SCRIPTURE OVERVIEW: The texts for Ash Wednesday are all ominous in nature, pointing forward to the redemptive power of God's grace. Lent is a time when Christians reflect on their mortality and sin, as well as on the creative and re-creative power of God. The original parents of humanity could not resist the seduction of the serpent, but that narrative stands beside the story of Jesus' lonely and painful resistance to the power of Satan. In Romans, the "one man's obedience" by which "the many will be made righteous" is the quality that endures. The Joel lection (not used by the writer) is an alarm bell in the darkness of the night. Those who are caught in this terrible moment cannot hope to save themselves, for they are powerless to do anything on their own behalf. They are powerless to do anything, that is, except to repent and to open themselves to God's intervening mercy.

QUESTIONS AND THOUGHTS FOR REFLECTION

- Read Genesis 2:15-17; 3:1-7. What if we heard this story with an ear of assurance that God still loves the creature and calls us into partnership in healing the world? How will open eyes expedite that mission?
- Read Psalm 32. How difficult is confession for you? Recall a time when you knew you were forgiven.
- Read Romans 5:12-19. What words would you write to the people you know who live in fear and under the burden of guilt?
- Read Matthew 4:1-11. What gives you the greatest strength when resisting temptation? Where do you look for strength?

Pastor Emeritus of Spiritual Formation, Saint Mark's United Methodist Church, Raleigh, North Carolina; blogs at avirtualchurch.com

Ah, Human. What have you done? Here you are, set in a beautiful garden. You have everything you need and free rein over it. Yet look at the choice you have made! God set the parameters clearly. But you made a choice that has marked human life since that day.

We know that consequences are a part of the natural order. We live in a world that does not spare us consequences, good or bad. We define our lives by our choices. We live or die in them.

Consider what Adam and Eve lost in their choice. They had it all. They had each other. They had relationship with God on a daily basis. They had purpose in the garden of Eden, "Till it and keep it." They chose to overreach, to desire the same knowledge as God. Their choices of disobedience and unfaithfulness took them from the garden, away from God's daily presence.

When choice and consequence take us from relationship with God and one another, we no longer live in paradise. We lose that place of plenty, that place of unity and love.

It's easy to blame a beguiling serpent when our own lack-luster faith and ego-self drive the poor choice of wanting to *be* God, with God's eyes and God's knowledge. Why is it not enough to be fully human, part of the story of beginnings, creatures set in a beautiful place to care for it and to share fellowship with God in paradise?

As we prepare our hearts for the journey of Lent, let us acknowledge the spot from which we start. Let us consider the choices we will make in the coming weeks that will prepare us for the healing that is Easter.

Guide me, O God, in ways that lead to life. Keep me from choices that take me from you and from those I love. Amen.

The awakening of self-awareness is sometimes shocking. It certainly shocks Adam and Eve. Realization of their nakedness is a new consciousness. This consequence prompts a quick response, "Let's sew some clothes." And sew they did.

The second creation story works to explain the human condition and human location in God's story. Sometimes I think how good life would have been if those people in that story had not messed it all up. Too often the weight of their sin has burdened my life and robbed me of thanksgiving for the garden living and goodness that surrounds me.

Awareness of the life that surrounds me is not all bad; in fact, it calls me into a contextualization with all creation and realization that I am part of the natural order, the oneness of God's creation. Open eyes? Check. Naked? Check. Ready to sew? Perhaps that is the question of my examen.

What will I see with these newly opened eyes? Do I see a world in need of repair? Do I see a people who need to be loved as God first loved us? What am I ready to do to cover not only myself, but all the others who need clothing and food? What am I ready to do for God and for the world?

This story of beginnings takes on an eschatological tone as responsibility and awareness of the human condition rest on new shoulders. Have we spent too long bemoaning our loss of paradise and our "fall"? Perhaps it is time to employ open eyes for good in the world. What will the rest of the story be? What can it be?

Open my eyes, dear God, to new awareness of the call you place upon my life, to the needs of those around me, to a place of service in your kingdom. Amen.

WEDNESDAY, MARCH 5 ~ *Read Matthew 6:1-6, 16-21*

Ash Wednesday

The woman at the cash register stared at the black smudge on my forehead as I swiped my credit card. Curiosity finally got the better of her. "What's that black mark on your forehead? Here's a tissue to help you get it off."

"It's OK," I said. "It'll wear off soon enough." The Ash Wednesday mark was still on my brow. I had come to the grocery story on my way home and almost forgotten the cross of ashes that marked me. The ordinary task of grocery buying crashed in on my Ash Wednesday reflection. Voices from speakers in the store barking out specials began to drown out, "From dust you came, to dust you shall return." And nothing remained but a black smudge.

Jesus' warning to "beware of practicing your piety before others in order to be seen by them" hits me right between the eyes. Is the cross I wear an outward piety easily wiped away with a tissue, or is it a sign for the world that my life, all that I am, all I have, all I do, belongs to Christ? The hypocrite in the room might just be me. Or could it be you?

There is a false "piety" in today's culture that is mocked for its outward show. True piety is found in the inward transformation of a life, the inner secret heart that spends itself in love and praise of God and humble service to humankind and all creation.

In this Lenten journey that begins today, locate your heart in the treasure that is Christ. Journey to a place that rises up from dust and ash to the reward that is Christ.

Lord, take the outward mark of ash inward and mark my heart again as yours. May my outward way so reflect your inward light that the world will not question whose I am. Amen.

It was just a small transgression. Really. I was a first grader and had proudly learned to write my name: Libby. Trouble was, I chose to write it on every page of a copy of the novel *Rebecca* that Daddy had borrowed from our next-door neighbor. The scribbling of a six-year-old did not get me into trouble—but the lie that followed did.

"Libby, did you write your name in Mrs. Booth's book?"

"No," I said. My adult memory hears me saying that and responds, "How lame can you be? Who on earth else would have done it? Do you really think you are pulling a fast one on your father? Do you not trust the daddy who loves you and is always ready to forgive you?"

The learning around this event is forever etched in my mind and heart. Clearly I was the guilty party. And just as clearly, I had no reason to think Daddy would not forgive me. He even said as he meted out judgment, "This hurts me more than it does you."

Sin can weigh heavy in our hearts, drying up our strength and wasting away our spirit. "I will confess my transgressions to the LORD," the psalmist says. A turning point in his life comes in confession. God forgives the guilt of his sin and goes on to say, "I will instruct you and teach you the way you should go."

We learn righteousness in the home of forgiveness and unconditional love. Childhood lessons shape us, teaching us the way we should go under an ever-watchful eye. In the care of a loving parent, I received another chance.

Laying one's life before God in confession exemplifies utter trust. We gain another chance to be free from the burden of sin and guilt in God's forgiveness and love. This is why we rejoice!

O God, here I come confessing once again. Set me right in your great love. Let all my life be praise! Amen.

The history of humankind since the Genesis story was written has been characterized as corrupt and sinful. The darkness that has covered the human story has indeed "spread death to all because all have sinned." This is hardly news.

The great reversal of what some call depravity, a people lost in unworthiness, happens in the Christ event. Fully human, fully divine, Christ comes to free us from the bond of sin and usher us into the fullness of human life that God has always valued and since the beginning called good. God comes among us, incarnate in Jesus the Christ, to remind us that we are God's own, beloved in the humanity into which we are born.

I imagine Paul writing this weighty epistle to early Christians who are feeling a growing uneasiness with their place in the Empire and the kingdom of God. First-century Rome is becoming a dangerous place for people of faith. Speaking again the story of Christ's saving love that continues us in God's grace must be at the forefront of Paul's mind.

I may not know the mind of Paul, but I know the work of Christ that sets us free from the burden of death and fear of the dangers of the world in which we live. Guilt and fear do no good in the world; receiving Christ's gift does. In Christ we are no longer counted as sinners but once again freed and set right in creation.

Lent is a season of emptying and clearing what encumbers us, creating in us a place for Christ to rise again. The call is clear. Let us not be weighed down in guilt, fear, and sin—but open to God's renewing promise in Christ.

Empty me, dear God. Make a place in my heart for you. Amen.

The Tempter comes to Jesus in his hunger. Jesus, Son of God, Son of David, is hungry, and the Tempter knows it. Yielding to his physical need is not in Jesus' plan. His hunger can be met only in the word that comes from "the mouth of God."

Temptation comes again from the heights of the Temple. "Jump," the Tempter says. "God's angels will bear you up. You won't get hurt." Again, Jesus rebukes temptation. Even Jesus will not put God to such a ridiculous test.

The third temptation is the call to worship Satan in return for all the treasures of earth. Jesus sends him away, this Tempter with his fantasies of power. Jesus remembers the commandment: Serve only God.

Temptation has not gone from the world. We see and hear it everywhere around us, calling us with a voice that sells us out at the drop of a hat. In business, politics, and even the church, we are tempted by power and the promise of favor. The acquiescence invited by the Tempter can be extraordinary machinations of people-pleasing and pleasure-seeking, accommodating worldly pleasure and earthly need. We won't even talk about the expectation that God will act on our behalf in ways incongruous with God's nature.

Twenty centuries give witness to the rise and fall of earthly powers and the work of the Tempter's hand. Jesus resists, coming again to trust that his life is *in* God and *for* God alone. Acknowledging that temptation is rampant in the world represents a first step into a new life. Name the enemy within and without, and prepare your heart to say, "Go away!" Turn again this holy season to the One who gives you the strength to say it.

Silence the voice of temptation that calls me, O God. And if silence does not come, grant strength to resist the noise. Amen.

FIRST SUNDAY IN LENT

Evil is persistent. After forty days and forty nights in the wilderness with no food or drink, Jesus is ripe for the tempting. But from his oneness with God, Jesus draws strength to resist all the charms and promises offered. Jesus remains true to who he is and what God calls him to do.

In the end, Jesus sends Satan away with words of Torah covenant: "Worship the Lord your God, and serve only him." If Evil has a face, it must look stricken. Instead of winning, Evil loses and skulks away for another day. The devil exits stage left, and look at what happens!

Suddenly, angels come and wait on Jesus. At the close of the fasting and tempting comes the consolation of angels who offer care. This wilderness drama has a great conclusion! Jesus resists and finds comfort in angels' attendance.

Consolation of the Spirit is real. Jesus knows it firsthand. Angels come as if waiting for their cue. Faithfulness through trial is the word in Matthew's temptation story. Jesus does not waver from his confidence in God. He never tries to use God or abuse his relationship with God. He is one with God and that brings him through temptation.

At times in my life, I would have found it easy to take a shortcut, to show somebody up, or to call somebody out. I could show off my piety rewarded with prosperity. But that is not the way of Christ. The way of Christ involves humility and obedience. I am to follow. Consolation comes as I am obedient, humble, and trusting.

In the wilderness of life today, may we be strong in faith standing up to temptation, trusting the Spirit to console us.

Come, Holy Spirit. Console your people who wander in desolation. Help us remain true to your plan for our lives. Amen.

What Only Faith Can See

MARCH 10–16, 2014 • KWASI KENA

SCRIPTURE OVERVIEW: Faith in God and deliverance by God are themes that dominate these scriptures. Abraham casts aside all baser loyalties and in daring fashion entrusts life and well-being to God's care. Abraham follows God's initiatives into new realms of loyalty and purpose. Paul reminds us that while Abraham models good works, his righteousness results from his faith. Nicodemus models an Abraham who has yet to leave Ur of the Chaldees. Nicodemus's comprehension of God's initiatives is shallow and sterile. The psalm for this day greets with joy God's invitation to renewal.

QUESTIONS AND THOUGHTS FOR REFLECTION

- Read Genesis 12:1-4a. In what area of your life is God calling you to leave behind the familiar to pursue some new opportunity?
- Read Psalm 121. Where are you experiencing God's grace during this Lenten season?
- Read Romans 4:1-5, 13-17. What does it mean to you to live faithfully?
- Read John 3:1-17. How are you discerning God's promises in your life?

Assistant Professor of Christian Ministry, Wesley Seminary, Indiana Wesleyan University, Marion, Indiana

College educators know about the image problem that confronts the new, young professor. The young whiz kid who earns a PhD by age twenty-four doesn't look old enough to be responsible for educating the next generation. In today's passage we meet seventy-five-year-old Abram. His body is advanced in years, but is his faith so mature that "all the families of the earth shall be blessed" through him?

You would think the life of someone who has "father of our faith" tacked to his name would be full of grand examples of unswerving faith in God. The opening verses of Genesis 12 appear to reveal such a person. Abram, an elderly man, willingly leaves the familiarity of home and family to follow God. Volunteering to become a stranger in a foreign land requires faith. Abram's spontaneous trust seems like a perfunctory first step taken by a godly patriarch whose faith will stand firm in the face of adversity. But Abram has not achieved patriarchal status just yet.

In Egypt, fear overtakes Abram and he twice misrepresents his relationship with his wife by stating, "She is my sister" (Gen. 20:2*b*). Would you or I deem a liar worthy of becoming the father of many nations? Perhaps God had faith in Abram's untapped potential.

Now we're getting a clearer picture of the way faith develops in people. God often has to smooth our rough places through challenging life situations. God's grace and mercy afford us opportunities to develop abiding faith. That Abram, fledgling faith and all, musters up enough courage to leave his country and kindred indicates his willingness to begin his walk with God. What step might God be asking of you today?

God of Abraham, keep speaking until you awaken faith within me. In Jesus' name. Amen.

Faith. The mere mention of the term turns our gaze inward. How many of us question our spirituality? "Do I have enough faith?" "Do I trust God?" While self-assessment is helpful, have you ever paused to consider how much faith God has in you, me, and all of humanity?

We, as Christians, affirm a God who can act in an omnipotent manner, yet often chooses not to do so. God places limits on personal power and respects those limits—often to our chagrin. We believe an omnipotent God should act unilaterally to end poverty, bring every evil deed to justice, and stop tragedies before they ever begin. With the snap of two fingers, God could have turned Abram into a mature spiritual man before promising to bless "all the families of the earth" through him.

Yes, Abram leaves his country and kindred (a definite sign of faith); but while in Egypt, he leads the pharaoh to believe that Sarai (his wife) is his sister. Abram fears the pharaoh's power to kill him and take his wife more than he trusts God's ability to save them both (Gen. 12:11-13). Nevertheless, God still believes that Abram will grow to become the "father of our faith." That took faith on God's part. God respects our free choice, even when it puts us at cross-purposes with divine intention.

When Abram doubts God's plan and has a child by Hagar because Sarai seems eternally barren, God continues to trust Abram. Only after more assurances from God does scripture record that Abram "believed the LORD, and the LORD reckoned it to him as righteousness" (Gen. 15:6).

Abram's story reveals both humanity's struggle toward faith in God and God's amazing faith in people like you and me. Why not pause today and appreciate God's faith in you?

Faithful God, you dare to trust me to handle your divine mandates, even when I struggle to handle my personal affairs. Thank you for having faith in me. Amen.

What Only Faith Can See

Speak the words, "We're going on vacation," and our thoughts turn to which clothes to pack or what sights to see. Say the words, "We're going on a pilgrimage," and we may take pause. Few of us have experienced a pilgrimage firsthand. Not so for the ancient Israelites; they made three annual pilgrimages to Jerusalem to participate in various feasts. The Israelites traveled up to Jerusalem, the city on a hill. As they went, they sang psalms of ascent. Some scholars believe travelers sang Psalm 121 on the way to Jerusalem.

Psalm 121 also belongs to the "songs of trust," along with Psalms 125 and 131. Why sing songs of trust? The purpose of the pilgrimage to Jerusalem is to join in corporate worship of God, to reaffirm faith in God as one people.

Imagine this scene. A voice begins singing, "I will lift up my eyes to the hills—from where will my help come?" As a question, the psalmist is asking, Will I look to the hills for help, the high places where people worship other deities? No! I must look beyond those places to find my help.

When we need help, whose name sits atop our list? Some believe technological advances provide the panacea for all ills. Others tune in to the latest talking head for advice to live by.

For the psalmist and all the pilgrims who respond to the psalm's opening question, help comes from the maker of "heaven and earth"—a central belief that other Songs of Ascent echo. Affirming God as a primary source of help in corporate worship does much to strengthen faith. Keep that in mind the next time you and a believing congregation recite the following line from the Apostle's Creed: "I believe in God the Father Almighty, maker of heaven and earth."

Dear God, maker of heaven and earth, I look to you as the source of my help. If I lower my gaze, remind me to look beyond the temporary help the world offers. Amen.

Islept well as the pitch-black and sticky night relaxed, freed from the cacophony of hooting car horns and the gossip of the day—until I heard the whack of wood on concrete. John, our night watchman, had just killed a poisonous viper that had slithered near the front door of our home in Ghana, West Africa. My wife, Safiyah, and I served there as missionaries. Friends had told us, "Get a night watchman to guard your house so you can sleep at night."

The Israelites trusted God to keep divine watch over them; a trust not available to followers of other gods. In verses 3-4, the psalmist declares that Israel's God does not slumber or sleep. This statement stands in contrast with Israel's neighbors who commonly believed that their gods "slept" during the winter months and revived during seasons of growth.

I once toured the temple of another religion. It contained many physical representations of their gods and a gong. When asked the purpose of the gong, the guide replied, "We beat the gong to make sure this particular god is awake."

The psalmist took every opportunity to affirm faith in the God of Israel. This God made heaven and earth. This God never slept. This God provided shade as a refuge. The belief that God could provide shade for the pilgrims indicated their belief in a huge God capable of shading them from the sun by day and the moon by night. The psalmist goes on to say that God will keep us from all evil. The psalmist places complete trust in God.

What about you? Of what do you boast about God? Which of God's characteristics do you rehearse to yourself and with others in corporate worship? Your declarations about God help you see life with the eyes of faith.

God, since you never slumber or sleep, free me from anxious nights and fearful mornings. Amen.

Y ou're sitting in my pew!" "I've been a member of this church long before you ever arrived." We could easily insert the phrase "membership has privileges." How many of us equate church membership with salvation?

In today's passage, Paul addresses the prevailing idea of his day: that Jewish heritage alone determines which people qualify to participate in God's covenant with Israel. But if Jewish heritage were the sole litmus test for "membership" in God's covenant, then we Gentiles would be left out.

Paul presents Abraham's experience with God as the prime example of justification by faith. What does it mean to be justified by faith? The answer eludes many of us. Intruding upon our understanding of what it means to be "right" in God's eyes are our concerns about not measuring up. Some ask, "Am I good enough?" Paul argues that justification, the act of God making humankind just or free from the guilt and penalty of sin, occurs by faith and not by works. We are in good standing because of what we believe and not because of what we do.

When we first met Abram in Genesis 12, he hadn't done much, other than leave his family and kinfolk to follow God. He hadn't been circumcised yet—a big covenant issue for Jews. He hadn't experienced the miraculous birth of Isaac. Last, God hadn't tested Abram's faith by asking him to sacrifice Isaac.

Jesus had not yet come to earth, but Paul reminds us that "Abraham believed God, and it was reckoned to him as righteousness" (Rom. 4:3*b*). Clearly, the message of justification is more about our willingness to trust the God who justifies the ungodly than about how many good deeds we've done or our spiritual pedigree.

Justifying God, thank you for making room for me to be in covenant with you. Thank you that faith in Jesus Christ opens the door to right relationship with you. Amen.

When I ask people in the United States about their relationship with Jesus Christ, many lower their heads and almost whisper, "That's a private matter." Today's passage focuses our attention on a private conversation. It seems faith is a private matter for Nicodemus too.

We could view Nicodemus's seeking Jesus out as a step toward discipleship. His questions will determine whether he comes to Jesus out of spiritual curiosity or spiritual snobbery. But why does he come at night?

Darkness, a commonly used metaphor in John's Gospel, represents a separation from God's presence. Darkness obscures what is clear in the light. Does Nicodemus want to hide his spiritual curiosity? Does he feel the need to protect his social standing as a Jewish leader?

For whatever reason, Nicodemus comes to Jesus at night to ask him a few questions. His first words betray collusion. "Rabbi, *we* know that you are a teacher who has come from God" (emphasis mine). "We" must have had a few questions they wanted Jesus to answer as well. So, Nicodemus comes representing himself and other inquiring minds from among his acquaintances.

Before this meeting, Nicodemus has formed predetermined categories into which he thinks Jesus fits. *You perform miracles, so you must be from God. I've got you pegged.* What categories have you created for God? Have you decided which people or sins are unredeemable? In response to Nicodemus's limited ideas about what God can and cannot do, Jesus replies, "No one can see the kingdom of God without being born from above." Nicodemus doesn't understand that seeing God's reign requires mind-expanding faith and spiritual transformation.

Limitless God, I pray for mind-expanding faith today. Amen.

SECOND SUNDAY IN LENT

Born again? Born from above? Born of the Spirit? What do you mean by all this, Jesus?" I can imagine Nicodemus's befuddled protest—the evening is not going as Nicodemus planned. He never voices the question that brings him to Jesus. Before he has cleared his throat, Jesus introduces a provocative spiritual conversation.

In John 3:3, Jesus uses the Greek term *anothen*, which carries a dual meaning. Some translators prefer its "again" meaning. That phrase, along with Jesus' later comments about water and Spirit, have caused some to see their combination as a clear reference to water baptism. Nicodemus, however, thinks Jesus is speaking literally about being born again. Even if he had interpreted the reference to mean "water baptism," he would have been nonplussed. In his tradition, baptism was reserved for proselytes, not people already established in the faith.

Other scholars translate *anothen* as "from above," which refers to spiritual transformation. The concept of being born from above would have been no easier for Nicodemus to grasp. As a Pharisee, he would have been conditioned to believe that keeping the law was the way to God's heart. But here Jesus talks about the kingdom of God and spiritual transformation.

In verse 8, Jesus introduces *pneuma*, another Greek term with dual meaning—both wind and spirit. The wind, Jesus reminds us, is unpredictable. By contrast, Nicodemus strikes me as a person who desires to live a neatly prescribed life and who may balk at the invitation to go whenever and wherever God's wind blows. How about you?

God, when your Spirit-wind blows, teach me to surrender my will and my way to yours. Amen.

Touchstones of Wonder

MARCH 17–23, 2014 • RAY WADDLE

SCRIPTURE OVERVIEW: All the readings affirm God's benevolent care of those who place their well-being in God's hands. While imperishable, God's love can be frustrated by human pride and faithlessness. Water is an important symbol of God's sustaining grace. In Exodus 17 the Israelites' dependence on water becomes a statement about their dependence on God. The manner in which they obtain their water stands as commentary on human pride and arrogance. The psalm recounts this episode as a means of warning the people against the kind of obstinacy that impedes grace. John 4 focuses on the full actualization of God's love in Jesus Christ through the "living water." Paul speaks of God's love being "poured into our hearts," a grace that comes in the death and life of Jesus Christ.

QUESTIONS AND THOUGHTS FOR REFLECTION

* Read Exodus 17:1-7. When have you complained to God about a situation, only to discover a clear rationale through God's guidance?
* Read Psalm 95. When have you put God to the test?
* Read Romans 5:1-11. How do you push yourself into experiences that enhance your character?
* Read John 4:5-42. Jesus offers the option of living water. What "risky questions" do you have for him? What "life-changing" responses have you internalized?

Writer and columnist; editor, *Reflections* journal, Yale Divinity School

During the six weeks of the Lenten season, churches often alter the rhythm of worship, seeking a different mood of the spirit. In many settings, the Alleluias are eliminated. In some sanctuaries, the organ goes silent. The point is to forge a zone of silence, invite self-scrutiny, impose discipline, acknowledge the looming theme of death in Jesus' story, and await revelation in pre-Easter humility.

I'm ready for this liturgical time of year. It's a way of fasting from wordy religious talk and letting some spiritual realism settle in. Time to give up illusions of control and perfectionism. Time to ask forgiveness, watch, listen, and remember basic facts of the divine relationship.

Psalm 95 provides a Lenten reality check. It says to look upon this earth and see the truth of God: "In his hand are the depths of the earth. . . . the sea is his; for he made it."

We can easily neglect this orientation. The habitual approach involves our gazing on creation and letting science do the talking. Yield to geologic principles. Concede the floor to particle physics. Make way for biochemistry. All these are brilliant tools, miracles of knowledge and theory. But the main event towers over it all, undergirding it: the work of a Creator.

This psalm carries a reminder of the nature of this God: A creator powerful enough to produce the universe will stand apart from it, unrivaled, invisible, eluding all imagery or description. The mysterious existence of life itself is the hard evidence of divine action. God didn't have to create it. But God did. Psalm 95's advice suddenly looks sensible: "O come, let us worship and bow down, let us kneel before the LORD, our Maker."

It's good to get back to Lenten touchstones of wonder and attentiveness. Alleluia to that.

Eternal Spirit, we are all sojourners in this life you have created. Make me an instrument of your compassion. Amen.

What would it be like—a chance encounter with the Messiah at, say, the water cooler or vending machine? How would it go? Would it be shot through with misunderstanding or a life-transforming moment?

The story of the woman at the well gives us a rare moment of dialogue between a regular person of the ancient world and a world-changing personality. Its realism is endearing. She is courteous but also feisty, and there's no evading the complications of her personal life.

Another realistic detail shines through: The woman doesn't understand what Jesus means. He talks of offering her living water, and she immediately thinks he means magic H_2O in a bucket that will take away the boring task of water-fetching, as well as her thirst, like a conjuring trick.

It's hard to blame the woman. She is coping with an intimidating scene, a face-to-face moment with cosmic revelation. The disciples and others reacted this way all the time, misinterpreting him, crudely reducing what he said to impossible earthly components. Even the learned Nicodemus: Born again? How can a person enter the womb a second time?

But the Samaritan woman hangs in there. The conversation continues. Her attention on him sharpens. She listens harder. She stands astonished, riveted by this stranger's insight into her life. In the end she is busting to tell others about his effect on her.

Spiritual conditions are no different now. Even two thousand years later the reckoning of faith looks familiar. I am standing at the place of daily routine every day, oblivious to the blinding potential of the moment. Then Jesus comes along. Will I turn away from all those wells that go dry and grasp the living water of the kingdom of God—or not? The encounter awaits.

Dear God, I pray to be attentive to the next encounter, the next revelation. Grant me understanding and courage. Amen.

I find it a strange, disconcerting image: the people of God quarreling with the Lord. In the Christian cultures I know—liberal, conservative, and in-between—we don't argue with God. We'd rather complain about one another.

In the Hebrew Scriptures, divine complaint is an honored tradition. Job famously challenges God. Prophets try to resist the divine plan when God taps them for service. In this Exodus passage, the whole group raises its voice against God's management of the precarious desert sojourn.

We modern Christians reluctantly aim harsh words at God or question divine arrangement. In the Old Testament, an argument with God suggests a real relationship. Anger assumes communication, emotional connection. It presumes a ground rule of engagement: The Judge will hear the bill of resentment and respond and make answer, if not amends.

I have a few complaints myself for the divine inbox. Why do we seem to be wired for tribal, limited loyalties rather than for universal love? Why the terrible maldistribution of riches and disasters and suffering and luck (and water) across the world? We are awash in mystery.

I read this passage again. I stand amazed that a relationship with the Creator of the universe is possible at all. In the ordeal of daily need in the boiling desert, this aspect is what the Israelites ultimately remembered. Frustration with God gave way to a greater experience: the mercy of God. It's what they learned and remembered, which is why we honor it even now.

Holy God, with gratitude I call your name. With conviction I admit my dependence on you. With hope I ask your blessing. Amen.

As a kid in Sunday school, I remember learning the basics of the moral universe, like the Ten Commandments. That included the enigmatic third one: "Thou shalt not take the name of the LORD thy God in vain." That implied avoiding a frivolous attitude toward God, avoiding certain curse words. These days the notion of taking God's name in vain covers a lot more ground than that.

Every day, the cascade of pleas to the Lord to destroy the opposition, endorse ruthless wars, or perform a miracle right here and now for our convenience all test the Divine to prove useful or worthy. Reading Psalm 95, with its river of praise for God's creation, restores a sense of balance—and just in time.

Whenever I get up early enough to watch the dawn aflame with color, this psalm could make a handy soundtrack. An uncommon calm fills the sky and me as well. Clarity asserts itself. The metrics of belief are made plain: God made this. God's creation speaks. It witnesses to God's decision to produce life and share it and be known by it. The proper response is mind-blowing awe, with some healthy fear and trembling thrown in.

The impulse to test God like the Israelites did at Meribah—to put God "to the proof" as this psalm says—signals hardened ingratitude, petulance, a refusal to attend to the mysterious fact of creation itself. So much goes unexplained in the brilliant, disturbing cosmos. But much goes unnoticed. Singing a song of praise to God is a way to reset the coordinates of this life: God is in charge of it all; I'm not. It's time to notice the big world again. It wasn't made in vain.

Step out into the quiet of a colorful dawn or dusk with notebook in hand and this psalm in mind. Record whatever thoughts come.

"Justified by faith," "reconciled to God," "Christ died for us." Romans 5 provides some of the church's cornerstone phrases. But stones can wear down with use, become weathered and mossy. To my ears, these phrases can too. Yet these phrases describe eruptions of experience close to the original action. Paul's words about Jesus were some of the first to circulate and win acceptance. His letters, written decades before the Gospels, stand as foundational witnesses to Christian history.

We have "peace with God" because of Christ, Paul says. What does he mean? Well, imagine if Jesus had not existed. No Jesus, no incarnation, no Word made flesh, no experience of a human connection to God. No peace—only stammering, guess-work, and doubt about God's presence.

Back to reality: Jesus lived, died, and rose again. Mind, heart and all the senses can follow him from Galilee to Gethsemane, from Calvary to Easter morning, revelation road, the work of God healing our broken connection to divine life. The human world stands reconciled with its Creator. Reconciliation with God is a new way of walking through the world, a way of meeting and filtering whatever comes next—pain, uncertainty, hostility, fear, the seven deadly sins, the unexpected grace moments—with a courage and confidence that didn't exist before.

Paul had a mind for making arguments and a temperament for making friends. He wrote in the great shadow of the One who inspired him, tracing the unmovable logic of God's love, clearing a way for readers and believers ever since. If God could raise his son on our behalf, then what could possibly defeat that love? Nothing anymore.

Author of all that is, I am grateful to you for language, poetry, and reason. Make me alert to your word, your thoughts, your will wherever I find them. Amen.

The Israelites' blunt question echoes through the centuries: "Is the LORD among us or not?" They had reason to wonder. Moses had led them out into the desert with no Plan B. Scorched conditions, no water.

Ultimately, only the Israelites' covenant with God saw them through. A covenant hammers out a two-way connection: The ancient Hebrews dedicated themselves to God; and, in the mystery of sacred history, the Almighty chose to dwell with them.

"Is the Lord among us or not?" The question lives on as a plea, a prayer, an outcry, sometimes a vain hope. The twenty-first century distorts it in new ways. We go to war, justified or not, and ask, "Is the Lord among us or not?" We go broke from overspending, causing all sorts of anguish, much of it avoidable, and ask, "Is the Lord among us or not?"

From the far corners of scripture, answers to the question come with remarkable variety. The Ten Commandments put a person in deep historical proximity to God's will for human life. Later, Jesus said to look into the eyes of those who suffer, reach out to them, and find the face of God. Indeed, Christ is Emmanuel, "God with us."

Keeping matters simple appears to be the point. In Proverbs the writer asks God to steer him clear of both riches and poverty, since each is a barrier to God. Poverty would make him bitter, riches arrogant.

It goes without saying that everybody suffers from bruises eventually. Crisis always comes too close for comfort. But in the desert experiences of the day-to-day, a person makes a hundred little decisions that keep God out or bring God within reach again. "Is the Lord among us or not?" rings every day with agonizing urgency. So do answers.

Describe a moment where you felt God's absence—and a moment of God's presence.

THIRD SUNDAY IN LENT

The first time I stood along the banks of a roaring white-water mountain stream, I was amazed at the pristine look of the water, the fresh smell, the thunderous current.

When Jesus talks of living water in this well-known story in John 4, his words suggest a spring of water rising from a serene, ultimate source. But I also think of water rushing down from the mountaintop—the beckoning sound, cool to the touch, detoxifying, incorruptible, unstoppable.

This is religion, Jesus seems to be saying: This living water is what I offer. Why not reach out to it? It's elemental, life-giving. Why settle for less? It's simple. Why complicate it?

But, of course, people do complicate it. We want to know who else is drinking from it. What are its origins? No, thanks, I've got my own water supply already.

With the woman at the well, Jesus could have talked about religion a hundred different ways. He could have prolonged the old debate between Jews and Samaritans. Instead, he moved beyond ideology or tribal loyalties, those things that derail a conversation in seconds.

Living water: It intrigued her. It stirred her own images of liberation from burdensome daily uncertainties.

Two thousand years later, each person still brings his or her own images of thirst and refreshment to the news of living water. No definition on earth can catch or exhaust its meaning. But as long as I live, the good news will make the sound of abundant, cascading water. I would be ungrateful if I did not reach out to it.

Eternal God, keep me mindful of your living water, so that I may drink deeply from it and share it with others. Amen.

Bringer of Light

MARCH 24–30, 2014 • JOHN W. ZWOMUNONDIITA KUREWA

SCRIPTURE OVERVIEW: First Samuel 16 reminds us of the bold risk that Yahweh took in the anointing of this young and unheralded shepherd. If 1 Samuel 16 causes us to wonder about the adequacy of all human shepherds, Psalm 23 reassures us that one Shepherd never fails. The New Testament passages consider the tension between light and darkness as a metaphor for the conflict between good and evil. In Ephesians 5, the struggle has already been resolved but takes seriously the continuing problem of sin. By means of the love and presence of Jesus Christ, even the power of evil cannot withstand the light. Then John 9 emphasizes the power of Christ as a bringer of light in the story of the man born blind.

QUESTIONS AND THOUGHTS FOR REFLECTION

- Read 1 Samuel 16:1-13. Reflect on a hard time when you had to move on with your life. What helped you move forward?
- Read Psalm 23. Where and how have you experienced God's provision in your life?
- Read Ephesians 5:8-14. How brightly does the Christ-light shine in your life?
- Read John 9:1-41. How does God display power and compassion in your life?

Founding Vice Chancellor, Africa University; currently E. Stanley Jones Professor of Evangelism of the Kurewa Chair, Africa University

God's message to Samuel stuns the mind, "How long will you mourn for Saul, since I have rejected him as king over Israel?" (NIV). Samuel takes the concerns of both Israel and Saul to heart; but Samuel, as the seer of God, has already suffered the pain of anointing Saul and then withdrawing God's favor. Saul's disobedience led to God's rejection of him as the first king of Israel.

Samuel's disappointment is understandable. I recall the jubilation and celebration of the African nations as they glorified their gallant sons who delivered them from oppressive colonial rule to liberation. The long road to independence was littered with promises of peace, economic development, and justice for all; but like with Saul, some leaders, though having been "anointed" through democratic ballot, were rejected.

God does not tell Samuel that his grief is understandable or that he should allow himself time to mourn this sad development. No, the Lord tells Samuel to get over it and find another king! Israel needs a king; now is the time for action.

When difficult situations confront us, we often feel that we need more time than we have to grieve, to think, and to respond emotionally. When circumstances do not allow us this time, we may need someone who urges us to move forward. God offers this service to Samuel. Moving on wasn't easy for Samuel, and it's not easy for us. However, God continually comforts, guides, and upholds us, helping us tackle each new challenge.

O God, give us courage to respond in obedience to the Holy Spirit's promptings and to confess sincerely, in spite of the consequences of our human failures. Amen.

Fill your horn with oil and be on your way; I am sending you to Jesse of Bethlehem. I have chosen one of his sons to be king." Samuel has accepted the Lord's pronouncement that Saul will not remain king; but even as he looks for a replacement among Jesse's sons, he looks for someone like Saul. He looks for someone who *appears* mighty and powerful—a figure whose very presence communicates strength and authority. After Jesse's sons parade before Samuel, the Lord gives the nod to the youngest. At the Lord's encouragement, Samuel sets aside his preconceptions about outward appearance. He anoints David, "and the Spirit of the LORD came mightily upon David from that day forward."

The anointing of David to the throne brings hope to the newly established kingdom of Israel; so it is with the message of hope for Africa with a new crop of leaders for its young nations. The transition of political power in Ghana has been remarkably peaceful; a woman head of state and government in Malawi has defied the lavish lifestyle of African presidents by flying commercial flights to regional meetings. The hope for a new Africa is increasingly being realized not only by the numerical growth of Christianity on the continent but also by the transformation and the renewing of the mind of the young generations of Africans.

May we too learn to set aside our preconceptions of outward appearance. As we look "on the heart," may the Lord come mightily to work through our leaders and our world.

O God our Father, we pray for heavenly wisdom each time we cast our vote for those you have chosen to be leaders over your people. Guide your church to teach faithfully that genuine authority to rule comes from you. Amen.

"The LORD is my shepherd; I shall not want." The psalmist expresses his unwavering trust in God. The countries of the ancient Near East, including Israel, used the term *shepherd* as a metaphor for kings. The shepherd provides those within his care all they need to prosper, including protection from danger. The king had a similar responsibility toward his subjects. The psalmist's affirmation of God as shepherd declares a loyalty to God with the intention to live out that loyalty.

God's sovereignty surrounds all our living: in green pastures, right paths, and the darkest valley. The rod (or scepter) of this shepherd king brings both authority and comfort. The final verses call to mind the gracious host who offers at table the very things the shepherd offers the sheep: food, water, protection from enemies. With God as our shepherd, we too can affirm that our cup overflows in all circumstances. God's guidance will finally lead us home to the "house of the LORD."

This psalm reminds me of a song I once heard a youth choir sing. The song narrates the story of a young passenger on a plane that was caught up in a terrible storm. The plane tossed up and down, causing great discomfort and fright to the passengers. The little boy remained calm in his seat—totally undisturbed by the circumstances. A passenger seated next to the little boy asked, "Young man, are you not scared with what is happening to the plane?" The little boy replied, "The pilot of this plane is my father; and he knows I am here!" May our living exude such confidence and faith in our Shepherd.

O God, Sovereign Shepherd, may all persons give praise and sing, "The LORD is my shepherd." Amen.

He leads me beside still waters, he restores my soul." As noted in Abingdon's *The New Interpreter's Bible* commentary on this passage, the words "restores my soul" might better be translated as "keeps me alive." God's provision is all-sufficient, and our lives depend upon it. The psalmist relies solely on God. But why does God the Shepherd furnish this opportunity? Why? "For his name's sake." God provides and nurtures because that is God's very character and nature.

A colleague pastor, Reverend Kuri, and I were about to have lunch, when he received a phone call. One of his parishioners, Takura, had been crushed by a tractor he was repairing. Immediately, we headed to the hospital and went straight to the outpatient ward.

Pastor Kuri tried to communicate with the man, "This is your pastor. Do you hear me, Takura? Can you hear me?" There was no response. "I am Kuri, your pastor. I understand you had an accident." Again, no answer!

Pastor Kuri, having realized the seriousness of the situation, picked up Takura's hand, clasped it between his two palms, and said, "Takura! I am sure you hear me now; I want you to repeat Psalm 23 after me: 'The Lord is my shepherd; I shall not want.'" To our surprise, Takura repeated the words of the psalm, up to verses 2-3: "He leads me beside still waters, he restores my soul." At that point, Takura stopped, took his last breath, and died peacefully. Indeed, God restored his soul, preparing a table before him even at his departure.

O God, may we learn to rely on you and your provision for our lives in all the circumstances in which we find ourselves. Amen.

For the writer of Ephesians, the "before" and "after" are clearly defined: darkness *or* light—before Christ and after Christ. We have a choice. Before Christ, we not only lived in darkness but *are* darkness itself. When we choose to live as children of light, we begin to identify with all that is "good and right and true." We long to discern "what is pleasing to the Lord." We not only avoid participating in evil but bring it to everyone's attention by exposing it. The way we live changes when we move from darkness to light.

As a pastor in a rural circuit, I have witnessed the conversion of lives from darkness to light. One notable example was a woman who attended church every Sunday. She looked sickly, frightened, miserable, and often sat in the back of the church. While other churchgoers realized she had a problem, no one could put a finger on it. One Sunday evening service, the woman came forward for prayer and healing. Her conversion experience changed her outlook completely as she began to reflect her inner transformation in the outward aspects of her life. She gained weight and looked radiant and healthy. One Sunday morning she testified, saying, "Since I committed my life to Christ I have discovered peace in my life. I have discovered new joy and genuine love for my husband and my four children. My life is now filled with new love to serve Christ, my husband, my children and my church." She who once was darkness—even to her family—became light in the Lord.

Often we shine less brightly than we could. Although the light of Christ envelops us, we let darkness in from time to time. When this occurs it helps to know that while we may slip into sin, the light of Christ continues to shine, stirring us from slumber and awakening us to a new day.

O God, each day may I awaken to the task of bringing light to the world, through the grace of Christ. Amen.

In Israel some rabbis taught that there was no death without sin and no suffering without iniquity. Some also speculated that a child could sin in the womb and that terrible punishments came on certain people because of their parents' sin. Out of this background the disciples ask Jesus whose sin was responsible for this man's blindness. In reply, Jesus changes the focus of the question from blame to revelation.

The Gospels offer several perspectives on the purpose of Jesus' healing: Jesus healed because he was compassionate; he felt a need to alleviate pain and suffering inflicted by illness or disability. Or, as we see here, John's Gospel advances the view that Jesus' encounters with affliction, sorrow, pain, disappointment, or loss of life offer opportunities for him to reveal God's work. So Jesus answers the disciples in this way: "Neither this man nor his parents sinned; he was born blind so that God's work might be revealed in him." Jesus heals him to show God's power and to display concern for the suffering.

As we consider this thought, we might reflect on the theological misconception from which the disciples' question arises and contrast this view with the man's absolute trust in Jesus. Jesus shifts the disciples' focus from the past, the cause of this man's suffering, to the future—how will God display power and compassion in the midst of suffering? The man born blind trusts that Jesus will reveal God's power in him and follows Jesus' verbal instructions. By hearing he goes to wash in the pool of Siloam, and he comes back seeing.

O God, may we both hear and see your power at work in our lives. And may we bear witness to both. Amen.

FOURTH SUNDAY IN LENT

This miracle raises the question of who really can "see," as well as the issue of belief and unbelief. the contrast between darkness and light noted in Ephesians becomes embodied in the characters of this story. Yet the man born blind, while in darkness, exhibits a faith that manifests itself in a witness before the Pharisees that is "good and right and true." He moves from physical blindness to physical and spiritual sightedness. His ability to see bears witness to God's power. The religious authorities, though physically sighted, come to question their own spiritual sightedness: "Surely we are not blind, are we?"

When questioned by the religious authorities a second time, the healed man gives evasive but compelling testimony: "I do not know whether he is a sinner. One thing I do know, that though I was blind, now I see." This confession in Jesus leads the Pharisees to expel the man from the synagogue. Hearing about his expulsion, Jesus finds him and speaks with him. Perhaps the healed man recognizes the voice and connects it to the face he longs to see. He responds, "Lord, I believe." In his eyes, Jesus, sinner or not, is a healer.

Some people we encounter may be put off by public testimony or declarations of faith. Might we reach these people by pointing to evidence of God's work in our lives? Sometimes actions speak louder than words.

O God, give us courage to speak aloud our testimony about the work of your Son in our life, community, and society. Amen.

New Life

MARCH 31–APRIL 6, 2014 • LORI L. J. ROSENKVIST

SCRIPTURE OVERVIEW: Ezekiel 37 presents a vision of the dry bones that represent the people of Israel after the invasion of the Babylonians—the people have no life. God calls Ezekiel to see the devastation and to prophesy to the dry bones with the message that they shall live. The psalmist cries out from the very depths expressing both a need and hunger for God and a trust in God's steadfast love and faithfulness. The story of Lazarus's death and Jesus' raising him to life calls forth our own stories and experiences of life and death. It draws us into a conversation that goes deeper than our intellect. It evokes our questions, our fears, our doubts, and our faith. The Romans text offers the good news that the Spirit that raised Jesus from the dead dwells in us. Each of these texts affirms life after death. Death is not the end; death does not have the final word.

QUESTIONS AND THOUGHTS FOR REFLECTION

- Read Ezekiel 37:1-14. When have you found yourself in a valley of "dry bones"? What hope can you take from God's urgent desire to "prophesy to these bones"? What does it say about God who seeks life for us, even when we may not seek it for ourselves?
- Read Psalm 130. What kind of pain do you need to be experiencing before you cry out for help?
- Read Romans 8:6-11. What signs confirm that Christ is in you or that the Spirit of God dwells in you?
- Read John 11:1-45. How would you describe the main purpose of this story in John's Gospel?

Editorial team leader and Associate Publisher, Logos Productions; writer/compiler for *Behold: Arts for the Church Year*; member, Lutheran Church of Peace, Maplewood, Minnesota

As we begin a new week together, the words of Psalm 130:1-2 can provide a way to gather our thoughts. "Out of the depths I cry to you, O LORD. / LORD, hear my voice! Let your ears be attentive to the voice of my supplications." Psalm 130 is part of a series of psalms identified as Songs of Ascent or Pilgrim Songs. Imagine, if you can, a procession of the faithful, moving as a group, praying or singing these words together.

The words of this psalm may not be as familiar to us as the words of Psalm 23, but this is probably the psalm we pray most often, most naturally, and most passionately. "Please help me, God. I'm out of options, and I don't know where else to go." Whether it's a broken relationship, a health crisis, or an impossible financial problem, we all know what it is like to feel alone at some of our darkest times.

When being treated in a hospital, patients are asked to rate their pain on a scale from 1 to 10. It is interesting to realize that no matter how objective this numeric scale sounds, it is completely subjective. The pain I might rate as a 6 may be a 10 to you, and the primary emphasis is that both of us are "right." The pain scale allows us to express our discomfort and gives us access to the relief we think we need.

Like the medical pain scale, there is no right or wrong time to call on God for help. All that is required is our trust, because as the psalm assures us, "With the LORD there is steadfast love." We are not alone.

I encourage you to use the words of Psalm 130 through the week as a touchstone for reflection. You could focus on one verse each day or, if you prefer, read the entire psalm daily.

God of my days, thank you for hearing my cry. Tune my heart to hear your voice, and empower me with your reconciling and eternal love. Amen.

In the antiquities section of the Art Institute of Chicago, I noticed a tiny gold sculpture, no more than three inches high. Two skeletons sat together talking, and I immediately thought about this text from Ezekiel. I imagined how this kind of informal reunion might have taken place between newly restored friends in the valley of the dry bones.

This text is dated to the sixth century BCE, during the final destruction of Jerusalem. Unlike the cries of the people in Psalm 130, Ezekiel's bones lie silent. As he surveys the valley, we can understand the desolation. What could possibly change here?

Hopeless as it seems, when God commands him to prophesy to the bones, Ezekiel does it. As I put myself in Ezekiel's place, I can imagine feeling a little reluctant. But Ezekiel intones the words God gives. Picture the startled expression on his face when Ezekiel hears that first "click" of bone knitting to bone. Extraordinary! And then the miraculous sight of flesh covering bone. Unbelievable but true.

These are not just any dry bones; these are the broken, scattered, exiled people of Israel. And God is not satisfied to abandon the people, even though they have lost faith and turned away. Instead, God asks Ezekiel to call the bones to life.

And amazed as Ezekiel may have been at all that has transpired, his words in verse 8 acknowledge that the task is only partially accomplished. "There was no breath in them." It is not enough for us to be functional human beings. God's desires for us are so much deeper. God calls us to a new, rich, and abundant life that we can't even imagine.

You might want to search for a copy of Gustave Doré's *The Vision of the Valley of the Dry Bones* as you explore this story further.

O God, here in my valley of dry bones, I hold on to hope and watch for signs of the morning light. Make me ready to recognize your hand at work in my life today, and restore me. Amen.

Ihave been the fortunate recipient of a life-saving organ transplant. In many ways, I found myself completely unprepared for the level of healing I would experience. Like Ezekiel's dry bones, I had grown used to living with some level of disconnection. As systems deteriorated and strength dried up, I learned to scale back my expectations. In my own way I got comfortable living in the valley of dry bones.

While I waited in that valley, I didn't think too much about what might be possible for me, how life could be different. I thought it would be wonderful simply to be stable—to have a functioning organ instead of a failing one. But after the surgery I was thrust into a powerful and unexpected new kind of aliveness. Not only did I mend from the surgery; I also experienced healing on a molecular level as blood chemistry began to change and my body began to find a new level of wellness.

It took time for me to learn to trust this new life I had been given, and, in truth, I had gone there reluctantly. I knew what I had in the valley of dry bones. I had no idea what might await me outside it.

My experience helps me sympathize with those bones in Ezekiel's vision. They have lain in the valley, peaceful. Though defeated and disconnected, they have accepted their fate. This broken people might not have dared to expect restoration. But God wants more for them.

God commands the exiled prophet Ezekiel not only to reconnect the bones but to reanimate them. God's desire, for them and for us, is a living, breathing, growing, worshiping community. Imagine the new life that might await you.

God of breath, you come to me from the four winds, refreshing me with your life-giving Spirit. Where I have been broken, knit me together. Where I have felt disconnection, restore. Fill me with hope, and give me courage to live fully in this day. Amen.

After spending time in Ezekiel's valley of dry bones, we return to Psalm 130. Just as those bones were knit together, so these two passages are knit together with themes of hope and redemption.

Verses 3-4 invite us to consider the weight of sin versus the liberating release of God's forgiving love. When we have received such a gift, we often find it easy to deny forgiveness to others—or even to ourselves. We prefer to keep track of injuries, holding them as close as we would a prized possession. In *Traveling Mercies*, writer Anne Lamott points out the flaw in our preference: "Not forgiving is like drinking rat poison and then waiting for the rat to die." Or consider Eugene Peterson's paraphrase of John 20:23 (THE MESSAGE): "If you don't forgive sins, what are you going to do with them?" Imagine these words about forgiveness being spoken to you. Where in your life do they ring most true? What, if anything, do you wish you could do differently? How much lighter might you feel if, instead of recalling injuries, you try to recall unexpected acts of kindness and moments of generosity?

Pastors often read Psalm 130 at funerals as a source of comfort. Perhaps it helps survivors link the original experience of this pilgrim psalm with their own life's journey. As we review the words, we can imagine that this would be an easy song to learn, memorable because of its repeating phrases and key words: *wait, soul, watch, hope, redeem*—brief but rich words. Slowly repeat them to yourself, and turn them over in your mouth. How do they begin to form a prayer for you?

Loving God, the gift of your forgiveness is almost more than I can imagine. Help me to be as open-hearted as you are, seeking restoration in all my relationships. And where I feel I cannot forgive, help me to wait and hope in your word. Amen.

Paul writes this letter to Christian believers in the capital city of the Roman Empire in 56–57 CE. Today's text talks about two mind-sets: life in the Spirit and life in the flesh. God's Spirit offers a new way of salvation, apart from the law.

Before his life as a Christian missionary, Paul had been known as Saul, a persecutor of the church (see Acts 7:54–8:3). Only after Jesus' resurrection does Saul encounter Jesus in a life-changing vision (see Acts 9). Consider the contrast between seeking death or seeking life.

In comparing this passage to Ezekiel 37:1-14, we note the obvious and more subtle appearances of themes like flesh and death, Spirit and life. What would it be like, for example, to read the Ezekiel passage and replace the word *breath* with the word *Spirit*?

Living out of a mind-set of the Spirit brings life and peace. We note that the Spirit is God's to give, not a possession to hold. With the Spirit comes empowerment. And thankfully, the Spirit moves in the past, the present, and the future. Paul makes a strong case for life in the Spirit and poses his argument to us personally. When he uses the phrases "If Christ is in you" and "If the Spirit of God dwells in you," he invites us to think about what kind of life might be ours if we live in the life of the Spirit.

Paul assures us that although we have experience with death, God's Spirit offers a life that exceeds any expectations we may have as mortal beings. God challenges us to live into this expansive promise. As you move through this day, return to the word *dwell*. How might you make more room for and attend to the Spirit who dwells in you?

God of life, forgive me when I set my mind on things that are not life-giving. Help me to dwell in you and in your word. Make me a sign of your new life. Amen.

This familiar story is dense with detail. The Gospel writer carefully sets the scene, which promotes the feeling that more is going on than meets the eye. The scene opens with the news that Lazarus is ill. Jesus' disciples fear that death awaits their rabbi if he returns to Judea. Only toward the end of this passage does Jesus announce the death of Lazarus, using the euphemism of his having "fallen asleep." The disciples feel that Jesus must not take the risk since Lazarus is only sleeping. Jesus clears up their misunderstanding by telling them "plainly" that Lazarus has died. This story pushes through present events to give us a glimpse of the true meaning of Jesus' ministry. Jesus has come among us to turn upside down our expectations of life *and* death.

Unlike Jesus' other healing encounters, this is not a first-time meeting. His friends Mary and Martha ask for his help. A deep relationship exists among these family members and Jesus.

And Jesus chooses to delay setting out after he has received word of his friend's illness. He offers some interesting words of preinterpretation: "This illness does not lead to death; rather it is for God's glory, so that the Son of God may be glorified through it." He interprets the death of Lazarus in the context of his own impending death. Jesus realizes this event will not only glorify God but will bring the disciples to faith. As he notes, his time is limited: "Are there not twelve hours of daylight?"

Thomas's words in verse 16 leave us on edge: "Let us also go, that we may die with him." What obedience! We cannot allow our fears about Jesus' death to distract us from the central truth of this story. Jesus intends this encounter to be a point of revelation. Jesus will show himself to be the Word of God made flesh, dwelling among us to bring new life.

Loving God, we turn to you in times of joy and sorrow. You know us through and through. Help us to trust your deep and abiding care for us in death and in life. Amen.

SUNDAY, APRIL 6 ~ *Read John 11:17-45*

In verses 1-4 we read that Mary and Martha beg Jesus to heal their brother Lazarus. In verse 17 we learn that Lazarus has been dead for four days. And this becomes the story's focus: How do we live with death?

The first time we meet Mary and Martha, Jesus is visiting in their home (see Luke 10:33–11:1). Some people read Luke's story and believe that Martha just didn't get it, choosing busy work over Mary's example of faithful devotion to Jesus. But in today's passage a different picture of Martha emerges. She greets Jesus with these words, "Lord, if you had been here, my brother would not have died. But even now I know that God will give you whatever you ask of him." It turns out that Martha has been listening all the while. And then she boldly states, "I believe that you are the Messiah, the Son of God, the one coming into the world." Martha is the only person in John's Gospel who confesses this truth about Jesus. She has listened to Jesus, seen his mighty signs, and witnessed with her life that he is the Christ, God's chosen one.

Jesus raises Lazarus from death—not to give Lazarus eternal life on earth in his present body but as a sign that Jesus has the power to give new life. He is a life-giver.

The resurrection of Lazarus reminds us that we don't have one life on earth, then die, then start another life on some other plane of existence. This story emphasizes our lives' ongoing transformation. Our new life with Jesus begins in baptism and continues eternally. We are at one with God right now—always have been, always will be.

God of new life, all too often the stench of death steals around us, and we despair. Give us courage to move the stone that holds us back, then unbind us that we might receive your transforming love. Amen.

The Palms

APRIL 7–13, 2014 • NIALL MCKAY

SCRIPTURE OVERVIEW: These texts raise questions about who truly welcomes Jesus and under what circumstances. Isaiah 50 recalls the hostility that inevitably follows servanthood. A moment of acceptance, even welcome, will not hide from the Servant the fact of the rejection to come. Psalm 118 claims that the city and the victory and the "one who comes" all belong to God. Any victory declared by human beings is bound to vanish as quickly as the day itself. The Philippians hymn asserts Jesus' own determination to be obedient even to death and God's consequent exaltation of Jesus above all creation. Even in the Gospel accounts, Jesus' entry is one of meekness and humility rather than of power and pride.

QUESTIONS AND THOUGHTS FOR REFLECTION

- Read Psalm 118:1-2, 19-29. In this week, we may recall "the stone that the builders rejected" becoming the chief cornerstone. When in your life has God taken a time of rejection and turned it into a foundational experience?
- Read Isaiah 50:4-9a. The writer notes that for Isaiah, suffering does not signal divine indifference but plays a part in the world's bigger story. When have you interpreted your suffering as part of a bigger story?
- Read Philippians 2:5-11. This "hymn" states that to know Christ is to know God. The author stresses Jesus' mindfulness. What earthly traits of Jesus are evident in your daily living?
- Read Matthew 21:1-11. Where are you in the Palm Sunday story? How do you respond to Jesus as he enters?

Minister, Uniting Church in Australia; currently living and studying in South Africa

MONDAY, APRIL 7 ~ *Read Matthew 21:1-5*

Our Bible reading rarely surprises us with something new. The familiar narratives allow us to read in ways that confirm what we hold dear and skirt around the challenging parts. This tendency is nothing new. The Gospel writers did not write to reveal an unfolding plot. They were aware that their audience already knew the stories. Instead, familiar accounts were retold to emphasize important aspects of God's revelation in Jesus—often things forgotten or things being stubbornly avoided.

When we hear about Jesus' entry into Jerusalem on the back of a donkey, palm leaves and cloaks covering the path ahead of him, we, like the earliest Christians, know the end of the story. We read from the other side of Easter. We know the hypocrisy of those by the side of the road, one week shouting, "Hosanna to the Son of David"; the next, "Crucify him." We know that the one who comes in the name of the Lord is rejected and humiliated.

But sometimes we need to set our foreknowledge aside and join the Palm Sunday crowd as if we were welcoming Jesus for the first time. We need to hope alongside the occupied people of Jerusalem. We need to feel their fervent yearning for a Messiah who will end the violence of the Roman Empire and the corruption of the Jewish leadership.

In hindsight we know that the people on the road did not fully understand who Jesus was. Nevertheless, their welcome and cries of praise gained authenticity because they grew from an authentic hope. Nowhere in the Gospels is their action condemned. May we, like them, recognize Jesus and welcome him with joy.

Our God, give us fresh eyes and open souls to recognize you working in our lives and our world. Amen.

Our culture promotes the notion that everybody needs a hero and that everyone wants to find a brilliant, talented role model to shape his or her life around. Some heroes like Hercules or Superman have amazing powers that they use to shape the world around them. These heroes and their similarly superhuman adversaries do not have to overcome their own weaknesses and inabilities. Their stories are moral tales and typically deal with the allure of power and the pressure of expectation. Other heroes are far more ordinary and share in the same mortality and frailty of "normal" people. These heroes, like Florence Nightingale or Sam Gamgee display loyalty, courage, and perseverance. They overcome hardship through extraordinary commitment rather than extraordinary abilities.

Psalm 118 asked us to put our confidence in the Lord, the bearer of steadfast love, giving thanks. This "hero" is good and extraordinarily committed; God's love endures. Putting our trust in God and modeling ourselves after the divine differs radically from following mortals.

The psalmist sings of God's bringing him back from the edge of an abyss. He expresses deep thanks for God's saving work. The people of Israel sang this "song" for centuries before Jesus' birth, yet many Christians "recognize" Jesus as the Lord of Psalm 118.

Jesus shares in our mortality and frailty. Jesus is the hero who proclaims that God's kingdom stands in opposition to the power of the princes and on the side of the oppressed. He asserts God's love, steadfastness, and goodness and holds the salvation and healing of the world dear. For Christians, only this kind of hero can save us and inspire us to work for the salvation of all creation.

Loving God, give us strength to trust in godly heroes who reflect Jesus' life and work. Amen.

Ihave spent most of my life in places where the climate has not allowed the traditional experience of four seasons. I do not think of snow in the winter, and only some trees lose their leaves in the autumn. Many of the plants brought to Australia and Africa from the north appear confused, dropping half their leaves in preparation for the cold, then sprouting new buds when the temperatures rise early. Eucalyptus trees, on the other hand, drop their leaves throughout the year, spreading a constant carpet underneath. While this frustrates gardeners who like neat lawns, in the "bush" country, the layers of leaves cover the ground all year round. When the earth is baked hard, these leaves protect and cloak it each day.

When I walk through bush country, the soft, tactile covering of the earth reminds me of Jesus' entry into Jerusalem. For him, the unyielding path was also covered by palm branches and the cloaks of the people. When the visitors and people of Jerusalem throw down palms and cloaks, they acknowledge the special quality, perhaps even a *royal* quality, in Jesus. The rich and wholesome "blanket" thrown on the rock-hard dirt signifies an act of care and welcome into Jerusalem that lessens the unbearability of the brutal confrontations to come.

The symbolic laying down of the palm branches resonates with the peaceful return of the servant of God in Isaiah 55 where the trees clap their hands and the mountains and hills burst into song. When they throw down their cloaks, the people of Jerusalem join with creation to praise Jesus, to cry out for healing and salvation. May we join our voices with theirs.

Creator God, may we join with all creation to welcome you into our lives each day. Amen.

The original writers of the Psalms did their work hundreds of years before Jesus' birth. Yet the evangelists seized the language and imagery of the Psalms to shape their story of Jesus as the fulfillment and realization of the hope of the Israelites. We Christians hear the words of the Gospel accounts: "the stone that the builders rejected" or "blessed is the one who comes in the name of the Lord"—and think of Jesus. And we are justified in doing so.

Psalm 118 reminds us that even before Jesus, people discovered the hope of God in unexpected places, and salvation came through events and people that were initially rejected. The Old Testament overflows with unlikely leaders, of shepherds and old women, of second-born and even twelfth-born sons who succeed, of prostitutes and handmaidens and itinerant prophets. Now as the psalmist rejoices in the beauty and glory of Temple-worship, God's inclusion of the rejected is not forgotten.

The psalmist's insertion of the verse related to the rejected stone that becomes the cornerstone seems out of place. To what building is he referring? What is the rejected stone? Perhaps a look at the modern church offers some clues. It has been far better at rejection than welcome, rejecting people on the basis of gender, class, race, education, and age. Sometimes this rejection has been tacit and at other times, explicit. Often the church has hidden its rejection of people behind the pretense of rejecting sin or bad theology. Despite our efforts, however, God builds the church on the rejected and despised; Christ is the cornerstone. That fact is our psalm of praise on Palm Sunday. Thank God that glorious and godly worship emerges from the lives of the outcast and the broken.

O God, we are blessed that you love us in all our brokenness. Amen.

The idea that actions speak louder than words has become an unquestioned truism where I live. From national political debates to school students learning about "values," there seems to be an underlying aversion to hypocrisy. We don't like the idea of saying one thing while doing another, especially if our actions are hurtful or destructive. As humans we need to find ways to bring coherence across our lives, to make our words and actions parts of the same whole. Unfortunately, when we put all our worth in action, we ignore the truth of the power of the word.

Words have the power to shape and sustain a community; they can give purpose and direction. Sadly, words can also cause division and prompt violence. As important as action is, without words, spoken aloud or written on our hearts, what we do has little form or coherence. Words shape our actions.

So we give thanks to God for the sustenance of the word spoken to the weary, which whispers hope in the morning. By words we learn and by words we begin to understand the world and our place in it. More important perhaps is that through words we receive our agency and purpose—the direction and ability to change the world and not simply to be passive consumers. It is a different collection of words, a different story, that enables us to stand and turn our cheek to those who have hurt us. Words allow us to circumvent our visceral impulse to retaliate in kind.

As Christians, only after being nurtured on the Word can we set our faces like flint toward the cross.

Jesus, our Lord and teacher, may your word be written on our souls. Amen.

Once a week I pack the kids in the car, pick up my wife from work, and head to a nearby church to share in their community dinner. The dinner began when a small, elderly congregation got together with a community group to provide a weekly meal for anyone who needed it.

I have participated in soup kitchens and welfare programs before, but the aspect I most appreciate about this dinner is that it is clearly a community event. It is not a place where the haves give to the have-nots; at the dinner everyone eats together. Tensions sometimes arise when the preconceptions of the socially respectable meet the basic needs of the homeless and the addicted. Yet, for over four years, the people at the community dinner have exemplified the self-emptying servanthood we read about in this passage.

For disciples of Jesus, obedience and exaltation are always intertwined. When we bow down to Jesus our Lord, we bow to one who takes the form of slave, to God who is also the truly human one. Theologians have tried to make sense of the paradoxical nature of Jesus, but it breaks categorical divisions and refuses to fit into a neat box. We cannot explain Jesus' identity simply, and even today it remains a mystery of faith.

Though this understanding cannot be rationalized, it still holds deep meaning for Christian witness and service. In places like the local community kitchen, in African orphanages for children whose parents died of AIDS, and in all other places where the hungry are fed and the sick cared for, the spirit of Jesus lives and the kingdom of God is at hand. Thanks be to God!

Our God, may we find ways to serve others and witness to your glory. Amen.

SUNDAY, APRIL 13 ~ *Read Matthew 21:1-11*

PALM SUNDAY

Some of us embrace the idea of Jesus as the Prince of Peace. The suffering and sorrow of violence and war horrifies us, and we cling to the godly ideal of peaceful relationships between individuals and communities. However, many of us have twisted the radical pacifism of the gospel into a paralyzed passivity. Shocked by the gruesome reality of the world, we close in on ourselves and avoid anything that might disturb us. While we feel impotent to end the violence of the world, we believe that if we build strong walls around us, we can maintain a peaceful sanctuary for ourselves.

For Christians, this approach will not suffice. Jesus' entry into Jerusalem causes turmoil, and Jesus' entry into our lives does the same. It stirs us up; everything around us looks different—so much so that we cannot help but act differently.

For the people of ancient Jerusalem this much-talked-about man comes riding in on the back of a donkey, and turmoil abounds. The final prophetic confrontation nears.

I expect that all Christian discipleship is surrounded by and causes turmoil. Our Prince of Peace does not "magic" it away. Rather, when we follow Jesus we find peace beyond the turmoil as justice is done; the world is transformed, healed, and made new.

Lord Jesus, may we find your path into and through the turmoil of your coming reign. Amen.

Voices of Holy Week

APRIL 14–20, 2014 • MICHAEL E. WILLIAMS

SCRIPTURE OVERVIEW: It is inappropriate to conclude that God disappears at the cross and only emerges again in the event of Easter. Christian proclamation of the cross begins with the understanding that even in Jesus' utter abandonment, God was present. The Holy Week/Easter texts bring together the common themes of death's reality, the powerful intrusion of the delivering God, and the manifold responses to resurrection. Paul argues that the gospel looks to many like nothing more than weakness and folly. The cross symbolizes defeat but is, in reality, the instrument of power and salvation. The psalmist sings of God's incredible generosity and "steadfast love," which come in times of opposition and threat: "With you is the fountain of life." John 20 honestly faces the reality of death. The Exodus passage reminds us that God always stands ready to deliver.

QUESTIONS AND THOUGHTS FOR REFLECTION

- Read Isaiah 49:1-7. When have you seen Jesus in those who serve you, and where have you been called to serve by doing so?
- Read John 12:1-11. When have you experienced God's extravagant love and when have you reflected that extravagant love to others?
- Read Matthew 28:1-10. The angel seems unsurprised by the women's fear. When have you missed the good news because of your fear of matters you don't understand?
- Read John 20:1-18. What weeds need to be pulled from your life to allow you to experience the new that God has offered in Jesus?

Senior Pastor, West End United Methodist Church, Nashville, Tennessee; storyteller, writer, General Editor of *The Storyteller's Companion to the Bible*

Mary speaks, When Jesus spoke I would hang on every word. Why wouldn't I? After all, he had called my brother, Lazarus, back from death. He wept from his own grief or perhaps because he shared ours. He was that kind of friend. Judas was jealous of my close friendship with Jesus. He never made a secret of that. In fact, all of his disciples were jealous of the love he showed toward my sister, my brother, and me at times, but Judas took no pains to hide his envy. I think they recognized that while they were simply his disciples, I was his friend. I learned as much, if not more, from his friendship as I did from his stories and teachings.

For someone who never sought to lord his presence over others, Jesus was an imposing figure. When he came into a room, all eyes went to him. When he spoke, all other voices fell into silence. This made some people, especially very powerful people, afraid of him. I never once feared him; but others did, and that made me fear *for* him. There were those who sought to end his life, silence his words. He spoke often of his death as if it were a tragic but certain ending, a sure thing. While I had no power to call him back to life, I could at least prepare him for the worst. Martha and I had prepared our brother's body for burial. At the sound of Jesus calling his name, our mourning turned into dancing as Lazarus limped from the tomb—his death clothes still carrying the fragrance of nard. My one remembrance from that time is that I poured my only treasure, my precious nard, over Jesus' feet. Love as extravagant as his calls forth a similar extravagance from us. Don't you think?

Loving God, teach us to reflect the extravagance of your love in our lives. Amen.

The servant speaks, You will not remember my name after tonight. "Good evening. My name is . . . and I will be serving you this evening. May I start you with a drink or appetizers?" The name that fills the empty space in my well-rehearsed speech doesn't matter. It matters only that you are welcomed, the dust of the road washed from your feet, the weariness of the journey left behind. It matters only that you are filled with drink and food and that your conversation is never interrupted. I am artful in what I do. You will hardly notice that I am here. Unless, of course, you need something more. Then I will be at the ready to serve you. I am less a person than a function, a wisp of smoke, having just enough substance to serve, to please.

What if, just once, you truly heard my name, saw my face, looked into my eyes and saw the pain that lies in hiding there. It is a face that is neither handsome nor homely, neither comely nor ugly—a face that is something beyond those superficial distinctions. It is the face of those who are invisible to you and, at the same time, indispensable to your happiness, your well-being.

What if you looked at my face and in it saw your own true face reflected? You are the servant, bringing drinks and dishes, washing the feet of guests, bowing to those who consider themselves superior to you. Taking orders and then following through on them, spending your life meeting the needs and wants of others. What if you looked into my face and saw yourself reflected in me and me in you? Then, after you have seen that we are one, you learn to serve from me.

What if you looked into my eyes and saw there a holy glance. What if you heard in my voice the voice of the Holy One?

Jesus, in you we have seen what it looks like to serve. Help us to follow your example and serve at your side. Amen.

Judas speaks, He tore the piece of bread from the round flat loaf and handed it to me. The one who dips his bread into the same dish as me, he had said; that one will betray me. He might as well have said "the one who dips my bread" because it was his before it was mine, his bread ripped from his loaf and offered to me. The others looked around in shock and revulsion. They looked into the shadowy depths of their own hearts asking "Could it be me? Am I capable of betraying the best?" And they knew the answer was, yes, they could. Given the right circumstances they would do anything—betray him, deny him, desert him in his hour of need. It simply wasn't their time. It was mine.

While the others faced their own forms of faithlessness, Jesus leaned in to me and whispered, "What you have to do, do quickly." He knew the dark and fearful secrets of my fretting and stumbling attempts to follow his words and ways. Perhaps he knew the role into which I had been cast. Did he cast me or simply direct the action, urge me on . . . to what? His destiny or his destruction or my own or both or all?

Will my simple act (that many will call betrayal) ever be seen for what I had intended? Will anyone be able to understand that I was opening the door to the reign he had spoken of since I first heard his voice? The reign of God established, the Romans gone, Jesus lifted up onto the throne of David our ancestor of blessed memory. Of course, things could go wrong. This play could turn out to be a tragic tale, the hero lifted on a cross rather than a throne.

There is no time for such questioning now. Doubt would only hinder the reign that I (rather, he) will usher in. What I have to do, I must do quickly. Isn't that what Jesus said?

God of forgiveness and love, help me to examine my own heart to see the ways I betray, desert, and deny Jesus. Amen.

MAUNDY THURSDAY

Peter speaks, Jesus always acts in ways that put us in a difficult position. When we told him that the crowds had no bread, he told *us* to feed them. We did, but only after he had come through for us—and them. Then when we traveled through Samaria, he stopped at our ancestor Jacob's well and began to speak with a woman from a nearby town. We objected, but he would have none of it.

Of all the things Jesus has done, this was the most bewildering and offensive. You heard me right, offensive! Rabbis do not wash their disciples' feet! Disciples wash the rabbi's feet. That is the order of things, an order set out by God. Truthfully, the servants are supposed to wash everyone's feet. Jesus had talked to us about serving. I for one would never have thought that it would include washing feet. The others may not have had the nerve to refuse, but I did. "Not my feet, you won't!" I told him as he knelt before me. Quietly but firmly, he told me that if he didn't wash my feet, I would have no part of him. I had been a part of him from the first. Was he about to reject me now? I would not allow such a mad reversal. I forced his hand. Well then, I told him, if you want me to be a part of you, then wash my whole body. That will show him. If he wants all of me, he can clean all of me.

At that Jesus laughed and began to pour water over my feet. What could I do? Then he began to tell us that we were supposed to do the same, to wash each other's feet. I will *never* understand this man.

God of time and memory, help us to remember Jesus washing his disciples' feet and learn from him how to serve. Amen.

GOOD FRIDAY

A *woman at Golgotha speaks,* There's nothing like a crucifixion to focus the mind. That's exactly what the Romans intend too. They don't want any of us to forget who is in charge here and what happens if you step out of line. The message comes through with such force that the men who followed Jesus fled to the hills. If not the hills, then somewhere far away; they are nowhere to be seen. A few women like me stand by helpless except to pray that his suffering will be brief, that death will come quickly. All we can do is watch him die.

Despised and rejected, those were the words that kept coming back to me. Jesus had read them from a scroll, the scroll of the prophet Isaiah. The phrase "despised and rejected" echoed in the space between me and this rabbi I had followed. How could I not have seen Jesus as the witness Isaiah described?

A lamb silently led to slaughter described Jesus perfectly. He could have called for an uprising; he could have called down an army of angels. He could have convinced Pilate of his innocence. The word from the palace was that he presented no evidence, called no witnesses, made no argument on his own behalf.

Still some of us respected rather than despised him, loved him rather than rejected him. It was from his life and the stories he told that we learned such respect and love. There may come a time when all of us, those who are here to watch him die and those who will only hear about it, will show the respect and love we learned from him. Who knows, one day we may be called upon to put our lives on the line for him.

God, who despises and rejects none of your children, help us learn from Jesus to respect and love all. Amen.

The angel speaks, It is little surprise that my message made no sense to the women, given what they had seen. Their teacher had been crucified. They had heard his last whispered words, and they had seen him unable to pull himself up for breath. When I said, "He is not here," they immediately thought that someone had opened the tomb and taken his body away. When I added the phrase, "He is risen," it shook their minds just as the earth had trembled earlier that day.

Of course, I had begun in the usual way, "Don't be afraid." Every messenger of God is taught to speak softly, put them at ease, tell them there is nothing to fear. These mortals are such an easily frightened lot, especially when anything outside their previous experience confronts them. No one ever expects the messages we angels deliver. My words of comfort did little good. The women were clearly terrified by my presence and bewildered by my words. I could see it in their eyes.

"Go, tell the others," I instructed them. I'm sure they had no idea that now they were the messengers of God (angels of a sort, if you please). They needn't expect a better reception from the others than they had given me. Their message, my message, God's message would prove just as frightening and confusing to the men as my message had been to them.

"He has gone ahead of you," I told them. Truthfully, he had been ahead of them all along and would continue to precede them wherever they traveled, and was also ahead of the ones who would come after them throughout the years. After all, if he did not continually precede them on their various journeys to God, how would they be able to follow?

God of all that is good, help us to hear without fear the good news of what you have done in Jesus. Amen.

Easter Sunday

Mary Magdalene speaks, I mistook him for the gardener—an honest mistake. After all, we were in a garden. When the gardener called my name it was with the same inflection I heard when Jesus spoke to me. "Mary," he said, and I knew. This was no gardener. This was my rabbi. When I called him "Teacher" in response, he knew that I knew. I wanted to kiss his hands, to throw myself at his feet, to embrace him. As I approached, he told me not to touch him. He had never kept me at such a distance before. I didn't understand, and it hurt my feelings.

My feelings are no longer bruised, and I comprehend Jesus' actions better. I have decided that I was not mistaken. Oh, he was Jesus all right; but maybe he was the gardener too.

Hear me out. What does a gardener do? A gardener plants seeds. Every word of Jesus was a seed to be planted; the stories he told sowed seeds through the minds, imaginations, and lives of all who heard them. We would bear fruit or blossom before he departed from us.

A gardener also pulls the weeds that would choke our growth. Jesus tore out the weeds from our lives and pruned the parts that would not bear the fruit of God's love. From me he weeded seven demons that were choking my mind and spirit. From Peter he pruned the arrogance, snipping off each denial with the question, "Do you love me," and then, "Feed my sheep." For each of us there were weeds to be pulled, there were branches to be pruned. Perhaps Jesus was the gardener each of us needed.

God of new life, pull up all the weeds that hinder us, and prune all the branches that do not produce fruit. Amen.

This Jesus God Raised Up

APRIL 21–27, 2014 • KATHERINE WILLIS PERSHEY

SCRIPTURE OVERVIEW: Psalm 16 and Acts 2 fit together, since the latter quotes the former. Both celebrate God's presence in human life and the powerful expression of that presence. In his Pentecost sermon Peter sees a messianic application of the psalm to the resurrection of Jesus. First Peter affirms that resurrection creates community, stressing the faith and love of Christians that arise without the experience of physical contact with Jesus. For later generations, belief and commitment are born out of the witness of others.

QUESTIONS AND THOUGHTS FOR REFLECTION

- Read Acts 2:14*a*, 22-32. How should the reader (or preacher) acknowledge Peter's troubling language of blame toward the Israelites without losing the point of the passage?
- Read Psalm 16. In what way does God provide protection and refuge for you?
- Read John 20:19-31. What does it mean for Jesus to bless "those who have not seen and yet have come to believe?"
- Read 1 Peter 1:3-9. How do Peter's words speak to Christians who do not live with the threat of persecution?

Associate minister, First Congregational Church (United Church of Christ), Western Springs, Illinois; author of *Any Day a Beautiful Change: A Story of Faith and Family*

Peter speaks these fiery words on Pentecost Day, but the theme of his address is pure Easter. The message Peter and his fellow apostles have for the Israelites (and, in good time, all the world) is extraordinary. Jesus died a horrible death, but God raised him up.

While Jesus' crucifixion took place in public, thereby becoming an all-but-indisputable fact, the resurrection of the Messiah is a different matter. On this topic we settle for the testimony of witnesses. To believe the Easter story we must first determine if we believe Peter. We know well Peter's less-than-stellar record as a follower of Jesus. We not only remember Peter's density and desertion; we cringe at the way he incriminates the Israelites. You crucified and killed him, Peter taunts; his accusation reverberates throughout history, leaving a shameful wake.

Why should we believe this imperfect apostle? Is his biblical interpretation pointing to the incorruptibility of Jesus' flesh persuasive? Is his confident delivery convincing? Can we perceive the power of the Holy Spirit at work in his words?

In all honesty, I can come up with no good reason to believe Peter—at least no reason that relates to Peter himself—or any of the other eleven witnesses with whom he stands that Pentecost Day. The person bearing witness of the good news may be a reformed scoundrel or a sinful saint, a relapsed drunkard or a child with a reputation for crying wolf. I believe Peter's testimony because what he says about Jesus is profoundly true in my own experience and that of others through the millennia.

Jesus, the holy man from Nazareth, the one through whom God did deeds of power, wonder, and signs, could not be held in death's grip—and because of this, neither can we.

God of Easter, we hear the good news with glad hearts; make us witnesses with Peter. Amen.

TUESDAY, APRIL 22 ~ *Read Psalm 16:1-6*

When reading the psalms, I tend to hurry through the harsh parts. I linger on the psalmist's intimate expressions of faith and doubt but avoid the vitriol spoken against the psalmist's enemies. Accordingly, I often skip past the line about the maligned others who choose other gods when I read Psalm 16— to my detriment. It casts a shadow, no doubt, but the contrast illuminates. Fixing our eyes on the darkness often makes the light more brilliant.

I know something about sorrow-multiplying idolatry. We all do, I think, even if we don't call it by its proper name. The false god I am most frequently tempted to serve is the god of absolute security. As a person who suffers from bouts of anxiety, I desperately desire assurance that nothing bad will befall me or my family.

I find it much harder to take refuge in the true God than to seek absolute security in a false god. The true God will not swoop in and catch my daughter when she tumbles from a concrete step or guarantee that the cells of my loved ones will never be besieged by cancer. (As it turns out, no matter how many metaphorical drink-offerings of blood I pour out, the false god can't do these things either.)

The protection our devotion to God affords us is not always the protection we think we want. But the boundary lines fall around us in a most pleasant place, indeed: They embrace us within God's eternal grasp. Nothing can remove us from that everlasting refuge. Even if our voices tremble, let us say to God, "You are my LORD; I have no good apart from you."

O God, we take refuge in you and trust that no matter what befalls us, we are yours forevermore. Amen.

The disciples cower behind locked doors, frightened and, I imagine, ashamed. They have failed their prophet, their teacher, their leader, their friend. If the tomb truly is empty and Jesus is walking the streets of Jerusalem again, are they ready to face him? Cowards in the hour of Jesus' death, they now allow their fear and shame to make cowards of them in the wake of his resurrection.

Suddenly Jesus stands among them. Isn't this the stuff of ghost stories? Don't only intangible haunts pass through doors? Aren't we to focus on the real and tangible body of Christ, present and fully alive? I used to roll my eyes at this kind of detail. But through the eyes of faith, Jesus' sudden appearance inside a locked room becomes more than a special effect thrown in for pizzazz. Yes, it signals God's impressive power, but God doesn't waste power on empty miracles.

In this passage, the Christ breaks and enters—and not just into a house. Jesus breaks the chains that bind God's children to fear and shame and enters their hearts.

"Peace be with you." This is what he says to the disciples gathered there. Not, "How could you deny me, Peter?" Not "Why did you not go looking for me when Mary told you she had seen me?" Simply: "Peace be with you." The disciples might have expected anger and disappointment. Instead Jesus greets them with the ultimate sign of reconciliation—his peace.

Jesus breathes on them. As they inhale the gift of the Holy Spirit, the disciples experience release from their cage of fear and the bond of shame and receive the authority to forgive—to break the shackles of sin that yet cling to their brothers and sisters.

Lord Jesus Christ, break into our hearts. Grant us the peace that delivers us from fear and the forgiveness that releases us from shame. Amen.

No wonder Thomas is ticked. No wonder he stubbornly announces that he won't believe a word unless he can see and touch Christ's wounds for himself. He has missed out on the encounter with Jesus Christ in the flesh, who grants peace and exhales the gift of the Holy Spirit. Wherever Thomas was that evening, he wasn't in the right place.

Thomas often gets a bum rap throughout Christian history; no one wants to be a "doubting Thomas." But how can we blame him? He becomes the first person pressured to affirm Christ's living presence without having seen for himself.

So Jesus does it again. He enters through the closed doors of the house. He issues the same greeting of peace and addresses Thomas personally, offering Thomas exactly what he needs to believe and offering it with no condemnation. Even as he concedes the special blessing in having faith without the benefit of proof, Jesus gives Thomas the chance to touch the hands and side of his Lord.

Sometimes we focus our attention on Thomas, whether we judge him or relate to him. Certainly, we find his struggle with belief and unbelief compelling. But we wisely turn our gaze to the One who was raised from the grave. Here we witness a resurrected Christ who willingly encourages a man to touch his tender wounds in hopes that he will believe in God's glory.

We may not have seen, but we believe. And if we do not believe, Jesus will find a way to make it so. The breath of his peace still rests upon us.

Jesus, give us what we need to see you for who you are and the courage to confess that you are our Lord and our God. Amen.

Enough is as good as a feast." Thus says Mary Poppins, ever the arbiter of wisdom. The children in her care want more, as children tend to do—as most of us tend to do, if we're honest. One slice of decadent chocolate cake is surely sufficient, but the temptation to go back for just one more forkful is fierce. More dessert, more money, more power, more time—we often struggle to make peace with *enough*, even though enough is not only enough, it is often preferable to profusion.

Here, the Gospel of John divulges that there is more to the story. It delights me to envision a host of undocumented miracles, conversations, and encounters with Christ. Sometimes that unrequited imagination even finds an object of fascination when an ancient manuscript or mysterious relic is discovered.

Yet even as John teases the reader about the many other signs Jesus did in the presence of his disciples, in the very same breath he confirms that the stories written in his Gospel are, quite simply, enough. In the text of our sacred scriptures, we encounter Jesus, who challenges and invites to believe that he is the Messiah, the Son of God.

We can choose to accept his invitation and live it out every day. We need nothing else to have life in his name: no hidden knowledge, no higher pathway, no magic prayer.

This story is enough. Our humble response is enough. Jesus is enough—and, sure enough, Jesus is as good as a feast.

Jesus, you are the Messiah, the Son of God. We entrust ourselves to you and give thanks for the life we are granted in your name. Amen.

Thomas sees and believes. The author addresses this letter to Christians who have not seen and yet believe. These believers find themselves in crisis; their acceptance of Christ makes them exiles. They have received the gift of salvation only to be faced with unthinkable persecution.

How can this reminder of the troubled history of the early church follow so quickly on the heels of Easter's glory? Surely, the good news that rang out last Sunday means that suffering is no more. And yet this epistle tells us that the faith of these early Christians—some who surely joined the unnamed class of martyrs—will be tested and refined by fire. Didn't Christ's death and resurrection put out the fire of evil and oppression for good?

Easter does not promise that we will be whisked away from suffering. Indeed, many believers throughout the centuries have experienced *increased* suffering because of their faith. Today, in some places in the world, openly professing belief in the name of Jesus Christ can be dangerous.

Jesus' resurrection brings new life, fostering the growth of a new community of persons who nurture and support one another. Christians rejoice in the face of persecution and pain, for as the author reminds us: We have an inheritance coming, one that is imperishable, undefiled, and unfading.

The promise of salvation doesn't render our life on earth meaningless, but an eternal perspective has an impact on how we approach each day. It gives us a new birth into a living hope. Life will overcome death.

The world around us may feel like Good Friday, and sorrow may touch our lives. But we are transformed by Christ in the here and now. The glory of the hereafter resides in our bones.

O God of living hope, no matter our circumstances, we rejoice with indescribable and glorious joy. Amen.

When I lived near the ocean, I always enjoyed driving the road that ran along the shore. On a clear morning, I would ponder the blue ocean and the spray of the breakers. I marveled at the curve of the land, how the mountains and the peninsula stretched to embrace across the bay.

But what I enjoyed most was the chance to observe the people on the sidewalk who were taking in the grand seascape. I caught fleeting glimpses of people who stood transfixed. Being in the presence of something so deep, so mysterious, so big, grasps people. I've heard it said that gazing at the ocean causes a soul to expand; the soul grows in response to what it sees.

I find it interesting that Peter in his sermon quotes rather extensively from this psalm to support his belief in Jesus' resurrection. (Read Acts 2:22-25.) This week's passages propel us to consider our response to what the Resurrection might mean for our lives. The Gospel emphasizes belief. The letter of First Peter weds belief to celebration: "You believe in him and rejoice with an indescribable and glorious joy."

Today's psalm sets the tone for such rejoicing. It serves to remind Christians—when read in the context of the other lectionary texts during the Easter season—that the Resurrection is not merely a doctrinal point to which we grant our intellectual assent. The Resurrection is something to behold and experience.

Our hearts are gladdened, our souls freed to rejoice. The Lord holds our cup and portion; our living is not restricted. And our bodies, often a source of pain, can rest, trusting that nothing can wrench us from the Lord's grasp. The believer will not descend to Sheol. The faithful will not tumble into the Pit. Easter reveals the breadth and depth of God's glory and leads to the path of life. May our souls grow in response to what we behold.

Lord, we believe; receive now the rejoicing of our souls as we delight in your wondrous presence. Amen.

Responding to Love

APRIL 28–MAY 4, 2014 • JEN UNGER KROC

SCRIPTURE OVERVIEW: What is the Easter message, and what are we to do with it? Two dimensions of the responses to God's act of raising Jesus stand out. First, repeatedly the texts speak of public worship. Second, the texts speak of changed lives. In 1 Peter 1 the Resurrection effects a new birth marked by obedience to the truth and to mutual love. The two responses—public worship and transformed lives—are not separate from each other in the texts. One leads to the other and back again.

QUESTIONS AND THOUGHTS FOR REFLECTION

- Read Luke 24:13-35. If you had a sudden encounter with the risen Christ, what plans would you change? What would you do instead? What would happen if you were to make those changes right now?
- Read Acts 2:14a, 36-41. Name a few ways in which following Christ means repenting from popular culture. Who will stand with you in mutual support as you seek to live out this repentance?
- Read Psalm 116:1-4, 12-19. How and when has God heard your cries? In what ways can you join the psalmist in offering praise, witness, service, or sacrifice as visible thanks for God's loving presence?
- Read 1 Peter 1:17-23. Who do you find difficult to love deeply? How can setting your faith and hope on God help free you for a genuine love?

Alto in the chancel choir at The United Methodist Church of Geneva, Geneva, Illinois

How do we respond to a love that breaks our hearts? Hopes awaken and then are dashed. We glimpse a new way, a different path, a kingdom of peace and love—here on earth. We take risks to allow ourselves to be caught up in that vision—to begin to think it might be true. To begin to open our hearts to God, ready to be used for that vision. Tastes of the sweet kingdom; the joy of sharing meaningful work together, work in service of a higher love.

These two disciples share in that sweetness only to lose it all, having witnessed the death of the one they have come to love and trust. They search their minds and hearts to discover how it could have happened, how it could have been prevented. Surely there could have been another way?

But there was no other way. And what the disciples have witnessed is not failure but a necessary and inevitable part of furthering God's reign—a reign larger and broader than they can possibly fathom.

In the fog of their sorrow and confusion, another comes alongside and joins their conversation. The two begin to explain but are stunned when the stranger begins instead to explain to them—to explain Jesus to them as if they had never really known him; to explain their own lives, their history, all that they themselves had known and witnessed and experienced.

In grief, with broken hearts, when they had left their familiar places, when all lay dead and shattered, they could hear what they could not hear before: God is not done with this story yet. Their hearts will not break forever.

God, we can do nothing but bring our broken hearts to you. Walk with us until our eyes are opened, and we can see you in our midst. Amen.

The disciples, intrigued by hearing their own story revisited in a new way, invite Jesus to stay the evening. An urgent hospitality: "Stay with us." A need to hear more. A sharing of the table.

The Gospel writer describes the disciples' response: new understanding, burning hearts, a sudden change of plans. Their original need to be in Emmaus seems irrelevant now. The greater need, even late in the evening after a long day's walk, is to hurry the seven miles back to Jerusalem to share the story, to be together with the other disciples, to see what this new thing might mean for all of them.

These two disciples move from grief, hopelessness, despair, confusion—to energy, burning hearts, urgency, insistent hospitality, a new plan. Trudging steps give way to flying feet. Seven miles back to Jerusalem in the middle of the night seems like nothing. It is as though the disciples themselves have been resurrected. Why? Because they spoke with a stranger and allowed themselves to hear something completely unexpected. How do we respond to a love that resurrects us?

Our lives can be full, even overfull, of our own expectations and assumptions. Shattered, when those expectations are broken. Confused, trying to make sense of loss and grief. And then—suddenly, unexpectedly, from a surprising source, reinterpreted, retold, redeemed. Can we also feel our hearts burning within us? Can we welcome the stranger, and acknowledge our need to hear more?

Lord, come to us. Make yourself known to us in the stranger we meet unexpectedly, in the stories we think we know so well. Let our hearts so burn within us that all our self-preoccupation, confusion, and grief burn away, and we change our plans to see where our new story takes us. Amen.

Peter's sermon brings his hearers to repentance, and, for him, the next step is baptism. Becoming a follower of Christ in the days of the early church went against cultural norms. It meant walking away from the way of life and identity that had shaped you up until that moment; recognizing a new Lord, and letting that Lord become the guiding force for every decision and plan from that time on.

For many of us today, born and raised in the church, this is not our experience of Christianity. Does that make following Christ easier or harder for us? Has it become too easy to confuse being Christian with simply being "a good person" or a good citizen? Do we feel we have nothing to repent from? Is there nothing that cuts us to the heart and moves us to cry, "What should we do?" What message is there for us to hear and welcome? How do we repent and change if we think we're already on the right track and doing pretty well?

What does following Christ mean now, today, in this culture, in your community? How do we respond to a love that calls us to repent?

Live into it—this very day! Take a step that has eluded you because it felt too countercultural. Reach out to someone you might normally overlook. Remember someone who is too often forgotten. Admit a need for repentance. Ask forgiveness. Share your joy; share someone else's pain. Take a greater risk in the name of the One who took every risk. And before the day is done, share your experience with another who seeks to follow Christ—not to brag but as a companion disciple humbly recognizing the need for community.

Lord of our lives, send your Spirit once again. Wake us from our routines and habits so that we can hear your call to repentance and renewal. Work in our hearts so that we can truly welcome you as our Lord and Messiah. Amen.

Can we imagine, in one great Pentecostal day, adding three thousand people to our lives? People we may have never known or have felt no connection to. Surely among three thousand people, there would be a few we don't even like. Only God's Holy Spirit can break down barriers of personality, culture, language, and nationality to create a unity greater than any division.

After that great day, many of the three thousand left Jerusalem and returned to lives and communities that knew nothing of their conversion. How will they sustain their new faith? We realize after a "life-changing" event how easily we can slowly but surely return to the old ways, to let go of the very revelation that cut us to the heart.

But . . . what if these newly baptized believers return to their homelands, not as individuals, but as freshly bonded groups of a new community? What if the unity they experience at Pentecost returns with them? Then it becomes all the more likely that the new Christians can sustain and even grow in their faith!

Peter assures us that the promise is for us as well, for our children, and for all who are far away. But we do not live into this promise alone, as individuals isolated within a culture that does not understand. We live our faith in community, in unity with others—even others with whom we may not share much else in common. (Or whom we don't like!) Our need for community in faith is too great to let these things stand in the way. How do we respond to a love that binds us to a community?

Perhaps our need for repentance includes repenting of our comfortable lack of connection. If the Holy Spirit brings connection and unity, let us seek it out and embrace it.

Come, Holy Spirit. Cut us to the heart. Cut away those things that divide us, so that we can be grafted together, growing together into your new church. Amen.

Ifeel so alone. No one understands. How did this happen? What do I do now? I need you to pray for me. Help."

In distress and anguish, we acknowledge the power of being heard. Of knowing that we are not alone. Of sharing the burden with someone who cares.

In distress and anguish, whom do you call? A trusted friend, a spouse or parent, a mentor? Someone who may have felt pain like yours and who understands what you are suffering? Someone who will listen, hear you, understand you, and love you, even if he or she cannot change the source of your pain?

The psalmist cries her suffering aloud to God, begging to be heard. She does not wait for invitation or approval before crying out her pain. God hears. God is there. God stays close.

And in response, the psalmist overflows with love and gives expression to her gratitude: "I love the LORD, because he has heard my voice and my supplications. . . . What shall I return to the LORD?" Having been heard, she offers praise, trust, public witness, service, and sacrifice.

God has freed the psalmist from isolation and fear—and in return, she feels an even stronger bond of love and devotion. The response to love received is love given. Love overflows. All those around her will see it. Her life becomes a fountain, overflowing with love.

How do we respond to a love that hears our cries of pain? Let us not reply to God's persistent presence with indifference.

Hear us, Lord. And by your grace, help us to respond with the kind of love you have for us. Amen.

Last year, I began taking mandolin lessons. Each week, my instructor would give me homework: scales to practice, chords to learn, or a song to play each day. When I returned the following week, he would ask me to demonstrate my new skills. He would easily know whether I had done my homework!

More recently, I've returned to martial arts. Again, I have homework: one hundred sit-ups every day for a month. Learn to do fingertip push-ups. Practice the first basic form three times a day. And again, my instructor can tell whether I've been diligent at home.

Peter reminds those in the Christian community to do their homework: Live in reverent fear. Set your faith and hope on God. Purify your souls by your obedience to the truth. That's a little different than practicing scales or doing sit-ups! What might Christian homework be? For the author of First Peter, conversion involves a deep commitment to mutual love, living a life consistent with the gospel. Have you done your homework today? Who will help you check it over?

How do we respond to a love that calls us to disciplined practice?

Just as in music or martial arts, the goal of Christian homework is not the homework itself. My mandolin teacher never expected me to give a recital full of scales, nor does my martial arts instructor think that sit-ups are the pinnacle of style. The goal of Bible study goes far beyond simply reading the Bible. But without the scales, a musician can never play a symphony; without sit-ups, an athlete will never build strength. Without meaningful discipline and love for one another, how can we shape our lives after Christ's example?

Lord, in all my practice today, teach me to set my faith and hope on you. Amen.

Peter writes to a Christian community in exile, separated from the homeland and from other believers. He writes to encourage his friends from afar but also to remind them to stay faithful.

This epistle urges them to hold on to their faith and their practices! To remember who they are! And what does Peter identify as both core and outcome of these practices? Is it regular attendance at worship? tithing? willingness to chair a committee or teach Sunday school? No. Rather, it is to love one another deeply from the heart, to have genuine mutual love.

This passage challenges me to use only one measurement to evaluate my spiritual practices: Am I becoming more loving? Am I loving God and neighbor more deeply from the heart? I suspect Peter would be unimpressed with hearing how many days I remembered to read my Bible, or even to pray, if that time spent did not help me grow in genuine mutual love. Indeed, how can mutual love even exist if I sit alone in my kitchen, reading and praying by myself? My study of scripture and time in prayer must drive me out of my house and into relationship and service, so that genuine mutual love can grow.

How do we respond to a love that calls us to genuinely love one another?

If genuine mutual love is where I set my sight and find my purpose, then perhaps I will still serve on a committee or teach classes—and surely I will find myself in communal worship and offer my gifts. But these actions will spring from love and commitment to my community, rather than from obligation or simple habit. I will express that love and commitment outside of my church walls as well. By the grace of God, let it be so.

Loving God, enter into my practices and habits so that they become a means of your grace. Amen.

The Shepherd's Voice

MAY 5–11, 2014 • KEN EDWARDS

SCRIPTURE OVERVIEW: Three of the texts use the image of shepherd and sheep. Psalm 23 and John 10 picture the familiar relationship of trust that sheep exhibit toward the shepherd. The shepherd places himself between the dependent sheep and the aggressive enemy to ward off destruction and exploitation. John 10 and 1 Peter 2 introduce the costly price paid for protection. The sheep's safety comes with immense and undeserved sacrifice. In 1 Peter 2, the shepherd's sacrifice makes possible the return of wayward sheep who have wandered from the shepherd's protection.

QUESTIONS AND THOUGHTS FOR REFLECTION

- Read John 10:1-10. What spiritual practices have helped you discern the voice of the Shepherd? Reflect on the image of the sheepfold. How does this image aid or hinder your thoughts about an inclusive Shepherd? Reflect on this thought: "Status does not exist in the mind of God."
- Read Psalm 23. What sights and sounds come to mind as you read this familiar text? How do your senses help you understand the nature of God as presented in Psalm 23?
- Read 1 Peter 2:19-25. Reflect on times when you have strayed or been tempted to take an easier path. Spend a day practicing attentiveness, and reflect on how this spiritual practice made you more aware of God's leading presence.
- Read Acts 2:42-47. What is the role of the community in the ministry of encouragement and support? Reflect on a problematic or confusing time when others offered help and support to you.

Senior pastor, Belmont United Methodist Church, Nashville, Tennessee

Imagine a watering hole in a primitive place where nomadic shepherds gather to water their flocks. The shepherds come from the hillsides with their sheep, and the flocks mingle together. From our vantage point it is impossible to tell one from another. The shepherds enjoy this rare moment of fellowship, telling stories, sharing food and drink. Finally, the time comes to depart. A shepherd stands, takes his staff in hand, and speaks. He speaks a word, or perhaps he speaks the names he has given to the individual sheep. The sheep that belong to the shepherd cock their heads to one side and begin to move out and away from the others and follow the familiar voice.

Jesus paints a similar picture in this text from the Gospel of John. The shepherd calls the sheep by name, and the shepherd leads them out. The sheep follow because they know the shepherd's voice. When I read this passage I always ask, "How will they know the shepherd's voice?" And how will *we* know the Shepherd's voice? How will we discern the voice of the Good Shepherd from all the other voices that threaten to drown out Jesus' voice? Our days are filled with many voices speaking loud and conflicting messages, voices that beckon us to follow, voices that seek to lure us down other paths. How will we know the voice of Jesus?

The sheep in our imaginary scene follow their shepherd because over time they have come to know the shepherd, to trust the shepherd's direction and care. They have developed a bond with one another. For us the bond is nurtured through time and the richness of spiritual practice until we come to a place of knowing trust and assurance. Then we are able to discern the familiar voice of the Good Shepherd from all others, give attention to his gentle leading, and confidently follow.

Gentle Shepherd, in moments of quiet and stillness we hear you call our name and prepare to follow where you lead. Amen.

Although I was not the man's pastor, I had been the one to offer pastoral care during the last days of his illness. His daughter had explained that her father had fallen out with the church when he was younger and vowed never to go back. He had attended church with her and in spite of his history with the church, he graciously received my hospital visits. On one visit he was obviously struggling with pain. When I entered the room, I asked if I could help make him more comfortable or get a nurse; he asked me to read Psalm 23 to him. I gladly accommodated his request. The next day he died, and death came as a release from his great suffering.

The daughter asked for one more favor, "Will you help the family with the service?" I was glad to help. I spoke only briefly at the funeral and related the story of his request for the reading from the psalm. When we arrived at the graveside, I invited those gathered to say the familiar words along with me. "The LORD is my shepherd I shall not want." The words were softly spoken and carried on the gentle breeze.

Later the daughter would tell me that hearing those words from the psalm, spoken softly and reassuringly through the familiar voices of family and friends, made her aware that she was not alone in her grief. Her community's presence and her community's shared affirmation of God's shepherding presence carried her through the days and weeks ahead.

"The LORD is my shepherd" is Israel's affirmation of faith; we too take comfort in knowing that God is our Shepherd on our life journey. God guides our paths, gives us hope and strength, and walks with us, even through those dark valleys of grief.

Loving Shepherd, guide our paths during the dark nights of grief and crisis. Amen.

My wife and I were driving from Durango, Colorado, back to our campsite at Mesa Verde National Park when we saw a young boy riding bareback on a horse and coming toward us on the shoulder of the highway. As we got closer to him, we could see that he was waving a red bandana and trying to get our attention. I quickly slowed the car and as we crested the small hill ahead of us we could see the reason for the look of alarm on the boy's face—sheep. Dozens of sheep had escaped their enclosed pasture and were roaming all over the highway. After thirty minutes of herding and pleading, the sheep began to make their way off the road, and my wife and I resumed our journey.

The passage from First Peter reminds us that the protection of the sheep comes at a cost to the shepherd; shepherding is a demanding vocation that can entail suffering. Peter notes how Christ, the Good Shepherd, suffered, and he implies that our vocation as Christians may bring suffering. Our redemption comes in following Christ's model.

The sacrificial life of the shepherd enables the wayward sheep to find their way home to protection; "For you were going astray like sheep, but now you have returned to the shepherd and guardian of your souls." We all go astray from time to time. Most often, we stray because we have quit listening to the voice of the Shepherd. The journey of faith requires attentiveness to God's leading presence.

I met a young man in college who said, "Every morning, before I get out of bed, I lift my hands toward heaven and say, 'Dear Jesus, take my life before someone else does.'" I never forgot that simple prayer and my morning prayer is much like it, "Dear Shepherd, I give myself to you this day. Help me be attentive to your leading presence all day long."

Patient Shepherd, we give ourselves to you this day and trust in your leading presence. Amen.

When I went to serve a church in the city, I developed a pedestrian relationship with the homeless. I learned their names and heard their stories. I became more aware of the hardships of life on the streets, of enduring unpredictable weather and the disdain of business owners. The church looked for ways to grow in our hospitality toward these folks who are among the most marginalized of our city. Where do these neighbors fit into the shepherding imagery of the Bible?

The leaders of the Hebrew story, Abraham, Jacob, Moses, and David, were all shepherds. But by the time of Jesus, we know that shepherds were not held in high esteem. For Jesus to use the image as a reference for himself would have been stunning and possibly scandalous. In this passage from John the shepherd enters and leads out through the gate. Those who pass through the Jesus-gate receive the assurance of nurture and protection. Jesus sets forth a beautiful rhythm of hospitality in these words as the shepherd leads in and out and welcomes the sheep as his own. We can easily imagine Jesus welcoming into the safety of his loving fold those who are often dismissed or overlooked.

We are surprised again and again by the wideness of God's inclusive mercy, and we keep finding ourselves shoulder to shoulder in the sheepfold with persons who are different from us. The sheep who follow the Shepherd are not all like-minded; they are not of the same class or race or political party. Some are financially secure and others are struggling, poor, and marginalized. Status exists only in the minds of human beings, never in the mind of God. In the voice of the Shepherd we hear the call to widen our circles and open our hearts.

Inclusive Shepherd, help us set aside our human inclination to value status, and open our hearts to welcome everyone into your sheepfold. Amen.

FRIDAY, MAY 9 ~ *Read Acts 2:42-47*

The description of those early church folks, gathering to pray, to experience fellowship, to break bread together, and to share their lives "with glad and generous hearts" presents a lovely image. The image is repeated over and over when we put aside our busy schedules and find our way to a place where friends in faith have gathered.

In my early years of ministry, I took part in a faithful covenant group. The members often studied the lectionary together to prepare for Sunday sermons, but we also loved one another, bore each other's burdens, prayed for one another, encouraged one another, and shared meals and stories together. Being together certainly made our hearts glad.

Our group had scheduled a day apart at a local retreat center for the purpose of sharing the stories of our calls to ministry. At this particular point in my life, I felt overwhelmed and was second-guessing my call to ministry. I struggled to find joy and peace in my daily life and work. I found it tempting to cancel my retreat participation because I did not feel up to the emotional demands of sharing any part of my story. The retreat took place on a beautiful, sunny day. I embraced my decision to join the group but still felt reluctant to share. Toward the end of our time together, I did find the courage to speak aloud some of my personal struggle. To this day I recall how the group members gathered around me, supported me, and prayed for me.

Through their voices of encouragement and support I knew the guiding presence of the Loving Shepherd and found my way back to a sense of joy and to a greater certainty that God had indeed called me. Like those early followers, I learned again that the journey is not a solitary experience but a sharing with those whose hearts are glad and generous.

Good Shepherd, we give thanks for those who share our burdens and support us in love on this journey of faith. Amen.

The church in which I was raised had a painting of Jesus in the main entry area. The painting depicted a happy Jesus holding a beautiful, white, soft lamb. Other sheep surrounded Jesus, and in my memory of this painting the sheep appear to be smiling and charming. The painting was idyllic and romantic, but the life of a shepherd was never idyllic. The shepherd faced periods of suffering, extreme hardship, constant threat, and the vulnerability of being outside in the elements day and night.

In this passage Jesus states that he is "the gate for the sheep." Only thieves and bandits attempt to enter the sheepfold another way. We imagine the shepherd bringing the sheep into the sheepfold at night. He brings them inside a stone wall enclosure or into a small canyon surrounded by steep hills on three sides. They will be safe from predators there, and he can watch over them. The shepherd lies down at the opening of the sheepfold and literally becomes the gate for the sheep, laying down his life for the sheep.

This passage reminds us of the Shepherd's sacrificial love for the sheep. Throughout the Bible we read the story of God's unrelenting love for us and for all creation. This love has unending patience; it persists and pursues; love is made real to us in the life and death of Jesus Christ.

We follow the Good Shepherd because we know that we have been loved by God, forgiven by God, and made new by God. All this is God's gift to us. We hear the voice of the Shepherd saying, "I love you and I will lay down my life for you," and in our hearts we know that we must follow.

Good Shepherd, we give thanks for your unending love for us, and we follow you with deep devotion and gladness. Amen.

My wife and I were visiting the Grand Teton National Park. We signed up for a ranger-led hike, an all-day outing that would take us into a rather remote area of the park. People of all ages and fitness levels showed up at the ranger station on the morning of the hike, and we gathered around as the ranger offered some instructions and warnings: "Fill your water bottles, pack some food for lunch, stay together, watch for grizzlies, and be careful along steep banks." The ranger's knowledge and experience reassured and relieved us. He led the way along a beautiful rushing river and up into a steep canyon of waterfalls, aspens, and giant lodgepole pines.

Throughout the day the group would stop as the ranger pointed out different animals and birds, offered the names of trees and wildflowers, and shared a little of the history of the park. He stopped to give us rest breaks and often came to the back of the line to help someone who was struggling up the rocky incline. The hikers agreed that none of us would have tried this hike on our own, but we felt confident and safe with our guide.

We do not travel on this spiritual "hike" on our own either. Psalm 23 paints a picture of the trusted, guiding shepherd, who leads us beside still waters, through dark valleys where we are apt to be afraid, and along the right paths that lead us closer to God. We can trust, letting go of our fear and reluctance, and move confidently toward the Shepherd's reassuring presence and voice.

Trusted Shepherd, we follow your voice and follow confidently and with assurance that you will always lead us closer to your loving arms. Amen.

Trust in God

MAY 12–18, 2014 • LUIS F. REYES

SCRIPTURE OVERVIEW: Since the beginning, Israel's faith has turned to God in situations of acute trouble. In such turning, Israel has found God utterly reliable and able to rescue. Today's psalm reading sounds those ancient cadences of reliability. The sermon in Acts 7 takes up those ancient cadences and places them on the lips and in the mouth of Stephen. Stephen's preaching evokes hostility in his listeners. In the end, however, it is Stephen who knows the joy and well-being of life as a gift from God. Both the Gospel and epistle readings turn the faith of the psalm and drama of Stephen's ending toward the concrete reality of the church. They tilt toward the need for a domesticated church to reengage its peculiar identity and its unusual mode of being. The language of "place" serves the practice of risky obedience.

QUESTIONS AND THOUGHTS FOR REFLECTION

- Read Acts 7:55-60. Recall a time when you have witnessed to your faith. How did that experience make you feel?
- Read Psalm 31:1-5, 15-16. When have you taken refuge in divine presence?
- Read 1 Peter 2:2-10. How do you understand being Christian as a distinctive identity? What sets you apart from others in the world?
- Read John 14:1-14. What demands of proof do you request of God? What is enough for you?

Lead Pastor, First United Methodist Church, Lombard, Illinois; native of Puerto Rico

We have heard these words read many times—usually shared at funeral or memorial services. In those moments, we hold on to them for comfort as we mourn the loss of a loved one. But I wonder if that is the intent of Jesus' words to his disciples. These men will be facing a future without Jesus' physical presence. Their discipleship journeys, like ours, will take them into questionable places and circumstances. So Jesus attempts to reassure them, "Don't be troubled. Trust in God. Trust also in me" (CEB). As residents of an anxious world, how do we remain calm in the midst of surrounding turbulence?

Jesus wants to calm the disciples' anxiety. Not knowing or understanding Jesus' message, the disciples must have many thoughts racing through their heads. Jesus invites them and us not to be "troubled" in spirit but to trust. This is not an easy task.

In these opening verses Jesus promises the disciples that they will be with him in an enduring relationship and place. In later verses he offers the promise of lasting fellowship, but here he speaks specifically of "dwelling places." The disciples will be with Jesus, for they know the way. Thomas, ever the show-me man, states that they do *not* know the way. But as they follow him in this life and the next, they will come to greater knowledge of Jesus.

A trusting relationship can develop out of human desire to know and experience God in our life. Jesus invites the disciples to trust his words, his actions, his message. He reminds them that in their journey together he has shown who he is. It is the same for us. As we move forward in faith, we will not allow trouble to hinder us as we trust and rely on God.

God of peace and comfort, help us to turn to you in times of high anxiety in our lives. Help us to trust your presence, and guide us into paths of discipleship. Amen.

My wife was at the church helping with the distribution in the food pantry. I decided to call Puerto Rico to check on my father who was in the hospital. But I was put on hold. The seconds felt like hours and then a voice said, "I'm sorry, sir; your father died early this morning." No explanation, no words of comfort. My wife found me weeping on the steps of the house.

I cry out with the psalmist, "I take refuge in you, LORD"—a cry that signals we have no other shelter. I traveled to Puerto Rico alone. Over two thousand miles and five hours later, I reached San Juan and from there I drove another hour to my hometown. To whom do we turn in times like these? We in the church are good at comforting others in the same situation. It is part of our ministry, another way we embrace our call. However, when the circumstances become personal, no words—even expressed with kindness and caring—can provide comfort.

Verse 3 offers a deep expression of trust in the One who can ease the pain, "You are definitely my rock and my fortress. Guide me and lead me" (CEB). The psalmist turns to the God who is rock and fortress; the God who rescues, delivers, and saves. It is to this God that we turn in times of crisis and despair. This God strengthens us to awaken every morning, holds us as we take one step at a time. This Rock and Fortress will comfort and embrace us in peace. Today, twenty years after my father's death, I realize how these words sustained me in that difficult time.

How much do we trust God? Or even better, how much do we embrace God's steadfast love in our lives?

Gracious and compassionate God, thank you for your love and care in all the circumstances of our lives. You are our rock and our fortress. We take refuge in you. Amen.

My son has received a unique gift. Our family moved out of the city of Chicago and into the suburbs. We worried about the lack of a diverse community, but from the time he stepped into his first grade class, there was no majority or minority. His friends' families come from many parts of the world and have, like us, a primary language. He has been blessed to live in a multicultural/multiracial community, full of tolerance and respect. But he has never forgotten his identity, his roots, and his heritage.

Today's reading presents similar issues: The Temple no longer exists, and the church has moved farther and farther from its place of origin. Now the risen Christ becomes the center of worship, the source of inspiration. The church has a new identity.

The danger always exists that we will lose the sense of who we truly are. Our text today clearly names the Christian community "living stones." They, like Jesus before them, will face rejection. Peter asserts the building up of a spiritual house, God's household—a unity of believers. The passage goes on to name the community "a chosen race, a royal priesthood, . . . God's own people."

This huge responsibility comes to them and now to us. With the risen Christ as the center of inspiration, we learn to live with our new identity. As members of one household, are we willing to embrace tolerance and respect for those who are different from us? God builds this house, and Christ is the cornerstone. We belong to one another, and we belong to God. That relationship calls us to live the core values of the risen Christ. Will we claim and embrace our new identity?

God, you trust us to carry the ministry of your son. Keep us humble, so that we can continue building your spiritual house in our communities. Amen.

THURSDAY, MAY 15 ~ *Read Acts 7:55-60*

This passage raises this question for me: How much do I trust God's support of me in the witnessing ministry? For the past three weeks, the texts have focused on Peter's preaching with the rich results of persons believing and being baptized. Stephen, the first Christian martyr, reminds us that not all Christian witness results in new Christ-followers; Stephen exemplifies the ultimate act of witness by giving his life.

Stephen speaks aloud of God's many promises that have been fulfilled in Israel's life as a nation. Despite this fulfillment, Israel has often turned from God. The people of the day have rejected Jesus just as they rejected Moses—not the most uplifting sermon, to be sure. The people cover their ears! They don't want to hear these words.

Many of us struggle to share our faith, to engage in conversation with others about our beliefs, our core values. We assume those conversations would be rude and disrespectful to others and, in some instances, an intrusion into other people's lives. But what is our call?

God has entrusted a message to us that we can't keep to ourselves. The majority of us embrace this call, and with joy we leave the safety of our sanctuaries and walk into the community as bearers of God's word. In our society we probably will not endure what Stephen did as we speak and live out God's message. However, we do have missioners responding to God's call in regions of the world that involves risk in doing so. Nevertheless, if we trust God is calling, we let go of fear, step out of our comfort zone and into the world. Then, like Stephen, we will see "the glory of God."

God, give us Stephen's passion for bearing witness to the powerful message of the gospel. Give us strength to overcome any obstacle in our journey; help us to trust that it is your voice calling us to witness to your love for all. Amen.

A current TV show deals with crimes, investigations, and the work of proving that those brought to justice are the guilty ones. Our Gospel lesson today gives a glimpse of what it means to prove something is true. In this case, it is not about innocence or guilt—it is about identity: "Lord, show us the Father; that will be enough for us" (CEB). Philip voices this request. We may wonder how he can request this now. Is the disciple still unsure of who Jesus is and who sent him?

Jesus' reply hits hard, "Don't you know me, Philip, even after I have been with you all this time?" (CEB). How would you feel if one of your closest friends or a member of your immediate family said to you, "I don't know you"? Jesus' question to Philip has resonated with me my entire faith journey. *How much do I know Jesus?* The biblical stories of Jesus are filled with details from his birth to his resurrection, his compassionate love, his passion for all God's children, his constant desire to bring good news to all. This is the Jesus we know.

But here in our text for today, the question becomes more personal. This question focuses on the relationship between Jesus and the disciple who has listened to him, witnessed with him, learned from him, but who still needs proof.

Do we not wonder sometimes? We may not make a brazen request like Philip's, but at times we don't trust Jesus' words. Then we begin to doubt our call and our response. Knowing and trusting Jesus provides the foundation for our faith journeys. Jesus replies to Philip and perhaps to us, "Don't you believe that I am in the Father and the Father is in me?" (CEB). Jesus proves through word and deed again and again who he is and who has sent him. May that be enough to sustain us.

God, thanks for your gift to us in the person of Jesus. It is enough. Amen.

As I grew up, I always dreamed of becoming a doctor. I wanted to help those in need. I walked into my first anatomy class at the medical examiner's building. What I saw was enough to make me hang up my gown, walk to my counselor's office, and say, "I don't believe my future is in medicine; what should I do?" The logical option was business administration—I have no reason why. Perhaps I envisioned my future working in an office doing the same things daily. However, during my senior year, I responded to God's call to ordained ministry. Now the question became, Do I see my future serving in parish ministry?

I remember a bus driver's asking me, "Why are you throwing your future away by becoming a pastor. You will not make any money and will not have a good life. You don't deserve that." I don't recall my reply. I trusted that the future of God's invitation was sufficient for me to walk into. My future lay in God's hands.

How much do we trust God with our lives? The psalmist looks to God for deliverance, shining countenance, and salvation. The psalmist's prayer and confidence in God's action on his behalf refocuses his concern from enemies and persecutors to the help of God. Our enemies are not necessarily traditional ones; often they surface in our fears of trusting in God, of placing our lives and all we are in God's hands. Our persecutors are the voices that tell us not to trust God and the future God has for us. So we will say to God once again, "Save me in your steadfast love."

Loving God, you know all—our past and our present. Help us daily to recognize that our future is in your hands. Amen.

This passage begins with Jesus' words to his beloved disciples as a message of comfort and possibility. Yet Thomas's concern, voiced in verse 5, may also be ours, "Lord, we don't know where you are going. How can we know the way?" (CEB). Many are the days that we don't know the way. We get caught up in routine and lose sight of Jesus' ways. We get frustrated, discouraged, or angry that events are not moving along or that we see no spiritual growth. I desire to trust, and when I find myself conflicted, I ask, "Do I know the way?" Jesus' steady reply comes to me: "I am the way, the truth, and the life." So back to basics. How well do I know Jesus?

If Jesus is willing to prepare a place for us where he is going, why can't we trust that the same Jesus is with us in our current situations? Do we value control more than we value Jesus' guidance?

Stop for a moment to consider the words Jesus offered to his disciples. In retrospect, we know why Jesus' compassionate words made so much sense. Do we perceive them as words of hope? Do we trust Jesus' statements?

At the close of today's passage, Jesus reinforces the power of prayer and his abiding presence. The disciples need only pray—believing and asking in Jesus' name—and it will be granted. The granting of these prayer requests does not serve the needs of the pray-er but to glorify God in Jesus Christ. Prayers offered by the community and for the community will undergird the "greater works" to be done. Do we know the way? God's steadfast love in Christ still guides us.

> *God of all generations, we thank you for your son, Jesus, who is the way, the truth, and the life. We confess our poor judgment, our lack of trust, and our need to be in control. God, have mercy on us and grant us your peace. Amen.*

Being There

MAY 19–25, 2014 • JERRY OWYANG

SCRIPTURE OVERVIEW: The psalm and the Acts reading address the ways in which the concrete faith claims of the community have credence outside that community. They undertake to make the faith credible to outsiders. On the basis of personal testimony, the psalm invites the nations to share in the new life given by God who has saved. Paul makes concrete confessional claims about Jesus in response to the religious inclinations of his Hellenistic listeners. The Gospel and epistle readings focus on the needs of the church community and seek to offer pastoral consolation. The psalm and Acts readings are a "journey out" to the nations and to attentive nonbelievers. The Gospel and epistle readings are a "journey in" to the life and needs of the church.

QUESTIONS AND THOUGHTS FOR REFLECTION

• Read Psalm 66:8-20. When have you felt that God tested you in a situation? What was the result?
• Read Acts 17:22-31. How do you attempt to learn the context of persons with whom you speak about Jesus? How does that learning affect their acceptance of your words?
• Read 1 Peter 3:13-22. When have you suffered for doing what is right?
• Read John 14:15-21. How do you experience the indwelling of the Holy Spirit?

Ordained deacon and senior pastor of Cornerstone United Methodist Church, a later-generation, multi-ethnic Asian American congregation, Placentia, California

The United States of America and many other nations have experienced a shift in ethnic and cultural diversity, as well as in faith traditions. These shifts have often led to conflicts with long-established Judeo-Christian values. How do we cope with world religions and contemporary philosophies that care little about the truth of Jesus Christ?

Paul finds himself in similar circumstances when he visits Athens—then the world center of intellectual and idolatrous life-styles characterized by the Stoics and the Epicureans. The Stoics asserted that a divine nature existed in every form of matter and believed that the "gods" controlled everything. True happiness came from accepting that things are the way they are and cannot be changed. Epicureans focused on personal happiness, arguing that the way to total contentment came in maximizing pleasure and minimizing pain. They believed that the "gods" residing in the universe never interacted with humans.

With quiet respect, Paul engages these thinkers to listen to his calm logic as he presents the truth of God and sows the seeds of the Christian faith. He carries his message to a land with a multitude of religious beliefs as he speaks to the heart of the matter by identifying the "unknown god." Paul quotes the words of earlier philosophers and poets: "In him we live and move and have our being" (Epiminedes of Crete, 6 BCE) and "For we too are his offspring" (Aratus of Soli, 3 BCE). Paul's "god" created the world, requires no support from humans, and is the Lord of all life.

When we look at our culture with its increasingly pluralistic religious spectrum, remember that we too face Paul's challenges; we carry the same message, supported by the same power that raised Jesus from the dead.

Lord, show me how I may expose the "unknown god[s]" of our world to the light and truth of Jesus Christ. Amen.

Ionce worked as an environmental planner for a large city. My first public hearing to discuss a large-scale project was nearly a disaster as I arrogantly presented myself as "the expert." I may have had the right answers, but I was misdirected in my approach with seasoned politicians. I failed to take into account my setting.

Paul, on the other hand, understands his context as he evangelizes the Greek world. He knows that when one forgoes the God of the universe, it takes an infinite number of gods to fill that space. The Stoics and Epicureans looked everywhere for satisfactory gods. The evidence of their spiritual hunger did not lay in their many gods but in their altar to an "unknown god."

Paul makes a simple point. If you don't have God in your life, you have two options: make pleasure your ultimate goal or decide that life is tough and you have to be tougher. Paul "admires" the depth of the philosophers' search and then introduces the Athenians to his God, a God involved in the affairs of creation and humanity. He and we worship a "known" God.

Paul evangelized the Greek world by taking the time to understand its context. Maybe we too can find common ground with our pluralistic culture by knowing what people believe and by putting the gospel into terms they understand. Without changing the message itself, we must present it in a way that can be understood. Into this world of constant change comes the message of love and righteousness found in Jesus, putting faith and morality together and revealing God's standard of grace and the sacrificial love of Christ.

As Paul clarified for others what they did not know, how can I shed light on the different objects of worship of our culture and share the gospel with those in a different context than mine?

This pivotal psalm of joy affirms a life rescued from the snares of death and overlooks the cause of the circumstances. When life unravels to the point of catastrophe, we wonder *Why?*—a question asked when we experience suffering, unanswered prayer, and the unfairness of life. It becomes a matter of faith when we direct the question to God as we ponder God's justice or even the very existence of God with an honest query. We often link our disappointment with God to how we think God is *supposed* to fix the broken aspects of our lives. When deliverance does not come as we expect, maybe we need to reexamine our expectations in the light of God's bigger picture.

Often we may find ourselves in that "dark night of the soul" that describes a sense of abandonment by God. Rather than interpreting an authentic confusion before God as punishment, my experience has been that such times are blessings in disguise. Distractions are stripped away, and I am invited to take a long and intimate walk with God for rest and refreshment. The end result is a fresh perspective on my circumstances that leads my soul to a unique, inner joy.

The psalmist praises God for saving him from death, echoing the purifying Exodus from Egypt experience and enthusiastically dedicating himself to personal worship with sacrifices and offerings. With utmost joy he testifies that God has always been faithful in the midst of severe troubles. He seems to be at a loss as to finding ways of expressing total elation and utter delight! He calls all God fearers to "come and hear" his witness: The Lord listened and gave heed to the psalmist's prayer, holding him in steadfast love. May it be so in our lives.

What is the importance of expressing joy personally as well as communally, especially when following an experience of fear or darkness?

Ionce brought my youth group to a simulation of the Underground Church (Christians persecuted for their faith in God) hosted at a Christian college. As teams of youth were sent across campus to find their "house churches," they faced interruption, detainment, questioning, intimidation, and separation by those acting as the "secret police." By the end of the evening, the youth had a somber reality check that simply being Christian was not enough to avoid the harsh realities of the nonbelieving world.

While many of us do not live where practicing our faith is against the law, let alone fatal, Christianity is under assault at many levels throughout the world. If we are "eager to do what is good," Peter says we need not fear ultimate harm. That does not mean that there will not be any unjust suffering. We are to distinguish our values from those of the world: "Do not fear what they fear." Our response and its manner are important. We are to respond to suffering with verbal witness—not silence. Peter states that defending oneself is appropriate—but we are to do so gently and with a clear conscience so that faith in God stands above any hostile reproach.

Suffering in any form may lead us to question God's goodness, especially when on a daily basis we face homelessness, long-term unemployment, critical health care issues, abusive relationships, or even oppressive political regimes. Peter's message, however, makes it clear that those who inflict suffering have only limited power over us. We, as people of God, receive blessing when we suffer. In that role, we continuously witness to the hope of Christ in us.

God of my life, when I encounter suffering for doing good, may I know the special blessing that comes out of faithfulness. Amen.

Many of us in the United States have difficulty grasping what it means to suffer for Jesus Christ. Our experiences of distress and hardship seldom result from being a follower of Jesus. However, in a pluralistic society even being a Christian in prison can invite persecution, and the author of this epistle writes to give confidence to believers across all time.

For many years, I have volunteered with Kairos Prison Ministry to bring God's love, hope, and forgiveness to the incarcerated. Although it is similar to the Walk to Emmaus and Cursillo programs, the harshest difference is that participants remain confined to their prison environs while I get to go home. Upon a return visit, I sometimes discover that these "prisoners for Christ" have been assaulted because of their faith.

This letter provides encouragement for innocent sufferers by reminding them that even Christ suffered unjustly in obedience to God. Peter encapsulates the ministry of Jesus in that if we are called to suffer for what is right, we must look to Jesus who suffered for our sins—and through that suffering has come to the place of highest authority. Ultimately, we will share in Jesus' triumph over evil as we live into our hope—by both word and action—remembering that baptism is our promise to God to live with purity of conscience.

Just as the flood had the power to destroy the sinful (and save the righteous), so too the waters of baptism bring power to the believer. Suffering, then, can set the context for the believer's greatest triumph, as we see in the victorious example of Jesus Christ.

How does knowing that Jesus suffered "for sins once for all" help you endure the distress that you encounter?

When my children were little, and I had to leave for a meeting, they would ask, "Where are you going? How long will you be gone? Who will take care of us?" When I replied with the name of their favorite caregiver, they would be thrilled! With this person in my children's presence, they would be well cared for, and they would not be afraid.

I imagine the disciples being childlike in their faith when Jesus speaks comfort to their hearts just before his arrest. Their world will be shattered; they will be confused, lost, and filled with anxiety. *Where are you going? How long will you be gone? Who will take care of us?* they may rightly wonder.

The Gospel writer wants us to trust in the promise that Jesus gives the believer comfort in the form of a blessing that the world does not enjoy: the Holy Spirit that stays and indwells the people of faith. Further, this Advocate will make known to us and remind us of Jesus' deeper truths.

An intimate privilege I have as pastor is being with a family when the "Do Not Resuscitate" order is carried out at the hospital bedside. As life ends and a rebirth is witnessed, Jesus' loving promise of the Advocate "to be with you forever" assures us with clarity that no one in God will ever be left alone—the presence of God is not only a promise but a power that enables life beyond the world's understanding.

Loving Jesus and keeping his commandments go hand in hand—it's not about "following the rules" but about being faithful to what we know about God through our relationship with Jesus. Then we do not have to ask, "Who will take care of us?"

Precious Lord, let me be at total peace with your Holy Spirit dwelling deep inside of me. Amen.

M y dad is being transported to the hospital for chest pains," the daughter said almost apologetically for calling so late in the evening. In the emergency room, I encountered the Friday night crowd of the injured: police-guarded assailants handcuffed to gurneys and assaulted victims of crime being treated. A hospital can be the common ground for grieving losses of health, innocence, or freedom—but it's not the only place for sensing abandonment. That happens anywhere.

Death, divorce, desertion. Add rejection, betrayal, and criticism—all can inflict mortal wounds to the soul, leaving a dull ache covered by layers of scar tissue that cancels out trust. When all the variations of these themes play out, we may feel like an orphan as life becomes shattered. As remnants of trust scatter across the backdrop of our contemporary culture, what would happen if we staked our lives on Jesus' promises? Do we believe that we can trust him?

The epistle of First Peter states that Christ suffered as a human; he knows, then, what we feel and identifies with our losses to bring us a hope in God that stands above any and all sufferings we may experience. For Jesus to have this intimate sense of "humanness" allows us to trust him with our feelings of aloneness and abandonment.

Jesus delineates between what the world knows and what the disciples know and have experienced about divine presence. Through God's grace the disciples will continue to experience Jesus' presence, even when he is not physically present with them. What they have come to know and cherish will undergird them even as they feel "orphaned." When our world shatters and we feel orphaned, we return to the truth of the statement: "Those who love me will be loved by my Father."

When have you felt orphaned or forsaken? What undergirded you through this time?

With One Heart

MAY 26–JUNE 1, 2014 • ANNEMARIE PAULIN-CAMPBELL

SCRIPTURE OVERVIEW: The entire Easter season focuses on the new governance that breaks the grip of all that is old, tired, deathly, and enslaving. The psalm shows the church using the ancient language of enthronement. Now it is Jesus through whom the drama of God's power is brought to fruition. In Acts, the community accepts the new governance as a bold witness in the world, sustained by a disciplined life of prayer. The epistle reading addresses people who are in the midst of suffering, hurt, and need. They are enjoined to hope for the time of God's eventual and full triumph. The Gospel portrays the church, under the power of God's resolve, being given a wholly new identity and vocation in the world.

QUESTIONS AND THOUGHTS FOR REFLECTION

- Read Acts 1:6-14. The disciples joined constantly in prayer with one heart. When have you experienced being part of a small praying and discerning community?
- Read Psalm 68:1-10, 32-35. How have you understood and experienced God as a bringer of righteousness to the disenfranchised?
- Read 1 Peter 4:12-14; 5:6-11. We are invited to unload our burdens onto God, with the promise that God will raise us up and sustain us. What burdens do you need to unload at this time?
- Read Luke 24:44-53. As you reflect today, where do you sense you are being called to continue Jesus' mission in the world?

Spiritual director; retreat giver and trainer of spiritual directors in the Ignatian tradition; a Roman Catholic currently working for the Jesuit Institute South Africa; psychotherapist with special interest in the interface of spirituality and psychology

MONDAY, MAY 26 ~ *Read Acts 1:6-14*

"W ith one heart all these joined constantly in prayer" (NJB). In this coming week we are journeying in the time of the Ascension. One theme of this week strikes me powerfully: the growing development of a community of prayer. Before, during, and after the Ascension we read that the disciples are meeting as a group that prays and discerns together. They seek to become more and more one mind and heart with Christ and with one another. Immediately after Jesus' death, the community of his followers scattered. But as the risen Lord began to appear to them, seemingly they began to gather as a tight-knit community sharing and praying together. By the time of the Ascension, Jesus' followers have become a praying community. Something powerful can occur within a community that prays and discerns together.

As a student at University, I met and prayed daily with two other students and an older retired woman each morning. Our time together allowed us to pray and to share with one another on a deep level. Out of this deep prayer, reflection on our lives, and honest sharing, we began to discern the Lord's invitation to each of us. Even when our responses to God's call began to take us to different places, we remained connected through prayer and regular e-mail. Despite no physical connection, a union of hearts and minds continued and sustained us in our different ministries. The apostlcs model for us here the vital importance of being connected not only with the Lord in prayer but also with the community of other believers.

Lord, help us to find communities of prayer in which we can discern your call to us and be supported in our desire to grow in relationship with you. May we actively participate in your mission in the world. Amen.

Here, in Jesus' farewell discourse, we see, perhaps most powerfully articulated, the relationship between Jesus and his Father—an extraordinary oneness in a union that existed before the world's creation. Jesus has lived his life in complete obedience to the Father; the desires of the Father and the Son are the same. And we are drawn into that relationship of the Father and the Son in which each gives glory to the other.

The plea is for us to be drawn into the intimacy of the relationship between Father and Son and to come to know the Father "the only true God, and Jesus Christ whom you have sent" (NJB). How do we come to know Jesus and the Father whose glory he came to reveal? How do we develop a relationship in which we, like Jesus, share more and more the mind and heart of the Father? I believe this occurs only by spending time in prayer, contemplating the person of Jesus. As we come to know the Son, we also come to know the Father.

Ignatius of Loyola encourages us to enter imaginatively into the Gospel encounters with Jesus using all our senses—especially sight, hearing, touch—and to allow ourselves to be present to Jesus. As we enter deeply into being with Jesus in the various moments of his life, we can come to a more interior felt-knowledge of who he is. Ignatius also invites us to engage in heart-to-heart conversation, as one friend speaks to another. In this way we deepen the intimacy that comes from the vulnerability of self-revelation. God constantly seeks self-revelation. Though God knows us intimately, the choice is ours to reveal the depths of our hearts and so enter into immeasurable relationship.

Choose an encounter passage from the Gospels, and allow yourself to enter into it using your imagination and your senses. Then talk with Jesus heart to heart about your experience, and hear what he says to you.

Today's passage was written for the Christians of the early church at a time when they faced persecution for their faith. It offers words of encouragement and hope, reminding them that if they endure insults for their faith, the Spirit of God, the Spirit of glory rests on them. It also speaks powerfully to us. Whether or not we have to endure religious persecution there is a cost to discipleship. When we choose faithfulness to Christ and his values, we willingly endure that cost. Sometimes we see this cost in the loss of life for the early Christian martyrs. In our own time, a person like Nelson Mandela bears witness. He endured twenty-seven years of imprisonment out of the compelling need to oppose racial injustice. At other times the cost may come in daily suffering borne in being present to a loved one with Alzheimer's or in raising a child with a serious disability.

The scripture tells us not to be surprised at being "tested by fire" (NJB). This testing is an integral part of the Christian journey. A dangerous and false teaching is making the contemporary rounds: Prosperity and lack of suffering signal God's favor. On the contrary, Peter tells us to be glad if we share in the sufferings of Christ because then "we will enjoy a much greater gladness when his glory is revealed"(NJB). Suffering offers a powerful means to deepen our union with Christ. It is not about suffering for its own sake but rather about accepting and embracing the sufferings that come in life, especially those that come through our living out Jesus' call in our life with faithfulness. Suffering can make us bitter or discouraged. It can even make us doubt God's love for us. But if we can enter into it as a way of uniting ourselves more closely with Jesus and sharing in his passion, we will grow into maturity in faith and be assured of sharing more fully in the glory of the risen Christ.

Lord, in hard times may we trust the assurance that by sharing in your suffering we will also share in your glory. Amen.

ASCENSION DAY

Now as he blessed them, he withdrew from them and was carried up to heaven" (NJB). In the forty days since his resurrection, Christ has continued to teach and mentor his disciples. During that time, the disciples' sense of dislocation (caused by confusion and grief) has lifted and their shattered sense of meaning and purpose has been renewed. The compassionate Christ helps them to see that his death does not signal the end but rather the beginning of a new mission and responsibility. Jesus is the Messiah who is revealed in scripture, and it is he to whom the disciples turn for interpretation of scripture: "Then he opened their minds to understand the scriptures." They will continue Jesus' mission by preaching repentance to all nations in Jesus' name. As he ascends to the Father they experience a profound sense of joy and return to Jerusalem to praise God in the Temple. They no longer feel fearful or lost. Seemingly, since they cannot lose the Lord, they no longer require his physical presence. Their unity with him and with one another provides spiritual consolation and profound recognition that Christ has entrusted them with a mission.

We who have never known Jesus' physical presence may take consolation in the disciples' experience. We who find ourselves united with Christ and with the Father through prayer and scripture have also been entrusted with a mission to witness to Christ, each in our own particular way. Jesus himself says, "*You* are witnesses of these things" (emphasis added). God empowers us to proclaim Jesus' story, call for repentance, and declare divine forgiveness. We are part of God's strategy!

Lord, remind me today of the mission with which you have entrusted me, and give me the courage to witness to your love in the world. Amen.

"Stay in the city, then, until you are clothed with the power from on high" (NJB). From behind locked doors of an upper room to the outskirts of Bethany the disciples come. The fearful community comes out into the light of day. Jesus breathed upon them the Holy Spirit; now they await the power from on high.

In my twenties I had the privilege of making a thirty-day silent retreat in the peaceful countryside of North Wales. I had gone abroad to study spirituality with no idea if or how I could carry out this work when I returned to my home country of South Africa. I desired to start a center for Ignatian spirituality, but I had no idea how to secure the funding or support needed. One evening at sunset I was praying this text at the end of thirty days of praying the life and ministry of Jesus. These words "stay in the city, then, until you are clothed with the power from on high" made a deep impression.

When I returned home, I prayed for clarity of vision, courage, and a sense of first steps. Within four months, my concerns disappeared as the Jesuits employed me to start the work. At other times, I regret to say I have not waited to be "clothed with the power from on high." That has resulted in my jumping into situations that were not God's desire for me or living out of fear rather than out of love. If we are entrusted by God with a particular mission, it helps to recall Jesus' last words that invite us to a trustful waiting on the Holy Spirit. Only then will we move out into the world with conviction, courage, peace, and perseverance.

Lord, you have not abandoned us to continue your work alone. Clothe us with the power of your Spirit so that our efforts may bear fruit and be to your greater glory. Amen.

For the writer of First Peter, evil actively assaults Christians. The struggle between the powers of good and evil is real. The devil wants to undermine our faith and trust in God and will encourage us to lose heart. Today's passage offers several responses to the reality of evil. The first involves our humbling ourselves before God. We bow down before the power of God, which overcomes evil.

A second response comes in our active and intentional resistance to evil. We remain vigilant, aware that following Christ is not without suffering and struggle. We may assess our area of greatest vulnerability and consider where the devil will try to undermine our confidence. Be alert, for he comes like a roaring lion. However if we place our trust in God, God will sustain us and raise us up. We rest assured that we can "unload all [our] burden on to [God], since he is concerned about [us]" (NJB).

Another response encompasses our rejoicing—both in God's care and concern for us and also in the understanding of our final restoration. We will be raised up in "due time," and the difficult times will not last for long. Ultimately we will be brought through these trials to share in the eternal glory of Christ.

When we remember that God supports us in our times of desolation and suffering, we can more easily stand firm against the temptation to despair. We place our confidence in the One who will not let us down. As the great mystic, Julian of Norwich, wrote in her *Showings*: "All shall be well, and all shall be well and all manner of thing shall be well."

Lord, may I unload my burden on to you and not carry it alone. When I feel discouraged, help me remember your promise to raise me up and restore me. Amen.

The theme of glory weaves its way through this psalm. The image of God here is one of a powerful, benevolent, and compassionate God who can disperse enemies, provide homes for the lonely, lead prisoners into prosperity, and rain down showers of blessings on the people. This God evokes a sense of awe and wonder and is called "Rider of the Clouds" (NJB). The people, filled with exuberant joy and delight, dance, sing, and make music to express their joy. Their God arises as a strong agent of change. This God works on behalf of righteousness for the socially disenfranchised: orphans, widows, the lonely, the prisoners. This psalm affirms that God sends rain on the parched land; the flocks and those who have no other resources receive a rich gift at God's hand.

In our postmodern, increasingly secularized world we can quickly forget our dependence on God and delude ourselves into thinking that we control our own lives. The more material possessions we have and the more we fill our lives with the constant input of social media, the more tempted we are to forget that we are God's creatures. We can then think that we have no need to rely on God.

However, when we face the uncertainties of life and situations over which we have no control, we turn again to the One who "brings us to life . . . and keeps our feet from stumbling" (Ps. 66:9, NJB). This God of righteousness comes to the aid of those who accept the truth that we are created by God and sustained by God in each moment. All that we are and all that we have is God's generous gift to us. When we allow ourselves to realize that all is gift, we affirm the awesome nature of our God. "Blessed be God!"

God of glory, may we be filled this day with wonder and awe at your greatness and be moved with gratitude to praise and glorify you, trusting in your compassionate love. Amen.

Where the Spirit Works

JUNE 2–8, 2014 • MARILYN CHANDLER MCENTYRE

SCRIPTURE OVERVIEW: The foundation of the Pentecost festival is that series of events recorded in Acts 2, a decisive proclamation that links new life in Christ to the activity of the Spirit of God. At the heart of the church's new life is its experience of the crucified, risen Lord, a reality also recalled in the John 7 reading. Psalm 104 celebrates the power of God in endowing the heavens and the earth with life, an endowment that is linked to the work of God's Spirit. First Corinthians points the reader to the reality that the gift of life, having once been made, remains with the Spirit-led person in the form of a heart reoriented to new and marvelous deeds of witness.

QUESTIONS AND THOUGHTS FOR REFLECTION

- Read Psalm 104:24-34, 35*b*. In what specific ways does this psalm invite us to consider our individual and collective call to be stewards of creation?
- Read Acts 2:1-21. How do you interpret the meaning of being "filled with the Holy Spirit"?
- Read 1 Corinthians 12:3*b*-13. How might the metaphor of the body be probed for more specific direction in discernment of community members' gifts?
- Read John 7:37–39. How might this promise that believers will be made sources of living water be linked to the actual and urgent ministries that connect spiritual good news with distribution and care of water for the common good? What do you perceive as particularly powerful and pertinent about the image of "living water" as a sign of faith?

Teacher at the University of California, Berkeley and Davis; a Fellow of the Gaede Institute at Westmont College; recent books include *Caring for Words in a Culture of Lies*; *Christ, My Companion*; *Reading Like a Serpent*

The Spirit of God still moves over the waters. The Spirit is sent forth to generate new life and to renew the earth. As I read this psalm, I am aware of how sorely the "face of the ground" needs renewal. I am conscious of record droughts and fires, melting ice, and disappearing species. We have cause to mourn the state of the planet. But I am also struck by the verb use in verse 30: "Send forth your spirit. . . . " "Send forth" suggests direction, energy, and urgency. God's urgency meets our own. When we suffer, God hastens to meet us. Where the earth languishes, where animals roam in destroyed habitats, and where humans suffer on parched land, the Spirit of God (in Hebrew, *ruach*—"breath") breathes with us the way a husband coaching a wife through labor breathes with her through the contractions.

A few years ago, I sat with a young family member for an hour near the end of her life and simply breathed with her. Each slow breath reminded me that the work of letting go is fueled by the same breath of life we receive as a new gift each moment.

Clearly God's Spirit animates life. God's absence brings death. We acknowledge our dependence on God for our well-being and for that of the whole creation. God's attentive self-giving allows us to flourish. We are learning new ways to attend to the earth. The sea and its creatures, the forests and the shorn mountaintops need healing. We participate in that task, recognizing the earth's story as part of our own, trusting the Spirit to bring our efforts to fruition and renew the face of the earth. As Gerard Manley Hopkins put it, "The Holy Ghost over the bent world broods with warm breast and with ah! bright wings."

Creator God, fill us with love for all creatures, both great and small, with whom we look to you for life and breath. Help us learn to care for them, even as you care for us. Amen.

I've always been struck by the public nature of Pentecost. The Spirit comes to anoint the disciples when they are gathered together. This is no private revelation. Unlike the scenes in which Jesus admonishes people to "tell no one," this time God becomes present in a way so visible, audible, palpable, and dramatic that no one present can fail to recognize that heaven has broken through and the Holy One is among them.

God appeared to Moses in a burning bush, and to the Israelites in a pillar of fire. God spoke to Elijah in a still small voice. In Jesus, God walked the roads as one of us. On Pentecost, God manifests in three new ways, all of which are rich with meaning. The rushing wind reminds us of God's immanence and power; the fire signifies the One who is the light of the world; the tongues denote the Word who was in the beginning, reflected in the life-giving communion of human conversation. Three signs of God's presence appear to them—the wind embracing them, the fire resting on each, and the gift of new language coming variously to those who had heard God's word and heeded it. In a consummate moment of community, Jesus' followers are not only called but called together.

The followers of Jesus still are called together. And life together requires more than private devotions, though they are as good and necessary as the food and rest we take. God calls us to engage in a *shared life* that binds us closer than brothers and sisters, whose common heritage is the breath of life and the bread of life and the Spirit of life that is "poured out" in these latter days, more present and abundant than we can imagine.

Spirit of God, keep us attuned to your voice and to one another's as we walk the paths you disclose. Amen.

That God created the Leviathan to play in the great, wide sea gives us reason to rejoice. It clearly indicates that God honors and cherishes play and delights in the creatures' pleasure. Play matters. Through play children discover how things work and come into relationship with each other and with the things of the earth. Play provides spiritual refreshment for adults. By playing, we reclaim habits of trust and delight. Pure play (as opposed to commercialized recreation) has no hidden agendas and stays open to surprise. It says yes to opportunity, takes risks in trust, and depends on the faith that ultimately we play in a space made safe by the One who created and cares for us all.

We acknowledge that the world is not always a safe space. Dangers, local and global, assail us on all sides. But the closing line of one of W. H. Auden's poems, "Leap Before You Look," redirects us to the great paradox we inhabit: "Our dream of safety has to disappear." That is, the dream of safety that clings to the securities of this world: our burglar alarms, our insurance policies, our system backups, the emergency button on our phones. While we need not give those items up, we need to recognize that our real security resides in roots sunk deep in the biblical story. Then with confidence we can say, "In life and death we are the Lord's," and "Our times are in your hands." Knowing that we are called forth, guided, held, and cherished by the God of all creation frees us to play, like the Leviathan in the wide waters of this world, and to delight in all the created beings that are given into our care.

God whose kingdom is for those like little children, teach us the trust we need to play with joy and confidence in your fields. Amen.

A healthy faith community recognizes, fosters, and puts to use its members' various gifts. Some churches take time to gather and identify specific gifts each member has to offer. These are not necessarily "skill sets" or talents. Sometimes a gift is a habit of being; a quality of presence; an inclination to kindness or patient listening; or incisive, timely, constructive criticism. Discerning gifts takes time, vulnerability, and commitment to stay in prayerful conversation about our life together, our common needs, our fears, and the faith that transforms those fears into a confidence that steps trustingly into the unknown.

Discerning our own gifts involves considering all we know about ourselves—our stories, our wounds, our weaknesses, our strengths, our talents, and also our desires and hopes—in light of our membership in the body of Christ. One thoughtful older woman, upon being asked about her gifts for her worshiping community replied simply, "I've been through things." A long life rich with story is a gift indeed.

As Paul notes, "To each is given the manifestation of the Spirit for the common good." We work together just as cells, hormones, and organs do in the physical body. This truth challenges us to a radical understanding of our relationship to one another in Christ. A brief elementary anatomy review can enrich our understanding of it: Some are catalysts. Some are hormones that transmit timely messages to the members that can act on them. Some are nerve cells that sense where pain is and report it so appropriate care can happen. Some are skin that protects, or digestive organs that distribute nourishment, or livers and kidneys that filter what is harmful. The precision of such analogies may help us get more specific about what the whole body requires to function healthily, according to God's good purposes.

God, as you have made us one body, unite us in one Spirit. Amen.

In a time when lack of access to clean water afflicts so many, the image of flowing rivers is both potent and poignant. Thirst is one of the hardest deprivations to bear—the one physical form of suffering Jesus named in his last hours on the cross. To bring water to dry fields or clean water to a person dying of cholera represents a powerful ministry. Jesus promises rivers of living water in desert country where his hearers know its significance.

Jesus is referring to the effect of the Holy Spirit on the lives and ministry of those within his hearing—and ours. Not only will the Spirit quench our thirst or give us unlimited access to the source that sustains our lives; but when the Spirit is "poured out" on us, we will become conduits of living water for others. The Spirit will empower and authorize us to bear God's own gifts. This is the ordination of all believers upon which Luther insisted: Our own hearts, transformed by the action of the Spirit will be like artesian wells where water from a deep source is constantly replenished.

Flow is a verb worth pausing over while reflecting on this passage and on life in the Spirit. What *flows* from us comes almost in spite of ourselves. We simply open a way and the water finds its course through the hills and valleys and rocky places of our lives into the open spaces where others may reach it. The Spirit that comes as wind and flame and Word also comes as water that finds its way through any terrain, persistent and patient enough to wear away the resistance of granite and make tunnels in any wall.

Gracious God, may your living water flow through us as we act as agents of your grace and bearers of your good gifts. Amen.

SATURDAY, JUNE 7 ~ *Read Psalm 104:24-34, 35b*

Biodiversity, a rather technical term, has come into common use over the past decade because it is a matter of public concern. Species are disappearing with alarming rapidity—some biologists believe at a rate one hundred to one hundred thousand times the rate of natural extinction—due in large part to poor stewardship of habitats and animal and plant populations. These facts add a dimension of sorrow to the joyful words in today's psalm about God's manifold works and the seas that teem with life. Today they call us to awareness and stewardship—to participate in ocean clean-ups or to support responsible agriculture or to help eliminate islands of plastic in oceans and chemical waste in rivers.

David Quammen, an author who writes with informed humor and grace about the lives of animals, argues for preservation even of those species we don't see as "useful"; not because they may prove useful at some point, but because utility isn't an appropriate criterion by which to decide whether a creature has a claim to its place on the planet. One reason to respect the many orders of creation is precisely that we may not yet understand why they are among us or how they may occupy an eco-niche of wider importance in the interlocking systems we inhabit. One argument Quammen makes about preserving a species of small, inedible fish is their beauty.

This psalm doesn't invite us to analyze or calculate but to celebrate life in its many amazing forms. Various and teeming, all have a place in the order of creation that is not open to question. The psalmist invites us here not only to celebration but to the humility that serves as a prerequisite to right worship and to awe.

God of all life, teach us how to care for creation and cherish our kinship not only with each other but also with beings of other orders in whom you also delight. Amen.

SUNDAY, JUNE 8 ~ *Read Acts 2:1-21*

PENTECOST

Peter's sermon, like many of Jesus' own, reminds listeners of familiar prophecies. He connects Joel's vision of the "latter days" to the events of his time, locates his hearers in the story unfolding around them, and breathes new life and meaning into ancient words. What Joel foretold is coming to pass even as Peter speaks. The Spirit has been poured out on the apostles and many others.

People have invoked the closing verses of this passage to support various "end time" theories. However, Peter does not speak them to invite speculation about the day or the hour of the Lord's return but rather to stir hearers to a keener awareness of what God is up to. Peter's words envision a new way of life in which the distinctions that put people at odds melt into an understanding of common good and common life in Christ. Old and young, male and female, rich and poor will take part in preparing for a new heaven and a new earth. What separates us carries less weight than what unites us in the Spirit. Poured out, the Spirit drenches us all.

To live in the Spirit implies not only living in sure hope of heaven but also living with eyes wide open to God's work in the world. Spirit-drenched people see how gifts are made fruitful, how the forces of destruction bring forth courage and invention, and how light overcomes even the great darknesses we face. We face them together, held in that light, breathing one breath, infused by the one Spirit who makes us sons and daughters of the one God. And this God is love itself—the force that moves galaxies, "the force that through the green fuse drives the flower" (Dylan Thomas).

God of all, bind us together with the force of your love. Give us courage in dark times and discerning ears to hear the dreamers and prophets among us. Amen.

Mirroring God's Love

JUNE 9–15, 2014 • SUE JOINER

SCRIPTURE OVERVIEW: Trinity Sunday is an appropriate time for the church to reflect on the dynamic tension between what we know of God and our attempts to formulate and articulate what we know. The Genesis text demonstrates that the God of Israel, the creator of heaven and earth, is unlike other gods and must be served and worshiped exclusively. The psalm asserts the same power of God but is more explicit about the implications for human life of God's governance. The Gospel reading reflects on the gift of God's presence in the church, a presence marked by moral expectation and demand, as well as assurance. The epistle reading voices the strange convergence of God's authority and God's remarkable grace known through the presence of Christ.

QUESTIONS AND THOUGHTS FOR REFLECTION

* Read Genesis 1:1–2:4a. How do you experience God in both light and darkness?
* Read Psalm 8. Look in the mirror of your life. How is God reflected in you?
* Read 2 Corinthians 13:11-13. What have you learned from the saints in your life?
* Read Matthew 28:16-20. When have you experienced God's love for others flowing through you?

United Church of Christ minister; director of Called Back to the Well, an ecumenical spiritual renewal program, Albuquerque, New Mexico; staff member, St. Michael and All Angels Episcopal Church

In these first two days of creation, God fashions both light and darkness. It is easy to see God in the light. In the mornings as I see the dark sky give way to light and as I watch the spectacular colors of sunrise fill the heavens, I know God is there. Later in the day I witness the light dance through the trees. This same light changes the color of the Sandia Mountains in Albuquerque to a lovely pink and purple, and I recognize God's handiwork. It gets more difficult for me as the light begins to fade and darkness approaches. I forget to look for God in the shadows. But on evenings when the brilliant stars fill the clear sky, I see God peeking through.

Why is it so difficult to remember that God dwells in darkness? Or, for that matter, how is it that we forget that God created darkness? Darkness is no accident or failure. It is the time of gestation and rest. Darkness evokes quiet contemplation on our often-busy days. We can embrace the goodness of the dark and remember that it is God's creation. It provides space for us to sit with the One who calls all of creation good.

Humans tend to separate things into categories of good/bad, light/dark, full/empty, right/wrong, and worthy/unworthy. We want to write off the less than desirable parts of our days. Yet God intends that we live our lives as a whole. We can uncover certain wisdom only in the dark. These first few days of creation invite us to embrace all of life. Can we perceive God in the darkness as well as the light?

Creator of all, help me to embrace all of life and to recognize the way you are at work weaving your goodness into the darkness and the light. Amen.

I am taking part in a program called Soulcraft. The program provides an opportunity for personal growth in the wilderness. Participants sleep outdoors and use nature-based practices to understand and embrace their lives more deeply.

I didn't discover the gift of creation until I attended college. Since that time, I have been drawn to nature. I greatly enjoy camping and hiking. When I am out-of-doors, I see things differently. I am more attuned to the natural rhythms of the day; I also find that my life begins to harmonize with those rhythms. I experience that as a relief, and I am reminded how we often ignore the wisdom of creation.

I knew I had chosen wisely when, at the first Soulcraft session, every assignment began with the words, "Go out on the land. . . . " Ah. I experience aspects of my life differently in this setting. The students don't look for answers in a book or from a wise teacher. Creation is our teacher. Our task is to pay attention to the wisdom of the wilderness.

I struggle to stay grounded. I am overly attached to my calendar, to my cell phone that contains more information than I can use in a lifetime, and to my work. Out on the land, I sought perspective and perceived this message: "Stop. Feel the earth beneath your feet and the way it holds you. Look up and find your place in the vast sky. Open your hands and receive the gifts that are there for you."

When we lose our way, we can remember that the earth and sky are God's gifts to us. God created them and saw that they were good. They ground us and convey to us a sense that we are part of something much larger. What can we do but receive the gifts God has for us?

Creator of earth and sky, help us to find our place in all that is. Open our hands and our hearts to receive the gifts you have for us. Amen.

What a delightful passage! Creatures, wild animals, birds, creeping things, cattle—and it's all good! These creatures fill the earth with their goodness. Then God says, "Let *us* make humankind in our image" (emphasis added). This is the first story of relationship. Humans are related to God and to creation. Perhaps the "us" in this verse offers a glimpse of the Trinity—yet another relationship! Even God comes to us as three-in-one. God breathes life into human beings so that we can relate to all creation. At the end of each day of the Creation story, God sees that it is good. But at the end of the sixth day, God sees everything and declares that it is *very* good. Some believe that humans were the grand finale and the words "very good" reflect on us.

But as I read this passage, I gain a different insight. I wonder if God is looking at the interconnectedness of all creation and calling that relatedness "very good." When we read this story in light of the One who became incarnate so that we could understand the depth of God's love for us, we see that God comes to us in relationship. After Christ ascended, the Spirit came to weave the motley crew of believers into a powerful church—God's people in the world. The church also reflects relationship. God connects with those early believers and helps them relate to the world around them.

God created us for relationship and teaches us how to be in relationship through the Trinity. We recognize that the story of Creation is one of relationship: of light and dark to earth and sky, to animals, to humans, and to God. We cannot exist without one another.

O God of all creation, help us to see how our lives are woven into the fabric of creation. Help us to celebrate and honor our relationships, for they are a reflection of you. Amen.

THURSDAY, JUNE 12 ~ *Read Genesis 2:1-4a*

God rested. God blessed the seventh day as a time to hallow the work of creation. Resting and hallowing are counter-cultural in 2014. We have the ability to be plugged in and available at all times. Because we have the ability to do so, we often believe that we should be plugged in at all times. We may resist rather than welcome stopping to rest. We struggle to take a break from our list of things to do. Perhaps we fear that all of our tasks and demands will overwhelm us if we step away. The world measures our worth through our productivity. Yet God rested.

What if we were to follow God's lead? What if we practiced sabbath? The concept of sabbath appeals to many, but it seems too impractical. As I read this passage again, it makes me wonder if we find stopping to rest too jarring. What if we took our cue from verse 3? It states that God hallowed the seventh day. Maybe that is the key.

Can we stop what we are doing and hallow our lives? The word *hallow* invites us to honor, make holy, or bless. What if we were to stop and bless our week? If we can reflect on what we have experienced in the week rather than focusing on all that remains on our to-do list, we might find it easier to rest and honor what we have just lived. A day of rest where we gratefully embrace our experiences can be a powerful spiritual practice. The spiritual practice of rest and blessing our days opens our hearts to embrace the fullness of our lives and creates space for God to work within us.

God of rest and blessing, teach us to practice sabbath and to honor the life you have given us. Amen.

Thin beautiful song of nature proclaims the goodness of all that God has created. As the human names all that God has made, awe floods the writer and begs the question, "What are human beings that you are mindful of them?" When we stand in the natural world and ask the question, "Who am I?" we receive the opportunity to see ourselves through God's eyes.

Our human nature leads us to quest for our purpose. We read books. We talk with wise companions. We pray. We agonize. We dream. We long to know why we are here.

The psalmist shows us that as we step into the earth and breathe in all of God's good creation, we will discover the answer. We are here as God's beloved to care for the earth as God would care for it. We are created in God's image, which says less about *how we look* and more about *how we are*. We have the capacity to love, forgive, show compassion, nurture, heal, and hope. We have been given some of the attributes of God so that we may use our likeness to treat one another, plants, and animals as God would.

With this capacity to love and care as God does, comes the responsibility to do so. God gifted us with the world and asks us to care for it, using our godlike attributes. The implicit assumption is that we will see the world as God sees it and nurture it rather than take advantage of it.

That opportunity fills us with awe. God creates us and calls us to be like God in the way that we care for the world and one another. What an awesome gift and responsibility!

We thank you, Creator of all, for making us in your image and giving us the opportunity to love the world as you do. Amen.

Ah, relationships. After a long struggle with the Corinthian church, Paul prepares his farewell. He tells them to "put things in order." He asks that the members lovingly invest in the building up of the church. His message doesn't translate as well in our disposable culture. When we tire of things, we get rid of them or throw them away. When we weary of the struggle, we feel tempted to walk away from it all. This certainly applies to churches. *Why should we stay? Isn't there a better church down the street?* Paul requests that the Corinthians—and we—live peacefully with one another.

Of course, sometimes we *must* walk away from a relationship or an institution or a situation. But that comes after attempts to find a way to live in peace together. It is curious that Paul mentions the saints. Is this an opportunity to gain some perspective? If we shift our gaze to those who have gone before, those who have "fought the good fight" (2 Tim. 4:7), perhaps we will better understand how to work through the issues that we face in our communities of faith. What can we learn from the saints? What loving legacy do we inherit from those who have gone before us? Do our churches today reflect the generosity and hope of the saints who built them?

Paul closes with a blessing from the Trinity—the grace of Jesus, the love of God, and the communion of the Holy Spirit. The Trinity demonstrates relationship sustained in grace and love. Communion refers to the close relationship of Christians. Any close relationship depends on love and grace to withstand the trials as well as to thrive in the good times. God as three-in-one gives us that love and grace in abundance and calls us to offer it to one another without keeping score.

Holy Trinity, help us to be loving and gracious in all our relationships. Amen.

TRINITY SUNDAY

Jesus' final words to his disciples are simple, "Make disciples." When church members find themselves lost in the many demands of stewardship, youth ministry, music and worship, building maintenance, outreach, and the multitude of meetings that seem to be far removed from mission, they may return to these words "make disciples." We refer to this passage as the Great Commission. The resurrected Christ returns to his followers to offer guidance so that they may continue his ministry of love, healing, and compassion.

Perhaps Jesus realizes that he places before them an impossible task just as God realized Moses' task was impossible—because Jesus offers the same promise. Rather than guarantees or strategic plans, he leaves them with five small, yet powerful words: "I am with you always." That is enough. That is more than enough. It doesn't seem very comforting, but we know that a promise like that is all we need to move mountains.

Jesus reminds us that our command to "make disciples" isn't up to us. He calls us to baptize in the name of a triune God. When we lovingly invite others into relationship, we are empowered by the God of creation, Jesus who redeems us, and the Spirit who sustains us. God's loving redemption is for all. We may be tempted to hoard it for ourselves, but clearly God intends that love to flow through us for the rest of the world. We are simply vessels, and our task is to allow ourselves to be both filled and then poured out for the world. We do not have what it takes if we depend on ourselves, but God's mercy will give us what we need to make disciples and fill the world with love.

Loving God, Gracious Christ, and Generous Spirit, flow through us so that the world will be filled with your goodness. Amen.

Letting Go

JUNE 16–22, 2014 • MISSY BUCHANAN

SCRIPTURE OVERVIEW: An essential biblical dynamic of threat and promise characterizes this week's readings. Implicit in the story of Hagar and Ishmael is the threat to Isaac and to God's promises to Abraham and Sarah. The psalmist captures the terror by unnamed forms of destruction that may threaten an individual or people. Paul raises the specter of that most universal threat—death—but does so within the context of the new life won by Christ's resurrection. Matthew describes various ways in which the enemies of Jesus threaten his disciples because of their association with him. Despite the reality and power of each of these situations, God's intervention proves to be more powerful still. The dynamic of God's threatened people always carries with it the assurance of God's presence.

QUESTIONS AND THOUGHTS FOR REFLECTION

- Read Genesis 21:8-21. Why is letting go so difficult for you, especially when you know that blessings have already been promised?
- Read Psalm 86:1-10, 16-17. How does feeling small in comparison to God make you confident in your daily walk?
- Read Romans 6:1b-11. In what ways are you tempted to make excuses for your sins rather than confessing them before God?
- Read Matthew 10:24-39. How might you rearrange your priorities so that you can grow toward a more radical and effective discipleship?

Passionate advocate for older adults; writer of a monthly column called "Aging Well" for the *United Methodist Reporter;* appeared on *Good Morning America*; author of several books including *Living with Purpose in a Worn-out Body*, *Joy Boosters*, and coauthor with Lucimarian and Robin Roberts of *My Story, My Song*; living in Rockwall, Texas

An older woman walked through her home for the last time. She pushed her walker past the bay window she had decorated each Christmas for over fifty years. She looked out at the huge oak tree that her children and grandchildren had climbed. There in her empty house, she stood at a crossroads. The time had come to move to an assisted living center. Even so, letting go of places and possessions she loved proved more painful than she had ever imagined.

Each of us faces change throughout life. Children grow up; loved ones die. Families move; jobs are lost. No matter our age, we struggle to let go of the things we love—a universal and timeless theme.

If we allow ourselves to think like Abraham, we can imagine his pain at letting go of his firstborn son Ishmael. We struggle to understand how a loving father can relinquish his child to the wilderness, but Abraham acts in faith because God has spoken, telling him to do whatever Sarah says. So, clinging only to God's promise, Abraham sends Hagar and Ishmael into the wilderness with bread and water.

Letting go. We are rarely ready for it. Some of us need to let go of anger or resentment; others of control, fear, or pride.

The point is, even in the messiness of life, we can count on God to keep God's word. The divine promise to bless Ishmael is all that Abraham has to hold on to in his time of fear and uncertainty, but it is enough. God's promise is always enough.

To what are you desperately clinging this day? In an act of faith, relinquish your grip and grab hold of God's promise instead. Like Abraham and Ishmael, you too will be blessed.

Forgive me, Lord, when I refuse to let go of my Ishmael. Give me courage to release my grasp and hold on to you instead. Amen.

Who among us has not felt that life was unfair? Maybe the feeling surfaced when a loved one betrayed you, when a manager gave you a pink slip, or when the cancer returned. Without notice, life turned upside down. Certainly Hagar could identify with the situation. As Sarah's handmaiden, she has dutifully fulfilled Sarah's command to have a child with Abraham. After Ishmael became a boy, Sarah's jealousy festered into revenge, and mother and son are banished to the desert.

Imagine Hagar as she falls to the scorched ground and sobs. Her deep guttural cries come from the broken heart of a mother who is helpless to save her son. Surely, Hagar cannot bear to see Ishmael's sunken eyes and bleeding lips, cracked by the relentless sun. She moves away, trying not to hear his cries as she waits for slow death to overtake him, then her.

She looks around—nothing but sun-baked ground and endless sky. The heat is oppressive. That's when the voice of an angel of God breaks through, "What troubles you, Hagar?"

It seems an odd question. Doesn't God know what is troubling Hagar? Of course, God knows the predicament. Perhaps the question is asked of Hagar so she can examine her own faith.

Hagar and Ishmael have not wandered beyond God's watchful gaze. Neither have you. God wants to hear your answer to the angel's question. What's the matter? What worries are causing you to fall to your knees in the sweltering wilderness? What is causing you to lose sight of God's promise of blessing?

O God, when life experiences overcome me, help me to hear your question and respond so that I can return to living out your promise. Amen.

You may remember the classic children's camp song about going on a bear hunt. As the children slap their thighs in rhythm, they encounter different obstacles—tall grass, a river, and a dark cave—while searching for a bear. They repeat the lines, "Can't go over it, can't go under it, can't go around it, gotta' go through it!" In many ways the psalmist paints a similar picture about our approach to God in prayer.

No doubt we can relate to the psalmist's cry of distress. At moments in our lives we all have crumpled to our knees and begged God to hear our cry. We too are "poor and needy." This passage reminds us that God wants us to work through those challenges in relationship.

God yearns for our authentic selves and doesn't want us to try to sidestep our emotions or go on a wild goose chase. We can approach God in confidence, knowing that we can bring the full extent of ourselves—the good, the bad, and the ugly—and ask for help to work through the messiness of life.

Notice too that the psalmist cries out all day long. That fact implies the idea that we incorporate prayer into daily life, not just during a worship service or before a meal. The psalmist cries out to God throughout the day. Why? Because persistent prayer brings us into regular community with God. The more we commune with God, the more likely we are to find comfort and encouragement when we have to slog through those tough times. If we turn to God in the ordinary moments of life, we will discover new perspective and understanding when trouble comes our way.

Father God, I confess that at times I pretend I am something I am not. Forgive me. Help me to bring my authentic self and my needs to you, knowing that you will work through life with me. Amen.

Not long ago I winced as I watched a former Olympic gold medalist attempt to make a comeback in her sport. Just a few years before, she had dazzled the world with a near-perfect performance. But on this day, millions of eyes watched as the young woman faltered again and again. Soon a trio of younger, better-trained athletes stood on the awards podium while the former champion stood in the shadows with tears trickling down her face.

That event served as a painful reminder of the way our culture views greatness. In the society of abundance, we view greatness in terms of money, scores, and fame—each fleeting and fragile. Yet the psalmist tells us that the true standard of greatness is God and God alone. If we place our trust and hope in the abilities of people, we will ultimately be disappointed because even the most gifted among us will falter. God's greatness will never fail or fade over time.

We may be tempted to think that God is just a few rungs above us on the ladder of greatness, but God is in a class all alone. We cannot even comprehend the fullest expression of God's power, holiness, and love for us. When we gasp at snow-capped mountains, we catch only a glimpse of God's power and creativity. When we count the fingers of a newborn baby, we find it impossible to take in all the mystery.

Our ongoing awareness of God's presence in the world helps us realize how small and powerless we are by comparison. If we truly want to understand God's character, we can begin by acknowledging God's greatness. The problem is, in the busyness of life, we forget to pay attention. When we do, we become less egotistical and more humble, less angry and more forgiving, less talkative and more prayerful. Then we will glorify God's name.

God, open the eyes of our minds to see your greatness all around us. Amen.

One day I was having lunch with friends at their retirement community where I visit weekly. Standing in line at the salad bar, I couldn't help but overhear a conversation between two older women as they discussed the color of fabric each had selected for her casket lining. I found myself smiling, amused at how easily they talked about death while filling their plates with lettuce and cottage cheese.

The two women chatted on about hymn selections and who would do their eulogy. Then the woman who was holding a cherry tomato with the tongs turned to her friend and said, "Well, one good thing about dying is that we won't be tempted to sin anymore. Praise the Lord for that!" Both women broke into uproarious laughter.

As I returned to my seat, I thought about this passage from Romans. Paul makes the point that in choosing to follow Christ, we die to a life that is ruled by sin and are resurrected to new life in Christ. He uses imagery of baptism, death, and resurrection. We die to sin, which has been snatching meaningful life away from us even when we did not know it. The power of sin no longer has a strong hold on us.

We still live in a fallen world. As the older woman at the salad bar understood, our sinful nature will remain with us as we live on this earth. But in Christ, we have changed hearts, changed attitudes, a changed identity. We belong to God.

Temptation will still come, but now we gain confidence in knowing that we are not helpless to resist sin. The bottom line is simple. We die so we can live. We die to ourselves so we can turn the world upside down for Christ! We die to our selfish ways so that love, hope, and joy will define us in new life.

O Lord, today I choose life in its fullest. I choose Jesus. Let me live boldly in your transforming power. Amen.

We live in a world of sound bites and tantalizing headlines. How many times have you glanced at an attention-getting headline and then delved into the story only to discover that the story is very different from what you had been led to believe? The disparity between headline and story can leave you feeling disillusioned, confused, or misled.

Today's verses from Matthew seem to have the same effect if taken out of context. Jesus' words almost shout from the page: "I have not come to bring peace, but a sword. For I have come to set a man against his father, and a daughter against her mother." What? Pitting family members against each other? It hardly sounds like the compassionate Jesus who commands us to love one another.

We are easily lured by a sound bite. Without understanding the context and culture of the passage, we scratch our heads at Jesus' words. Yet Jesus is giving his disciples a quick look at the opposition they will face. He is warning them that following in his footsteps comes with a cost.

Jesus sets this hard truth before us too. Authentic discipleship requires ultimate commitment to Christ. There will be times when the good news forces a choice between our family and friends and our faith. No one knows the human heart better than Jesus. He understands the pain of ostracism and rejection, especially by people you love. He knows too that commitment to him will conflict with the world's values. But he commands it anyway. Are we willing to walk away from someone or some situation because we love God more? May we affirm that life in Jesus is worth the risk.

O God, I confess that I have grown comfortable with easy discipleship. Renew my resolve to move toward a more radical gospel life. Amen.

The minister leaned his head down to the children gathered around him on the sanctuary steps and asked them to count the hairs on his head. The children giggled as a few of them tried to sort out single strands on his slightly balding head. After a short while, the minister lifted his head to tell the children that God knew exactly how many hairs were on each of their heads. The children looked at one another with wide eyes. Finally a preschooler with long, curly red hair announced, "Wow, God must love us a lot to count that high!" Indeed God does.

Just when we think our lives don't matter. Just when we feel the ache of loneliness. When it seems that others have forgotten us or simply don't care, we remember this scripture. We wonder how God is so big and yet so small. Big enough to create the universe. Small enough and intimate enough to know the number of hairs on our heads.

The disciples hear this message when they need it most. Jesus has presented the tough reality of what it means to be a disciple. Certainly following this man is not for the fainthearted. They will face danger and persecution. Knowing that their hearts race with anxiety, Jesus tells them not to be afraid. Three times. "Have no fear"; the small beginnings of their mission will yield a great harvest. "Do not fear"; those who kill the body cannot kill the soul. "Do not be afraid"; the Father in heaven cares for you. Jesus speaks these words to us as well.

Christ-followers need not fear what others say about us or what they can do to us. God who cares for the sparrows loves us far more. God is close enough to count the number of hairs on our head. We can trust God with our lives because God knows every detail of our lives and loves us still.

Compassionate God, when I am afraid and stumbling through life, let me reach to my head, feel my hair, and remember how very much you love me. Amen.

From Life to Death

JUNE 23–29, 2014 • BETH LUDLUM

SCRIPTURE OVERVIEW: God's unthinkable call on Abraham; it jeopardizes the long-delayed, but now realized, promise. Yet in the end, Abraham's faith and God's grace prevail. Psalm 13 is the classic example of a psalm of complaint. It shows that a prayer of complaint is a vigorous, active form of hope in God. Thus the psalm moves from a situation of need to a resolution in joy and confidence. In the passage from Romans 6, Paul juxtaposes three pairs of opposites: sin versus righteousness, freedom versus slavery, and wages versus gifts. For Paul, sin is a power that exceeds the abilities of human beings to contest. Only God is a match for the power of sin. We cannot earn or achieve eternal life; it is a gift from God. Matthew 10 makes a strong claim about the identification of believers with Jesus and, in turn, with God.

QUESTIONS AND THOUGHTS FOR REFLECTION

- Read Genesis 22:1-14. What places in your life seem to be dead ends but may, at God's initiative, become surprising, alternative, life-giving paths?
- Read Psalm 13. What anger, fear, or sorrow do you need to raise to God? How can you share stories of God's faithfulness in order to bring hope to others in their times of darkness?
- Read Romans 6:12-23. How does your daily life reflect your salvation? In what areas do you still allow sin and death a foothold?
- Read Matthew 10:40-42. Where can you practice offering and receiving hospitality as you seek the presence of Christ in community?

Program Director in Collegiate Ministries, General Board of Higher Education and Ministry of The United Methodist Church; member of an intentional community connected with Edgehill United Methodist Church; Nashville, Tennessee

Would you go? If God called you to the hardest task, the most painful journey, with the most uncertain ending, would you follow? This story is startling, even disturbing, because of Abraham's beautiful, terrible obedience. Without questioning or complaining, Abraham departs early in the morning to do as he's been told—to offer up his child.

Abraham's God has made other drastic requests. But this child is Isaac, the long-awaited one born to aged parents, a promise fulfilled. And, as any parent can understand, he was a beloved child who brought incredible joy, hope, and pride to his parents' hearts. Still, Abraham obeyed.

We're often willing to obey God, to follow the path we are called to travel . . . to a certain extent. "Yes, God, I'll go anywhere . . . but that place." "Yes, God, I'll do anything . . . but that work." Nearly all of us have a "but"—an exception to which we cling.

Our Christian ancestors, particularly Ignatius of Loyola, spoke about the necessity of cultivating "holy indifference" in order to follow God. Holy indifference required setting aside all emotions and preferences until nothing could be held back from God. No longer a "yes, but." Just a "yes."

Whether full or empty, used or laid aside, John Wesley developed a holy indifference to the circumstances of his temporal existence in light of God's desire. His covenant prayer, still a touchstone for people of faith, reflects his commitment to remain true to the path laid before him no matter what.

How did Abraham go forward, even when God asked him to perform the hardest task? Only by holding everything in life so lightly that nothing kept him from obeying God.

God, I don't always understand the path that lies before me. When you call me to hard places, to tasks I do not understand, I am afraid. Give me courage to let go of my caveats and conditions so that I may utterly and completely follow you. Amen.

It is perhaps one of the most simple and profound responses of obedience found in the Bible. Three times, to God and to Isaac, Abraham responds, "Here I am." Perhaps this isn't simply a response of rote obedience or functional identification.

When a friend of mine was struggling through a period of depression, she couldn't handle being home alone. Many nights I slept on her couch, available when she woke to simply say, "Here I am." For the child awakened by a nightmare; for the spouse separated by time and space; for the one who is lonely, sick, incarcerated, or institutionalized, it may be the most longed-for assurance: "Here I am."

Those words of presence are a marker of relationship. They are an acknowledgment that begins in the present moment but is rooted in a relational past and extends toward the next step of the journey. They are proof of a readiness to act, to go, to respond to a need or request with—or for the sake of—another.

For years, God had journeyed alongside Abraham, leading, guiding, and protecting. In foreign lands, on difficult roads, in hard-to-believe promises, God's presence remained steadfast. God was always there. God and Abraham responded to each other, journeyed together, and knew each other. So when God called with the hardest request, Abraham knew the only appropriate response: "Here I am."

Though Abraham's obedience is essential, it is possible because of its solid foundation. God's presence, their lifelong journey together, had built a relationship so solid that when one called, there was only one possible answer: "Here I am."

Help me to know you so deeply, to walk with you so closely, God, that when you call I can answer, "Here I am." Through relationship, may I come to know your constant presence, that I may be always ready to follow you. Amen.

Oh, how we want to be model Christians. We want to be bearers of the good news, bringers of hope to the world, witnesses to the light. And yet, sometimes, bearing that hope seems impossible.

"How long, O LORD?" We know that lament, don't we? When children squabble and bills pile up. . . . When the needs of the community far outweigh our ability to provide. . . . When depression blocks the light. . . . When illness cripples bodies and chemotherapy saps strength. . . . When our own sin, selfishness, and brokenness drag us far from the path of discipleship we desire. . . .

We know what it is to lose our way, to sense death's fingers grasping at us, to feel abandoned and alone. When we get to that point, the psalmist assures us, it's time. It's time to vent our pain, fear, and anger at our God who is big enough to handle it.

It's time to acknowledge that sometimes we feel that God has forgotten us and that the world is drowning in sorrow. It's time to pull back our veil of perfection, to show our scars, and to allow others to share their secret sorrows.

Maybe it's even time to issue God an ultimatum, to remind God and ourselves that finally, God is all we've got. God is the difference between life and death, light and darkness. God *must* come to save us.

It might seem easier to settle for platitudes that offer a band-aid of hope. It might seem easier to try to be strong and self-reliant. But we know that God promises more, and our journey toward light must begin with this crying out, this acknowledgment of the world's brokenness. For only after death may resurrection come.

God, give me the courage to be honest with you, the faith not to give up on you, and the love to offer truth and honesty to others. Amen.

Growing up on a farm, I knew well the first signs of spring. I would eagerly watch and wait as the cows grew heavy with calf, as ice started to thin and crack on the creek, as winter wheat began to turn a vibrant green even beneath a frosting of snow. But before it all, sometimes even before the groundhog Punxsutawney Phil emerged for his famous weather prediction, life would stir in the flower bed in front of our house. Though winter lingered, the first crocus that broke through the frosty earth was a promise, a signal that spring was coming.

In the midst of the winter of the psalmist's despair, a surprising refrain breaks forth: He begins to sing of God's salvation and steadfast love. Even as he acknowledges the darkness that surrounds him, his stubborn praise pushes through, claiming the promise of God's faithfulness and refusing to give darkness the final word.

Too often our lives and our communities are frozen by the troubles that surround us. In the dormant season of the soul, we see only our own exhaustion and insignificance and the world's great brokenness. While faith confesses those realities, it also proclaims that another reality is emerging and is, in fact, already present, if we can but see and claim it. God is steadfast, faithful, and true in every season of our lives.

"Share every story of God's faithfulness," a wise Christian couple used to remind our college Bible study group. "You never know when your story of God's faithfulness will be the reminder that carries another believer through his or her darkness."

A crocus doesn't mean that spring has arrived. But, like the stories of God's faithfulness, it reminds us that spring is near, life rises up, and death never has the final word.

What stories of God's faithfulness carry you through the darkness? How can you tell your stories so as to offer hope to others?

As usual, Paul states the difficult truth clearly, without beating around the bush: You once were dead, living in sin. Now you have been given life. So live like it.

When I first met Kris and Kristine, they were an average young couple. They enjoyed spending time with friends, staying up late to watch movies, and going camping on the weekends. When they had their first child a few years later, everything changed. Although they were the same people, they began living into an entirely new reality. The change was not always easy, but they willingly embraced new habits, sleep schedules, and social activities. Their highest priority was to live fully into their new reality, becoming the best parents that they could be.

Think back on a major transition in your life: landing your first job or getting married or having your first child, perhaps. In the days after the change, you were still, in many ways, the same person you had been before. Sometimes you might even have been tempted to live like nothing had changed. But the new path, the better path, required a different way of living—and, ultimately, offered great rewards, such as maturity, partnership, and love. As you embraced the new reality, you became the adult, partner, or parent you were called to be.

Our Christian life is like this, Paul says. Once we have been saved, we still have the option of living the old life, choosing sinful behaviors or ignoring the needs of the world. Old habits are tempting and easy. But the better way, the life-giving way, is to practice living into our new identity as Christians, becoming like Christ in action and character. After all, how we live determines who we become, and that faithful response to Christ brings eternal life.

God, show me the ways I continue to embrace sin and follow death. Give me the courage to turn instead to you and live into the abundant life you have promised. Amen.

At the Passover meal, Jewish families around the world pour an extra glass of wine or set a place at the table for the prophet Elijah, in hopes that he will return and usher in the messianic age. Christians later adopted a similar tradition, setting a "Christ plate" at the table, ready to welcome any stranger as the presence of Christ himself. For centuries, churches have lived out variations of this practice, creating space at the table for all who gather and recognizing the presence of Christ in the breaking of bread.

At the intentional community in which I live, church members, neighbors, unhoused friends, and wandering students gather every Sunday for a potluck meal. Each week the food selection is as motley as the people who come. Hearty stews and elaborate desserts sit alongside corn dogs and Popsicles™, but there's always enough—and there's always blessing. Among people of diverse age, race, and class, community forms with stories and laughter. We who host recognize that we feast in the company of prophets and angels and that we are blessed by their stories and presence.

Jesus prepares to send out his disciples to teach and to heal. After numerous instructions about the nature of their mission, Jesus closes with words of hospitality, welcome, and reward. Though they may face danger and hostility, Jesus promises that any who receive them, who offer hospitality in their name or honor, will experience his presence and will reap the spiritual blessings of their labor.

We who have been brought from death to life have a new mode of being in the world. To embrace life means to extend Christ's welcome to others, particularly to the stranger, the prophet, and the child; and in them, to find Christ.

God, help me to recognize you in the people around me, to provide them hospitality and welcome. Amen.

The disciples take little with them, so they will literally rely on the goodness of others to survive. They cannot be picky about food or accommodations; they will accept whatever is given from whoever will give.

We find it hard to rely on others. Particularly for cultures or families that celebrate self-sufficiency, receiving hospitality can be more difficult than offering it. To give out of our abundance to those who have less makes us feel good. To be the one in need, especially when we can offer nothing in return, challenges our independent, prideful hearts.

As Jesus commissions his disciples, he makes an astounding promise: "Whoever welcomes you welcomes me, and whoever welcomes me welcomes the one who sent me." As if to diminish the anxiety of relying on others, he promises that they will actually be the presence of God in Christ to those who receive them.

For a year after college, I lived and taught in another country. From the moment I arrived, my students and their families overwhelmed me with hospitality. They lavished food, clothing, and gifts on me. They invited me to their homes, took me to famous sites, and helped me bargain in the marketplace. I had absolutely nothing to offer except my presence and gratitude, but I came to realize that perhaps that was enough.

This final lesson is one of the most difficult and joyous. Though we often feel more comfortable bestowing hospitality, our willingness to receive graciously is a gift. As humble strangers, we can become the presence of Christ to those who welcome us. We offer the opportunity to be a blessing and to be blessed. As our communities learn to give and to receive, we become the body of Christ.

Gracious God, thank you for the ways you have blessed me through others. May I receive what others have to give so that I become the presence of Christ in their midst. Amen.

God's Gracious Will

JUNE 30–JULY 6, 2014 • LAURA JAQUITH BARTLETT

SCRIPTURE OVERVIEW: The Genesis text tells of Abraham's quest to find a bride for Isaac from among his own people. In opting for Isaac, Rebekah makes herself the instrument for the preservation of the promise; God's intentions are sure. A hymn honoring the marriage of the king is a good pairing with Genesis, since the psalm deals with the future birth of Jacob and the sustaining of the family and nation. Romans 7 depicts a battle of human life. Here the strong desire to do good and serve God rightly is threatened by the enemy of sin. Jesus' prayer in Matthew recalls that knowledge of sin's defeat often comes to those "infants" to whom God has granted revelation.

QUESTIONS AND THOUGHTS FOR REFLECTION

- Read Genesis 24:34-38, 42-49, 58-67. Think about times in your life when you can identify God's guidance in how a situation played out.
- Read Psalm 72. How do you convey your concerns about protecting the poor and needy to persons in authority?
- Read Romans 7:15-25a. Paul asserts that the more we want to do what is right, the more we seem to do what is wrong. The problem is that we rely on our own will instead of God's. Choose one habit or activity and, using prayer, practice turning that piece of your life over to God this week.
- Read Matthew 11:16-19, 25-30. We need not understand God's gracious will in order to benefit from the offer of rest for our souls. What burden do you need to lift up to Christ this day?

Program director, United Methodist adult retreat center in the foothills of Mt. Hood, near Portland, Oregon

Coincidence? In my family, that's one of our favorite questions, and it's always asked with a wink and a bit of a mischievous smirk because it's obviously a trick question. The members of my family don't actually believe in coincidence.

Was it a coincidence that I didn't get the wonderful music job I had applied for—on the same day I finally acknowledged that my middle school daughter desperately needed me to take a leave of absence to homeschool her? All the job signs had been positive, and it seemed to be a great fit. I'd been praying daily for God's guidance in seeking a new path, and I felt sure the music position was the right move. Then the homeschooling opportunity dropped into my lap, and I found myself confused and panicked about how to handle the possible job offer. A few hours later, the phone rang, and I heard these words: "We've decided to go with the other finalist." Coincidence?

Abraham sends his servant on a potential Mission Impossible. His goal: find a suitable wife for Isaac, a woman who is willing to travel far from her homeland to marry a man she's never met. In the patriarchal milieu of the ancient Middle East, this mission may not have been an impossible task, but the servant does not seem optimistic about his chances for success. He prays hard—not to his own god, mind you, but to the God who is most likely to influence the situation. He prays to the God of his master, Abraham. Not only does the servant effortlessly cross paths with Rebekah, but she immediately agrees to leave her home and family to marry Isaac. Coincidence?

When hearts open fully to God through prayer, the resulting blessings may be predictable (a willing spouse for Isaac) or unexpected (a new vocation as a homeschool teacher). Either way, it's no coincidence.

God of the ages, help us to trust your guidance in our lives. Amen.

It's difficult to resist the temptation to interpret scripture through the lens of my twenty-first-century lifestyle. Why would Abraham send a servant to carry out such an important errand as choosing a wife for his son? (Never mind that I know nothing of the cultural marriage traditions of that time and place.) And my feminist hackles are raised when I read that the servant assumes Rebekah will fetch water for him and for his camels. (Forget the established customs around "well etiquette," which both Rebekah and the servant knew and respected.) My modern sensibilities take particular offense to the idea that Rebekah will be expected to leave behind everything familiar to her in order to marry a forty-year-old stranger waiting in another country. I want to shout, "No! Don't do it, Rebekah! Stand up for your rights!"

But even allowing for the vast cultural differences between my life and Rebekah's, I acknowledge another force at play here. Seemingly, no one demands that Rebekah say yes to any request made of her. In fact, her family wants her to stay home at least ten days longer (vv. 55-61), but Rebekah makes it clear she will leave immediately. This woman makes up her own mind and decides to follow God's call.

Through her very obedience, Rebekah models independence. Through submission, she demonstrates strength. As a willing servant of God, she becomes one of the matriarchs of our faith.

Rebekah's story reminds me of another young woman whom the angel Gabriel asked to submit her own will and future plans to God's will and vision (Luke 1:26-38). Like Rebekah, Mary affirmed her identity as a willing servant of God. In doing so, she changed the course of history.

O God, give me the strength to be your servant. Amen.

Long live the king! Even those who have not been raised in a monarchy know how to exalt a king or queen—if not from following world news, then at least through exposure to fairy tales or Disney movies. Whether benevolent or corrupt, the ruler holds the power and resources to control the direction of the country—and thus the lives of those who reside there. A wise and effective monarch is a gift to all the people and certainly worthy of praise!

The people do not honor the king of Psalm 72 for his riches, his power, his military expertise, or his political skills. In fact, this king is not feted for any of the attributes we normally associate with governmental leaders. Verses 12-14 get to the heart of the matter. The following characteristics bring about celebration of this ruler: focus on the poor, the needy, the weak, help for those who have hit rock bottom, and redemption of their lives from oppression and violence. His most precious subjects are the ones who are most helpless.

How would our world differ if every head of state used Psalm 72 as a governmental guidebook? Listen up, all you rulers! If you want your people to revere you, if you want your foes to bow down before you, if you want gold and abundant food, if you want enduring fame, here is the secret: Alleviate poverty, put an end to violence, address the causes of oppression, and protect the most vulnerable people in your system. Long live any leader who understands this truth!

Using a globe or a world map, touch a country and pray that its leader will govern with God's sense of justice and righteousness. Continue this practice for different countries throughout the week.

Please make your bed now," I tell my younger daughter. The response varies, but it's rarely what I want to hear. "I don't feel like it!" You can't make me!" Or her current favorite, "I don't care." When she really wants to push my buttons, she shortens it to the curt, "Don't care."

What I've finally learned on this parenting journey is that if I walk away without engaging in debate, the task usually gets accomplished after I've left the room! My daughter is trying to assert her independence and let me know that I don't have control over her—even though she generally understands the importance of whatever chore I've given her and fully intends to complete the job. She prefers to think of it as exercising her own free will, rather than following the mandate of a dictatorial mother. I celebrate her appropriate development (even as I battle my frustration over the process).

Perhaps we are all stuck in the black hole of adolescent angst when it comes to conforming our will to God's. Paul points out that, like my daughter, we don't suffer from a lack of desire to do the right thing. My daughter says, "No, I won't do it!" but then she follows through on my request. Most of us, however, say to God, "Yes, I'll do it!"—and then we somehow miss the mark.

Paul addresses the power of sin to permeate human existence—even those who choose to respond to God in obedience. When we fall short in the obedience category, are we trying to tell God that *we're* really the ones in control? From his own experience, Paul understands that's a dangerous and fruitless path. The irony is that the more we think we can handle life on our own, the more we need God to shine the light of love and grace on the road ahead. Like a loving parent, God is ready to do just that.

God of love, help me understand that in giving up control to you, I gain control of my life. Amen.

My brother taught me how to play Spider Solitaire on my computer, and I can't say that I'm grateful. I really enjoy the game! What could be wrong with a bit of solitaire as a stress-reliever during a complex task or as relaxation in the evening after finishing work projects? The problem comes when "one quick game" somehow turns into "Where did that hour go?" And even without completing my work projects, I can easily rationalize that I deserve the reward of a game or two.

Am I possibly addicted to Spider Solitaire? It may not be a clinical diagnosis, but Paul understands the fundamental dilemma: "I can will what is right, but I cannot do it." No matter how many times I will myself to stay on task, my computer mouse finds a way to click on that spider icon.

Once I complained to my brother about my difficulty in staying on task and away from the game. He lit up in recognition. "Let's just agree that Spider Solitaire is of the devil!" Though he was joking, my brother had identified the fact that we can't seem to stay away from that which is evil, even when our eyes are wide open to the danger.

The only time I've successfully resisted the lure came one Lent when I eliminated the game as part of my seasonal spiritual discipline. With the help of prayer and other daily rituals, I stayed Spider-free for an entire forty days.

Spider Solitaire may not be akin to "this body of death," but the good news is that the discipline of prayer and spiritual commitment can save us from the evils that assail us. With God's help, there is "no condemnation" (Rom. 8:1). So I join with Paul in affirming, "Thanks be to God through Jesus Christ our Lord!"

Dear God, thank you for the saving power of Christ Jesus! Amen.

How easy it would be simply to skip over these words of Jesus! Most of us in First World countries no longer understand the culture of children calling to one another about marketplace games. We have no context to understand this reference, so we logically choose to jump ahead in the reading. And then we get to the name-calling: "He has a demon!" "He is a friend of tax collectors!" Again, our contemporary perspective makes it hard to engage with these labels.

But if we dig just a bit deeper, we find ourselves even less eager to linger and reflect on Jesus' meaning for us. These challenging words indicate Jesus' unhappiness with his contemporaries! These people are desperate for leadership, and yet they rejected both John (because he *did not* eat and drink) and Jesus (because he *did* eat and drink). It's a lose/lose situation, but the people Jesus addresses are the ultimate losers.

So what about us, reading these odd words from our comfortable vantage point in the twenty-first century? Are we willing to listen to our own prophets? Do we dare to admit that our primary concern involves building up the institutional church rather than building the kingdom of God? Can we acknowledge that Jesus also addresses us today—and that we lose when we do not listen?

The Gospel of Matthew spends a great deal of time exploring the "kingdom of heaven." The Gospel is full of good news about how disciples of Jesus (that means us!) can enter God's reign of love and transform the world. Today's verses remind us that too much is at stake to ignore Jesus' radical call. May our prayers today strengthen us for the task.

Pray the Lord's Prayer (Matthew 6:9-13), and focus especially on verse 10.

Jesus tells us that God's "gracious will" includes the gift of rest for the weary and the heavy laden. The director of the retreat center where I serve always ends his welcome speech with these words: "It is the practice of our staff to hold each group in prayer as we anticipate your arrival. We've been praying for you and will continue to do so throughout your retreat." The retreat center provides a box in the lobby where guests are invited to leave cards with prayer concerns or suggestions for how we might ask God to bless them.

The staff of my retreat center provides hospitality for many kinds of events, both sacred and secular. The "church folks" are pleased to know they are being held in prayer, and they nod with recognition when told about the prayer box. But the most significant impact of our prayer ministry seems to come for people who do not have a faith community of their own. They often seek out the director to express their delight at being held in prayer. They eagerly and gratefully avail themselves of an opportunity to share their deepest heart concerns with persons who will lift those up to God.

The staff has discovered that people long for rest, not only through the hospitality of food and lodging but also through our willingness to take on their burdens in prayer and share them with God. Few gestures offer more comfort than having a heavy weight eased from one's shoulders. As a follower of Jesus, I can extend Christ's comfort to those who come through the retreat center doors weary and carrying heavy burdens. When I participate in God's gracious will by offering the gift of rest, I find that I am the one who has been gifted.

Ask one other person today how you can be in prayer for him or her.

Walk in the Light

JULY 7-13, 2014 • JEFFRY WELLS

SCRIPTURE OVERVIEW: Genesis 25 marks the beginning of the narrative of Jacob's life. The theme that stands out in starkest relief is the election of Jacob to be the heir to the promise—Jacob, who has no claim to be the heir except that which the grace of God bestows. Psalm 25 reflects a general sense of alienation. Yet the psalmist expresses confidence in following God's paths and truths. Paul sets out two polarities in Romans 8: those who "live according to the flesh" and those who "live according to the Spirit," a cosmic duality related to the rule of sin and the rule of God. The parable of the sower and the seeds in Matthew 13 is an object lesson in the mysterious grace of God.

QUESTIONS AND THOUGHTS FOR REFLECTION

- Read Genesis 25:19-34. When in your life have you experienced the favoritism of parent, friend, coworker, or boss that created division?
- Read Psalm 25. The writer notes that if we pray for peace, we must work for justice. Pray and fill in the blank: "Redeem [*state your concern*], O God, out of all its troubles."
- Read Romans 8:1-11. "If Christ is in you, . . . the Spirit is life." Do you more often follow the Spirit or the flesh? What distinction do you draw between the two ways of living?
- Read Matthew 13:1-9, 18-23. How bountiful a harvest do you produce for God?

Lead pastor, Community United Methodist Church in Massapequa, New York; chair of the New York Conference Board of Church and Society; writer

On the surface, this story is a caricature of recognizable and deplorable human behavior: parents who favor one child over another; a mother who manipulates those around her to get what she wants for her favored child; a youth who makes a foolish and shortsighted decision; and a cunning child who takes advantage of a sibling for selfish gain.

At a deeper level, the story is about how God works in the world. We acknowledge that God bestows mercy on whom God chooses (Exod. 33:19). In like manner, God will choose whomever God wills to advance divine purpose in the world. God had promised Abraham that he would have many descendants and that they would be a blessing to all the nations. This promise now resides in the lap of Isaac's family. The calculating, manipulative, and unethical Jacob would seem like an unlikely candidate to carry forward God's promise to Abraham. Yet, perhaps God saw that Jacob would be clever and farsighted enough to succeed, whereas Esau had already demonstrated an inclination to be ruled by immediate and passing desire.

God endows each of us with particular gifts and abilities and then tries to encourage and inspire us to develop and use those gifts. That rarely happens fully or without the distortion of human sin. Still, God calls us to particular tasks or endeavors in the service of love and mercy. God knows that there are no perfect humans to be found to accomplish holy purposes; so instead, God chooses people like us—people who are available (willing or not). Neither does God always choose the firstborn, the rightful heir, the one with seniority, or the obviously qualified. God does not allow human conventions or traditions to get in the way of God's will. Seemingly, God does choose the person most able to accomplish God's desires.

God, give me clarity, wisdom, and strength to accept your call so that you can bless the world through me. Amen.

This passage raises a serious question about God's relationship with human beings. We could read into this story that God foreordained the described outcome. Did God cause Esau to be foolish and Jacob to be manipulative and greedy in order to achieve God's will? That conclusion would not square with our understanding of free will with which God endows us. When read carefully, we note that the scripture does not say God predestined Jacob to become the "child of the promise"—only that God foresaw it.

Does that reading imply that God does not intervene? Absolutely not! God continually influences and inspires us to choose the right, good, and loving word and action, yet grants us the freedom to make that choice. We are capable of choosing good or evil. We are "at liberty" to think, speak, and act either in accord with God's will and desire or in trying to thwart God's purpose. Thankfully, God is not constrained by our choices. In fact, as in the story of Jacob and Esau, God often uses even our foolishness and our sin to accomplish God's will.

Surely God did not desire Esau's flippant disregard for his birthright and Jacob's cunning trickery against his brother. However, seeing what each of them will do, God uses their actions to fulfill God's promise.

In a multitude of ways, we separate ourselves from God and fail to heed the Spirit's guidance. Yet, God graciously offers to fix our brokenness, heal our wounds, and clean up our messes. Moreover, our loving God—not one to be easily turned aside—continually works around our flaws, mistakes, and willfulness. God moves us toward the promise of God's dream for humanity: the beloved community of hope and love and peace.

Gracious One, continue to offer me your vision, show me what you desire from me, and use me to further your will and purpose. Amen.

How does the word of God light our path? First, we need to know to what word we are referring. The psalmist uses *word* and *ordinance* to speak of the Torah. This psalm refers specifically to the written word, the set of commands that bring life—instruction, history, poetry, and stories passed down and codified in scripture. It is this word that guides our feet and lights our path. Obedience to God's ordinances brings joy.

As Christians we are addressed by the living Word of God—the Word that was with God "in the beginning," the Word that "became flesh and lived among us," and the Word that speaks to our hearts and minds by the power of the Holy Spirit.

What, then, must we do to allow word and *the* Word to light our path? Listen to the psalmist's commitments in these eight verses of this longest of the Psalms. The composer vows to swear an oath, to remember and observe laws, to offer praise, and to acquire learning. As we grow in our spiritual lives through prayer, study, worship, we incline our hearts to God's instruction and guidance. Making ourselves open to the word and Word requires a great deal of effort and intentionality on our part. The living Word continues to teach, instruct, and lead us.

God communicates with our heads and our hearts—but only if we watch and listen attentively. We have to see with eyes of faith and listen with ears of faith. We pray; study; worship; practice love, mercy, and justice; and share scripture with others. As we make an effort in each of these areas, we listen for God's communication through scripture, tradition, reason, and experience. In faith and trust, we open ourselves to allow the word and *the* Word to light our path.

Illuminating God, your word is a lamp and a light for our journey. Help us to grow in the Spirit of Christ so that we will be able to sense the ways you are guiding us and live obedient to your will and desire. Amen.

Paul does not say that the Spirit is good and the body is bad. When he writes about "flesh" and "Spirit," he describes two different "ways of being" in this mortal body given to us by God. Material and physical concerns dominate the "flesh" way of living, which is always self-focused. We turn from God, allowing our lives to be ruled by our own desires, values, and concerns. The "Spirit" way of life focuses on God. It worships God and has no idols. Life lived in the Spirit is ruled by God's desires, God's values, God's preferences, and God's concerns. Rather than being self-absorbed, it is absorbed by concern and love for the other— God, neighbor, and the creation as a whole.

God did not give us bodies with all of our wonderful senses of touch, taste, smell, sight, and hearing in order that we deny ourselves the pleasures of food, sex, music, bird songs, flowers, reading, nature walks, and so on. God *does ask* that we be disciplined about enjoying these pleasures. Paul argues that such discipline comes from the Spirit, not the flesh. Yet, we are inclined to gluttony, hoarding, overindulgence, and addiction. Recognizing our lack of self-discipline, which even God's law could not keep in check, God came to dwell among us to overcome our bondage to sin and offer us a way to live in the Spirit of love and self-giving.

The Spirit-centered life permits an integration of our physical and spiritual lives. When we let go of our self-centeredness enough to allow God's Spirit to rule our thoughts, words, and actions, then we can be freed from bondage to self and to sin, and the Spirit way of life can reign over the flesh.

Holy One, inspire me to live a disciplined, obedient, and joyful life. I give thanks for the body you have given me and for your Spirit that dwells within me. Amen.

God desires that the Spirit within us determine our embodied lives. Only this can accomplish the balance and integration of flesh and spirit that allows us the chance for a truly loving and harmonious relationship with God.

This passage makes it sound as though living in the Spirit is an isolated, individual act. But we know from Paul's work as a whole that he saw this as a collective endeavor. Living life according to the Spirit requires life together in the body of Christ. There, we begin to experience the transformation of the world as we participate in and witness glimpses of what God's dream for humanity actually looks like.

The ability to live a different sort of life in obedience to and in loving relationship with God and the ability to participate in the transformation of the world—for this reason God came to live among us in the person of Jesus Christ. As Paul makes clear, the law was too weak in the face of sin. Only the Spirit of life and love in Christ could break sin's power over us.

Jesus came to offer us first, redemption and second, a Spirit that could radically reshape our whole orientation to life and turn us back to God. That Jesus had to die on a cross and then be raised from the dead to accomplish this redemption shows the power and attraction of the flesh-determined way of living. In this earth-shattering and mind-blowing act, God wipes the slate clean for all of us, places us in the relationship of beloved children, and offers us God's own Spirit to dwell in us and break the chains that bind us to sin.

Redeeming Lord, help me live according to the Spirit that dwells within me and to savor the new life God has been offering me all along. Strengthen me to let go of my need to control and, instead, offer myself into your hands. Amen.

Jesus teaches us that if the seeds of God's living word are to take root and grow and bear fruit, then we have to become good soil. We might need to have our pH adjusted. We may need extra nutrients, and perhaps some compost. We could use a little Miracle-Gro™.

Getting the right mix is not easy. We know from experience that life does not naturally lend itself to making us into "good soil." Many factors shape whether we will remain hard, rocky, thorny soil or will develop into healthy soil, in which seeds of the gospel can take root and flourish. Did we have loving parents, a nurturing environment, and a moral and spiritual upbringing? Were we taught compassion and generosity or did we learn, instead, to always "look out for number one"? Have we been hurt or traumatized in some way that makes it harder to open up to God and to people around us? Further, are we willing to make the commitment and put in the effort to grow in the Spirit and thereby improve our soil quality?

Becoming good soil requires conscious and intentional effort. We spend time looking into ourselves. We ask ourselves: "What are the hard, dry, rocky, or thorny parts of myself that I need to work on?" We open ourselves to God's nurturing and cultivating until we become soil worthy of God's garden. Through study, devotions, prayer, worship, and building relationships in small groups, we gain strength, support, encouragement, and inspiration to grow and bear fruit. But perhaps we first have to listen! What do we hear? Does our hearing lead to understanding?

Seed-sowing God, by the power of your Spirit help me to be open and vulnerable to the ways you till, fertilize, and water me to become good soil for your kingdom. Amen.

I passionately desire to bear fruit for God's beloved community of love on earth, so I fervently want to be good soil for the seeds that God continually scatters. Jesus tells us that if we are good soil, we will hear the word and understand it. God's word will then infuse every aspect of our lives. It will guide our thoughts, words, and actions and, therefore, equip us to bear sweet and abundant fruit for the kingdom.

If we reflect honestly, we know that we cannot produce fruit by our own will or power. We have to turn our wills and our lives over to God. That intention on our part makes us receptive to the Sower's seeds. God's strength and might empower us to bear fruit.

Thus, becoming good soil requires humility and submission. It demands that we recognize our incompleteness, our failings, our participation in sin, and our utter dependence on God. It requires that we reflect deeply and regularly on God's word and seek to live it daily. It expands our desire to connect with God in prayer. When we are good soil, we have a sense of awe and wonder and a desire to praise and serve the one who is the great Sower of Seeds and the Gardener of all Creation.

The Great Gardener continually scatters seeds, knowing that some will land on good soil. Our task is to keep striving, with God's help and with great intentionality and desire, to be the best soil we can be for God's garden.

> *Gardener of Creation, I lift my thanks to you for your forgiving love and grace. I want to be used in the making of your beautiful garden of love. Nurture and guide me to bear much fruit. Amen.*

Our Father

JULY 14–20, 2014 • DANNY WRIGHT

SCRIPTURE OVERVIEW: This week's texts depict a broad span of settings of God's activity, from Jacob's encounter in solitude to the broader context of Creation itself in Romans. The texts also tell of God's commission of human agents, weak and inadequate, to carry out divine tasks. Jacob may not be totally aware of God's plans for him, but the reader knows. Paul declares that the people in whom the Spirit of God dwells are very much in tune with the pain of creation. They also long for God's final deliverance. Just at the point of the reluctance of God's agents to carry out the tasks, the parable from Matthew about the wheat and weeds gives hope. God will take care of the weeds in God's own time. Psalm 139 is a moving statement on the ubiquitous nature of God's presence.

QUESTIONS AND THOUGHTS FOR REFLECTION

- Read Genesis 28:10-19a. What "certain place" or places has God used to reveal the divine plan for your life?
- Read Romans 8:12-25. What "sufferings" derail you from living in God's grace and experiencing God's hope?
- Read Psalm 139:1-12, 23-24. What is God's searching of your heart prompting you to deal with?
- Read Matthew 13:24-30, 36-43. When have you tried to do what you thought needed to be done instead of asking for God's guidance in the matter?

Associate minister, New Paradigm Christian Church; chaplain at Midas; living in intentional community with the Moria Project in inner-city Indianapolis

Most of us have stretched the family rules to play our "cards" in our own favor. We tend to revert to our own best interests and try to make everything turn out as we desire. When we get caught, we may have to shuffle out of sight to avoid the fallout. The heavy heart weighs more with each step.

Jacob is putting the miles between himself and the heartache and havoc he has spun. He searches for a place to put the loathsome journey on pause and try to escape to anywhere but here and now. When he finally stumbles upon that "certain spot," he sprawls out on the ground and grabs a rock for a pillow. As he drifts off to sleep, the craziest thing happens. He dreams of a ladder with angels ascending and descending while God stands and stares at the weary traveler. The same God that Jacob had referenced as "your God" when talking to his father, Isaac, now promises divine presence to the deceiver and guarantees a future beyond his wildest dreams and any of his best deserving.

Grace is like that. It always comes to us when we least expect it and where we never would have found it for ourselves. Grace is more than a dream. It is a gift and a reality infused into our existence. Our God is the giver of every good gift and does not need a GPS to find us when we are on the run. Jacob didn't have a pillow, but I sure am glad he packed that oil.

God, may we forget our pillows, carry the oil, and be ever ready to sleep long enough for you to wake us in your grace. Amen.

We struggle to recall and recollect. We do what we can to create slogans that will remind us: "Remember the Alamo," "Never Forget," and "WWJD." We wear bracelets and necklaces and buy T-shirts that rip off Madison Avenue. We create alternative subcultures, circle the wagons, build our own museums, and write our own books and songs. We career through the world with as little touch as possible and miss God's presence that was with us all the while. We wrestle with life and dance without recognition.

Before Jacob goes to sleep, God's presence is in that "certain place"; yet Jacob remains unaware. Now his dream has opened wide his eyes, and he can see what he could not see before. His father's God was becoming his. The road will not go from crooked to straight immediately, but this revelation transforms his journey forever. There will be no return to life as he had known it. Things are different now.

Promises made and presences recognized lead to Jacob's giving that place a new name because it served as the gateway to a new world. Jacob now moves forward "plus one" in traveling companions and his life would never be the worse for wear. God begins the recalibration of a soul and signs the adoption papers. Jacob has time to reflect on a journey that has been longer than he realizes and that will end up changing him—and us. It's what happens when you become a resident—not just a guest—in Bethel, the house of God.

God of our waking and God of our dreaming, write your story with our lives. Amen.

We too often live in a now that is shallow and a here that is only represented by our physical presence. We are not even scratching the surface and yet the architecture of time and structure and atoms and DNA swirls all around us. A work is transpiring that punches no time clock and does not start and end its day after a bus ride with two transfers and a three-minute walk. Every so often, we sense that someone lurks in the shadows and that time has more layers than we realize. We perceive that there is more to this existence than the stuff the eye records and the ear gathers in audio waves for the brain to assimilate and decipher.

Yahweh has searched our souls and knows us better than we know and understand ourselves. God is the one who understands the true character of those who pray. The psalmist, in the opening verses, employs verbs that speak of God's perception of us—inside and out: "know," "discern," "search out," and "are acquainted." God observes our activity and inactivity and even knows the syllables that will form in our mouths before we speak. In the passing of time and scurrying activity, as well as the moments of placid inactivity, we are in God's loving vision, recipients of divine attention. The psalmist notes that God hems him in "behind and before." He is surrounded by God.

"Where can [we] go from [God's] spirit? In Acts 17, Paul writes that the omniscient, omnipresent God gives us life, breath, and everything else as we live, move, and have our being in God. Our lives are saturated with God. May we, like the psalmist, feel the guidance of God's hand upon us.

Father, we thank you for knowing, loving, guarding, and guiding us in your light. Amen.

On multiple occasions, I have lost my keys. I usually ended up going around in circles, sure that they could not have gotten very far away. It has been years since I lost that last set. The last wallet I lost either flew off of the back of the truck or was left in a movie theater. I am telling you this because when I call in the coast guard and go on an all-out search, my items still remain lost. Much of my searching is in vain, but God searches and finds.

The psalmist desires to be real and genuine. He knows that God has searched him before, and he longs to be searched again. He wants to shed anything that is less than what God requires and only walk the everlasting way. In these verses, the psalmist comes full circle. Initially God's searching nature is the object of his awe—"such knowledge is too wonderful for me." He steps forward confidently asking God to search him and test him! The psalmist believes that God will find no "wicked way" in him. God's all-knowing power will assure him of "the way everlasting." He gives himself over to the sovereignty of God in all parts of his life.

Our full commitment to God demands that we submit to God's searching gaze, even as we affirm that God knows our every movement. God's searching is never in vain.

The Gospel of Luke tells us that Jesus came to seek and save the lost. You and I are proof positive of his success. The God who created us knows our thoughts, tests us, and searches for any wicked ways in us. God, in divine mercy, searches and finds and redeems. It's a good thing God is searching, and not me.

Lord, search me and test me. Root out my wicked ways. Lead me in the way everlasting. Amen.

Some people wake up afraid for their lives, and others have not eaten in days who search city dumps hoping for scraps that can stave off the hunger. Others experience atrocities that we cannot even begin to imagine but keep on caring for the poor and the forgotten. They hold little hope that anyone will intercede in the plight and heartache that they experience. The rest of us have vending machines, pet stores, and ubiquitous Wi-Fi, yet we often lead lonely, separated lives even within our own homes and bedrooms. Spouses ignore each other while their children sneak out the window and proceed to crush their parents' hearts. People still hold strong feelings against others because of skin color, accent, or clothing they choose to wear.

But we are not meant to live our lives enslaved to the power of the flesh. Our hearts' longing for God cause us to cry out, "Abba! Father!" We instinctively know that we want to belong to a family in which all people have standing and receive nurture. The very Spirit of God transforms our now and offers guarantees of the not yet. We are joint heirs with Christ—heirs of both his suffering and his glory. The creation itself groans as it awaits redemption.

In John 16:33, Jesus promises that this world will give us trouble and then notes that we need not fear because Jesus has overcome the world. This groaning world offers us struggles through paschal rhythms of our own, but God meets us in those mini-deaths and creates mini-resurrections that will ultimately lead to the once-and-for-all shedding of the power of sin. We have hope because we have been adopted and are heirs together with Jesus. We cry out to a Father who always hears. Paul reminds us "that the sufferings of this present time are not worth comparing with the glory about to be revealed in us."

Father, remind us of the hope we have because you have adopted us. Amen.

Growing up, I belonged to a group of persons who practiced a fundamental form of Christianity. The group was always on red alert. Phasers were never set to stun. We lived our lives on a witch hunt and tried our best to rid our existence of anything and everything that might even reek of a hint of that rancid, rotten smell that comes from the touch of the evil one. We would shut the gate at the entrance to the cave at the foot of the mountain and sequester ourselves from the possibility of defilement. We were vigilant about protecting our ivory tower and ensuring the safety of our generation and the ones to follow. We were responsible for our spiritual sanctity and security.

In other words, I spent much of my younger life tiptoeing around the edges of society because it was wrong to dive into the fray and mix with the godless. My Christian culture believed it was not right to live in the middle of a world gone wrong.

Yet, Jesus makes it clear in this parable that the good seed that he has sown in the world exists alongside the bad seed that the "enemy" has sown. The slaves of the householder react to the weeds with anxiety. They want to pull the weeds out immediately. But the householder counsels patience. To pull up the weeds might damage the wheat. The servants and the seed remain faithful to the process.

In the world, in faith communities we find wheat and weeds. Jesus' words, while speaking patience, also carried notes of judgment. At the appropriate time the weeds will be bundled and burned. It was never my place or the responsibility of the self-proclaimed keepers of the holy and referees of the right and wrong to call one soul in and another soul out. Our zeal could result in damage to the wheat.

Lord, help us to reserve judgment and wait patiently for your justice. Amen.

Listening is essential to life and central to discernment. We cannot move forward if we are incompetent with this ability. We never seem to get enough professional training in this skill, and people who practice it well are not the first to be chosen for the team at recess. We need to learn to listen.

Everyone needs someone in his or her life who is willing to listen—to listen hard and long, with patience and passion. Some words are more artfully crafted and deserve mass production. In order for that to happen, they need to be written down, read, told and retold, heard and heard again for the first time. These verses fall into that category. These words, initially spoken to disciples who fail to understand, are recorded for the edification of many. Jesus' words resonate far beyond those within earshot.

Jesus tells stories of what the kingdom is like and connects those stories with everyday experience. But this explanation moves far beyond the everyday to the end of the age. In these verses Jesus explains the various pieces of the parable, revealing the Son of Man as the one who sows good seed. The devil sows the weeds. Both weeds and wheat will grow together until the harvest. And on the day of judgment, the Son of Man will dispatch angels to reap.

The Word made flesh reveals truth. And at this story's end, he punctuates the truth by pointing out that people with ears to hear should listen. His words were often difficult to understand; but Peter tells us there is nowhere else to go because Jesus has the words of eternal life (John 6:68), and James reminds us not to be hearers of the word only, but doers.

Word of Life, help us hear and obey the words that give life. Amen.

Love Prevails

JULY 21–27, 2014 • PETER VELANDER

SCRIPTURE OVERVIEW: In the Genesis text, Jacob the trickster is tricked. Yet through a combination of patience and perseverance he ultimately wins Rachel, which sets the stage for all that follows in the story of Abraham's family. Psalm 105 addresses a forgetful community that has lost touch with the God of the Exodus. Remembering becomes a powerful experience when it focuses on both God's actions and God's judgments. Romans 8 also serves as a reminder of God's way, of God's movements from knowledge to action, from saving grace to promised glory. The scribe of Matthew's short parable brings out of the storehouse both what is new and what is old. There is no true future without a remembrance of the past.

QUESTIONS AND THOUGHTS FOR REFLECTION

- Read Genesis 29:15-28. When have you experienced or witnessed a similar story of love, scheming, and perseverance? Where do you see God in this story?
- Read Psalm 105:1-11, 45b. The psalmist acknowledges God's presence and reliability over time. If you had written this psalm, what occasions of God's faithfulness would you mention?
- Read Romans 8:26-39. Paul speaks in sweeping generalities about the circumstances that might make us feel insecure about God's love for us. What circumstances in your life have caused you to feel this way?
- Read Matthew 13:31-33, 44-52. What experiences of the new and the old have been important to you in your faith journey?

Editorial director, *The Upper Room* daily devotional guide and *El Aposento Alto*; member, Trinity Lutheran Church, Bellevue, Tennessee

As often happens, the story of God's people reads more like a soap opera than holy history. It is fitting that we begin our week together witnessing some of the best and worst of human behavior because God meets us in these and all circumstances.

How can we not admire Jacob's devoted love for Rachel—a love that works hard and waits patiently for seven years to be together with his beloved? We all desire that kind of devotion from another human being.

We also recognize the scheming of someone like Laban. Many people take advantage of others' best intentions. Whether Laban's trickery is born out of compassion for his older daughter or of simple greed, he uses Jacob's love for Rachel to create an opportunity for himself.

And how do we explain the oddest part of the story? Veil or no veil, it seems Jacob should have recognized the woman he has desired for so many years. Perhaps a little overindulgence at the celebration left Jacob vulnerable to Laban's scheme.

Jacob's love prevails but not with a happy ending. The years that follow bring growing animosity between Rachel and Leah, which fills their home with conflict, struggle for acceptance, and competition for attention.

Humans, with their mixed motives, make for messy love. Relationships with people we believe we can trust sometimes turn sour. Perhaps you can recall moments in your life that have been tainted by jealousy, deceit, or broken dreams.

It is in this messy world that God meets us. When we are untrustworthy, God is true. When we are impatient, God is long-suffering. When we experience disappointment, God brings hope. When human love fails, God's love prevails.

Redeeming God, my ability to love is imperfect. Fill me with your Spirit that I may grow closer to your example of perfect love. Amen.

God has a destination in mind for us: a life surrounded by God's love and grace. What's more, God knows that we can't find our way there on our own. Life's varied circumstances cloud our experience of God's love and grace. At times it seems impossible for us to feel confident that love will prevail. In today's reading, Paul offers two promises that help us persevere during those times when God's reign seems far away.

Sometimes despair fills us so completely that we don't even know what to pray for or how to pray. Paul tells us that in those moments, God comes to us, and the Spirit prays on our behalf. That's the first promise. When our pain stretches beyond words, when circumstances leave us at our wits' end, God's Spirit intercedes on our behalf.

The second promise that Paul offers us in difficult times is this: "We know that all things work together for good for those who love God." He does not say that all things are part of "God's plan." The promise of Romans 8:28 is that God will be with us; even in the most difficult circumstances, God can work for good. This powerful promise does not deny the impact of tragedy or distress in our lives. And we need not accept those events as "God's plan." Rather, we can live in the hope that God's love will meet us in our darkest hour and work for good. It is comforting to know that we do not have to live in denial of our heartbreak to believe in the promise of God's steadfast love and presence in our lives.

Loving God, when we have no words for our pain or distress, help us to rely on your Spirit's intercession and claim the promise that, for your children, all things work together for good. Amen.

The kingdom parables are familiar to us. Small acts of love and kindness "planted" like the tiny mustard seed can result in remarkable outcomes. Seemingly insignificant acts of mercy mixed into the community like yeast into flour can change the whole community, causing it to "rise."

Another aspect of these parables relates to our contemplation of God's prevailing love. The amazing plant that emerges from the tiny seed and the airy loaf, fully leavened by yeast, do not happen instantaneously. The process takes time. It requires patience to see the results. And waiting is not easy. I'm reminded of my children planting seeds in paper cups and putting them on the windowsill. They plant and wait. Children especially become inpatient. When will something happen? When will the seeds grow?

We can see the signs of God's "kingdom come" all around us every day. But we also experience God's reign as coming—that is, not yet here. Sometimes the areas where we await the coming of God's reign hold our attention more than the places where we see clear evidence of God's kingdom. We become obsessed by the broken relationship with a family member or friend. Our spirits are troubled by the senseless acts of violence we witness in the world around us. Tragedy abounds. Where is the mighty tree that grows from the tiny seed? Why is that flat dough not growing to rise over the edges of the bowl?

We are often called to live faithfully as we wait for God's reign to come—for God's love and grace to be fully evident in circumstances where we desire them most. We can wait because we know God is true to God's word.

Timeless God, grant us the patience to plant the seeds and mix in the yeast, knowing that you are faithful and that your reign will come. Amen.

What causes you to feel at risk or condemned? The first and last time I cheated in school was in the fourth grade. I stealthily erased and moved a decimal point on a returned math test. One more correct answer would give me a higher grade. I approached the teacher saying that I thought my answer was correct. He looked at my paper, then looked me straight in the eye and asked, "Did you change your answer?" I could move a decimal point, but I couldn't lie to my teacher's face. I was caught.

I remember an overwhelming feeling of guilt. I felt criminal —as much as a fourth grader can feel criminal. I knew God was not happy with me and that in some way I had failed everyone who was important to me.

Guilt causes me to feel separated from God's love. In today's reading Paul lists some other circumstances, much weightier than moving a decimal point, that can make us wonder if God's love is secure. Hardship, like unemployment; distress, like coping with illness; persecution, like that person at work who has it in for us; famine, whether it is food or affection that we hunger for; nakedness, or any other form of vulnerability; peril, like the anxiety that precedes a test; or the sword, when we, or someone we love, serves in harm's way.

What causes you to feel at risk or condemned today? Your list will be personal and specific.

Hear Paul's words: "In all these things we are more than conquerors through him who loved us." In those moments that we feel most insecure, God chooses to reach out to us in love.

Embracing God, when I feel surrounded by peril, help me to feel your strong arms holding me securely in your love. Amen.

FRIDAY, JULY 25 ~ *Read Romans 8:38-39*

Yesterday we considered a list of circumstances that can cause us to feel at risk or condemned. The apostle Paul reassured us that in all of those circumstances we could be more than conquerors because God's love prevails. But we are not easily convinced, and Paul knows this. Even the most confident among us can be shaken by circumstances beyond our control. Often we find ourselves plagued with fear and challenged with feelings of loneliness or alienation.

Paul's argument for God's prevailing love has escalated as we have moved through this week's passage from the book of Romans. First he told us that when we are too desperate or weak to pray, God's Spirit takes up our cause and prays for us even as we are silent before God. Then he claims that all things work together for good for those who love God. With stirring words he tells us that God is on our side and that none of the circumstances that cause us to feel at risk or condemned can overcome us—because God's love prevails.

Now Paul "closes the deal." Even after his fervent defense of God's prevailing love, Paul can imagine us saying, "But what about . . . ?" His final list is adamant, ending with, "Nor anything else in all creation will be able to separate us from the love of God in Christ Jesus our Lord."

This passage from Romans has provided a touch-point for me in what have felt like the darkest moments of life: when a parent or grandparent has died, when my children have suffered, when I have faced personal failures. In these times, and when great tragedy strikes somewhere in the world, or when the TV news causes me to wonder *Where is God?* Paul's manifesto reminds me that ultimately God's love prevails.

Faithful God, convince my sometimes trembling spirit that your love will always carry me. Amen.

God's reign has a singular focus—love. Many other character-istics grow out of this focus; for example, forgiveness, jus-tice, compassion, and service. But the growth starts with God's audacious gift of love bestowed upon us, which is the source of every good human act.

Jesus asks us to use our imagination to understand how incredible this gift is. He asks us to consider the giddy excite-ment that we would experience if we stumbled upon hidden treasure or a priceless pearl. Our minds would immediately begin to spin with plans for laying claim to such a valuable pos-session. Both examples remind me of the questlike behavior of a character like Indiana Jones. The prize is so great that the risk taken to receive it is almost limitless. Such is the value of God's love and presence in our lives.

We acknowledge God's love as a gift; it requires no merit or effort of our own. We know that by grace we are saved and invited into God's reign. The parables suggest that if we recog-nize the value of these gifts of love and grace, we will greatly desire their full presence in our daily lives such that we earnestly pursue and nurture them, holding them close to our hearts. That is our quest.

It's one thing to receive a gift; it's quite another to let it change the focus of our being. That's the invitation we receive in these parables. The gift is ours by the grace of God. The question is this: Will it make a difference in the way we live?

Inviting God, your gift is great. Provoke me to live into your reign, to pursue it fervently in my life so that your gift can have its full effect in and through me. Amen.

Throughout the week we have "zoomed in" on specific stories or circumstances that have demonstrated both the challenges that we face in our walk of faith and the steadfastness of God's presence in the midst of those circumstances. We have taken a "close-up" look and have been reminded of particular events in our lives when we have found ourselves waiting for God's reign or feeling separated from God's love or longing for God's presence in more palpable ways.

Today the psalmist invites us to "zoom out"—to consider the long view of God's faithfulness. "[God] is mindful of his covenant forever, of the word that he commanded, for a thousand generations."

When we find ourselves in trying circumstances, we can turn to scripture for reassurance and direction. Our prayers can bring us strength and clarity. But we can also do what the psalmist does—take a step back and reflect on God's faithfulness to us over the long haul. A recitation of God's presence with us in the past can give us more confidence about the future.

In today's passage we read of God's faithfulness for "a thousand generations," beginning with Abraham and continuing with Isaac, Jacob, their families, and the community of faith. The psalmist continues with testimony to God's work through Joseph, Moses, and Aaron. I can do the same. When I take the long view, I remember stories of God's faithfulness told by my parents, grandparents, aunts, and uncles. When I consider my own span of years I can clearly see God's constant work in and through the circumstances of my life.

The practice of zooming out, of remembering, gives us confidence and strength as we meet the future.

Steadfast God, remind us of your faithful presence over the years and in all circumstances. Teach us to meet the future boldly, remembering your reliable presence. Amen.

"Thy Name Is Love . . . "

JULY 28–AUGUST 3, 2014 • E. BYRON ANDERSON

SCRIPTURE OVERVIEW: The heavyhearted psalmist gives voice to the feelings of many when he states, "Hear a just cause, O LORD; attend to my cry." In the Genesis text Jacob wrestles with a "man." At one level, this story is about human struggle with God, but at another level the story tells of a human being's struggle with himself or herself. Yet even in the midst of our struggles, the enduring word is one of God's grace. Romans 9 also deals with suffering: Paul's personal anguish over Israel's failure to receive God's messiah, the Christ. Matthew 14 reminds us that God's mercy is real. Obedient disciples become agents through whom God's provisions are served to hungry people.

QUESTIONS AND THOUGHTS FOR REFLECTION

- Read Genesis 32:22-31. Consider where and when you have wrestled with God. What marks do you bear from that wrestling? How do those marks inform who you are today?
- Read Psalm 17:1-7, 15. Spend some time reviewing what has been in your heart, your spoken words, and your missteps over the past day or week. Conclude each part of your review with "Show me your steadfast love, O God."
- Read Romans 9:1-5. Paul expresses concern about the division between Israel and the growing Gentile Christian community, a division that increasingly becomes "us" against "them." Who are "they" in your life, and what will you do to overcome your separation from "them"?
- Read Matthew 14:13-21. What is your deepest hunger and how have you sought to satisfy it?

Styberg Professor of Worship, Garrett-Evangelical Theological Seminary, Evanston, Illinois

If you know Jacob's story, you know that he hardly models holiness in the sight of God. Yet, somehow, Jacob is the one who prevails in the wrestling match with God. Jacob is the one who becomes Israel. Jacob is the one who receives God's blessing. How did this happen?

The story of "Wrestling Jacob" begins in the night, a time of vulnerability when every shadow hints at a threat to life, a time when we are most susceptible to being wounded, a time when all that haunts our minds and hearts seems to get the best of us. (There is a reason we fear nightmares but cherish daydreams.) More, it begins at a point where Jacob is alone, dispossessed of both family and property. He is neither here nor there, no longer in his own land and not yet with his brother and family. He is nowhere and has nothing. Perhaps you've been there.

Jacob and, like him, the Christian desert mothers and fathers, discovered that readiness for encounters with God often comes when we find ourselves at the point of nowhere and having nothing. Vulnerable and alone, we can do no more than trust in God, in God's love, and in God's promise, even when it seems, as it must have seemed to Jacob, that God is on the attack. Perhaps at this point Jacob and those desert mothers and fathers show us what holiness looks like and how it develops—not from a life of easy choices but from a life of persistent wrestling with God. When we wrestle with God, we discover, like Jacob, that we are no longer who we were. Moreover, we seem to have acquired a limp.

Grant me, O God, the tenacity to wrestle with you through the darkness of my life that, when the new day dawns, I may radiate your transforming love and grace. Amen.

When I was in ninth grade, a favorite teacher was helping me with a vocation project—what and who did I want to be when I "grew up"? One of his statements to me, which my fourteen-year-old self shrugged off because it seemed a silly play on my name, was "Don't forget the importance of being earnest." (My first name is Ernest.)

What's in a name? What is the purpose of a name? "Wrestling Jacob" evidences a concern with names: names given, names revealed or withheld, names changed. In biblical times, a name reflected a person's character. "Jacob," the one who seized his brother's heel or, from a more psychological perspective, the one who tended to overreach. Also, knowing a person's name afforded power over that person.

Jacob the "overreacher" wrestled with God, prevailed, received a sought-for blessing, and was given a new name: Israel. But God never reveals the divine name to Jacob. Jacob prevailed in wrestling, yet he had no power over God and could not know the fullness of God's nature. God remains mysterious, unnamed, unknown, and uncontrollable. Unbound by a single name, God remains free to act, free to grant mercy and blessing.

When in baptism we receive the name "Christian," we begin a journey of seeking to understand the nature of this name, of trying to comprehend who we are and who this God is that wrestles with us, challenges us, and blesses us. As we continue that journey we discover, as Charles Wesley noted in his hymn "Wrestling Jacob," a God whose name and nature is Love, yet who remains, at some level, unknowable and uncontrollable. What is in your name? Who are you?

God beyond all names, grant me the power to live up to the name you have given me in Jesus Christ, that in name and nature I may bear witness to your love. Amen.

Where the story of Jacob's wrestling with God challenges us to explore our name and nature, the psalmist invites reflection on the truth or falseness of what we present to others and to God. Such reflection changes the question from "Who are you?" to "What have you done?" Is our cause that we bring before God a just one or a partial truth? Knowing Jacob's story as we do, we know that Jacob could not, in truth, appeal to a just cause in the court imagined by the psalmist. So God's visit in the night tries Jacob's heart, tests his strength, and brings about his transformation.

The psalmist, who unlike Jacob can be certain of his righteousness, reminds us that the truth of our lives cannot be concealed from a God who searches us and knows us, who is acquainted with all our ways (Ps. 139:1, 3). There is always the risk that, if we seek our day in court, the truth about our nature will be on trial as much as that of our accusers. Whatever you feel about making oaths, the challenge, "Do you swear to tell the whole truth and nothing but the truth, so help you God?" is a challenge to truthful disclosure of our nature. Such a challenge may lead us to more strongly assert our self-righteousness. But if we are honest with ourselves, such a challenge will also lead us to self-examination and confession. Then, having come through the night of testing and investigation, we can awaken to a morning of blessing and assurance, a morning that reveals God's love.

Try my heart, O God, and test my ways. Then, in your love, give me a new heart and set me on a straight path for your name's sake. Amen.

THURSDAY, JULY 31 ~ *Read Romans 9:1-5*

The question of God's covenant with Israel lies at the heart of this reading from Romans. As we saw in the reading from Genesis, God bestows on Jacob the name "Israel" as a marker of God's covenant with God's people. But Paul, who sees himself as a Jew "according to the flesh" and a Pharisee "according to the law" (Phil. 3:4-6), has been called to a mission among the Gentiles. This mission forces him to wrestle with the question of Israel's continued place in salvation history and what it means to include non-Jews in God's saving covenant. This question of Israel's place in salvation history has plagued Christianity throughout the centuries, often to the detriment and death of the Jewish people. Somehow we as the church concluded that the only way God could include "us" was if God some how excluded "them" (Israel).

What is it about our tendency to exclude others and our desire to reserve some special benefit for ourselves? Such tendencies, along with our history of human violence, surely must signal our human brokenness. Even in our increasingly diverse world, we are becoming more segregated. What began, perhaps, as a "sibling rivalry" quickly became a kind of tribal warfare, not only between Christian and Jew but among Christians as well.

For Paul, however, there can be no "us" or "them"; there is only God's invitation to listen, to obey, to follow, and to live as God's covenant people. God's justifying grace knows no limits. God in Christ has broken through all human hostilities between family and tribe, gender and race. That truth is worthy of the doxology that concludes this reading: "God [be] blessed forever. Amen."

God of unbounded grace, do not let me contribute to further division in our world. Grant me the courage and conviction to work for the unity of your covenant people. Amen.

Paul's grief and deep love for his "own people" Israel, expressed so clearly in this reading, could make it easy for us to focus our attention on any person or group of people who have rejected or turned away from the good news of Jesus Christ. But to focus our attention there would be to miss Paul's emphasis here and throughout this letter on the covenant faithfulness and steadfast love of God. As Paul reminds us, this is the God who made the people Israel, gave them the covenant and law, ordered their life and worship, and from whom has come God's promised anointed one, Jesus. This God is faithful!

The judgmental streak in me, prompted in part by Paul's listing of God's gifts to Israel, wants to say, "But look at the way they (whoever "they" are) have squandered these gifts!" Yet two things happen as soon as this thought appears. First, I am judged for the ways in which I too have squandered God's gifts to me. Like the writer of Psalm 17, I am called to account for the thoughts of my heart, the words on my lips, and the steps or missteps I have taken.

Second, I am confronted again by a story of love and compassion, by God's continuing good news to the world. These two things together turn my attention in a new direction; they turn me around; they "convert" me, for conversion is the turning around of our lives. As a result of this conversion, the judgmental streak is silenced—at least for a time. In place of judgment, it becomes possible for me to focus my attention rightly on the generosity and love of God, a generosity and love that extends even to those who seem least worthy of such love and grace— even to me.

Convert me, O God, that my life may signal your generosity and love for all people. Amen.

Although this story has no direct connection to the story of Jacob with which we began this week, it does have some similarities. It leads us to a wilderness or deserted place. It takes place in the evening, the threshold between night and day, dark and light. Those who come to this deserted place at evening are vulnerable, sick, and hungry. And, in this place of vulnerability, sickness, and hunger, people encounter God.

There are also some *differences* between the two stories. Here, in contrast to Jacob's story, those who have come to this place do not wrestle with the unnameable God but come face-to-face with Jesus. Here the vulnerable receive healing rather than injury. Here Jesus senses their need, has compassion on them, and feeds them. Even more, he not only feeds them but invites them (in the Greek) "to recline" on the grass. This posture isn't for a picnic but for a banquet—at which all will eat and have their fill.

When we find ourselves trudging along the way of discipleship—and many days it does feel like trudging—we are often led into wilderness places, even when we would not choose such places on our own. Our resistance to those places comes, in part, because we do not expect to find in these places filling and satisfying banquets, much less the healing we so desperately need. Yet, as Psalm 23 suggests, a banquet with cups overflowing is exactly what we should hope to find and what we have come to expect from God, even when we find ourselves in the "valley of the shadow of death" and in the presence of enemies rather than friends.

Compassionate God, when I am at my most vulnerable, help me to trust you to provide what I need. Amen.

The Gospel of Matthew's account of the miracle of the fishes and loaves suggests that this story is about more than a miracle. When the writer tells us that Jesus took the loaves and fish, blessed, broke, and gave them to the disciples and to the crowd, he gives us a clue about how the early church understood what was happening when it gathered to break the bread and share the cup at the Lord's Supper. Just as God provided manna to Israel throughout its forty years wandering in the desert, so too God provides bread in the wilderness for the church.

This understanding figured so prominently in the early church that the story appears in some form in all four Gospels. Even more, when we pay attention to the framework provided by "take, bless, break, and give," we also discover that this story connects with *all* the feeding narratives throughout the Gospels. The loaves and fish provided in this wilderness connect not only to the bread received in the upper room (Matt. 26), but also to the bread of life (John 6), the resurrection meal in Emmaus (Luke 24), and the meal on the lakeshore (John 21).

So it is that Sunday after Sunday the church continues to gather around the Lord's table. Thanksgiving is offered; bread and wine are broken, poured, and shared. There is enough for all, and all who come are fed. While it is no longer a complete meal, it demonstrates the ways in which God now feeds us and satisfies our deepest hungers in this brief wilderness of our lives. And it anticipates the time when we are no longer in the wilderness but are gathered at the heavenly banquet.

Do not send me away hungry, O God, but receive me at your banquet table and fill me with your life-giving bread. Amen.

The Gift of Faith

AUGUST 4–10, 2014 • JONATHAN WILSON-HARTGROVE

SCRIPTURE OVERVIEW: The Genesis text begins the story of Joseph. Things would have turned out very differently for Joseph (and for Israel) had it not been for the watchful care of the One who called Israel into being. Psalm 105 briefly recites the saving events in Israel's life, and this week's portion remembers the story of Joseph, stressing both the hiddenness and the crucial significance of God's mercy. In Romans 10 note the manner in which Paul brings the past to bear on the present in terms of God's saving activity. Notice also Paul's insistence on the universal availability of salvation. The Gospel lesson of Jesus stilling the storm points to the inexplicable wonder of God's redeeming love, which can be appropriated and answered only in doxology.

QUESTIONS AND THOUGHTS FOR REFLECTION

* Read Matthew 14:22-33. What signs of God's power have you witnessed? How do those signs point you toward a specific act of trust in your life today?
* Read Psalm 105:1-6, 16-22, 45*b*. What struggle does this psalm speak to today? How does it give you hope?
* Read Romans 10:5-15. How have you experienced Christ's love? What news do you have to report, and who needs to hear it?
* Read Genesis 37:1-4, 12-28. What conflict do you most identify with right now? Whose dreams do you despise? In what ways are you kin to those enemies?

Director, the School for Conversion (www.newmonasticism.org) in its work to help beloved communities unlearn habits of social division through experiments in the way of Jesus; author of several books, including *The Wisdom of Stability, Common Prayer,* and *The Awakening of Hope;* learn more at www.jonathan-wilsonhartgrove.com

In the mid-nineteenth century, Johann Christoph Blumhardt pastored a small church in a German village. He did his work faithfully. There was nothing exceptional about it—nothing, that is, until a couple in the church told him about problems they were having with their daughter. Pastor Blumhardt met with them to pray and visited with the daughter. As he attempted to figure out what was going on, Pastor Blumhardt realized that he might be dealing with a demon like those he had read about in the New Testament. This was half a century before the Pentecostal movement began at Azusa Street. Germany's historical-critical scholarship was preparing to explain away demons in the modern world. But here in a small German parish, Blumhardt revealed Jesus' power in an exorcism.

As in Jesus' day, the good news of liberation from a demon's power spread quickly. People came to see what new thing was happening—what power had been unleashed by Pastor Blumhardt's ministry. God was indeed doing a new thing, and Pastor Blumhardt wanted to be faithful to it. He began to realize that many people came for the wrong reasons. He began to tell the "thrill seekers" that the exorcism wasn't a healing for its own sake but a sign meant to point people toward God's kingdom.

The miracle of Jesus walking on water follows immediately after the feeding of the five thousand in Matthew's Gospel. Jesus knows what Pastor Blumhardt learned centuries later: We are often more interested in the miraculous signs of God's power than we are in the kingdom movement that they point us toward. Jesus calls the disciples *oligopistoi*—"little-faiths." He is talking to all of us. It's one thing to see the power of God and know it's real; it's something else entirely to trust the Lord who asks for everything, even as the storm rages about you.

Lord Jesus Christ, Son of God, give us faith to trust our whole lives to your kingdom movement. Amen.

John F. Kennedy's biographers have noted that he was groomed by an ambitious family to become someone important. He was America's favored son, even before he survived a boat wreck during his service in World War II—a feat reminiscent of yesterday's story, in which Jesus walked on water. He was elected to the White House as the youngest president in history, and the collective voice of the nation echoed Jacob's blessings of his beloved son Joseph, the favored one.

But election comes with temptations. Those who wear the "long robe with sleeves" (AKA the coat of many colors) can forget that it is a gift—that everything, in fact, is gift. To live in the way of the gift is to learn to walk in humility—to admit limits, to acknowledge contingency, to listen to others. Privilege warrants responsibility. Joseph learned this lesson down in Egypt, where he lived as a slave and a prisoner before he rose to be the savior of his people.

Though he had used the cocksure language of a Cold Warrior in his campaign speeches, JFK learned the fragility of his power during the Cuban Missile Crisis of 1961. Astounded that his military advisors were prepared to unleash a nuclear holocaust, he reached out to his enemy Nikita Kruschev through secret communication. Kruschev responded favorably, and two world leaders who had been humbled by the thought that they might have destroyed the world decided to pursue peace together. On this day in 1963, they signed a test ban treaty—the first public attempt to de-escalate nuclear arms. The decision would cost Kruschev his political career. It may well have cost Kennedy his life. But he was learning what Joseph teaches us—that we are blessed so we might serve, even when it entails great suffering.

Lord, teach us to follow our dreams to your peculiar way of the cross. Amen.

In 2003, as the United States waged its "shock and awe" campaign against Baghdad, I was with a Christian Peacemaker Team delegation to Iraq, praying for an end to the madness of bomb after earthshaking bomb. One morning after a blast, team members walked down the street to talk with neighbors and assess the damage. Some of the team members stood on the sidewalk taking pictures. A police car drove by, stopped, and asked what citizens of the country that was dropping bombs on their city were doing on the street snapping pictures. We were all arrested and driven to a local police station. As team members sat together in that place, all wondering what might happen to us, someone in the group started singing, "Paul and Silas bound in jail / ain't nobody to post their bail." I joined in, glad to sing a song that both named our predicament and reminded us that we were not alone.

Scholars tell us that most of the psalms in scripture were recorded in their present form when Israel was exiled in Babylon. Sitting together in bondage, wondering about their future, they started to sing. The call to extol God's deeds among the nations in our psalm today is a song of hope designed to lift God's people above their present struggle. It invites divine light to shine on our darkness.

The psalmist addresses his people who seem to be suffering from spiritual amnesia. They have forgotten their past and the ways God has upheld them. These opening verses call the people to wonder and praise. When we fall prey to spiritual amnesia, may we sing and recount the mighty works of God on our behalf.

Lord, shine the light of your glory in this present darkness that we might press on in hope. Amen.

The noted community organizer Saul Alinsky used to say that if you want to know a people's power, you need to listen to their songs. Think, for example, of the civil rights movement and its freedom songs. It's hard to imagine the Montgomery bus boycott without hearing "We Shall Overcome." People who had little in the way of economic resources or political power demonstrated the power of nonviolent social action to the whole world. In so many ways, the songs summarized that power.

These songs of ancient Israel summarize the power of God's movement, much like the freedom songs of the civil rights movement. Taken out of context, they can seem like exuberant praise we utter for God to serve our own ends. But in this psalm, we see that the excitement—the unreserved praise of the people—is in response to God's actions in their particular story. The psalm recounts God's decisive actions in Israel's history. God "summoned a famine," "sent a man," and then intervened through the king. Joseph's life is surrounded and directed by the hidden purposes of God. No matter how bad events and experiences might seem, we worship the God who can make a way out of no way.

When we sing this song anew in our own context, it invites us to share the same hope embodied in Israel's Exodus movement and in America's civil rights movement. For those of us who feel the pain of injustice and oppression, this song helps us keep our eyes on the prize and hold on. But for those of us who sit in comfort, this song is an invitation to consider how our prayers unite us with God's suffering people. For if the psalms are the prayer book of Israel, if they are the songs at the heart of the church, then they are songs we are meant to sing with all of God's children, uniting us in the movement that leads to justice and peace for all.

God, give us grace to sing the songs of Zion while in a strange land, always looking to you for our help. Amen.

The Sisters of Charity community in Calcutta relates the following story. When Mother Teresa received the regular shipment of shoes, she would invite all the sisters to come and take a pair, knowing that each of them spent much of the day on her feet. Only after everyone else had selected a pair would Mother take her shoes. They seldom fit. When she prayed in the chapel, she would take off her shoes and kneel barefoot. Those who knelt behind her could see her twisted and calloused feet.

At the close of today's passage, Paul celebrates the beauty of feet that carry the gospel. He emphasizes proclamation—how can anyone hear about Jesus unless they are told? And how can they be told unless someone is sent to proclaim the news? Strikingly, Paul, in this urgent call to evangelism, does not focus on the need for a golden tongue but on the necessity of feet. Preaching the good news relies less on lofty ideas and persuasive speech than on a willingness to go. To go and tell the good news about an event that has changed everything once and for all.

Because Jesus took on flesh and lived among us—because he loved us while we were still his enemies—we know what God's love looks like. We know that we have not been abandoned in our troubles but that God is with us, even now. I appreciate the ancient icons of the Ascension of Jesus in which all eyes are turned up to the heavens and the feet of Jesus form the focal point, hanging down from a cloud. Those feet still bear the scars of the nail that was driven through them when Jesus was hanged on the cross. The feet bear the message: "I've come to stand with you; I've suffered to love you." Indeed, how beautiful are the feet of those who bring the good news.

Guide my feet, Lord, so that they show forth the beauty of your love. Amen.

In small Southern city, toward the end of the 1960s, the federal government sent in facilitators to integrate the public schools. One of them, Bill Riddick, was no fool. He knew that as a government representative he could not impose an integrated system on the people. The transition would require local leadership. The people would have to work it out for themselves.

Seeing the societal division generated by the stereotypes of racial division, Riddick had a flash of insight: Only the extremes could unite the community. So he invited a radical black activist and the local Grand Dragon of the Ku Klux Klan to cochair the committee for integration.

The result was no less than a miracle: Working together through the facts, this poor black woman and poor white man realized that they had quite a bit in common. Their kids weren't getting a quality education. They realized their fighting wasn't helping the people they loved. They became friends and went to work together to improve public education.

The salvation in today's story comes at the moment when Joseph is remembered not as the annoying dreamer but as a brother. Reuben convinces his brothers that they ought not kill their own flesh and blood. The irony of the story is that they end up selling Joseph to their cousins, the Ishmaelites. Their "family values" only extend so far. Still, everything hangs on the moment of recognition. If we can see, even for a moment, that we are all sisters and brothers, then it's possible for even the worst of enemies to become friends.

God, grant us eyes to see our own flesh and blood in the faces of those whom we would call enemies. Amen.

Joseph Bernadin lived a successful religious life. A priest in the Catholic Church, he rose through the ranks to become a Cardinal, overseeing thousands of parishes in the archdiocese of Chicago. He was widely celebrated as a man of great faith. But in his book *The Gift of Peace*, Bernadin chronicled the terrible storms he faced in his final years: a false accusation of sexual abuse by a man who was mentally ill. Then in the midst of the turmoil surrounding this accusation, he learned he was dying of cancer. And yet, Bernadin said these last years of his life taught him to pray. He learned what faith means, almost as if for the first time.

We often consider Peter, who steps into the spotlight in today's Gospel lesson, to be a man of action. He stands boldly to proclaim that Jesus is the Christ. He assures his Lord at the Last Supper that even if everyone else betrays Jesus, he will stand true. He pulls out his sword in the garden of Gethsemane and takes off the ear of the high priest's slave in a single swoop. Like Bernadin, Peter stood at the ready to make a bold move.

But today's passage suggests that stepping out onto the water is not Peter's primary act of faith. The bigger challenge— the place where Jesus invites Peter to expand his faith and trust—comes in his standing in the midst of the storm, watching the waters churn about him when he's going nowhere fast. Responding when God calls is obedience. Continuing to obey when you cannot hear God's voice, standing true when you feel like you're slipping away, is faith. Faith, it seems, is something we learn only through trials.

Lord Jesus, teach us to trust when we cannot see and so come to know your inconceivable power. Amen.

The Unity of God's Family

AUGUST 11–17, 2014 • BO PROSSER

SCRIPTURE OVERVIEW: Genesis 45 portrays Joseph in a moment of triumph. The trials of the past are over, and his trembling brothers are now in his power. Joseph acknowledges God's hand in the events of his life and is reconciled to those who attempted to do him harm. Psalm 133 is a brief but exuberant song to the spirit of unity and fellowship that can exist among the members of the family of God. Paul delivers a resounding "no" to the idea that God has rejected Israel. God's election is irrevocable. The story of Jesus and the Canaanite woman in Matthew 15 illustrates the wide umbrella of God's mercy. The woman's faith and persistence serve in a curious way to minister to Jesus. As she becomes a means of God's grace to Jesus, he extends God's mercy to her.

QUESTIONS AND THOUGHTS FOR REFLECTION

- Read Genesis 45:1-15. Are you more like Joseph, his brothers, his father? Why do you think so? Where do you find unity in God's family with this group?
- Read Psalm 133. What words might you use to describe the blessings of unity that God has bestowed upon you?
- Read Romans 11:1-2a, 29-32. When is a time you have felt forsaken by God? Who are some people of the Bible who have shared this feeling? How has God affirmed God's presence with you?
- Read Matthew 15:10-28. What aspects of your faith need further explication? What rituals do you think define "clean"? What healing are you asking Jesus for?

Coordinator for Missional Congregations, Cooperative Baptist Fellowship, Atlanta, Georgia; Sunday school teacher, Smokerise Baptist Church

The older I get, the more certain I am that unexpected twists and turns fill our lives. Joseph, beloved by his father, is sold into slavery by his jealous siblings. While in slavery, Joseph endears himself to Pharaoh and rises to leadership in Egypt. In today's reading, Joseph reveals himself to the siblings who had sold him into slavery!

Pay close attention to verse 7. Joseph gives glory to God, dwelling on the blessings and not on the hardships. His reconnection with his brothers is a source of joy. He could have been righteously indignant; yet, he simply declares, "God sent . . . me to preserve . . . you!" What a declaration from someone who had justification for retaliation!

Several years ago, one of our church youth ran away from home. Her mother did not support my ministry. However, the night her daughter went missing, she called the police and then she called me. "I'll be right over!" I immediately replied.

I had no desire to be ugly or self-righteous. I would only make a bad situation worse by retaliating. We found the daughter later, and I helped the girl and her mother reconcile. My calling, our calling, comes in preserving the faith of others rather than being selfish or indignant.

Life is too short to allow self-righteousness to rule us. Joseph would have been within his right to lash out at his brothers. My situation could have called forth personal retaliation. Instead, Joseph expressed gratitude for the reunion of his family, and I was thankful for the mother who chose to trust me in a difficult time. That's what family does for one another. We have been sent to preserve one another! Thanks be to God!

God, help me to act justly, to love mercy, and to walk humbly with you. Amen.

Joseph has been estranged from his father and his homeland for many years. Rather than retaliate against his brothers for their wrongful treatment, he showers them with love and hospitality. Then he tells them to go and get their father and all their households and return to Egypt. He promises to care for them all. Then there are embraces and tears, lots of tears.

Can you imagine? Perhaps the brothers, remembering their treatment of Joseph, cry tears of shame. Then come the tears of relief knowing that Joseph does not plan to retaliate. Maybe both parties—the brothers and Joseph—shed tears of sadness for the lost years of relationship. Finally come tears of joy at discovering that Joseph is not only alive but is ready to care for them in a time of danger. And certainly tears from Joseph knowing that God has brought him to such a time as this. Hear his words to his brothers, "I will provide for you." Joseph models faithful obedience. I'm not sure that I could be so generous and high-minded.

Nobody can upset me like my family. They know the buttons to push and the strings to pull. I know families that have come apart because of frustrations and strained relationships. But not Joseph. He chooses to preserve his family and to provide for them.

Someone in your family may be in the midst of famine today. Someone in your family may be feeling enslaved today. Someone in your family may need your forgiveness, your preservation. Follow Joseph's example, and choose obedience.

God, help me to be an obedient child to my immediate family and to you. Help me reach out to hurting family members and bless them in abundance. Amen.

Agreat gospel hymn opens with the line, "What a fellowship, what a joy divine, leaning on the everlasting arms!" Many of us have sung that hymn repeatedly in a variety of congregational worship settings. We sing it with gusto, leaning on one another and leaning on Jesus.

The members of one church in my town have been fighting with one another for years. Their anger runs deep; their relationships are dysfunctional; and their witness is poor. The congregation finds reasons to fuss, to delay decision making, and to block church growth. They have run off a number of ministers. Many of the congregation's members can't remember when the church turned so angry, but they have done nothing to reverse the trend for the better. Theirs is a sad church of sad Christians who are going through the motions of doing church with no real purpose.

On the other side of town is a congregation filled with loving members. Their joy is palpable; their relationships are close-knit; their witness is vibrant. The members of the congregation find reasons to encourage one another, to decide quickly and confidently, and to grow spiritually and numerically. Many in this congregation will tell you that the spirit of joy and unity has been present since the church began. This is a joyous church filled to overflowing with joyous Christians doing exciting and meaningful ministry in their community and around the world.

How can two churches be so different? One has chosen not to preserve one another, not to care for one another. One has chosen to exist for the benefit of all. It seems to me that God blesses a cooperating "family" of believers. The psalmist thought so. "How good and pleasant it is when kindred live together in unity!" And therein we receive God's blessing.

Thank you, God, for the unity of a fellowship of believers who serve and worship you with joy. Amen.

Several years ago while pulling out of my subdivision, I noticed a car parked in a secluded spot in a cul-de-sac. What really got my attention was the silver hose that was taped to the tailpipe of the car and running inside the passenger side window! The car was already filling up with exhaust fumes. I had stumbled upon a suicide attempt. I acted quickly and called the rescue squad, which responded immediately. The driver was pulled from the car and given medical care. Though he had been unconscious, his attempt was not fatal.

The police officer taking my statement affirmed my action and told me that I had disproved the driver's assumption. He said, "The man told us that no one cared for him, that he had no reason to live, that even God had forsaken him!" Then the policeman noted, "I guess now that man knows that *you* care and that God cares!" You just never know!

The Romans raise a similar question: "Has God rejected his people?" Paul answers with a resounding no! Paul traces his lineage as if to say, "I am a Roman and a Jew. For as far back as I can remember, God has been with us. We are together in God."

Perhaps today you may feel lonely or forsaken by family, friends, even God. Seriously consider claiming the presence of God in your life. May you recognize and realize today that you are loved, and we are unified in the love of our heavenly Parent.

Place your hand over your heart; feel life pumping through this vital organ. Focus on God's love for you as your heart beats, as your blood flows. Know that we are unified in God through Christ Jesus our Lord.

If I have heard these words once, I've heard them a million times, "That's not fair!" I have no good reply to that complaint other than to respond, "You're right. Life's not fair; get over it!" (My daughters have heard that response more times than they care to count.) I know that is not a "fair" response.

Several years ago, a young man who was interning with our church came to me requesting a salary increase. He was a good employee, but he was a full-time student and a part-time worker. He actually wanted to be treated to all the benefits of full-time staff. He began his case for a raise with those words, "It's not fair! The full-time people get all the benefits and salary increases." He didn't get a raise and soon found another place of employment.

God's mercy is a mystery; while none of us understands this mercy, it serves as a unifying principle. Saints and sinners, good persons and not-so-good persons, friends and enemies—we all share the disobedience of sin and the unity of God's mercy. How often we forget the first part of these unifying factors.

None of us is entitled to God's election. None of us is exempt from the need for repentance. *All* of us have sinned and fallen short of the glory of God. Yet, God in infinite wisdom and grace has granted forgiveness to each of us. For sure, it's not fair; it is mysterious. For sure, it's not fair; it is merciful. And God includes us all. We are the family of God, united in our disobedience and in God's mercy.

While mysterious, that's *fair*!

Thank you, God, for your mysterious mercy. Thank you for the gift of salvation in Jesus the Christ. Thank you for inviting me into your mysterious and merciful family. Amen.

In the verses prior to this passage, the Pharisees and scribes have come seeking an explanation about the actions of Jesus' disciples. In responding to them, Jesus says, "Listen and understand." Peter then seeks further clarity about Jesus' teachings. Jesus replies, "Do you still not understand?"

It seems to me that we all need to understand Jesus more clearly. Most of us seek understanding in order to live better, to follow Jesus better, to serve God better. Many of us think we know Jesus' teachings, but there is a difference between knowing and understanding.

We may, like the Pharisees and scribes, believe that legalistic rituals make us godly people. We may find ourselves committed to outward conventions without a conversion of the heart. Possibly we arrogantly think that we know what Jesus meant in his teachings but that Jesus directs his teaching to others—surely not to us.

And some of us, like the disciples, have heard Jesus' teachings and still desire a simpler explanation. We have followed Jesus but have doubts about total commitment. We too think that Jesus' teachings are for others—surely not for us.

Yet we all eat in the same way. We all digest in the same way. We all speak out of mouths influenced by hearts. We all have been tempted in some way or another, knowing these temptations are to be avoided—yet tempted just the same.

We, with all others in God's family, need to "listen and understand."

Practice this breath prayer today: "God, help me to listen; God, help me to understand." Pray these words in sync with your breathing. As you inhale, "God, help me to listen. . . . " As you exhale, "God, help me to understand. . . . "

More often than not, we end up petitioning God to intervene in our lives. Several people have suggested that we pray only two prayers: (1) Help me, help me, help me. (2) Thank you, thank you, thank you.

Today's passage builds upon yesterday's focus on ritual cleanliness. With few exceptions, Jesus makes it clear that he has indeed come first to the house of Israel. This woman, a Canaanite, would not have been accepted by the Jews. Jesus' disciples try to run her off and ask Jesus for help. Jesus ignores the woman; yet she persists. She knows that she is not ritually clean in the eyes of the Jews. But she also knows that Jesus is the only hope for her daughter. She confronts Jesus humbly, kneeling at his feet, agreeing with him that she is no more than a dog. She willingly accepts the label if she can get the crumbs from under the table. And so it is that her persistence and willingness to accept second-class status gets first-class results, and the woman helps Jesus expand the boundaries of his ministry. It is she—not the Pharisees with their ritualistic entanglements nor the disciples with their lack of understanding—who receives Jesus' words of commendation: "Woman, great is your faith!"

All of us would do almost anything to bring healing to a loved one. All of us kneel humbly and beg and plead for God's healing power. All of us remain united in our asking. People of all stations in life came to Jesus, hoping against hope, asking for Jesus' help. And the rest of the story? Jesus responded! We all have been blessed beyond our expectations. Thanks be to God!

Make a list of the many things you've asked God for in the past few days. Now, make a list of the blessings you've received in the past few days. Pray the breath prayer, "Help me, help me, help me. . . . Thank you, thank you, thank you."

I Choose You

AUGUST 18–24, 2014 • STEVE GARNAAS-HOLMES

SCRIPTURE OVERVIEW: All the texts bear witness to the rich and powerful sovereignty of God, who generously gives life. In the Exodus text, both the future of Israel and the future of God's plans for all humanity are imperiled. At one level, the infant is saved only by the cunning of his mother and sister and by the compassion of the Egyptian princess; but, truthfully, Moses is saved only by God's grace. Psalm 124 looks beyond the birth of Moses to the moment of the Exodus and celebrates with great joy God's redemption of the people. Only by God's help can humans find life and freedom. In Romans 12 Paul calls for the transformation of the person through the power of God. We are to "be transformed," thus placing primary emphasis on the activity of God in the life of the Christian. The Gospel reading is a confession of Jesus' identity as the Messiah. Matthew emphasizes the rootedness of the church in the disciples' recognition of Jesus' messianic nature.

QUESTIONS AND THOUGHTS FOR REFLECTION

- Read Exodus 1:8–2:10. How do you evidence trust in God's intent for your life?
- Read Psalm 124. When have you experienced God's coming to your rescue and setting you free?
- Read Romans 12:1-8. What practices do you employ to renew your mind? What are your spiritual gifts?
- Read Matthew 16:13-20. Who do you say that Jesus is?

Poet, musician, pastor of St. Matthew's United Methodist Church, Acton, Massachusetts; writes a daily meditation "Unfolding Light" (www.unfoldinglight.net)

MONDAY, AUGUST 18 ~ *Read Psalm 124*

As you prepare for the white-water rafting trip, the guide hands you your life vest. "This is for when you get dumped in the drink," she says and smiles.

God does not promise that life will be smooth, that we will never have to navigate raging waters. God promises that we have been set free. "The snare is broken, and we have escaped." We have been set free not only from all past dangers and difficulties but future ones as well. The snare is broken; it will never work again. It's not because we are especially good or lucky. It's because God chooses to save us. God is "on our side"; not against other people but against all that diminishes life.

Notice the psalmist's intriguing choice of words. He opens with two *if* statements and moves on to three *then*s. The water imagery overwhelms: the flood, the torrent, the raging waters. And then we encounter the trap—escape, snare, snare, escape. On either side of the trap is escape, rescue, freedom.

God does not promise a happy ending every time; but no matter how circumstances end, by God's loving grace we will be free. We may suffer, but it can't entrap us. Bad times will happen. Enemies will attack; people will be angry. We will get dumped. But we will not be swallowed up alive.

Troubling waters will sweep over us, but they can't hold us. Disaster and disappointment may come, but they can't contain us. All the evil that we suffer, even death itself, cannot define us. Only God will hold us forever, tenderly, faithfully.

Trust this hope, even as you hear the rushing of the torrent and especially when you hear the raging of the waters.

O Lord who made heaven and earth, for the many ways you have rescued me and set me free, I give thanks. Help me to trust your grace. Amen.

I Choose You

Archbishop Desmond Tutu is world famous because of his role in various peace and justice movements in South Africa and around the world. Millions of people—including me—know a lot about him. But because I've met him and worked with him a couple of times, I don't just know *about* him; I know *him*. I know the sound of his voice, the energy of his presence, the feel of his spirit. To me he's not simply an international symbol or a historical figure; he's a person.

Peter and the rest of the disciples have spent a lot of time with Jesus. They have witnessed his miraculous healings and listened to his teaching. It may seem odd that Jesus even raises the question with this inmost circle of friends: "Who do you say that I am?"

Sometimes all we see of Jesus is our beliefs about him; we miss the actual person who loved and wondered, who had feelings, and who encountered life with people in real situations. Clearly we can know a lot about Jesus without knowing him.

Who is Jesus to you? What kind of relationship do you have with him? No matter *what* he is to you, *who* is he to you?

Read the Gospels and let him come to you through the veil of time and doctrine, through the barrier of all that you're "supposed" to believe about him. Let him reach out to you in your particular needs and wonderings with his particular loving presence. Give him time and freedom to become more real to you, more present, more alive, and more fully himself: not dictated by theological claims but revealed to you by God. Listen for his voice. Even as he asks, "Who do you say that I am?" he will reveal himself to you.

Jesus, you who know me fully, be with me that I may come to know you more deeply. Amen.

In hindsight, we might feel compelled to tell Jesus, "Jesus, you're making a pretty rash decision by founding your church on the 'rock' of Peter. It's more like building a house on sand if you're counting on impulsive, flighty, unstable Peter. He's moody and often violent. He doesn't understand you; he blurts out crazy things; he's given to extremes; and when you need him most, he will abandon you. Jesus, don't do it!"

And I can imagine Jesus' reply, "I know. Peter was a pretty rough draft, huh? But that changed, didn't it? Once he took on the yoke of the church, he did become a rock. You all couldn't see it then, but I did.

"And I choose you too. You are part of that same church. The amazing thing is that it's comprised entirely of people no better than yourself. I chose you not because you're better than others but because I've put my Spirit in you. I've given you tremendous power—not the power to coerce other people or to control your life (heck, I myself don't even have that power) but the power to bind people, to create community, and the power to loose and set people free.

"You know you're no better than Peter. You don't believe you have special gifts. But you do. You can't see it now, but I do. I have given myself to you in ways you can't see. I am within you. I am alive in you with such strength and courage and compassion that the gates of hell cannot prevail against my love in you and your unity with one another.

"Now get to work. Don't just go around saying great things about me. Let me live in you. Let's see what we can do together."

Jesus, Anointed One of God, live in me, that I may be a faithful part of your presence on earth. Amen.

Advertising tells us, "Be unique! Express your individuality by buying the same pair of pants that thirty million other people wear." And we fall for it. We become conformed to this world to avoid the anxiety of being ourselves. We want people to think well of us and to like us. We want to fit in. We go along and submit to peer pressure, to socialization, to other people's expectations. And we often compromise who we really are in doing so. We distort our souls when we choose to conform ourselves to this world.

So let's not do it. We won't take on a false self because we're afraid to be our true selves. We will choose transformation through the renewing of our minds—not just changing our minds but changing our mindfulness. We allow the rebirth of consciousness. Rather than conforming to other people's expectations, we focus on discerning God's will, on discerning what is good and acceptable and perfect.

Of course we can't always know the will of God. But we can remain open and prayerful, always paying attention. Discernment draws us ever deeper into listening, into silence, into wonder. It draws us toward our true selves, toward the God within, toward a place of true freedom. We free ourselves from others' desires and those of our own. We seek only what delights God.

Let this be our worship: to be free of other people's definitions of us and to be God's continual re-creation. We will not be conformed to this world but transformed by the renewal of our consciousness. Then our lives will embody what is good and acceptable and perfect.

By your mercies, God, I pray only for attentiveness to your will and courage to carry it out. Amen.

After a brain injury, Brian was confined to a wheelchair, with limited use of his hands and extremely slow, slurred speech. It required great effort for him to come to church. His mere presence was a gift to the congregation. He would share during the prayer time, working slowly on a sentence that might take a couple minutes to complete. We in the congregation learned to wait—not impatient waiting, wanting him to hurry up and get it over. We employed a patient waiting, and the listening became prayer itself. Brian taught us that—not intentionally but simply by praying with us. His praying was a gift to us.

Who we are and how, is a gift. We do not have superpowers; our gifts, abilities, and presence, while perfectly ordinary, are of immeasurable value and power. What seems unremarkable to us might be a great gift to someone else. Don't bother to envy other people's gifts; God chooses each of us to bear different gifts. Our particular gifts are just what the world needs.

And so we present our bodies and our gifts. We are to "be transformed." We do not transform ourselves; the transformation itself comes as a gift rather than an achievement. And our gifts exist for the benefit of building up the community.

What are your spiritual gifts? They may be as ordinary as your praying. What are the ways God blesses the community through you? Give thanks for them. Give attention to them. Nurture them. Respect them. Share them.

God uses you for the mending of the world. Give thanks, and give your whole self to God.

God, giver of all good gifts, help me to see my gifts honestly, to treasure them gratefully, and to share them generously with the joy and confidence of Christ. Amen.

The young girl could not have envisioned the great events of the human story that she carried as she stood on the river bank watching her baby brother. She could not know her significance in the Exodus story—nor could her mother or Pharaoh's daughter or the Hebrew midwives or Pharaoh and, least of all, Moses himself. But God uses all these people, each in his or her time and place in that complicated arrangement to achieve God's desire for freedom and redemption.

Rembrandt's monumental painting *The Night Watch* depicts an official portrait of a militia group. But in the midst of the dignified soldiers, there's a little girl in a white dress returning from market with a dead chicken tied around her waist. The subjects of the painting took offense at her presence there. But Rembrandt said, "It's my painting, and I needed a highlight there, so I put her in. If you don't like it, make a better painting."

Few of us are able to see our place in God's "plan," but we trust that God needs us there. This is God's world, and God has brought us to this time and place, with our particular gifts, for God's purposes.

I don't believe that God has everything planned out. I do believe that God has an intent for our lives, purposes beyond our seeing. God will use us to bring justice, healing, and blessing to the world. Trust God's loving intent. Be mindful of God's great purpose. God can use your life as part of the salvation of the world. Give thanks, and give your whole self to God.

Creating God, I am yours. Use me as you choose. I trust your will. Use me in this time and place. And if I should ever find myself in the wrong time and place, use me there too for the sake of your grace. Amen.

The river was exceptionally high with spring runoff. Dangerous spots lay before our group of rafters. As we climbed into the white-water raft, one person suddenly had doubts, saying, "I just can't get my mind around it." "To heck with your mind," the guide said. "Put your body in the boat, and your mind will come along."

Paul knows that we hesitate, we hold back. He urges us to "present [our] bodies as a living sacrifice." Our community and the world need more than religious ideas. They need us to put our bodies on the line. We become a living sacrifice as we commit our comfort, security, and well-being to God's purposes. We give over our whole being: our thoughts, choices, and actions; our time and money; our love and prayers for the singular purpose of serving God's grace in the world.

We have been set free by the transforming of our minds, and we give God both mind and body. Our worship extends beyond the hour on Sunday; our whole life becomes an act of worship, a prayer, a hallelujah. Let God's love flow through our breathing and our heartbeat. Let God's justice break forth in everything we do. Let every word be a word of healing, every act an act of praise. Let every moment be holy. May every person we meet be the person God most desires to bless. God will saturate our being with divine presence, and the realm of God will unfold in our lives.

May we embody the grace God chooses for us and, by God's mercy, may our lives be good and acceptable and perfect.

Gracious God, loving redeemer, receive me, transform me, and use me for the healing of the world. In the name and Spirit of Christ. Amen.

Setting Our Minds

AUGUST 25–31, 2014 • MICHELLE M. HARGRAVE

SCRIPTURE OVERVIEW: In Exodus 3, Moses is drawn to inspect the bush because it is an oddity, but the real miracle he encounters is the presence of the living God. Not even Moses could be prepared for the challenge that ensues. Psalm 105 recites God's great acts of mercy in Israel's life; in this instance, focusing on Moses and Aaron. The key verb here is "sent," and its subject is God. In Romans 12, Paul takes the notion of covenant demand and expounds on it. Christians do not simply keep rules; they are transformed and readied for new life in the world. Paul provides an inventory of new life for those who are changed and renewed by the gospel. The Gospel reading is one of Jesus' most acute reflections on the obedience expected of the faithful. He announces his own destiny of suffering obedience and invites his disciples to share in that radical destiny. For the faithful, there is no "business as usual."

QUESTIONS AND THOUGHTS FOR REFLECTION

- Read Matthew 16:21-28. When does your concern for security or your vision of the future get in the way of Jesus' work?
- Read Exodus 3:1-15. How has God come to you and opened your life to new possibilities?
- Read Romans 12:9-21. Who helps you grow in your ability to practice the qualities of Christian life that Paul describes?
- Read Psalm 105:1-6, 23-26, 45c. Psalm 105 recites the ways God has remained faithful to the people Israel. How has God been faithful to your ancestors? to you?

Lead pastor, Fairmount Avenue United Methodist Church, St. Paul, Minnesota

Y ou are setting your mind not on divine things but on human things." Jesus responds sharply to Peter's insistence that Jesus stop talking about his coming death. Yet Peter's outburst reveals the concerns anyone would have in this situation: we all prefer life over death, safety over danger, the continuation of Jesus' powerful ministry instead of its end. We want to protect the things we value and cherish.

In setting his mind on human things, Peter sees the only possibility he can imagine. His best possible future involves the Jesus he currently knows and understands. Suffering and death lie beyond the scope of his vision, and he cannot hold them in tension with the hope and healing of Jesus' teachings. He cannot see a path that includes both death and Jesus.

In setting his mind on human things, Peter does not listen to what God says through Jesus. He does not hear the hint of resurrection in Jesus' words. In refusing to hear Jesus, Peter also misses a chance to support him—a very human behavior. We foster this attitude when a loved one who is sick asks to talk about dying, and we insist on recovery. We do this when a friend expresses concerns about work performance, and we play the cheerleader instead of replying, "Tell me more about that." Refusing to hear, we refuse to let God move into death, pain, and heartache and work something new.

We cannot easily set aside our perspectives to make space for what God has in mind. Jesus tells us that God sees differently from us, that God's intent comes from a vision larger than ours. God imagines possibilities humans cannot fathom. In Jesus' words God prepares the disciples and cracks open their minds just a bit to ready them for what is coming.

God, help me to see and to hear the possibilities your mind holds for me. Amen.

It is difficult for us to take up our cross and follow Jesus when we set our minds on human things. When we think like humans, we seek not only to protect what we have but to increase it. Our human mind keeps an eye on our place in the world, gauging our status, our stuff, our social circle.

So Jesus' words to Peter are counterintuitive. They make no sense to the human mind. How can we experience life if we deny ourselves? How can we save our life if we lose it? Why would people follow Jesus if it doesn't mean improving their lives and increasing their happiness? We aren't so different from Peter, who probably stands there looking at Jesus, confused.

Yet because of Easter, we know that God's mind, God's way, God's reign takes an innovative initiative that differs from the get-ahead/fall-behind, life-and-death approach we know so well. Because of Easter, we can see the wisdom of Jesus' teaching. The cross, an instrument of suffering and shame, becomes a pathway to resurrection. Following Jesus, setting aside (as much as we can) the human mind of getting and protecting, does not guarantee a peaceful and prosperous life. But following his path leads to a life of meaning and purpose, inexplicably soaked in hope and love.

When Christians give of themselves to others—teenagers building a roof for a widow in poverty, businesspeople working with the homeless to mentor them into the job market, friends taking an evening to pack hundreds of nutritious meals for people they will never meet—they discover joy they could not have imagined beforehand. As we learn to release our lives into the possibilities of God's mind, we experience a richer life than we can imagine on our own.

God, help me to let go of all that keeps me from living fully in you. Amen.

Setting Our Minds

The biblical stories of God's call provide windows into the way persons who think very human thoughts and worry about very human things come to glimpse a piece of God's vision, possibility, and thought.

Moses meets God in the middle of his workday. While moving his father-in-law's flock from one place to the next, minding his own business, he notices a bush burning nearby. God invites Moses into the holy space and introduces the ancestral history of God's connection with Moses' people. Then God gets down to business. After explaining what God has witnessed with regard to the people in Egypt, the Holy One says to Moses, "So come, I will send you to Pharaoh to bring my people, the Israelites, out of Egypt."

Moses cannot embrace this possibility right away. He thinks of himself as a shepherd who cares for someone else's flocks. Or perhaps he thinks of himself as a murderer on the run. Going back to Egypt where he had killed a soldier seems a pretty foolish action now. But here God speaks through a voice in a flame on the mountainside and invites Moses into a new way of thinking about himself and an entirely new future.

Often just a word from someone awakens us to new possibilities. A woman in my childhood church walked up to me by the coatrack one day and told me I should consider being a pastor. That simple comment changed my life (supported, of course, by many other people and experiences over the years.) Yet sometimes we need a shock to disrupt our thought processes. Sometimes we need a jolt, a two-by-four up side the head, to help us see what might be possible. God showed up in voice and flame to open Moses' mind to something completely surprising. How has God come to you and opened your life to new possibilities?

God, open my eyes and my mind to consider my life and my purpose in new ways. Amen.

Meeting God in the burning bush does not satisfy Moses' desire for understanding how he will free the Israelites. Seeing the impossible and chatting with God do not suffice for him to grasp what God sees in him.

So Moses asks two important questions. The first is, "Who am I?" He needs to understand how God views him. He needs a new perspective on himself. God's answer is not what we expect. First God says, "I will be with you"—a strange response to the question, "Who am I?" However, with that reply God assures Moses that he will not be alone. He will not have to accomplish his task by his own strength; God's presence will be enough for him to do what is needed.

The second part of God's answer promises what is to come: "When you have brought this people out of Egypt, you shall worship God on this mountain." God says "when," not "if." God assumes Moses' success and offers Moses a glimpse of his future.

Moses' second question is basically, "Who are you?" God responds, "I AM WHO I AM." Again, God replies to Moses' concerns with a promise of presence now and in the future.

Moses has more questions, and God remains patient. God listens and responds. Each answer reveals a bit more of God's self and God's future. This ongoing revelation allows Moses to move forward. He sets aside his view of things because he has seen a tiny bit of what God sees. He has received a hint from God's mind of divine things. And so he goes to Egypt.

God, hear my questions, be patient with my concerns, and show me a new way forward. Amen.

Glimpsing God's future, like Peter, and answering God's call, like Moses, are not the only expectations of us as Christ-followers. Living fully into God's vision for our lives means growing in two distinct directions: growing in our love of God and growing in our love of all people as shown in the way we treat them. In Romans 12 Paul encourages us in both kinds of love, explaining in careful detail what this means. Depending upon how you sort them, this passage mentions twenty or more specific descriptions of love lived out.

Every week I meet with a small group of women in my congregation, and we talk about our struggles and growth related to service to others and connection to God. My conversation with these women makes me mindful of the need to grow in both directions. I remember that praying is not enough nor is service to others, if I want to follow Jesus.

So every week I gather with these six women to talk, listen, and pray together as we struggle with how to love God more deeply in daily, practical ways. Every week I face the questions of whether my heart has sought God's presence; how I have prayed, studied, worshiped, and recognized God's love in my life. I listen as the others share their experiences and learn new approaches I might try. As the women speak aloud their experiences, I better understand how God is moving in our lives. I am encouraged by their faith and by their expectations that I will continue to grow. During the week I know I am held in their prayers.

It takes practice to learn to see God's perspective. But setting our minds on divine matters is easier with friends.

God, help me find the support I need to live the life you are inviting me into. Amen.

Most of Paul's list concerns relationships with one another. Like his words in 1 Corinthians 12–13, these verses offer directions for living with love in our communities. While many Christians find it rewarding to serve others in Jesus' name by helping at food pantries, building homes, and giving money to good causes, truly loving one another requires effort. Paul notes that saying we "love one another" is not enough. Our words manifest in appropriate action; we are not haughty nor do we claim that we are wiser than we are. When he writes, "Live in harmony with one another," then "live peaceably with all," he must have known we would need to be told more than once.

The church offers an amazing setting to practice these behaviors. We also have the support of others who are trying to live in love as well. Like many congregations, mine has expectations for how to behave when conflict occurs and a plan for addressing it. My community calls its plan the Rule of Christ. It lists biblical principles and practical steps to help us live in harmony with one another.

We practice these behaviors in the church because it only gets harder when we try to follow these commands in the wider world. Paul gives specifics about dealing with enemies—feed them, give them something to drink, meet their felt needs—that we may find challenging. The practice of releasing anger after a raucous church committee meeting prepares us well for that same process on the highway, at the office, or in our families.

It takes work to set aside our ways of thinking and move into God's way. "Setting our minds on divine things" (Matt. 16:23) takes practice, prayer, and perseverance. The support of the faith community is essential.

God, help me live with others the way you desire. Amen.

We join the psalmist in praising God. This psalm reflects the Israelite experience in Egypt. Joseph and his family are welcomed; they become fruitful and strong. Then the Egyptians begin to hate the Israelites. And in response, God sends Aaron and Moses. Their history involves the positive, the negative, the positive. And through it all weaves God's presence and guidance. We too have such experiences. Can we see God at work?

The psalmist recalls stalwarts of the faith and God's intervention in Israel's history. Our experience of God is also anchored in history. Moses' conversations with God, Peter's struggle with Jesus, and Paul's understanding of Jesus' words are more than useful teachings and wise advice. They are part of our ancestral history, our faith history. Like the psalmist, we remember these biblical ancestors when we praise God.

We carry the history of those who have come before us in the church. We remember those who have shaped our denominations, written our hymns, wrestled with our theology, built our churches, taught us in Sunday school, and preached to us over the years. Members of our families, churches, and communities convey God's presence to us. All these people have encouraged our relationship with God, and they become part of our praise.

This week we considered the challenges of viewing circumstances from God's perspective instead of our own. Today, on this day of worship, we rejoice in everything that has supported us in this effort. Today we remember all those who have gone before us and all those who walk with us now who make it possible for us to believe that God is present with us in trouble, that God can bring new life out of death, that following Jesus' path of love is the richest experience we can know. Praise be to God!

God, thank you for all those who came before me who led me to you. Amen.

The Sacred Struggle

SEPTEMBER 1–7, 2014 • DIANE LUTON BLUM

SCRIPTURE OVERVIEW: Exodus 12 provides instructions for keeping the Passover. Yahweh defends those who seek Yahweh's shelter. In the end, the people stand liberated from all false loyalties and allegiances and vow an allegiance to Yahweh alone. Psalm 149 sounds a strong note of realism. The rule of Yahweh binds Israel to an understanding that the social order must reflect the moral integrity of the world's ultimate King. The reading from Romans 13 marks a point of transition within Paul's letter. Paul here urges his readers to trust the fact that faith in Christ makes a difference. Matthew 18 speaks to the importance of trustworthiness in the life of the believing community and provides measures for the restoration of confidence and for reconciliation.

QUESTIONS AND THOUGHTS FOR REFLECTION

- Read Exodus 12:1-14. This text includes detailed "recipes" for reenacting the dramatic struggle of the Israelites to escape from the power of death and slavery. Recall ways that you and your family of faith reenact pivotal stories of God's deliverance.
- Read Psalm 149. How do you respond when you are compelled to "sing a new song"?
- Read Matthew 18:15-20. Recall a past or present relationship in your life that has been broken by sin. How might you practice the process described by the Gospel for restoring community with this brother or sister in Christ's body?
- Read Romans 13:8-14. Paul encourages us to become fully awake to our opportunities for loving action in light of God's future. Where do you struggle with temptations that waste opportunities and put off timely, faithful action?

United Methodist minister and spiritual director, Nashville, Tennessee

The struggle for freedom from bondage is rarely enacted without sacrifice. In early Israelite religion the sacrifice of animals held a routine place in the worshiping community. The sacrifice provided a sacred meal and an act of worship.

The Israelites would not be allowed to leave Egypt without significant sacrifice. The mystery and power of the plagues represent a part of the sacred struggle God will enact to release the Israelites from degrading slavery. While sacrifice may seem unnecessarily violent, it is, in this instance, an action that ends the greater violence of bondage and oppression. True sacrifice always entails the giving up of something valuable in order to realize something of greater and enduring value.

As the sacrifice necessary for the liberation of Israel from Egypt receded into history, the coming generations would be challenged to relive a crucial part of their formation as a community of faith. The blood of lambs that had marked the homes of the Israelites, saving them from the deadly plague, would become central in the celebration of this memory. By slaughtering specially selected lambs from the flock, the Israelite households would recall the sacrifice made with God to bring their freedom. In the annual observance, young and old alike would confront death: death to the animal selected for the Passover meal and, through that death, the recollection of the life and freedom gained by this holy sacrifice.

What sacrifices have we experienced in our journey with God as individuals or as a people of faith? In Jesus we receive courage to seek justice for others and for ourselves, risking comfort and familiarity in the sacrifice for liberating action. Our willingness for loving sacrifice empowers us to be a doorway, not a doormat, in our relationship with God and others.

God of the oppressed, open our hearts and lives to your liberating power, through the sacrificial love we see in Jesus. Amen.

The biblical narrator pauses to recount a recipe for the remembrance of the saving event of the Exodus. A horrific plague that results in death to firstborn children and animals is brought into a carefully prescribed religious observance for generations to come. All in the Israelite community will be expected to relive these sacrifices in order to appreciate and participate in God's salvation.

While the "recipes" for the recall of this liberating moment may seem foreign to our contemporary culture, these verses reflect changes that had already come about in daily life for Israelite families. The urgency of the event in Egypt is brought from memory into the spiritual practice of annual holy days. Each element of the Passover observance takes on theological significance. The keeping of this menu invites families to select the animal for slaughter, grouping households so none is left out and nothing is left over. Choosing the foods for this week of feasting, fasting (from foods with yeast), and worship would carry the story out of the past and into the living faith of the present.

We often look to the high holy days of our Christian calendar, Christmas and Easter, as if the events we celebrate unfolded only long ago. But, like our ancestors of Israel, we are invited to hear the echoes of God's continued saving action on our behalf in the present. The blood of the lamb, Jesus, slain during Passover week, calls each of us to examine all forms of bondage from which we still need deliverance. Where are you and I chained to social and economic systems that prevent our freedom for love in the name of the God of the Exodus? Where are our personal relationships broken or oppressive? Where are we yearning to be freed for loving obedience to God's intention for all to live in wholeness, justice, and peace?

God, may we live the stories of your saving power in our present lives and in the future to which you lead us in love. Amen.

Many of our congregations might greet the psalmist's invitation to sing a new song with resistance! Music and praise, like any vital part of our human celebrations, can easily become a place for struggle as we move from the past into the present and from the present to embrace God's future and unique purpose for our lives.

Israel's praise reflects for us a dynamic invitation to saving relationship with God. Even as this psalm encourages our expressions of love and joy in God's care and guidance for us, it also celebrates God's delight and pleasure in us. When we praise God not only with our words but with our bodies (in dance) and with our instruments (the drum—yes drums! And the lyre), we offer ourselves, wholly and without reserve. This celebration in worship signals our call to honor God at all times with all that we have and all that we are—nothing held back from God's transforming grace and power.

What new song does the psalmist want to emphasize in these verses? Verse 4 provides a strong clue to the psalm's orientation: "God will beautify the poor with saving help" (CEB). This is the God we recognize from the Exodus—the God whose passion for justice lifts up the poor with hope, power, and the promise of liberation. Jews living through the Babylonian exile can sing and dance this song as strangers in a strange land, as captives of an empire. Living hope can be practiced in difficult historical circumstances, including those of our own age. A generation ago in the United States, songs like "We Shall Overcome" became a compelling celebration of God's justice—for the present and the future. Where will you and I embrace the new song God gives in our generation? Notice God at work in this sacred struggle.

Holy One, allow us to glimpse your delight in our acts of praise and thanksgiving. We offer all we are into your care. Amen.

Why on earth is there an expression of anger in the middle of an otherwise lovely psalm of praise? This raging note of prayer suddenly changes the mood from that of the opening verses. Lest we forget, specific and real historical circumstances gave birth to each of the Psalms. The compositions that survive as Israel's sacred texts bear evidence of the struggles of ancient peoples in a chaotic world. Not only would Israel experience a violent sequence of events to gain freedom from Egyptian bondage, but settling in the "promised land" would entail generations of battles. The period of the Israelite monarchies would require struggles within the twelve tribes of Israel and struggle with external enemies.

The faithful ones mentioned in verses 1 and 5 would carry the heart of Israel's praise in their fierce commitment to God's sovereignty, resisting the temptation to bow down to human rulers. The enduring words of Psalm 149 gave expression to God's saving help and liberating power in a variety of historical situations. We need not fear its forceful call for revenge and action—we recognize these kinds of words in our own nation's declarations toward perceived enemies. We see these dynamics in the best-selling electronic games that children play. We also recognize these feelings in our own hearts over oppressive relationships and personal competitors.

How can we join in singing God's new song in the strange land of our changing present and our own unknown future? Can anger fuel faithful expressions of faith? How can anger over injustice link our lives with those who are oppressed and with God who delivers us from all forms of bondage, from generation to generation?

God of passion and compassion, shape our anger to bring your justice and peace to our relationships and our world. Amen.

The Gospel of Matthew provides loving and practical guidance for all the followers of Jesus who would live in community as the body of Christ. One of my beloved teachers ended nearly every class by saying something like, "All this theology is good, but the deep question is, Can we stand each other?" Many of us participate in groups where the opportunity for true relationship development remains limited. We live on the surface and trade on appearances. In groups that form us spiritually in the way and identity of Christ, we receive the invitation to move from pseudocommunity to *real* community. In this process, whether it is the two-person community of a marriage or a dozen people in a Bible study, we begin to experience the challenges of our human differentiation. We misunderstand, we compete, we hurt one another inadvertently. This harder place, where we "sin against" one another is exactly where the living presence of Christ in our midst gives us courage to offer healing honesty for the broken places in our relationships.

Reflect on the value of these opening verses: going directly to the person who has hurt us *before* involving others in a triangle that can escalate the conflict, saves many relationships. So much hurt comes from our limited, finite awareness of the other and from our own self-centered words and actions. A loving brother or sister who speaks the truth of our wrong to us in love becomes an extension of God's reconciling love. If, as the process in these verses suggests, the offending person is unable or unwilling to own his or her missteps, disciples of Jesus are still invited *not* to exclude this person from relationship but to see him or her as a focus for mission. We follow Jesus and put his love into action. There he is in our midst as we gather in this work of love.

Move us, redeeming Lord, to be part of your grace-filled healing in each of our relationships, especially the hardest ones that we lift to you in prayer. Amen.

Paul calls the Romans to love in ways that reflect far more than good feelings or sentimental romance. *Agape*, the word he uses to describe what God intends that we embody, moves us to grow well beyond the survival instincts that we often refer to as "only human." The human being, created in the image of God, is intended for life in the same love we witness in the life and teachings of Jesus.

Given our struggles with human nature, it helps to recall the commandments that spell out what love is *not*: It does not live in our willingness to take life, livelihood, or healthy life circumstances from another. Love does not live by holding another person in our debt. Love does not live in greed that seeks more than we need at others' expense. Love does not live in us when we break the covenants of committed relationship. Love does not live in us when we are consumed by the desire for others' possessions or to acquire more through dishonesty and violence. Love for self and for neighbor requires an awareness of our inner motives and drives. Love vigilantly prevents the thought or desire for what is wrong from becoming harmful action. When we live in love, we first do no harm to ourselves or to others.

One of my family's (often quoted) favorite movie characters makes a long, humorous journey into becoming a person of love. At a crucial moment in his story, just as he has failed again in the pursuit of the woman he loves, he exclaims, "Why, I don't even love myself!" The practice of God's love in the world begins with the regular rediscovery of God's passionate love for each of us. The love I experience for myself in this divine light will be the same growing love available to everyone I encounter. Paul challenges us to grow in this active love, grounded in genuine human struggle.

Help us, God of love, to do the work of love in all that we are and with all whom we meet. Amen.

Paul's missionary zeal reaches beyond the Romans he addressed to our twenty-first-century communities of faith. In an age when addictions threaten health and life for rich and poor alike, Paul warns us to celebrate in ways that do not spiral down into the darkness of wasted opportunities. As followers of Jesus we do not "party" with one another to escape from loving service and faithful living; we gather to live ever more fully in the light of day that dawns when we become part of God's work of love in the world. Where are you and I addicted to behaviors or substances that reduce our engagement with this life and our faith? Where do we tolerate or support the addictions of others when we know their choices lead to death rather than life and love? The journey of recovery and health begins with an awakened heart and an illumined mind.

A congregation I served as pastor was blessed to worship in a century-old sanctuary with lovely stained-glass windows. Morning and afternoon services revealed the exquisite colors and symbols of our faith. But I came to value a special gift this church provided the neighborhood: In the darkness, a spotlight came on from within so that passersby could glimpse the richly illumined figure of the Good Shepherd gazing down on the street and sidewalk below. From time to time a neighbor or a church member would alert me to the failure of the light within (a timer out of sync with the season or a bulb needing replacement). Those of us who gathered on the inside were tempted to forget that the world needed the light that shines from within the community of Christ as much or more than we needed to enjoy the illumined windows from inside. Are we awake to God's light for our world? When does God's light shine from within our communities and our individual lives of faith?

Holy One, light our paths and illumine our human struggles so that we may become vessels of your light and love to all. Amen.

Choosing God—Freeing the Soul

SEPTEMBER 8–14, 2014 • CATHERINE CAVANAGH

SCRIPTURE OVERVIEW: Exodus 14 narrates the Exodus event in stylized liturgical statements. It tells of God's utter commitment to Israel and of Israel's fearful doubt. This is a narrative "toward faith." Exodus 15 recites the joyous song that celebrates God's putting Yahweh's enemies to embarrassing flight. Yahweh's sovereign power to liberate is decisive for the world, as it is for Israel. In Romans 14 Paul struggles with the issue of freedom within obedience and moves us beyond the letter of the law to its spirit. For Paul, the attitude of faith shapes human conduct. The parable of the unforgiving servant in Matthew reminds all would-be disciples that law must be tempered with mercy in their dealings with one another if they expect to receive mercy from God.

QUESTIONS AND THOUGHTS FOR REFLECTION

- Read Exodus 14:19-31. What habits of mind or body hold you enslaved? What steps can you take to choose freedom in answer to God's call?
- Read Exodus 15:1b-11, 20-21. Do you give yourself time to celebrate God's goodness? Are you able to refrain from celebrating the downfall of someone who has hurt you?
- Read Romans 14:1-12. Do you ever catch yourself judging the religious practices of another? How might you overcome this? What good can you learn from religious practices that differ from your own?
- Read Matthew 18:21-35. Who needs your forgiveness? How will choosing to forgive free your own soul?

Works in chaplaincy in an Ontario Catholic high school; member, St. Francis Xavier parish, Brockville, Ontario; find her online at www.soulsider.blogspot.com

The Israelites have chosen to follow Moses, to walk away from bondage. But how helpless they must feel as they stand before the waters of the Red Sea, the angry Egyptian army bearing down on them from behind as the water bars their way forward! Two possible outcomes loom: to drown or to be cut down by the sword.

But then God steps in. In their most helpless moment, in their time of utter desperation, when nothing can save them, God changes everything. A lesson lies hidden here, a truth we so often forget. When we choose God, there is always another way, another perspective. Our human minds are so small, our imagination so limited that we cannot fathom the possibilities that God opens for us. Only when we give over power to God, when we choose the right thing to do—the only right thing to do—to save our people, to escape bondage of whatever sort, to take the path God calls us toward, do we allow God's love to shine most brightly and show us the way.

This does not mean we will avoid suffering—even if the Israelites walk through on dry land. It does not mean we can abdicate personal responsibility for our neighbor nor do we get to live in a world without conflict. The risks may seem great if we give up the greed, the addictions, the anger that hold us in bondage. But if we dare to walk away, if we dare to take the path out of slavery, then God will be there parting the waters and strengthening our hearts. Trust in God means making compassionate and courageous choices and believing a way can be found to truth and love.

Dear God, open our eyes to the bonds that hold us. Give us the courage to take the first step away from the things that enslave us. Help us embrace freedom, and believe that you will show us the way across the seas, the deserts, and the mountains that rise up to challenge us. Amen.

In their escape from Egypt, the Israelites disengage from violence. They choose not to fight their oppressors physically; they resist by refusing to continue as slaves. And when they do, God holds them close and opens impossible paths to freedom and hope.

It would seem that the Israelites recognize the importance of "Thou shalt not kill" long before their arrival at Mount Sinai. In the long and detailed story of their escape from Egypt, not once does scripture record the Israelites engaging in violence. There is one notable exception, of course: Long before he encounters the God of the burning bush, Moses kills an Egyptian overseer in a misguided attempt to help his people. He is shunned and forced to flee, rejected by the Israelites and hunted by the Egyptians.

Moses eventually discovers the way of peace. In his efforts to free his people, he leaves all violence to God. It takes great courage. God sends the plagues to warn the Egyptians, and God closes the waters of the sea so easily parted for the Israelites. Moses chooses God's way and leaves judgment in God's hands.

The celebration that follows is irresistible but at the same time troublesome. Moses and the people do not first celebrate God's compassion for them; they exult over God's power as a warrior. Already, in the first moments of freedom, violence holds them in awe, hinting at a future full of strife.

We see this so often in history: The oppressed often turn into oppressor, forgoing the lessons of their captivity. In the end, only Jesus refuses to answer violence with violence. And we are left with the question, Whose example shall we follow, and what choice shall we make?

God, guide us in wisdom away from the temptation of violence. Help us choose the path of freedom and peace, in the footsteps of Christ. Amen.

During the eight years that I lived in rural Africa, I would often listen at night to the sounds of drums in the distance. Somewhere in the dark night, people who had much less than I in terms of material wealth, education, and security, were celebrating together.

All the major moments of my life have been marked by song and story. Weddings, funerals, graduations—all carry a beat in my memory. Music and celebration transcend every economic bracket and every age. They bind communities and impart the values of each generation.

Stories and songs shape us and move us, reminding us of where we come from and who we are. Collective memory drives scripture. It pushes us to think outside of ourselves to ancient times and otherwise forgotten situations. Immediately after the Hebrew people's escape from Egypt, even as the waters of the Red Sea settle back into place, the people turn to song and story.

Moses, Miriam, and the Israelites sing to us across the ages, reminding us that sometimes we need simply to pause and celebrate the moment. We can appreciate their jubilant song of deliverance and the human relief that compelled them to sing for their God.

Freedom deserves celebration in song, fellowship, and prayer. God calls us, just as God called the Israelites, to look out for those who are enslaved and suffering and to draw them to ourselves in compassion so that they too may join the celebration.

Loving God, open our eyes to your goodness! Be with us in our celebration, and show us who among us needs our solidarity and compassion so they too may be set free to rejoice in you. Amen.

In the summer of 2012, I had the opportunity to participate in a Peace and Justice Pilgrimage to the Holy Land. One warm evening in Bethlehem, as my companions and I sat sipping drinks on a patio in Manger Square, the Muslim call to prayer erupted from the mosque directly beside us, which faced the Church of the Nativity. The singing drew Muslims to the mosque, which, given that it was the holy month of Ramadan, was soon packed to capacity. Undeterred, Muslims filled Manger Square, the men on one side and the women on the other. They spread their mats on the ancient cobblestones and began to pray beneath a sliver of a moon. No worshipers paid us any attention as they bowed and knelt, absorbed by their prayer. My companions and I sat awed at this example of devotion to God, so foreign from our own experience.

Diversity challenges us. We can so easily look at the rituals of another person or another religion and see the contradictions and absurdities. In the wake of 9/11, we heard much of the backlash against Muslims in North America, universally branded as potential terrorists and frequently treated as second-class citizens. While their lot has improved, we still treat those who approach God differently from us with suspicion.

But Paul tells us unequivocally, as does Jesus, that we are not to judge another, even on their religious practices. "Who are you to judge the servant of another?" Paul queries. We don't ask this question of ourselves frequently enough, absorbed as we are by our own preset assumptions, both cultural and religious. Yet we should. In conversation and acceptance, we can grow in our ability to love our neighbor as Jesus instructed us.

Dear God, help me to celebrate difference without judgment or fear. Let me never be a stumbling block to those who reach for you. Amen.

If only we Christians listened to Paul. "Accept [those] whose faith is weak, without passing judgment on disputable matters" (NIV). If we could achieve that alone—the ability not to pass judgment on others—we would be straying into the realm of the miraculous.

Humans appear to be judgmental by nature, and to some extent this is a strength. We need the ability to judge our own actions. We are called to make discerning, informed choices. The trouble starts when we turn that judgmental eye on others. Paul himself seemingly falls prey to this very fault. Immediately after his advice above, he states, "Some believe in eating anything, while the weak eat only vegetables." Paul has just judged another person as weak! But he quickly clarifies. We can't help judging actions as right or wrong, weak or strong, but we can refrain from contempt and from thinking that God loves us better than another.

In fact, our ability to judge our own thoughts is critical to growth in faith. "Let all be fully convinced in their own minds." Conscience, right living, good choices—all these are the cornerstones of lived faith.

But faith does not exist in a vacuum. It operates in the real world, in love of neighbor and acceptance of stranger. Relationships reveal God to us, both in the wisdom others share with us and the lessons we learn from our own actions. Thus Paul tells us that we may judge our own actions but not our neighbor's. For them, we reserve love alone. Each time we gaze on another with love, we learn something of the infinite God.

Dear God, help me to bear up my brothers and sisters and refrain from judging them. Help me to love as you do, with open mind and heart and without restraint or limitation. Amen.

The war for independence in Zimbabwe created many victims and much horror. An already divided people stretched the power of the human heart to heal when independence and majority rule was finally declared on April 18, 1980.

But amidst the lingering hate, one individual after another found the will to forgive, to move forward by recognizing the humanity of those on the other side. One of the more touching stories I heard involved a former "freedom fighter" who had joined the rebels after a night of abuse at a checkpoint. Several years after independence he randomly encountered the soldier who had tortured him. Somehow the two made peace, and dropped the veil that had hidden their shared humanity. Even as Zimbabwe continues to struggle, hope and forgiveness erupt spasmodically, a gift of God.

Love would be easy if we didn't also have to forgive. Jesus tells us forgiving seventy-seven times isn't enough, not even close. We need to treat others, all others, as if they were our children whom we would forgive endlessly and forever. This is the love we reach for, a love so deep in our bones that nothing can stand in the way of forgiveness.

I wish I could offer a solution as to how to achieve this when we find ourselves betrayed again and again, made to suffer at the hands of another, or, worse, made to watch those we love suffer. Jesus makes it clear that it won't be easy, as he utters the words "Forgive them" (Luke 23:34) from the cross. But forgiveness is more about *our* soul than that of the one who deceives us. If we cannot forgive, we are the ones whose souls fester in a prison of pain. We are the ones who suffer. In his parable, Jesus tells us to forgive for our own sake. Only in choosing forgiveness can we be free.

Dear God, open my heart to forgive the one who hurts me. Free me to live with you. Amen.

Jesus weaves his teachings into stories that bring truth alive to his listeners. Parables open the mind and heart in ways that a list of instructions simply cannot duplicate. When Jesus talks about a king forgiving a huge debt as a role model for our forgiveness of others, he is trying to bring alive his profound call to us.

As always, Jesus makes it clear that we are the ones who benefit when we choose to follow his teachings. The one who cannot forgive ends up in a prison for the soul. Those who choose not to forgive are the focus of the teaching—not the one who has not been forgiven. Yet we spend much of our time thinking about the ways we have been hurt rather than the one aspect we can control: our ability to forgive.

Jesus' way of teaching with parables illustrates that life itself can be our teacher. When we hear a story or reflect on a memory, we can make connections to the truths that Jesus imparts. The Bible converses with real life, deepening relationships, guiding choices.

The faith of a hermit may be very little faith in the end. The one who struggles with real life, complex relationships, and difficult situations has so much more to lose but also so much more to gain. Love arises in our interactions even where there is grief and sorrow. And no matter what happens to us, we are always left with the ability to forgive and continue to love. This is Jesus' lesson on the cross and in every story he blessed us with. It is a lesson for eternity.

Dear God, open my mind to your teachings. Help me to choose love and forgiveness even when I face hate and betrayal. Help me to love as you do. Amen.

Walking in Jesus' Footsteps

SEPTEMBER 15–21, 2014 • BOE HARRIS~NAKAKAKENA

SCRIPTURE OVERVIEW: The reading from Exodus 16 concerns Israel's primary memory of food given in the wilderness, given where there are no visible sources of life, given in the face of restless protest, given wondrously—and saving Israel from both hunger and despair. The verses from Psalm 105 recall the marvel of God's grace during the wilderness years and the people's joyful response. In the Philippians text Paul wrestles with the question of God's will with respect to his own leadership. Paul not only explains the meaning of his incarceration but goes beyond that to explain the meaning of his life: "Living is Christ and dying is gain." Matthew 20 reminds the reader that in the kingdom of heaven God's mercy is often surprising, even offensive. People are valued not because of their economic productivity but because God loves and engages them.

QUESTIONS AND THOUGHTS FOR REFLECTION

- Read Exodus 16:2-15. When have you forgotten the power of God to redeem any situation?
- Read Philippians 1:21-30. What footprints of faith are you leaving for others to follow?
- Read Psalm 105:1-6, 37-45. When you "enter the circle" of sacredness, how does your recollection of God's saving work ring out in prayer, song, and praise?
- Read Matthew 20-1-16. Consider secretly giving someone a small token of honor or friendship—a secret between you and God. Your spirit will truly smile.

A Northern Traditional and a Jingle Dress dancer who plays the Native American traditional flute; of Ojibwe and Dakota heritage, she shares her ministry of dance and music at churches, schools, and cultural awareness programs; attends St. John's United Methodist Church in Seaford, Delaware

Let my people go" declares Moses, and Pharaoh does just that. The journey out of bondage to the Promised Land begins. God saves the people from the Egyptian army by parting the Red Sea. Yet not long into their wilderness journey, the Israelites seemingly forget their excitement at leaving Egypt and begin to complain of hunger. Their recollection of food in Egypt is all the more tantalizing in their current setting. They complain to Moses and Aaron, expressing their desire to have died in Egypt with their fill of bread and meat, rather than dying in this land of nothing where starvation will surely take their lives.

Forgetting the work and power of God to redeem, the Israelites give way to hopelessness and despair. Coming from a "cushy" life in Egypt, they have not known this kind of struggle, the struggle for day-to-day subsistence. What will sustain them?

As an American Indian, I often find the word *exodus* calling to mind my own people. I reflect upon a time in our history when we were forced to leave our homelands and travel to lands not known to us. My people moved from a place of promise to a place of bondage. Some tribes were forced at gunpoint to march for thousands of miles with little food or water. Hopelessness and despair could easily have overwhelmed them. What sustained them? Perhaps part of the answer for the Native people came in their strong sense of community and faith.

For the Israelites the answer to sustenance came in God's response to their complaints. For us today who find ourselves hopeless and despairing, what sustains us? Part of the answer comes in the sharing of biblical stories like today's passage. Reading of other persons' struggles and despair reminds us that we are not alone in our difficulties. God will hear and respond.

God, our Sustainer, help us to trust in you always. Amen.

The chosen ones have allowed their circumstances to affect their faith. Their trust in the Lord is wavering. Have they so quickly forgotten their release from bondage and God's saving action on their behalf at the Red Sea? God breathed God's life into this people and God claims them as God's own. God does not abandon them. Have the Israelites abandoned God?

Then Moses tells Aaron to relay the following message to the whole congregation of the Israelites: "Draw near to the LORD, for he has heard your complaining." God sends manna in the mornings and quail in the evenings—making known among the people God's power, presence, and promise. Once again God saves and redeems.

When the Cherokees walked the "Trail of Tears" from their homeland to Oklahoma territory, hunger weakened their bodies. Often their food was rotten. As they walked, they said their prayers and sang their journey songs; they asked, "Has the Creator heard us? How will we survive?"

The Creator had breathed life into the Cherokee and claimed them as God's own. The Creator had not abandoned the people. Had they abandoned the Creator?

From heaven above, the Creator sent manna, bread of life, to the Cherokee people; but this was spiritual manna. The spiritual bread of hope, strength, and trust. Thus their spirits were fed, their faith renewed, and their journey continued.

When we despair, do we lose faith and trust in our Lord? In these times, we need to continue to trust and draw near, never believing that God has abandoned us. We live in a moment-by-moment relationship of faithfulness to the Lord and affirm the knowledge that God will never leave us. Only we can separate ourselves from God.

Creator God, giver of all life, may we stay forever faithful to you. Amen.

WEDNESDAY, SEPTEMBER 17 ~ *Read Philippians 1:21-26*

Jesus walked many miles sharing God's love and grace with all people. Now that Jesus no longer walks the earth, are his footprints deep enough for Paul to follow? It is Paul's time to walk. Every footprint Paul leaves proclaims the gospel of Christ, the glory of God's works. Paul spreads words of encouragement and hope to others. Now with Paul in prison, are his footprints deep enough for others to follow?

In Paul's letter to the Philippians he states that he believes his imprisonment has actually helped share the gospel. His imprisonment results from his dedication, love, and commitment to proclaim the gospel of Christ. Paul felt others seemed to have been empowered by his circumstance and made confident in the Lord, daring to speak the word with greater boldness and without fear.

Paul speaks of his desire to depart this earth and be with Christ. But he also realizes that his physical presence with these young Christians is necessary to their growth and development. All that matters to Paul, despite his lack of certainty about his fate, is that the gospel of Christ continue to be proclaimed.

Paul, as a disciple of Christ, walked the journey of Jesus in his time and place. We, in our time and place, take up the journey. Jesus left footprints deep enough for Paul to follow, and Paul left footprints deep enough for others. Will our footprints be deep enough for future generations to follow?

O God, we thank you for the footprints that your son Jesus has left and for the book that tells the story of his journey. Help us to leave footprints of care, love, and proclamation of Christ in our time. Amen.

Ihave a friend whom I call my Indian sister. She is of the Eastern Cherokee people, and I am of the Chippewa and Dakota people. We share our cultures through song, dance, and stories. Our grandparents' journeys involved great struggle to keep our people's traditions alive. Their existence depended on standing firm in one spirit, striving side by side with faithful connection to the Creator, the giver of all life.

My friend and I feel a deep connection to our ancestors. Their spirits and blood flow within our being. We tell their stories and bring them honor and respect. We continue the journey for our children, grandchildren, and great-grandchildren.

I think of Jesus, a man from a tribe of people. He came from a land of strong cultural traditions of music and dance. He wore his traditional clothing and spoke his native language when saying his prayers or singing his songs. Jesus, a tribal person, closely connected to his ancestors.

Jesus respected the sacred worth of all beings that his Father God had created. He walked with the outcast and the marginalized. He called upon those he gathered to stand firm in one spirit, striving side by side with one mind for the faith and future of the gospel message. Jesus and his early followers are our ancestors of faith; we share a deep connection to them.

Paul stresses the need for unity within the church. He encourages the Philippians' "progress and joy in faith." As followers of Christ we tell the stories—his story, our story—so others might stand firm in their faith, walking side by side and with one mind for the faith of the gospel and to be one in the spirit. What stories are you telling?

Father God, giver of sacred worth, we thank you for the stories of those who walked before us, those who walk with us, and those whose stories have yet to be told. Help us to hear and tell the stories. Amen.

Many social and ceremonial gatherings help Native Americans stay connected to their heritage, culture, and the Creator of all things. One gathering is called a powwow in which people from many tribes dance, celebrate, honor, respect, mourn, feast, sing, and connect.

Many Native American ceremonies and the powwow take place in a circle. The sacred circle is cleansed before anyone's footsteps walk within it. The dancers who enter the sacred circle are also cleansed. The cleansing ceremony involves the burning of special herbs. Someone with a fan in hand will spread the smoke over each person, while praying for this one who will enter the sacred circle. This act is part of Native American spirituality: taking the reality of everyday life and cleansing it away in order to walk into the circle of spirit. In the center of the circle the Creator lives. We come into the circle with equal status; each of us walks our own journey toward the Creator. I am not to judge but to honor the journey of those who walk with me.

Many different dances occur within the circle. I am honored to dance the healing dance or the prayer dance. The cones on my dress represent prayers; as I dance, the prayers ring out their requests to the Creator. I dance the prayers of the people.

As Christians we gather to dance, celebrate, honor, sing, and connect with God. We come together to recount God's wonderful deeds—deeds like those of the Exodus, being brought out of slavery, bread and water in the wilderness, and a land of riches. Like the psalmist, we "enter the circle," remembering God's goodness to us and affirming our obedience. Our prayers ring out; God saves; and we are brought out with joy and singing.

God, may we this day recount your marvelous works and once again affirm our obedience to your statutes and laws, knowing that remembering and obeying you will bring us joy. Amen.

Telling the stories of our ancestors can bring understanding, while carrying the message of hope for peace among the many peoples of our earth. Throughout the human experience many groups have been treated with less than sacred respect.

The history of my Native ancestors lives within my heart, spirit, and soul, for I am the living history of their experiences. My father attended an Indian boarding school from age five on. The boarding school, operated by a church, focused on religious instruction, English education, and vocational instruction. However, the primary focus seemed to be taking the "Indian" out of the child. How can a church that respects the sacred worth of all God's created people strip people of their birth identity and attempt to recreate in them a new identity? This experience that my father and other Native children went through has resulted in generations of trauma and unresolved grief. When I asked my father about his time in boarding school, he would not speak of his experiences, other than to say that he did what he had to do to survive. Someone must tell these stories. In the telling comes the taking of responsibility, repenting, and finding paths to forgiveness.

God offers the Israelites presence and sustenance, making the wilderness a place of care and support. They arrive in a good land. Their salvation story begins generations back with God's promise to Abraham. We worship a God who keeps promises. We tell of the glorious deeds of the Lord, of God's might and wonders. In our wildernesses we recall God's ancient promise; only then can we tell a new story of the healing of the nations and the peace and grace offered in the name of the one who saves and redeems.

Creator God, help us be bearers of truth and doers of justice. Amen.

The four great values of my tribal people are wisdom, courage, respect, and generosity. Being generous means providing for your family members and relatives, as well as needy ones in the community. When an important occasion arises, people honor one another with a "giveaway." The giver distributes much of what he or she has to other people; sometimes the giver releases everything.

At the end of a powwow, the lead dancers have a "giveaway" in the circle, in front of everyone. Items are placed upon a blanket. A spokesperson for the one hosting the "giveaway" speaks from his or her heart and knowledge of this person and his or her relationship with the community. Then the giveaway begins. Gifts are passed out to as many people as the person can give. The elders are honored, for they are the wisdom keepers; the children are honored, for they are the keepers of the future.

How this ritual stands in contrast to today's parable! The workers come and are glad for employment. The landowner goes out early and secures laborers. Then he returns throughout the day, offering the same opportunity to others. We hear the frustration when all receive the same pay at the end of the day.

Jesus is speaking to "insiders," those who labor from early on. What a surprise to us all to learn that God's grace is offered to those early, midday, and late! The tribal people honor one another with a giveaway. God honors us with the gift of grace. The wise and the young, the early and the late—all become recipients of God's giveaway.

We are called to reflect God's love, grace, hope, and generosity. When we have given to the least of these and walk a humble path, we have walked in the footsteps of our Lord.

Dear God, we are thankful for the many ways you give to us. May we become generous givers of those gifts to others. Amen.

Divine Power, Authentic Humility

SEPTEMBER 22–28, 2014 • BRUCE T. MORRILL, S.J.

SCRIPTURE OVERVIEW: The theme of God's mercy surfaces this week. In Exodus 17 Israel is not sure that God is faithful or reliable. By requesting water and voicing an urgent need, Israel appears to be testing God to find out about God's power and inclination. Psalm 78 praises Yahweh for grace in liberating the people from Egyptian bondage. Yahweh's mercy sustained and supported them. Philippians 2 begins with a statement about the need for human kindness and compassion and then moves to the work of mercy that motivates human love—the incarnation of God in Jesus Christ. In the reading from Matthew, the mercy of God, which is extended to those who normally receive no mercy, illustrates not only the inclusive nature of God's grace but also how different the kingdom of heaven is from the kingdoms of this world.

QUESTIONS AND THOUGHTS FOR REFLECTION

- Read Exodus 17:1-7. What circumstances have you experienced that gave rise to questioning God's presence?
- Read Psalm 78:1-4, 12-16. What glorious deeds of the Lord "speak" to you in the present moment?
- Read Philippians 2:1-13. How does Paul's exhortation to abandon "selfish ambition and conceit" come to bear on your life?
- Read Matthew 21:23-32. When have you found yourself changing your mind about where God's power is at work?

Roman Catholic priest and member of the Society of Jesus (the order popularly known as the Jesuits); Edward A. Malloy Professor of Catholic Studies and Professor of Theology at Vanderbilt Divinity School; author, *Encountering Christ in the Eucharist: The Paschal Mystery in People, Word, and Sacrament*

This confrontation occurs not just in the holy city of Jerusalem but at the epicenter of the Jews' relationship with God, the Temple. Matthew has just recounted how in this very place the blind and lame are coming to Jesus for cures (v. 14).

Jesus has brought his mission of teaching and healing—which reveals what God's will is on earth as it is in heaven—from the roads and lanes of the countryside into what, for his people, is the most sacred locale on the planet. Here at the center of the world brews the crisis over whether and how that world belongs to God. To the marginalized—the sick and the children crying out "Hosanna to the Son of David" (v. 15)—discernment of heavenly power at work on earth is clear. Why should the powerful men of the Temple care if that's how those at the bottom of society see things?

When recovered from disease and illness, the people were obliged to procure the Temple services of the priests who would offer the proper sacrifices. Being healed, not just cured of body but also rectified with God and reintegrated into God-fearing society, cost money—money that the afflicted often did not have. Having "overturned the tables of the money changers and the seats of those who sold doves" (v. 12), Jesus' cures proclaim that God's favor, divine grace, is utterly free. And so we find the chief priests and scribes asking Jesus about his authority. Jesus brilliantly responds on their turf and puts their rules into play with his question about John the Baptist's reputation and authority. After all, so much power on earth really is, in the end, about reputation. The powerful men's inability to respond to Jesus' question exposes their blindness and humiliates their claims to divine authority.

Teach us, Lord, to pray, "Thy kingdom come, thy will be done on earth as it is heaven," such that your words resonate in our attitudes and actions. Amen.

Holiness clearly is not a matter of mere words nor the workings of divine grace about instant notoriety, flashy results, worldly fame. Yet, such misperceptions have plagued the church and its members repeatedly. Televangelists gain social stature through powers of rhetoric, physical presence, and telegenic appeal, all channeled into messages of sneering condemnation for their whipped-up Christian public's enemies. Then these self-promoters fall like lightning from the starry firmament of popularity, and the crowd feasts on the exposed details of their secret sexual lives and financial malfeasances.

What do you think? Who has been doing the will of their father ("on earth as it is heaven")? Why are we so easily lured by preaching that gives a quick read of isolated biblical passages that assure us that we are the good sons who labor in the vineyard when joining in society's sadistic derision of whichever sinners are the current object of obsessive scorn?

Jesus warns the religious people, "You did not change your minds." You did not change your minds when you witnessed tax collectors and prostitutes believing the announced salvation. Do these and other such "sinners" become instant paragons of perfection? Surely not, not if we imagine holiness as utter loveliness, providing us a sense of the world's rightness through surface-level evidence of their goodness. Holiness has everything to do with Jesus' refocusing faith away from Temple religion to table fellowship. Jesus' relocation of the reign of God is a scandal to the scribes and Pharisees who ask, "Why does he eat with tax collectors and sinners?" (Mark 2:16). What is our answer? What does the very question itself offer us, his disciples, who earnestly desire to be with him?

Lord, help us to know you here on earth, sitting side-by-side with the tax collectors and prostitutes. Amen.

Is the LORD among us or not?" It's a perfectly fair question. Think of the poor who suffer from lack of drinking water (a distressing image not just from biblical times but also underdeveloped countries today), with death closing in on their children, their elderly, their livestock. Water is a necessity, after all. Thus did God create us!

Is the Lord with us or not? How great are the adversities that can force us to question God's presence and fidelity, the faithfulness of God for which we so truly yearn. When we experience the betrayal of that faith, how bitterly we might lash out. I recall years ago a father, distraught over his unwed twenty-year-old daughter turning up pregnant, noting, "I've had it! I've been saying my prayers daily all my life, never missing church on Sunday, and what did it get me? I've had it with God. I'm done!" There was no shortcut through the pain, but over time he proved faithful to his daughter and grandchild—and to prayer and worship.

More recently I watched the film *Winter's Bone*, the riveting tale of a seventeen-year-old Appalachian girl holding together her poverty-stricken family—a mother immobilized by depression, two much younger siblings—in the wake of their missing father's apparent death at the hands of a methamphetamine circuit. At great personal cost she pursues the bodily remains of her father, without which they have no proof of his death for creditors ready to take possession of their farm. Just as with the Israelites in their trek toward their divinely promised land, so it is for this girl who must quickly become a woman: The land holds them together as a family, a people, a home. Its loss means devastation. Her perseverance through horrific adversity is her profession of faith.

Who in my life, Lord, is struggling with the painful question, "Is the Lord among us or not?" Help me to comfort the afflicted and to afflict the comfortable. Amen.

When the going gets tough, when panic sets in, or we become worn down by diminished resources—material, spiritual, or psychological—we respond by jumping ship, changing course, doubting the trustworthy, and adopting an alternative.

From biblical times forward Christians have employed the language of "discernment of spirits" as a means for grappling with periods of personal impasse, of indecision, of conflicted desires, of lost sense of direction leading to despair. In his *Spiritual Exercises* the sixteenth-century mystic Ignatius of Loyola provides Rules for the Discernment of Spirits to help sort out the changing moods and attendant thoughts that evolve during times of intense contemplation and decision.

Ignatius distinguishes between experiences of consolation and desolation in prayer. We know consolation when we find ourselves inflamed with love for God through the created things with which and whom we carry on our lives. Our hearts overflow with gratitude through them for God alone. We experience a profound rightness about our feelings, words, and actions.

Desolation, in contrast, is just the opposite—fueled by not only heartbreaking circumstances but also, often, path-changing temptations that lead us from the consolations of faith, hope, and love. Ignatius counsels that in times of desolation we should resist letting our practiced habits of faith slip away and, worse yet, attempt decisions about a course of action. Rather, we should persevere in those practices—spiritual and bodily—that have nourished consolation in the past while claiming anew the conviction about our life-with-God-and-others known in consolation. God "answers" but not by human-estimated "results"; rather, by faithfulness through time.

> *"Make me to know your ways, O LORD; teach me your paths. Lead me in your truth, and teach me, for you are the God of my salvation; for you I wait all day long" (Ps. 25:4-5).*

If asked why we pray continuously with the Bible, Christians may answer in terms of nurturing and sustaining relationship with the living God. The only assurance we have that our claims to discerning the presence and action—the power—of God are not our own idolatrous projections of omnipotence rests in our constant turn to the sacred scriptures. When hearing, especially in the worshiping assembly, biblical accounts of God's deeds among people, we encounter not the static object of our psychosocially shaped power plays but, rather, the living God. We only know who that God is by recounting what that God has done.

The Book of Psalms comprises an important part of the treasury of biblical faith that Christianity receives from Judaism. When we pray the psalms, a key part of the rabbinic Judaism that Jesus practiced in synagogue, we join him in an encounter with the God whose eternal mercy and justice recur in moments of human history, making them revelations of the One whom "no one has ever seen" (John 1:18*a*). When we recount the mighty deeds of the Lord, we invite God to share that memory with us. Indeed, it is God who prompts our remembering and, across the whole arc of biblical books in their various genres, draws us into the reality of who God is for us by transmitting the qualities—the character—of that divine wisdom we deeply desire yet so often miss.

Christians join in word and sacrament so as to know him who has made God known. Jesus, "God the only Son, who is close to the Father's heart" (John 1:18*b*), gives us a portion of his life in God, the heart of which is freedom for the oppressed, mercy for sinners, justice for the poor. When we put those liturgically shared words into action we experience consolation in life as worship of the one true God.

Incline our ears, Lord, to know you in recounting together your glorious deeds. Amen.

The God of biblical faith empowers genuine humility, that is, honest recognition of who we are in relationship to God. This is not the groveling humility that bullies, batterers, and regimes demand of the human bodies and spirits they crushingly oppress. No, the humility to which the letter to the Philippians calls us draws upon the human vocation bespoken by every book of the Old Testament and, as Paul presents it, fully realized now in the crucified and risen Jesus. That humility is realized, however, only insofar as the members of Christ's body, the church, take on the mind of the One in whom the Spirit sealed them in baptism. Humility rests for us in Christ.

To "confess that Jesus Christ is Lord" is to assert the divinity of the man God raised up as messiah ("Lord" being a Jewish title for God). What is this God like? This is the One who called the wandering Aramean Abraham, along with his wife Sarah and entire household, into a covenant that set the course for humanity's dignity. And therein lies the key to genuine biblical humility: the recognition of who we are in God's presence. To be humble means that we ask continually: How does God see me or us or them in these circumstances? How do I see myself, my neighbor or spouse or child, in the light of God's word?

The baptized ask continuously to see with the eyes of faith, to look on others as Christ looks on us: with love. (See Mark 10:21.) In so doing, we share in the life of the One who has loved humanity to death. Thus did Jesus fulfill "the law and the prophets," the good life we can know by joining humbly and with full dignity in his divine mission for human justice and peace.

"Where can I go from your spirit? Or where can I flee from your presence?" (Ps. 139:7).

"Glory to God!" A common Christian utterance; yet, when we stop to reflect upon it, doesn't its meaning largely evade us? To the extent we consider how totally other than us creatures God surely is, the notion of glory may remove God to an even greater distance. Perhaps biblical reading can even reinforce the trend when, for example, we hear the climax of Luke's Christmas account of the shepherds on night watch in the fields:

> Suddenly there was with the angel a multitude of the heavenly host, praising God and saying, 'Glory to God in the highest heaven, and on earth peace among those whom he favors' (Luke 2:13-14).

After centuries of charming crèche scenes and children's pageants we can hardly hear how scandalous Luke's story would have sounded in his contemporaries' ears. Shepherds! Of all people, shepherds first receive the heavenly announcement of earthly salvation? Shepherds were at the bottom of the social ladder, despised and distrusted as shiftless, wandering ruffians; transients viewed as thieving and detestable as gypsies in today's Europe. (What parallels might we draw in our own land?)

This turn to a Christmas story is no digression from our praying with Paul's Philippians hymn, celebrating God's glory in raising the humble Jesus from death, death on a cross. God's glory resides in humanity's acknowledging God for who God is. Jesus' intimate relationship with the Father reveals God's glory in the one human who carried out God's message and mission of boundless mercy to the full. If we wish to know God, we must take on the same mind as Christ Jesus, seeking God's loving will where people most readily judge God could not possibly be. To be humble, to seek and promote human flourishing where it is being defeated to the point of death, is to glorify God in Christ.

Rest in Jesus' prayer: "All mine are yours, and yours are mine; and I have been glorified in them" (John 17:10).

Signs and Blessings from God

SEPTEMBER 29–OCTOBER 5, 2014 • BRUCE BLUMER

SCRIPTURE OVERVIEW: The Decalogue in Exodus 20 need not be considered a litmus test of righteousness or religious purity but rather a declaration that lies near the heart of the covenant relationship between Yahweh and Israel. The Torah is the way the people say yes to God's saving initiatives. Psalm 19:1-6 links the gift of the Torah to other acts of divine creation. The balance of the psalm celebrates the strength and beauty of the Torah and moves the reader behind the Torah to its Giver, thereby proclaiming the gospel of the well-ordered life. In Philippians 3 Paul speaks of himself as leaning into the future in response to the manner in which Jesus Christ has invaded his own life. The parable in Matthew 21 presents a direct and bold affirmation for living in accordance with the gospel, producing "fruits of the kingdom."

QUESTIONS AND THOUGHTS FOR REFLECTION

- Read Exodus 20:1-4, 7-9, 12-20. What "signs" does God post for your protection and instruction?
- Read Psalm 19. How comfortable are you with silence? What parts of your day lend themselves to communing with God in silence?
- Read Matthew 21:33-46. What fruit of God's kingdom do you bear?
- Read Philippians 3:4b-14. What specific steps can you take day by day to press on toward the goal ?

Executive Director of the Dakotas United Methodist Foundation; committed to mission work on the island of LaGonave, Haiti; funding that work with sale of his book *I Saw God Today*; Mitchell, South Dakota

Have you ever noticed how many signs exist in this world? There are so many different signs in so many places: Hospital this way. No parking. Don't Pass. Curve to the left or right or squiggly. Airport ahead. Watch out for trucks or animals that might be crossing the road.

Signs exist for a reason. They are helpful, instructive. They may be a bit directive at times, but they are there to protect us, to warn us, and to make our life easier.

Maybe we could consider the Ten Commandments as road signs placed in the Bible for a reason. While they can be directive, they instruct, protect, and warn to assist in our journey.

Stop—and remember you have only one God, no idols needed. Wrong Way—when you use the Lord's name in vain. Slow down—and take your sabbath. Caution—your parents deserve honor. Road Closed—to killing, adultery, stealing, bearing false witness, or coveting.

"Moses said to the people, 'Do not be afraid; for God has come only to test you and to put the fear of him upon you so that you do not sin.'" Moses asks us to pay attention to the road signs. God has laid out the obvious hazards of sin for us, if only we heed the signs. We become living and holy sacrifices when we demonstrate God's good, pleasing, and perfect intent for us. That signals God's will fulfilled through us.

What indicates that God is working on us? How is the Lord pointing us in the right direction: the sometimes squiggly path toward being who God intends us to be? We just have to follow the road signs.

O God, the signs are clear. Lead us in the path away from sin. Amen.

Recently I spent several days at a monastery for a personal retreat. It is the monks' custom to speak little, even during meals. My time there helped me focus on words *and* silence and the other ways that God speaks.

The first part of Psalm 19 tells us that creation itself pours forth praise for God. The heavens pour "forth speech" and declare "knowledge" of the Creator. The speaking and declaring comes without sound. When has God's creation spoken to you? What message comes through a beautiful sunrise? What do you hear in the whisper of a bird's song? What tune does the wind in the trees play for you? What does the changing moon say? What do crashing ocean waves tell us?

We tend to fill the silence and stillness and wonder of God's creation with words and noise. Think about an argument that you may have had with someone or perhaps a political debate you've watched. What was the purpose of those words—to change someone's mind or straighten him or her out a bit? Someone once said that we "devour" others with our words. Our goal is to consume others and, in the end, attitudes don't change and people are angered or feel condemned. When we fill our lives with words, we also miss God's communication.

Spend some time today without words, contemplating God's creation. Sense the warmth of the sunshine on your head and feel the Creator. Experience the wind blowing on your face and feel the Creator. See God's brush in the clouds and feel the Creator. Examine a unique-looking rock and feel the Creator. The messages are there; they remain unspoken. Know you are God's own design and feel the Creator.

Help us to be still, O God, and speak to us through your creation. Remind us that we are stewards but for a time, and we are to care for all you have created on this earth. Amen.

WEDNESDAY, OCTOBER 1 ~ *Read Psalm 19:7-14*

The second part of Psalm 19 moves from the celebration of God's creation to the celebration of the word of God. Verses 7-9 note the law of God / the six evaluations of the law / the six results of the law:

1. Law / perfect / reviving the soul
2. Decrees / sure / making wise the simple
3. Precepts / right / rejoicing the heart
4. Commandment / clear / enlightening the eyes
5. Fear / pure / enduring forever
6. Ordinances / true and righteous / altogether

Regardless of the Bible version you are reading, write the words out so the law, evaluations, and results align in the format above. Read through the chart a few times, and make the connections. At first it may seem as if some of the words don't belong together. But as you read them again, see how God's words are not condemnation but a celebration that is as desirable as gold or as sweet as honey. We become aware of the celebration of God's word and the reward for keeping true to *the* Word.

Then knowing we all fall short, knowing we all have faults and sins, and knowing we need to be aware of God in our lives, the psalmist offers this simple, yet elegant, prayer:

Let the words of my mouth and the meditation of my heart
   be acceptable to you,
O LORD, my rock and my redeemer.

We are aware of your perfect word and our need to have you in our lives, O Lord. Hear us when we pray, forgive us when we fail. You are our strength. You are our redeemer. Amen.

Within two weeks my wife and I experienced two fun events. We attended the stage production of *The Lion King*, and our first grandchild was born. If you've seen the movie or play, you may know where I'm going with this. The theme song of the play is titled "The Circle of Life." At the beginning of the play, a new baby lion is presented to the gathered animals. As the son of the king, the lion cub is the future king; the animals bow and cry out in celebration. Shortly after we viewed the play, our first grandchild was born. All four grandparents and three of the four great-grandparents have been able to hold her, and it causes me to reflect on the circle of life.

So how does this relate to today's scripture? The vineyard illustrates God's kingdom and the landowner represents God. The tenants (we sinners) at harvesttime first injure and then kill the landowner's slaves. The landowner sends more slaves who are likewise harmed. Finally God sends the Son whom the tenants cast out and kill.

God expects us, like the vineyard, to produce fruits of praise and glory. God expects us to share our blessings with others: to feed a hungry world, mend a broken relationship, forgive ourselves and others. We sin; we do not pray. We neglect others and think only of ourselves when the needs of humanity are so vast.

Again and again, we try God's patience. Again and again, God sends love and grace, and we reject it. So God sends more. God's love is unparalleled and unending. It's a circle of love, patience, and grace. When our lives of prayer and praise cease, there will be others to take up the chant. The circle of life is a blessing. The circle of God's grace is the circle of our lives.

Creator God, we bow and celebrate your great love for us. We praise you, God of abundance, for your continual circle of love and grace. Amen.

Many people who wear glasses consider it a minor detail. I hate wearing glasses. I used to have what my eye doctor referred to as "pilot's eyes," because my distance vision was so good. But change took place. As I aged, my once good eyes have become older eyes, and I've "graduated" to bifocals. Nothing seems as clear as it once did. And so it is for me as I consider verse 42 where Jesus says, "Have you never read in the scriptures: 'The stone that the builders rejected has become the chief cornerstone; this was the Lord's doing, and it is amazing in our eyes?'"

This passage addresses Jesus' listeners whose leaders are not receptive to Jesus, the Messiah. The parable of the tenants is clearly a veiled allusion to Jesus' being put to death. Jesus tells the story so that the listeners actually condemn themselves: "Put those wretches to a miserable death, and lease the vineyard to other tenants." One commentary I read interpreted verse 42 allegorically: the stone represents Christ; the builders are the church (in other words, us); and the chief cornerstone is God's building something new through Jesus. The Jews, having been offered the kingdom and refused, now forfeit it to the new community of God's making. If we don't produce fruits, God will take the kingdom from us and give it to those who will. Those who reject Christ will fall and be crushed.

Most of us enjoy the freedom to worship without persecution. Most of us enjoy access to the scriptures without worry. Many of us have resources like this daily devotional or the internet to read and digest God's word.

God warns us that these freedoms may be stripped from us when we are no longer fruitful. God wants us to build something new through Jesus the Christ. We multiply our gifts into opportunities to serve and glorify. And it is amazing in our eyes.

Reveal to us the blessings you have given to us in the kingdom,
O God. May we use them to do good works for you. Amen.

Ihad the privilege of hearing Ray Buckley tell stories. He has you laughing one minute and crying the next. He talks a great deal about the values his family of the Lakota and Klinket tribes have taught him. He challenges his listeners to consider their own stories.

Paul begins this reading with *his* family story. His circumcision shows the Jewish heritage; he then moves to his membership with the tribal and ancient people of God, a Hebrew of Hebrews, in regard of the law, blameless—his credentials are impeccable. But Paul continues on to say that knowing Christ surpasses all these qualifications. In gaining Christ, his remarkable family pedigree is rubbish.

Think about the past. What are our family stories? What stories will be told about us when we are gone? The histories of our parents and grandparents, our family and our life experiences have positively and negatively influenced that story. Some people tell stories of support and lifting up. Other people's stories hold tragedy and hurt. Regardless, our story has been molded and influenced by our heritage.

But Paul releases his and our history, casts it aside, and tells us that we have a new life with faith in Christ. When we know the power of the Resurrection, we understand the power that comes in our new relationship. But it's a process. We share our sufferings. We try to be obedient. We celebrate God's revelation of the light to us. Whatever has shaped us in the past, we know that Christ is available to shape our future.

Gracious God, let our story continue to be written in relationship with you. Help us to be positive models in shaping other people's stories. Amen.

I stood there and looked at the 6,730 pounds of rock that were sitting in the street beside my house and tried to decide if 3.365 tons sounded more than or less than 6,730 pounds. The landscape delivery personnel couldn't dump the rock in my yard because of the trees, so they dumped 3.365 tons (I decided that sounded like less) of rock on the street in front of my house.

The pile of rock couldn't stay in the street all weekend, and the pile wasn't getting any smaller by my contemplating if 6,730 pounds or 3.365 tons sounded better. I made a ramp, got a wheelbarrow and a shovel, and started hauling rock.

It took a lot of shoveling before I even made a dent in the pile. My back, legs, and arms were tired. I was discouraged and wanted to give up. I felt like leaving the pile of rocks with a sign, "Welcome to my new mountain." My family helped some, but basically I just kept taking shovel after shovel, filling the wheelbarrow, pushing it up the ramp, and dumping rock around the house—over and over and over.

Paul states that he has not attained or perfected his relationship with Christ. Since Paul's conversion experience, his life has become more complicated—not less. Life in Christ does not give answers to life's problems; it raises more questions and sends us searching for new answers. Forgetting those things that lie behind and reaching forward to those things that lie ahead, we press toward the goal for the prize of the upward call of God in Jesus Christ. Paul's progress comes through God's grace with the ultimate goal of knowing God forever. He has not reached the goal but is pursuing it, pressing toward the prize of eternal life. With vigor, Paul moved toward Christ day by day—over and over and over.

Help us to know you, Christ. Let us press onward, day by day, seeking the prize of an eternal relationship with you. Amen.

Expectations

OCTOBER 6-12, 2014 • RAQUEL MULL

SCRIPTURE OVERVIEW: The narrative in Exodus 32:1-14 reflects on the blindness of the people, but the focus is also placed on Yahweh's intense anger and on Moses' intervention. Yahweh's mercy prevails, and Moses is revealed as the quintessential mediator. Psalm 106 recalls the folly of the people in making the golden calf. The sinfulness of the Israelites is laid to their forgetfulness. The inability or unwillingness of the people of God to remember is a damning sin, and Israel rightly should be destroyed. The Philippians text stresses the need for faithfulness to the gospel. Matthew's version of the parable of the wedding banquet offers a negative example of faithfulness in the form of a guest who comes to the wedding without the proper attire.

QUESTIONS AND THOUGHTS FOR REFLECTION

• Read Exodus 32:1-14. We understand God's wrath against the Israelites; do you trust something in your culture more than you trust God?

• Read Psalm 106:1-6, 19-23. We go through our everyday life without noticing the shadows and the mystery of breath. When have you forgotten what God has done for you?

• Read Philippians 4:1-9. Sometimes we think we have to celebrate big, important events in order to rejoice. Speak aloud about the event that made you smile inside and rejoice.

• Read Matthew 22:1-14. The people's refusal to accept the king's invitation enrages the king. How do you handle rejection?

Born for Tobacco People and born to Salt Clan of the Diné Nation (Navajo); director of Four Corners Native American Ministry, Shiprock, New Mexico

What a wonderful way to begin a new week, with praise to the Creator! I am Navajo and live on the reservation in Shiprock, New Mexico. From my bedroom window and the window of my sewing studio, I can see the huge volcanic remnant rising from the desert floor with its grandeur and stark massiveness. In the morning, the rising sunlight reveals crevices and fault lines. Praise comes easily when viewing nature's splendor and beauty. I find it more difficult to praise if the kids don't have their backpacks ready for school or have nothing to pack for lunches or we're running late and the gas tank is registering empty.

In my culture, the traditional believers rise to meet the morning sun as it lightens the eastern sky and to offer thanks for a new day. We customarily give thanks for our family, what we have, and where we are. The sun serves to remind us of when to stop and pray: daybreak, noon, sunset, and night.

Monday is a new beginning for the week after several days of refreshment and relaxation for many of us. What is your attitude as you begin this week? Is it one of hopeful expectation as you prepare to see what God is doing around you?

The psalmist offers some reminders of how we can begin our new week, as well as the rewards of deliberate living. "Who can utter the mighty doings of the Lord, or declare all his praise?" Finding time to praise God is a challenge in the face of our busy schedules, especially if we think we are pulling more than our share on the job or in a relationship.

Perhaps we can learn from the elders—let the sun remind us to stop and utter praise to the One who created us and this universe.

Creator of the universe, help us to stop for a few seconds every day to praise you for your steadfast love and your goodness. Amen.

Have you ever found yourself caught up in a situation and, after all is said and done, asked yourself, "How on earth did that happen?" I think this is Aaron's experience. Moses has been gone longer than expected, and the people are getting worried—not about Moses but about how they will survive. So they present their solution to Aaron, "Make gods for us."

Aaron, in his defense, wants to appease this crowd. He is one man against a mass of scared people. They followed Moses expecting to be led into a land of milk and honey; all they have is the word of one man who seemingly has deserted them.

Aaron casts the image of a calf for the people. Then, encouraged by a positive response, he gets completely carried away. He builds an altar and assumes the authority of Yahweh and then proclaims a festival that the people gladly embrace.

A young woman I know was left at home while her parents went to a doctor's appointment in another city. Being normal seniors in high school, her friends said, "Your parents are out of town. You have the house to yourself; let's have a party." The woman agreed, and the party quickly got out of hand. Friends invited friends who invited friends who brought alcohol. The young woman got scared and didn't know what to do. A neighbor came to her rescue and kicked everyone out, but my young friend still had to deal with the consequences of joining in with the crowd.

When people engage in gossip at the office, do you listen, jump in, or walk away? A family member has just died—an estate must be probated and people are choosing sides. Do you join the majority or do what is right? Sometimes, we, like Aaron, can get caught up in the mob mentality without ever meaning to do harm. How do you wait patiently for God to act?

Lord, give us the patience to wait for your word and the wisdom to know your will. Amen.

So, who brought the Israelites out of Egypt? In this passage, if you listen to God, Moses did. If you read Moses' plea in verse 11, God brought them out "with great power and with a mighty hand." This question becomes one related to who takes responsibility for these people. God or Moses?

Of course, the answer is both—both God and Moses take responsibility for this perverse and stiff-necked people. Notice that Moses does not disagree with the Lord's assessment of the people's character; but he reminds God who they are: the descendants of Abraham, Isaac, and Israel. Moses doesn't defend them because they are really good people and deserve a break. No, he defends them because they are the descendants of men and women with whom God has a special relationship and to whom God has made promises—promises related to these very same people. If God were to consume them, God could not keep the promises made to those who had believed in them for so long.

God agrees to make Moses' family a great nation. But Moses realizes that if God forgets the promises to Abraham, Isaac, and Israel, the possibility of God's forgetting *this* promise is probable. Moses determines that the best way forward comes in helping God fulfill the promises already made. Selflessly, faithfully, he helps God keep God's word. Moses forfeits personal gain and gratification to uphold promises he has made, to lead the Israelites to the Promised Land.

How do you see God's promises being fulfilled in your life? What does that fulfillment generate in your life? How are you, like Moses, upholding your word to those who trust you?

Lord, may our "yes" mean yes and our "no" mean no. Amen.

Navajos have a philosophy of life they call *hozho*, or peace and harmony. In the traditional religion of the Navajo, Native Americans maintain this harmony through careful living and restore it through the chants and rituals conducted by a medicine man. It is not uncommon for a family to go into debt to pay for a ceremony to restore *hozho*, which is crucial to our mind-set and culture.

Paul writes, "The peace of God . . . will guard your hearts and your minds in Christ Jesus." I had never thought of the peace of God as capable of guarding my heart and mind—and guarding them against what?

Paul reiterates three warnings in behavior that promote faith, which fosters peace: He advises the Philippians to stand firm in the Lord, to remain united, and to imitate his example among them. Paul then goes on to note three themes that support faithful living. The first is this: "Do not worry about anything." We remain confident in God's ability to provide. And perhaps the Philippians have only a short while to practice, for "the Lord is near." In Paul's estimation, Jesus' return in glory will be soon. Finally, "Rejoice in the Lord always." Joy comes through acknowledging the work of God through Jesus Christ.

Through correct living, my heart and mind are in balance with the universe. Peace can guard my thoughts as well as the behaviors I choose. Paul tells us the same thing: Think only on the things that are good, pure, honorable, and worthy of praise. *Hozho* may be the Navajo religion, but it has much in common with Paul's approach. Both encourage us to know the peace and harmony that comes only from the Creator, and we focus our thoughts and energy on what is good.

Lord, help us recognize those things that move us away from your peace, which guards our thoughts. Amen.

Traditional Navajo culture has many taboos and sayings that reinforce beliefs or practices. We are not to say our names aloud too often or our ears will turn inside out. If a man sees his mother-in-law coming down the street, he crosses to the other side so he doesn't look her in the eyes. The first saying emphasizes the desire to be less self-focused. The second is in deference to the mother-in-law's role as the matriarch. These practices, if followed, promote peace and harmony, *hozho*. If not followed, judgment and rejection.

The dominant culture may or may not understand the importance of these practices or their continued influence on Native culture. In reading Matthew, we can understand the revenge of the king against those who killed his messengers. But we probably can't grasp the unnecessary violence done to the ill-clad guest who not only got kicked out of the party but was bound hand and foot and cast out into the outer darkness.

What is so special about the wedding robe? The wedding robe implies that the guest accepts the responsibilities associated with witnessing the marriage. The liturgy of the wedding service in the United Methodist hymnal asks those in attendance this question: "Will all of you, by God's grace, do everything in your power to uphold and care for these two persons in their marriage?" (no. 864) The proper response is, "We will." The couple is making promises to each other, to God, and to the witnesses. The ejected guest, by his improper dress, was responding "no."

We come to God's wedding party, clothed in humility, confident and eager to do everything in our power to uphold the vows we made at our baptism. Discipleship is not easy, nor is it always understood completely. But we come prepared to uphold our promises.

O God, may I wear my discipleship well. Give me courage to be your disciple in the world. Amen.

The king throws a party, inviting many people to join him in the celebration of his son's wedding. Many people in the city respond positively to the invitation. Everything is ready; the table is set. The king sends his slaves out to remind the people to come to the feast, but the expected guests choose to ignore the reminder as well as their previous decision to attend and do as they desire. Many of the king's slaves face ill-treatment and death at the hands of these guests. In his rage, the king sends troops to kill them and burn the city. The king then invites guests in off the streets.

Even with the understanding that the initial guests are the Jews and the ones pulled in off the streets are Gentiles who gladly come to the kingdom feast, it's harder to understand the ill-prepared guest who is thrown into "outer darkness."

We know that there is an expectation of guests at most parties; simply replying and showing up entails a commitment of some sort. When the guests arrive, their presence reflects a commitment to the host. And commitment is exactly what Jesus is talking about here. If we consider that the wedding feast represents the covenant relationship between God and the people, the expectations are clear.

So what is the wedding garment? Fruits of the kingdom? righteousness? Maybe both and more. When a king issues an invitation, he expects a great deal of the guests. There is a measure of expectation, a measure of preparation; and there is judgment. We come to God's banquet wearing the garment of authentic discipleship. We commit to Jesus and to life as a Christ-follower. The guests at the king's wedding feast knew what was expected of them as God's people. Are you as clear in your commitment and expectation?

Lord, help us to live up to your expectations of us. Amen.

Hindsight is 20/20. Sometimes we look at other people's behavior and say, "I can't believe they did that! What were they thinking?" We tell ourselves that we would never have followed Aaron and worshiped a golden idol. We would never refuse an invitation to be part of God's kingdom. We would never kill God's messenger.

Think back on this week and reflect on your actions and thoughts. Did you lose your temper? Did you criticize someone without talking to him or her first? Did you drive faster than the speed limit? Did you ignore the needs of another? Did you forget some of God's mighty acts?

Here is the good news—someone is standing in the breach for us, just as Moses stood in the breach for those stiff-necked Israelites. Christ has our backs when we fail, and we do fail.

Another question: For whom are you standing in the breach? Who needs your prayers for intervention that she or he might recognize their own weaknesses and shortcomings and turn to God? Moses began with intercession for the Israelites before he confronted them with their sin or carried out judgment.

Think back on your week and remember the people you have talked with. It could be the server at the restaurant or your child's teacher or maybe someone closer—your child. Who was tired, discouraged, or in sin? That person needs someone to stand in the breach for him or her.

Hindsight is 20/20. We all wish we had made different choices in some past situations; but since we can't change the past, we must focus on what we do from this moment on. We, like Moses, can make a difference in the lives of others. Let us not exchange the glory of God for an idol or forget what God has done for us.

Lord, open my eyes that I may see the person who needs my prayers. Motivate me to pray for that person. Amen.

Public Faith

OCTOBER 13–19, 2014 • HEIDI HAVERKAMP

SCRIPTURE OVERVIEW: In Exodus 33, Moses successfully argues that without Yahweh's merciful presence Israel is no nation and that Yahweh's and Moses' efforts have come to naught. Psalm 99 mentions Yahweh's royal rule, which brings to mind the human agents of that rule: Moses, Aaron, and Samuel. Each of these leaders facilitated Yahweh's conversation with the people and Yahweh's rule over them. The opening lines from First Thessalonians raise a question about the church's understanding of evangelism. Paul and his coworkers experience a change in themselves because of the Thessalonians, who become a living proclamation of the gospel by virtue of their ready acceptance of it. In the Gospel reading, Jesus answers a question with a question and confuses his "audience" both then and today.

QUESTIONS AND THOUGHTS FOR REFLECTION

- Read Exodus 33:12-23. How might you, like Moses, ask God to accompany you in a shared mission or journey?
- Read Psalm 99. Here, God is the exalted king over all the earth but also a king in relationship with his people and leaders, answering when they call. How do you respond to these contrasting but complementary images of God's power?
- Read 1 Thessalonians 1:1-10. In what public ways do you display your faith?
- Read Matthew 22:15-22. As you look at yourself, where do you see the stamp of God's image? the stamp of the "emperor"?

Priest and vicar at The Episcopal Church of St. Benedict, southwest suburbs of Chicago; she blogs at vicarofbolingbrook.net

Matters have been precarious for the Israelites. There was that incident with the golden calf, among other things. Now God has decided to take a break from accompanying them and to send an angel along instead.

Moses doesn't like this plan. He wants God to come with them. He also desires an identity for the Israelites as a community sent in God's name: to make him and them into a "we"—a way to be distinct as people. Moses knows his relationship with God is wrapped up with that of Moses' people.

For most of my life, I practiced a private faith. I prayed mostly for myself or for close friends and family. But in college a friend pointed out to me that in scripture God speaks to people as a group as much as God does to individuals. Jesus too speaks, not only to individuals but to crowds and the disciples as a group. Paul's letters are, all but one, addressed to communities. As Americans, we tend to imagine that our relationship with God is individual and personal and hasn't much to do with our neighbors, coworkers, or wider communities.

I have loved being part of the churches, schools, and neighborhoods where I found myself, but I had never thought to talk to God as a member of those communities, in the first-person *plural*, as "we." My life as a Christian had played out thus far entirely in the first-person singular: "I."

But we don't live in isolation; our lives intertwine with the lives of those around us. What could it mean to offer prayer as "we"—as a member of the communities that are part of our lives? What could it mean to understand our identity and our relationship with God as being intertwined with that of our brothers and sisters?

God of all people, you did not create us to be alone. Help us to see how you have intertwined our lives and our salvation with those of our neighbors. Amen.

We might cringe if someone congratulated us for being a "good example." Paul praises the Thessalonians for being "an example to all the believers in Macedonia and in Achaia," which might sound cloying to our contemporary ears.

But Paul names the Thessalonians "imitators of us and of the Lord," a high compliment, since in most letters he's urging communities to become his imitators, not thanking them for already doing so! Paul feels close to the Thessalonians. He acknowledges in this letter how welcome he felt when he visited and his delight at their readiness, despite persecution, to open themselves to faith in Christ. They became an example to other Christian communities, even without Paul's personal witness (1:8), because of their joy, trust in Christ, and hospitality.

Whether or not we feel like exemplary Christians, we set an example for others—even if we don't intend to. A quote attributed to Saint Francis goes like this: "Preach the gospel at all times. If necessary, use words." What we do and how we live speaks the gospel (or not!) more powerfully than any words we can say. How we welcome a stranger, how we trust in God despite our worries and fears, how we seek joy despite the struggles of our lives—these convey more powerful witness to the gospel than any words or explanations of faith we offer.

If we think too much about how others see us, we may seem superficial. But, if like the Thessalonians, we focus on hospitality, joy, and faith and let the "example" part take care of itself, we may find that being an example brings great joy and fullness of life in Christ.

Holy Spirit, descend on me with power and show me how to live my life with such joy and love that I may inspire others to do the same, that the whole world might give itself over to your saving grace. Amen.

People have employed this passage to tell Christians to avoid political confrontation and to accept the authority of the governments without complaint. However, in this passage from Matthew, Jesus is in the midst of a weeklong denunciation of the ways religious institutions have failed God's kingdom: the cleansing of the Temple; comparing religious leaders to dishonest sons, wicked tenants, and fatally underdressed wedding guests; and generally proclaiming their corruption and doom. He scarcely mentions political institutions until some folks in this passage come knocking to ask him about Caesar.

Jesus offers a theologically sound but mysterious answer to his conniving opponents—almost a riddle. It's pretty clear what belongs to the emperor, but what are these "things that are God's"? Doesn't everything belong to God? What does that mean for the emperor? And what is Jesus implying about the loyalties of the religious institution of the Temple by directing this question so pointedly at its disciples?

As people who most likely have great affection for and loyalty to the religious institution of the church, we must avoid becoming like Pharisees and blinding ourselves to the church's weaknesses. We, as religious people, are not the sole proprietors of "the things that are God's," nor is the church. The church cannot faithfully criticize the government without examining its own failures to embody God's reign.

Yet Jesus does not despair for religious institutions. Why would he spend a week before his death teaching around the Temple, constantly preaching about its culture, if he didn't believe the issue was worth addressing? May we put the kingdom of God before institutions, never mistaking one for the other.

O God, guide us as we seek your kingdom, which lies in the midst of us. Amen.

When I was young, I imagined that God looked a lot like George Washington. But I've never really pictured God as a king like the psalmist does. Maybe that's because I've never lived under a king—or queen for that matter (although it is interesting, in this context, that as a child I imagined God being like the President). And although one of my guilty pleasures is following stories about Queen Elizabeth II and her family, my comparing any of her fine qualities with God's qualities strikes me as odd. She's dutiful and gracious, but Queen Elizabeth isn't really very powerful.

What contemporary titles would give expression to the power of God? "The LORD is commander-in-chief; let the peoples tremble!" Or "The LORD is boss"? Or "The LORD is mayor." "The LORD is our president!" doesn't sound very grand or magnificent. Not many figures in a democratic society have absolute power over others. And those who have power over us can be dismissed from office by the electorate or held accountable by the public in some way. Even the power of employers only goes so far—we can quit jobs, report abuses, or waste our work time texting friends or messing around on Facebook.

But in our society, our cultural lack of totalitarian metaphors may not matter much. God is powerful not because God has power over others, like a king or boss or dictator, but because, as the psalmist points out, God is holy. God is the Being that precedes all beings. God is like nothing we know or could ever understand. God's ways are not our ways (Isa. 55:8); God's power isn't like human power. And yet God has entrusted us with a powerful commission in Christ to set ourselves against the powers of the world, to serve the least powerful, and to spread the good news.

God, you are holy and mighty. Help us to live out your power, justice, and mercy in our own lives and communities. Amen.

Paul had a special relationship with the Christian community at Thessalonica, and we sense this in the tenderness and affection of his language in this letter to them. As with most of his letters, Paul opens with thanksgiving—a kind of "thank-you" note to this Christian community that is still forming its identity and faith. For Paul, saying thank you to the Thessalonians involves more than gratitude. He wants to help these new Christians claim an identity *together*.

Like Moses, Paul wants this community of Christians to see themselves as a chosen "we"; a group called by God to a new, shared identity. How does he do it? He uses inclusive language: "our" God and Father and "our" Lord Jesus Christ. He says, "We always give thanks for all of you." He claims their persecution as a shared badge of honor, admiring that they were able to receive God's word with joy nonetheless. He names their entire community as an example to other believers.

Finally, letters were rare in the ancient world; Paul could have been encouraging this shared identity through his letter writing. Does this seem a manipulative thing for Paul to do? I don't think so. My mom taught me to write thank-you notes when I was a child. For her, saying "thank you" acknowledged not only a gift but also a treasured relationship. And for Paul, it is not only his relationship with the Thessalonians that matters but also their relationship with God and Jesus Christ. Offering thanksgiving acknowledged the gifts of the community and staked a claim on their relationships to one another, to him as teacher, and to their newfound faith in Christ.

Write a letter to a community of faith that is dear to you (your church, campus ministry, 12-step group, Bible study), expressing thanksgiving for the ways you share an identity in faith.

Many people prefer a private life of faith to a public life, choosing activities like prayer, devotions, and reading scripture. Others prefer more public activities of faith: service to others, leadership, teaching.

Moses exemplifies a public person of faith who also had a rich private life of faith: his personal and active relationship with the God of Israel. Scripture tells us, "The LORD used to speak with Moses face to face, as one speaks to a friend" (Exod. 33:11). Moses' brave and risky public life was only possible because of the intimate, private relationship he had with God. And his private relationship with God grew only as he stuck his neck out to lead and serve God's people. In this week's passage his private faith also required taking a risk.

Moses asks to see God's glory, and the Lord responds, "You cannot see my face." (Strange, since we heard in 33:11 that they spoke "face to face"). Moses requests an intimacy with God that moves beyond the focus of their relationship so far: the task of leading the Israelites. Moses may be saying to God, as Dr. Karla Suomala states, "You know me, by face, by name, in every possible way, but I don't know you and I can't see you" (workingpreacher.com). God demonstrates both authority and tenderness in response to Moses' risky request: God won't (or can't) show Moses the fullness of the Divine Presence but will give Moses a "back" view.

Like Moses, we are called to serve God and God's people in our public lives. And also like Moses, we are invited into a more personal relationship with God. Moses took risks to grow in both areas; may we do so also!

O Lord, our God, you are full of glory and power, but you also reach out to each of us, inviting us to lives of public faith and also to know you more and more. Amen.

The Romans referred to Caesar as a god. The coin the men pull out of their pockets reads *Tiberius Caesar, august son of the divine Augustus, high priest.* Yet, here stands Jesus, Son of God, in the Temple, the place of the Jewish high priest. You can cut the irony with a knife.

Christians of the Roman Empire found it an ongoing challenge to live under the rule of two Lords: Jesus Christ and Caesar. Christians hid themselves and their worship, since their faith clearly challenged the lordship the government claimed to have over their lives.

Perhaps our lives today aren't so different from these early Christians. Even if our political leaders don't demand that we call them "Son of God," government and civic commitment do place certain demands on our lives: taxes, jobs, laws, jury duty, schooling, mortgages, garbage pickup. There are also many "high priests" we turn to for leadership in our lives: financial planners, therapists, book authors, health professionals. And there are many "lords" who hold authority over us: family, employers, our emotions, our physical bodies, even the weather. Some "lords" over our lives may be explicitly harmful: disease, abusive relationships, addiction, discrimination.

And yet, none of these institutions, leaders, or powers has the ultimate claim on us or on our deepest identity. What image are we truly "stamped with"? Whose "likeness" and "inscription" (RSV) do we bear? Genesis 1 tells us that we're created in the image of God, that we're stamped and inscribed with God's likeness. May we be so bold as to remember that claim on our lives above and beyond anything else that vies for our allegiance.

Lord Jesus Christ, we belong to you. Help us to see the likeness of God inscribed on our souls and bodies and know that we are marked for love and grace above all else. Amen.

From Generation to Generation

OCTOBER 20–26, 2014 • GARY L. BARCKERT

SCRIPTURE OVERVIEW: Deuteronomy 34 narrates Moses' death and Joshua's succession—both the end of Moses' life and the continuation of his influence. Psalm 90 is ascribed to Moses, and the tone suits the setting portrayed in Deuteronomy 34. In First Thessalonians, Paul continues his recollection of the relationship between himself and the Thessalonians. Paul and his coworkers acted out their love of neighbor, a love that is possible only because of their prior love of God. The Gospel places Jesus in a setting of controversy with the religious leaders of the day. The exchange about the greatest commandment demonstrates that the religious authorities in fact observe none of the commandments because of their inability to understand properly what Jesus calls the "first" and "second" commandments.

QUESTIONS AND THOUGHTS FOR REFLECTION

- Read Deuteronomy 34:1-12. What consequences of sin have you experienced? How have they refocused your vision on God and God's purposes?
- Read Psalm 90:1-6, 13-17. How are you numbering and counting your days? In what ways does that numbering bring gratitude to God?
- Read 1 Thessalonians 2:1-8. How do you nurture and encourage the next generation of Christ-followers?
- Read Matthew 22:34-46. What theological positions or assumptions keep your life misaligned with the two great commandments of loving God and neighbor? How might you remedy that situation?

Member of Seattle Presbytery; Executive Director, "Sharing Alongside," a pastoral outreach ministry to families that have no faith community; Shoreline, Washington

Come to the top of Mount Nebo with me. Even on a hazy day, the view 4,030 feet above the Dead Sea impresses. I stand there on a 100° day looking out over Jericho and the Dead Sea contemplating the deep soul tremor that Moses might have experienced. He knows his leadership is transitional between God's promise to Abraham and future generations. His unique task of leading two generations from Egyptian slavery comes to a close, and Joshua's task of leading the current generation in conquest begins.

Imagine the memories that flood Moses' mind and heart: the story of his birth, the pitch-lined basket, the princess rescuing him from the river, growing up in the palace, murdering the Egyptian, tending sheep, the burning bush he could never erase from his soul, the plagues, the daunting Red Sea, forty discouraging but trusting years in the wilderness, Mount Sinai's Commandments, and finally Mount Nebo.

You too are a transitional person of God's promise for the next generation. Hebrews 11 lists generations of those who lived with "the assurance of things hoped for, the conviction of things not seen," and then concludes with deep irony: "All of these died in faith without having received the promises . . . since God had provided something better so that they would not, apart from us, be made perfect" (vv. 1, 13, 40). The challenge: Be faithful so the next generation will step up and follow with fresh faith.

What is the story of your calling? How do your gifts of leadership and God's purpose connect in service? What is your vision and strategy for preparing the next generation to follow God? If you reviewed your personal history, what experiences would stand out?

God of Abraham, Isaac, Jacob, Moses—and the church—grant me a fresh vision of your purpose and fresh energy to follow you with renewed commitment for the next generation. Amen.

When you're up to your neck in alligators, it's hard to remember that draining the swamp was your initial purpose. When immediate circumstances become overwhelming, retaining focused perspective and commitment to God's intentions can be nearly impossible.

Moses saw "alligators" more than once between Egypt and Mount Nebo. Two stand out: (1) at Mount Sinai he saw his charges worshiping the golden calf and in fury smashed the tablets; and (2) at Meribah, in his angry frustration with the people's complaining, he struck the rock twice instead of speaking to it. The memory of Meribah comes calling as he stands on Mount Nebo. He had taken the Israelites' antagonism toward him personally. Anger made it impossible for him to represent God faithfully in that moment.

Living with people we find frustrating exposes our fundamental needs and vulnerabilities. Focusing greater energy on them and the circumstances they create is tempting. Subsequently we temporarily lose sight of and confidence in God's purposes at that time.

God allowed Moses moments of failure and responded with both consequences and grace. Moses will not enter the Promised Land. However, the consequences of failure do not signal God's condemnation but rather serve as motivation, drawing us back to divine grace.

What "alligators" thrash your vision and threaten your potential of serving God's purpose? How might you get beyond the "alligators" and refocus your vision and confidence in God's purposes? How has God's grace come to you after your frustrating experiences?

> *O God, unite my heart with yours and wean me from all reactions that would prevent me from being a faithful steward of your promise. Amen.*

So teach us to number our days that we may get a heart of wisdom" (Ps. 90:12, ESV). Death will sweep us away as surely as it has everyone since our first parents. A colleague of mine, now deceased, said, "We're all penciled in!" Earth is our home—for a while. Both our life and death are for real. This is true for all God's creatures, great and small.

I am mindful of this fact as I write. The wife of my Swedish immigrant friend of forty-three years is dying. Yesterday I took my guitar to their home and sang a few old hymns. We prayed. Tearfully he stood at the foot of her bed, numbering her days in his mind. Then he recited John 3:16 in Swedish.

Psalm 90 affirms God's permanence even more than indelible ink! From everlasting to everlasting—as far backward and forward as we can imagine! God is our primary residence forever, our permanent address. Another colleague noted, "We are so much in God there is no way out." I think the psalmist sensed this when praying: "Satisfy us in the morning with your steadfast love, so that we may rejoice and be glad all our days."

I still recall the time when this verse first exploded in my heart with peace and joy. I imagined waking every morning with this initial conscious thought: Everyone in my home is permanently satisfied and content because of their grounding in the knowledge that God steadfastly keeps them! What peace! What joy!

What difference would your contentment in God's holding on to you make in how you approach each of your tasks and relationships? While you are here on this earth, with what attitude will you live? As you number your days, what wisdom grows in your heart?

Gracious and loving God, give me a fresh experience of being steadfastly loved by you, and free me to share. May I not take my days for granted but live in grateful service. Amen.

The psalmist affirms that God infuses divine work into our human activity, work and activity that will have an impact on future generations. "Let your work be manifest to your servants, and your glorious power to their children. Let the favor of the Lord our God be upon us, and prosper for us the work of our hands" (ESV). How is it that *God's* work and *our* efforts synchronize daily in accomplishing God's will?

Moses' staff provides a poignant reflection. Ordinarily used for walking and climbing, it possessed no inherent divine power; but through it God parted water, caused plagues, and brought water out of a rock at Horeb—guidance, deliverance, and provision. I support the following principle: God initiates; we cooperate—a principle reminiscent of Jesus' reminder, "Apart from me you can do nothing" (John 15:5).

My prayer before I meet with an individual or family is this:

Lord, may I listen carefully for how you are already present and active so I might facilitate and accelerate your work. May I not inhibit or convolute what you're already doing. Give me eyes to see; ears to hear; and a heart of wisdom to understand, so I don't deter the process in motion.

The disciples could have proclaimed Jesus' resurrection until they were exhausted, with no significant impact. Only with God's infusing presence could they proclaim, teach, heal, and suffer with godly impact.

When have you recalled times of awareness that something "larger" happened than you alone could have accomplished? In what part of your life do you most need God's infusion of guidance, deliverance, and provision?

O Lord, keep my mind, heart, and work in harmony with you so your will may be accomplished on earth as it is in heaven. Amen.

The Sadducees and Pharisees blatantly confront Jesus: the Sadducees in verses 23-33; the Pharisees in verses 15-22 and again in verses 34-40. All these encounters occur on the same day! Both groups are doing their best to entrap Jesus and put him on the defensive. His responses surprise and wither them.

In verses prior to today's passage (vv. 23-33), the Saddu-cees ask a patently disingenuous question based on disbelief. Jesus quickly silences them on two counts: "You know neither scripture nor the power of God." Lack of understanding and knowledge translates into misdirection! Lost!

The Pharisees see themselves on the side of being "right"— right in God's sight and right as opposed to any who in their view are "wrong." They ask, "Which commandment in the law is the greatest?" Jesus answers correctly (a left jab) and adds the second greatest commandment (a right cross). The Pharisees now find themselves on the defensive. Their actions don't look so "right" with respect to loving others as themselves. Their theology is orthodox; but the underbelly of their practice is, in fact, self-serving. "You blind guides! You strain out a gnat and swallow a camel" (Matt. 23:24). A scalding indictment!

Read the questions Jesus asks about identifying the Mes-siah (the knockout!). "No one was able to give him an answer, nor from that day did anyone dare to ask him any questions."

Which of your theological positions or assumptions conflict with the two greatest commandments? Which of them would Jesus ask you to lay aside in favor of being a humble servant?

Consider your impact on the next generation given your responses to the questions above. What actions and attitudes will bring about your desired legacy?

Almighty God, may my thoughts and actions be in accord with your intent for my life. Amen.

Paul and the other apostles entered Thessalonica, capital of the Macedonian region of the Roman Empire. They declared the gospel of God at great risk to themselves in the face of opposition. Now Paul writes to this community as he begins to lay out the characteristics of life in Christ.

Paul describes the state of his and the apostles' minds and spirits as they came to Thessalonica to proclaim the gospel. They were courageous, confident, bold, and fearless—in God. Based on this way of relating with this faith community, Paul makes clear what being apostles of Christ entails. Apostles are courageous, proclaiming the gospel in the face of adversity. Apostles are persons of integrity: they do nothing from "deceit or impure motives or trickery." And the third characteristic involves the way of relating: Apostles come as nurturers and encouragers. Paul affirms his and his coworkers' strong feelings for these people: "So deeply do we care for you that we are determined to share with you not only the gospel of God but also our own selves, because you have become very dear to us." Three necessary ingredients in the life of a Christ-follower are these: courage, integrity, and relationship.

Paul grounds his life in a relationship with God, a call that drives his entire life, a deep affection for people, and an integrity that will not manipulate them to meet his needs. Godly authenticity, credibility, and authority! Suffering did not govern his thinking, emotions, or will.

How does your life reflect these characteristics? What or who is the center of your grounding?

Eternal God, you do not change. Ground me in you that I may serve with boldness, integrity, and affection despite opposition. Amen.

Every generation needs nurturing and encouraging parents—nourishment and clear guidance. Paul adopts this metaphor of child rearing when describing his relationship with the new generation of Jesus' followers in Thessalonica. Their birth into trusting Jesus Christ was painful, and survival through infancy was treacherous. Almost immediately they found themselves in cultural, political, and religious conflicts—at complete odds with customary neighbors and, in some cases, family members.

We too have the opportunity to replicate, change, and add our story of trusting Jesus Christ as we nurture and encourage the next generation. "Things that we have heard and known, that our ancestors have told us. We will not hide them from their children; we will tell to the coming generation. . . . that the next generation might know them. . . . and rise up and tell them to their children, so that they should set their hope in God, and not forget the works of God, but keep his commandments" (Ps. 78:3-7).

Dale served as moderator of my presbytery (the governing body of a group of Presbyterian congregations) in 2011. He preached at the November presbytery meeting and shared the following incident. Before going on a Southeast Asia mission trip, he took one of his daughters to college. As he was leaving her on campus, she asked him, "Dad, if your plane goes down, what are your final words to me for the rest of my life?" His answer: "Trust Jesus."

Consider the next generation, especially those you hold dear. Are you at odds with any because of your faith? What is your multigenerational story of hope in God, and how are you telling it? When they suffer, whom will they trust? Your godly boldness and gentleness will have consequences far beyond your lifetime.

O God, help me nourish the spirits of those I love. Amen.

From Generation to Generation

Prayer and Work

OCTOBER 27–NOVEMBER 2, 2014 • THOMAS R. STEAGALD

SCRIPTURE OVERVIEW: The texts remind us that human decisions, relationships, and communities must be rooted in God's reality. The psalmist expresses that only Yahweh's grace and power render viable the life of the redeemed. The story of the crossing of the Jordan in Joshua 3 illustrates this principle: apart from Yahweh's grace, Israel's life could not be sustained. Paul does not deny an authority due him because of his previous relations with the Thessalonians. At the same time, he can reverse the image and speak of himself as an orphan when separated from these people. The possibility of mutuality emerges from a clear acceptance of the gospel's authority. Matthew 23 singles out the scribes and Pharisees for flaunting their positions and for engaging in pious activity to receive praise and be courted by others. Their craving of honorific titles shows their failure to acknowledge the empowerment of Jesus as teacher and God as Father.

QUESTIONS AND THOUGHTS FOR REFLECTION

- Read Joshua 3:7-17. When has faithful memory given way to faithful hope for you in a hard time?
- Read Psalm 107:1-7, 33-37. When have you read the Bible through your tears? How did that reading affect your life experience?
- Read 1 Thessalonians 2:9-13. How do you honor both prayer and work in your life? How do you integrate the two?
- Read Matthew 23:1-12. Where in your life do you witness judgmentalism, heroism, and honoring the dead? Where do you find yourself in this "little Triduum"?

United Methodist elder; Upper Room author, *Shadows, Darkness, and Dawn* and a new book in 2013; his reviews and articles have appeared in *The Christian Century*, *The United Methodist Reporter*, *The Circuit Rider*, and other journals and portals; Shelby, North Carolina

The back story of this text—all that has brought Israel to the edge of the Jordan and the Promised Land—reads like a case study in developmental psychology. Think of the long captivity in Egypt as a kind of extended gestation for Israel and the rescue from bondage a most difficult labor and delivery. The wilderness wailing of the hungry and thirsty Israelites was infancy (the terrible twos!); while at Sinai, Israel received basic instruction, the Commandments, the elementary dos and don'ts. The golden calf? Predictable adolescent rebellion, followed by a harsh "grounding" in the wilderness. Then, Moses, their "parent," dies.

Now, standing at the edge of the Jordan River, Israel is no longer a child and must make its own way into the future. But for a moment, as the Israelites look forward, they also glance back. They are leaving the wilderness to be sure, but they need to bless the ties that bind them to the past.

This passage illustrates a ceremony of reassurance, of reminding, of renewing. Yes, things have changed; but no, things are the same. They do not have Moses, but they have Joshua and the promise of God's blessing on him. Just as God parted the Red Sea to give their ancestors a way *out of* bondage, God parts the Jordan to make a way *into* freedom. The memory and the promise give them faith. Just as God miraculously provided for the previous generation, God will provide for them.

This important scene suggests an important truth: God has been with us, and God will be with us. Memory is a crucial part of faith. Hope is crucial too, and some would say hope is the more important. Perhaps. But faithful memory gives shape to faith's hope. Memory and hope together produce faithfulness, enabling disciples to enter the land of God's promises, whether geographically, emotionally, or spiritually.

Lord, may I remember all your blessings and trust in the blessings to come. Amen.

Among the rest of what we might notice in this text is something we might *not* notice—the command to *"stand still* in the Jordan." The command is reiterated, interpreted: when the "soles of the feet of the priests . . . rest in the waters of the Jordan," God will act.

Rest is an important word in the Hebrew scriptures, thick with connotations derived from the biblical accounts of Creation. The ancient poetry of Genesis 1 is as countercultural as it can be. In our world, the world as we conceive it, we imagine that all good things come by means of hard work—and specifically by *our* work. Our calendars, so crammed with human activity, leave little room for God to enter, much less act.

The biblical writers view God's world differently. Our first clue comes in the Hebrew understanding of time. Days begin at sundown: "There was evening, and there was morning, the (whatever) day." It is in the *evening*, when humans customarily quit working, when they rest, that God begins working.

In today's text, rest plays a key role. This rest, this standing still, does not signal merely the absence of toil; rather, as the priests stand still, the Israelites will be able to see what God is doing for them: providing for them what they cannot provide for themselves. *Only* when the soles of the feet of the priests rest in the waters of the Jordan will the waters be cut off and a path made so that the people can walk on dry land into their inheritance.

God will work for the Israelites but only when they cease their own efforts. Prayerful resting is crucial to prayer, to faith, and to testimony. Having seen God's power, they will remember God's faithfulness to them in coming days and tell others of what they have seen.

God, help me to stand still, to notice your work in my life and the world, that I may bear witness to your provision. Amen.

Tears make a powerful prism. Reading the Bible through tears reveals the wide spectrum of God's care and provision. God is the source of all blessing and the resource in every trouble.

In my earliest days and faith, I concluded that the gospel existed for the righteous, that God came near the "good girls and boys," that "real" Christians did not suffer or cry or have problems—and they certainly did not get into trouble. I suspect some people still believe in some form or other that God's care and bounty are reserved for the faithful, the obedient, the chaste.

Later, after many troubles (some of them my fault, some of them not) hurled me into my own private wildernesses, I began reading the Bible through my tears. I found many passages like this one. I began to see that the gospel is about redemption, the reclaiming of lost things. I began to trust that God hears the prayers of those who are in trouble, that Jesus welcomes sinners to his table, that God is a compassionate God.

What good news! Sometimes we imagine that our faults and failings remove us from God's presence. The Bible helps us see that troubles may be the platforms for God's best care. Just as God heard the prayer of the wayward Israelites and brought them to their home at last, God hears our cries and desires to gather us in from the wastelands to make the dry desert of our lives into a garden of new beginnings.

If you are in a wilderness now—and maybe you stormed off into it or wandered away or just got lost somehow—God hears. There is no weeping that does not sound to God's ear like a prayer and no darkness or depression stronger than God's embrace. There is no trouble that God cannot redeem. Even in bad times, God is good.

Lord, help me trust that you are able to redeem any circumstance and situation of mine or another's for your purposes. Amen.

The only Latin phrase I know, *ora et labora*, I learned in a Bene-dictine abbey. The phrase means "prayer and work," the organizing principle of monastic life. I go to a nearby abbey now and then to pray with the brothers. I slip into the loft, a stranger in a strange place. This loft is their home. Split rows of seats face each other across the long, cool chancel, shimmering with history, hope, and daily faithfulness. A few minutes before the appointed hours, the monks stop whatever they are doing and gather here. They take their seats, close their eyes, pray to be able to pray. They silence themselves, calm their spirits—and wait.

When the monks do speak, they sing, chanting the psalms appointed for the day and hour. They pray the entire Psalter each month, calling back and forth, as if to remind one another of all they are saying—of all they might forget to say if they were praying alone; if, indeed, alone, they remembered to pray at all.

After prayer, the brothers return to their abbey's work—whether raising chickens, making cheese, teaching school. They will soon return to prayer. Then they go back to work. On it goes, day after day, week after week, year after year: a deter-mined and unceasing intersection of *ora et labora*, each task sup-plying the raw material for the other task, each in turn. Praying together does not curtail their individual jobs. Their practical tasks do not replace their scheduled prayers. *Ora et labora*. Prayer and work. Both each day. Separate and together.

The monks' pattern challenges us to keep our prayers and work, our devotions and careers, our petitions and ministries sep-arate, and together. Paul seems to have viewed his own ministry in Thessalonica as a matter of both prayer and work: "unceasing thanks" and "labor and toil." Not one without the other but an intentional, disciplined integration of prayer and work.

Lord, let my prayers guide my work and my work give way to prayer. Amen.

It may be more blessed to give than to receive, but receiving is critical as well—especially with regard to the word of God. Without receiving the word of God, the gospel simply remains words or ideas. I ponder that thought as I read this text once again, and the most beautiful and arresting part of it, which is the reason for Paul's unceasing thanks: "When you received the word of God that you heard from us, you accepted it not as a human word but as what it really is, God's word, which is also at work in you believers."

Paul describes his ministry among these Gentile converts in terms that we, in our quick-fix culture, find almost incomprehensible: labor and toil, working night and day, not wanting to burden them, he says, but proclaiming the gospel of God, urging and encouraging, pleading. That was his giving. But their receiving is the source of his thanksgiving.

If the temptation for any preacher (though some do not see it) is to convert people to the *preacher*, the proof of Paul's ministry is that he did not want that. He did not want the Thessalonians to be converted to Paul, to his way of seeing or thinking. No, Paul wanted the Thessalonians to receive his proclamation as God's word. He wanted to be the *means* of their conversion to God and God's purposes.

The voices of propagandists, unscrupulous salespeople, and self-help gurus fill our world, hoping to sway us to their way of thinking. Not Paul. What he gave, what the Thessalonians received, was neither offered nor received as a human word at all. It was neither human wisdom nor temporal strategy. What Paul proclaimed, what the Thessalonians accepted, was an *eternal* word, God's word, at work in Paul's giving and their receiving.

Lord, may I receive your word today as your word to me, and may your word be active in my life. Amen.

ALL SAINTS DAY

Among the saddest realities of our day is that the church seriously disregards the Revelation of John. This disregard takes two basic forms, I think. Some "teachers" disregard Revelation by manipulating it to serve their fear-mongering purposes. It is an insult to read Revelation as we would a fortune cookie or tea leaves or a Rorschach blot. But many look into Revelation's pages and find whatever they choose to see.

Even more unfortunate is that "teachers" who know better than to manipulate the text find themselves so cowed by the mystery and symbolic language that they ignore Revelation altogether and abandon the book to irresponsible interpreters. If some preachers lament the hold that doomsday teachers have on their congregants, they have no one to blame but themselves.

I greatly enjoy teaching Revelation. It is so full of mystery and power. I appreciate today's scene especially—the elders falling on their faces, the angels and living creatures, the vast multitudes in heaven that no one can count: the saints!

I sometimes ask my students, "Who are these elders?" They answer this or that, with "the patriarchs and disciples" being the go-to answer. I say, "It doesn't matter. They are face down! John doesn't care if we know who they are; John wants us to know who the Lamb is. That's what's most important."

On All Saints we remember the elders and the multitudes— those whose rest is won. It is good and natural to remember them, to recall their faith and witness. But in heaven and in any gathering of the saints on earth, John would remind us that the center of our praise, the real focus for all the saints, is Jesus.

Today, O Lord, help me remember the faithfulness of those who have gone before. Especially lead me to remember the faithfulness of Jesus. Amen.

SUNDAY, NOVEMBER 2 ~ *Read Matthew 23:1-12*

Today we are completing what I sometimes call "the little Triduum." *Triduum* means "three days" and usually refers to the springtime sequence of worship services from Maundy Thursday evening to Easter Sunday. But there is another Triduum, a *little* "three days" in the fall of the year: All Hallows Eve (October 31), All Saints (November 1), and All Souls (November 2). This little Triduum and the focus of these days has something to say to us by way of prophetic reminder.

All Hallows Eve (Halloween). Judgmentalism is in no short supply in our world and culture. We are well-practiced in profiling, identifying, scapegoating, condemning others—and not least the hypocrites in the church. On Halloween we dress up, playfully acknowledging that we can wear masks, that we are capable of mischief, that we are sometimes at home in the darkness. Think of this day as a kind of confession.

All Saints. We also often see heroism in our world. People make the sacrifice, pay the price, give themselves for the sake of others. The church has its heroes too: saints. On All Saints we acknowledge our debt to those who came before, and we call ourselves to spiritual heroism, remind ourselves to be more than we have yet become—more faithful and more selfless—for the sake of future generations of believers.

All Souls. All Souls is a day to remember all the dead: sinners, saints, and all the rest who, like most of us, are not so much one or the other but a mixture of both. We remember the dead with God's compassion and mercy—forgive them their faults and amplify their virtues—and we pray mercy for ourselves. We commend all souls and our own souls into God's hands. We remember that we are dust, and we give humble thanks.

Lord, help us to acknowledge and confess our sins, that we might be more forgiving of all souls whose source and home is in you. Amen.

Heeding God's Direction

NOVEMBER 3–9, 2014 • CLAUDIO CARVALHAES

SCRIPTURE OVERVIEW: This week's passages speak of ultimate commitment or of the return of Jesus, or they speak in parables that reflect a protagonist who has been delayed in an anticipated appearance. Living so far from the time of the texts makes it difficult to appreciate the urgency with which the issues arose in various communities and the crises they precipitated. In the Bible, eschatology provides the framework for ethics, the context in which believers are called to right conduct. It is the coming advent of God that demands from and warrants for the people of God a distinctive style of life. The text from Joshua 24 resonates to eschatological themes in its insistence on unswerving loyalty to Yahweh. Israel is given an opportunity at the Shechem assembly to define itself by identifying its God. Israel is shaped by its understanding of the nature of God in whom the people are asked to hope. Jesus calls for readiness to face the delay of the bridegroom. A lack of preparedness results in a devastating verdict from the bridegroom: "I do not know you."

QUESTIONS AND THOUGHTS FOR REFLECTION

- Read Joshua 24:1-3*a*, 14-25. What gods do you choose to serve? How does that service manifest in your life?
- Read Psalm 78:1-7. What ancient landmarks guide your spiritual life?
- Read 1 Thessalonians 4:13-18. How does your faith affect your view of death?
- Read Matthew 25:1-13. Where do you "buy" oil for your lamp? What practices keep your light burning?

Ordained in the Independent Presbyterian Church of Brazil; now a member of the Presbyterian Church (USA); currently teaching at Lutheran Theological Seminary, Philadelphia, Pennsylvania

Our bodies and hearts still carry the marks from yesterday's worship services, if we were able to attend. What did you learn yesterday in church? What were you called to do? What vows did you renew in your faith?

In today's text, Joshua gathers the tribes of Israel to infuse in them the desire to live together under God's word. The Israelites have left their nomadic ways and now will settle in the land of promise. They will no longer be wilderness wanderers but permanent residents. This marks a major shift in their understanding of themselves as a people. Joshua knows that gathering around God's word is fundamental to their identity. All the Israelites present themselves before God at Shechem and hear God's word. Isn't that what we do when we gather together as the people of God—to worship and hear God's word?

God's call to the people of Israel through Joshua reminds them of who they are—based on those who came before them. Joshua begins by saying, "Long ago your ancestors. . . . " The Israelites do not find themselves in their current situation because of *their* efforts but because of the work and presence of those who came before them. Their ancestors created the opportunity to receive the gift of being God's people.

I believe we hear the same words today: "Long ago your ancestors. . . . " We are here because of our ancestors, those who prepared the way for us to be where and who we are. This remembrance gives us the strength to keep going, reflecting God's call in our daily lives. We are not alone but surrounded by a cloud of witnesses. As a consequence, we too gather together and prepare the way for the ones who come after us. How faithful are we in this mission?

Make a list of names of your ancestors, those who prepared the way for you to be where you are. Say a prayer thanking God for them.

Today's text continues with the theme of the ancestors but with a twist. Yesterday Joshua called the people of God to remember their ancestors. Today, he asks that they remember the liberation events of God in their lives and also the idolatrous ways they have lived as the people of God.

Joshua encourages the Israelites to "put away the gods that your ancestors served beyond the River and in Egypt." The people have to ponder the important events that gave them life, while looking at their choices that moved them away from God. This discernment entails a decision: "Choose this day whom you will serve." What is faith, and what is idolatry?

How are we to understand this passage today? One approach is to notice how we engage what we have received from our traditions. We ask ourselves how they can be renewed, reformed, and reinvented. *Tradition* means "handing down," and at this point we face a decision: What shall we keep, and what shall we change? What will we hand down to our sons and daughters from what we have received?

Some of our ways of living require keeping, while others require renewal. Discernment between the two is the work of God's people—together! If we do not consider our life of faith together, it is to everyone's detriment. If we do this work with openness and trust in God, pondering and praying together, we can find ourselves responding, "As for me and my household (church), we will serve the LORD."

God of our lives, help us to discern together what we need to keep and what we need to renew to be better servants of Jesus Christ in this world. Help us be to be open and to listen attentively to one another. Amen.

This is a harsh text. We are not used to such a threatening God. Joshua challenges the people's sincerity with regard to their commitment to Yahweh. Does he really believe they will not follow through or does he simply want them to consider their decision more seriously? He tells the people that if they don't turn back to God, God will harm them. For me, Joshua focuses less on the anger of God and more on the need to live a life of justice, mercy, and love. The Israelites face the danger of living as if they have no commitment to God and to one another.

Today, if we choose to live on our own, we trap ourselves in a life of arrogance that trusts and depends on our own efforts and capacities. But in life we always need somebody else; we always need the presence of another to hold our hand and get us through when we are not doing well. When we choose to hold the hand of lesser gods of the "River and in Egypt," we also allow others to fall to the mercy of an economic market that does not care for those who cannot afford it.

To decide to follow God is a choice to serve the least and the last. God's call to us, as it was to the Israelites, is simple: To serve the Lord is to serve one another, and to obey God's will is to live a life of care and attention to God's word and others. A covenant with God is always a covenant with the people of God.

Joshua reaffirms the covenant of the Israelites' ancestors and challenges them to live it out fully. They will "put away the foreign gods that are among [them], and incline [their] hearts to the LORD." This covenant comes to each generation with a challenge and a need for confirmation and reaffirmation. We willingly choose to place ourselves in the service of God and the least of these.

God, today I once again choose life and choose to serve you with all that I am. Help me serve you and the least of these. Amen.

To hear and heed God's direction has been a central theme for the week's readings. Today's passage encourages us to pursue God's guidance as we struggle with our history and what to make of it. Our ancestors surround us, and our decisions are, in part, a result of their choices and stories.

The psalmist engages his readers with a precious but dark history. He sees a line of continuity of faith grounded in the past to be lived in the present and passed on to future generations. For the psalmist, history is not a collection of dead events. On the contrary, it can inform our current living, enlightening our present and creating hope for the future.

The psalmist's backward look fills him with joy. He bears witness to God's glorious deeds, God's power and wonders throughout the history of God's people. Because of that view he considers himself and the people who live with him a fundamental part of it! The glorious deeds of God bring peace to the present living of the people of God.

The might and wonders of God surround the people with trust and power. For this reason we need to tell our children. If the children know about this mighty history, they will grasp a better sense of life and know that God holds their future.

What glorious deeds of God in previous generations can we note? What can we tell others about the miracles and mercy of God in the history of people? How are we relaying this story about the wonders of God to those who will follow us in this journey of faith?

God, I will tell the future generations about your mighty acts of love in my life and in the world. Amen.

Although planted in the present, the psalmist always looks backward and forward. He reaches for wisdom and finds it in the history of his people. God's care for the people engenders a trust of God in the psalmist. He conveys the necessity of these past events being remembered and urgently told to future generations. For him, a good grasp of God's presence in the history of the people corresponds to his having a better grasp of himself, his purpose, his faith, and his future.

For this reason, when Christians celebrate Communion, the liturgy often notes a long list of historical events that attest to God's power so people will remember. They can then relate to that power-filled moment of a God alive in the history of God's people. This same God promises to continue to be active in the lives of God's people today.

The psalmist reminds his people of the decrees and laws God has established for God's people. It reminds me of a verse from Proverbs: "Do not remove the ancient landmark that your ancestors set up" (22:28). His children and his children's children will know about them. That knowledge will ground them, giving them reason to hope and trust that their lives will be always guided by the presence of a wondrous and powerful God.

My mother used to read *The Upper Room* meditation to me every morning; I was not allowed to leave the house without reading the Bible and praying. That time together gave me the courage to face the world every day. The telling of these stories deeply affected my faith and my notion of their connection to my past, present, and future.

God, our mother and father, help us not to forget your works or your commandments. We will relate our understandings and interpretations to the next generation as well. Amen.

SATURDAY, NOVEMBER 8 ~ *Read 1 Thessalonians 4:13-18*

Our previous passages stressed our need to know about our ancestors, our past, and God's marking the history of God's people. Now the apostle directs our attention to the future. Early church believers eagerly anticipate the parousia, the day of the Lord's coming, in their lifetimes. But several members of the faith community have died and Christ has not yet returned. The Christ-followers are becoming concerned.

Paul assures them that they need not "grieve as others do who have no hope." Christians live in the light of a special hope: that of Jesus Christ's resurrection. Upon the Lord's return, both the living and the dead will be gathered to Christ; they "will be with the Lord forever."

The apostle wants to inform these Christians in Thessalonica about what is to come and how to relate with death. One mark of Christians comes in the way we deal with death. Death is not the end but a transition into God's arms. We pass from life to fuller life, where all our tears will be wiped away. We do not grieve in despair. We grieve the death of persons close to us because we lose their presence, their joy, and the ways they made our lives and the life of the world better. But we do not grieve in desperation because we will meet again. Those who go before us will rise first and then those who still live will join Jesus.

Our beliefs about the future influence our direction in the present. With a past lived in God's hands and a future that is already in God's hands, we venture into daily life without fear. We live every minute of our lives in trust and confidence, holding in our hearts this eagerness to be with Jesus and our ancestors in that glorious day.

God of the future, prepare our hearts to meet you on that jubilant day! Amen.

Our last passage for this week also speaks of the future and of our preparation to encounter Jesus. Matthew employs a metaphor to talk about the kingdom of God: bridesmaids waiting for the bridegroom. This story emphasizes the need for vigilance, preparation for the future, and anticipation of future possibilities. This passage does not address outsiders but those who are within the church. In the face of Jesus' delayed return, these insiders fail to be obedient, thereby becoming outsiders.

In some ways, we will never be ready for what is coming. But we can attempt to organize ourselves in a conscious manner. In this text, the oil will keep the bridesmaids' lamps working. If we venture into an interpretation that says that we are the lamps and the oil is the Holy Spirit, we can say that without the Spirit we lose our light. We may feel the need to go to "dealers" to get our "oil." However, we don't need religious dealers who promise us a rich life if we give money to this or that ministry.

We too may feel the pressure of a long-delayed bridegroom and find ourselves unprepared when he does come. We can fail to be obedient in the lengthy time of waiting and allow our lights to go out. When this occurs, we may find ourselves in the place of the foolish bridesmaids who come late to the banquet hall, knock, and hear these words, "I do not know you."

The oil of the Holy Spirit will keep our lamps burning. Then we will be prepared to meet our savior Jesus Christ. Having been fed by the precious oil of the Spirit day by day, we then can gather in worship, where God replenishes the oil through the presence of our brothers and sisters.

Holy Spirit, feed our lamps and make us ready for that day when Jesus calls us into his kingdom. Amen.

Walking in the Unexpected

NOVEMBER 10–16, 2014 • JUDITH JENKINS KOHATSU

SCRIPTURE OVERVIEW: In the book of Judges, we find a woman confidently leading a patriarchal nation as though it were an everyday occurrence. The psalm reminds us that the need for mercy reduces each and every one to a posture of outstretched hands and upturned eyes. To sing such a song on the way to worship, as was traditionally done, is to prepare the mind and heart for the possibility of whatever blessing may be given upon arrival. In First Thessalonians we overhear an apostle's exhortation to live openly and expectantly regarding God's future—alert to the coming of Christ but also aware that the Christ may come in sudden and unanticipated ways. Finally, a parable in Matthew runs counter to our instincts to safeguard that which we treasure, challenging us to consider the ways in which faithfulness involves a strange coupling of risk and reward.

QUESTIONS AND THOUGHTS FOR REFLECTION

• Read Psalm 123. Where is the pilgrimage time or spot in your living?
• Read Judges 4:1-7. What call from God mediated through an unexpected source are you likely to ignore? Why?
• Read 1 Thessalonians 5:1-11. We need to be appropriately equipped as we make our way through life. How does your spiritual practice equip you for faithful and obedient living?
• Read Matthew 25:14-30. Where are your growing edges in investment management?

Clergywoman interested in urban and interim ministry and spiritual formation; appreciative of the interaction of theology and science; Pittsfield, Massachusetts

This week I invite you on a pilgrimage. You choose the destination; the road is the scripture passages for this week. A pilgrimage involves a journey with spiritual intent, a physical journey or one into our minds and souls.

Some psalms were written as pilgrimage songs. Picture yourself just inside the walls of the ancient city of Jerusalem. At last you feel safe from the hazards of the road. You turn your eyes toward your destination. What do you see? Consider how your eyes seek out that for which you long. Older translations liken that attention to that of servants toward the one they serve or a lover toward his or her beloved. More modern translations use the image of a dog looking to the hand of its owner. This humble image is one you might know and also experience. How is it for you to gaze upon the Holy with such intent? The purpose of such gazing is to steady oneself, to renew stability in a world of uncertainties. As you contemplate your pilgrimage, what is it that you seek?

In our technologically oriented world, we may not be consumed by the concerns of arduous foot travel through bandit-occupied hills, but many people and things clamor for our attention, imploring us to make them the focus of our lives. The words of the African American spiritual "Guide My Feet" from *The Faith We Sing* can provide our prayer mantra as we stand amid the clamor and search for God.

In faith we claim that God stands with us amid the clamor! We experience God's presence in the middle of daily life—no matter how blessed or traumatized that living is. God is the expected in the face of unexpectedness. As you quiet into prayer, what do you seek as your steady point? What do you find?

Still Point of our living, enable us to "lock on to" the beacon of your justice, mercy, and love so that we may walk humbly as we share these qualities with others. May it be so.

Sometimes our pilgrimage takes us to unexpected sources of wisdom. The biblical account regards Deborah—in a time of male brawn and frequent military action—as a person of wisdom, a judge. Her "day job" includes mediating and settling disputes of both civil and family natures. But her job description also includes mediating God's word to the supposedly faithful people of God. How odd this situation must have seemed to some: a vulnerable female—subject to the risks of childbearing and endlessly occupied with child rearing—as the go-to person. That was hardly the picture (then and perhaps even now) of a strong leader.

Those who mediate God's wisdom come in all sizes and shapes. Think back over this past week. Where, in whom, have you encountered the holy wisdom you sought? Who satisfied the judicial needs of your faith life? How were you opened to hear a holy truth from a source that your societal upbringing had discounted?

It also takes strength to seek wisdom. Imagine Barak, the muscle power in his people's time of need. While he would automatically answer a summons from a male judge, what enabled him to respond to this female judge? How do we respond to the unexpected sources of God's wisdom? Do we have to wait until we are desperate (as in twenty years of occupation and in the face of nine hundred chariots) until we open ourselves to God's wisdom? Might we be a Deborah and not merely a Barak?

Holy Sage, give us the gift of knowing that we don't always know. In that revelation equip us with the courage to seek your holy truths, even when they crop up in unlikely situations. Encourage us to act thoughtfully sooner rather than later when a more conventional sign might appear. May it be so.

My family and I are stuck in pre-Thanksgiving traffic on the Mass Pike, and voices rise from the back seat of the car, "Are we there yet? Are we almost there?" We were barely an hour into an eight-hour drive to New Jersey to Grandma's home. The early Christians at Thessalonica give voice to similar concerns in their desire to know the day of the Lord's return. They want to be ready. Paul replies that for faithful Christians the "when" doesn't matter since they are already living their faith.

The question of "when" continues to rise on our lips as we plan our days, program our future and that of others. We contemplate what we might do—someday, sometime. It applies to clearing off our desk, tidying up the kitchen, cleaning out the attic, making that career move, or deepening our spiritual life.

Paul suggests that the Thessalonians just get on with it; "it" being the life that Jesus taught. Just do it—live in the light! Paul suggests. He states that they, and we, are already doing it!

We're still waiting over two thousand years later for the sign —the *right* sign. It is time to live our faith in the moment, this very moment. Listen for God's prompting and follow it. Such seemingly impetuous action, such living in the now, may be frightening. Notice that Paul addresses his words to a community of believers, not merely an individual. Walk your life with the support and guidance of your community. The important aspect is the timing—now! We have no other assured moment except the one we now occupy. Live fully in God's way—now.

Creating God, I don't need to move with the speed of the rabbit, but empower me to move with the constancy of the tortoise. Direct my energies to the now, so that my living will attest to your love, peace, and justice. May it be so.

In today's parable, the landowner goes on a journey and leaves three servants in charge, entrusting them with unimagined responsibility. I feel in a similar position when my spiritual director asks me, "What are you going to do that God isn't already doing?"

We know the outcome: Two of the three servants invest the enormous sums entrusted to them. The third one aims to be risk-free and buries his sum in the ground. The landowner returns and commends two industrious servants while severely chastising the third for his risk averseness. Two servants share in the landowner's living; one gets to reside in outer darkness.

I don't have much capital to invest. I do have a life, certain gifts and talents, some experiences—and I am more or less in charge. Our lives, with which God entrusts us, is divine capital. We choose how to invest. So what have you done with God's gifts to you? Are they invested or buried? Are you simply warming a pew or actively participating in God's work?

Think about your investment in your journey of faith. Which gifts are you using that surprise you? What gifts that you maybe yearned for have returned a lower yield? Where are you residing—thanks to your investment strategy: in the full life of Christ or in the outer darkness?

When my daughters were young and experienced an undesired alteration in their life's course, they would reply, "When I'm big, I'm gonna be in charge of myself, and I'm going to do what I want!" The good news is that we *are* in charge of ourselves, and God stands ready to assist!

Blessed God, lead us on paths of due diligence and courageous risk-taking so that our gifts may increase holiness among us. Amen.

Paul, after calming the fears of the early Christians about the timing of Christ's return, turns to the practical—how to prepare ourselves for daily living. The obvious cautions are "keep awake and be sober." How often do we plow blindly through our day, oblivious to the godly word available at every turn?

God speaks to us during our meditation or devotion time—who needs more communication! Often I self-medicate (our current description of addiction), sometimes with the overpowering idea that I need to get on with the predetermined program. Or maybe I'm preoccupied with the "what ifs" and paralyzed to proceed. Or perhaps I'm so stimulated that I barrel through my day communicating only with myself. None of these serves as a great approach to pilgrimage.

Paul even provides us with some equipment-for-life advice. People of his day would have been familiar with the Roman soldier's garb—the helmet, the breastplate. Notice that Paul draws our attention to the protective gear, not the offensive paraphernalia. What competent cyclist goes out without a good helmet or jogger without a good pair of running shoes? Even inline skaters or skateboarders take the precaution of knee and elbow pads. Paul commends to us the gear of faith, love, and the hope of salvation.

So as you dash out the door today, how have you equipped yourself: slings and arrows or protective gear that allows you to receive and respond to the day's offering? Paul urges us to encourage one another, to build each other up. We are safe—protected. Therefore, we can share the bounty of God's grace. Unlike the Roman legionnaires, we come not to conquer but to liberate.

O God, call my attention to the attitudes and equipment I need for today's mindful jog through life. Amen.

I've added two verses to the reading. When we left Deborah, she was sending for Barak to amass his troops to overthrow Jabin. This is an important battle. Never before have the hill people (the Israelites) overpowered the technologically superior plains people. Barak realizes the import and makes a deal with Deborah: I'll go fight, if you come with me. We might wonder about Barak's distrust; does he not believe that a woman can bring the word of God with clarity and decisiveness? Or is he prudently realizing the power of accompaniment?

Often we think that our spiritual journey is a solitary one. Are we shy about asking for companionship on such a journey, or are we determined to do it ourselves? What is your spiritual journey like? Who accompanies you?

Our scriptural narrative generally supports the notion of accompaniment, of shared creativity—even Jesus had the company of the Holy Spirit during his time in the desert. Companions can point out things we might miss or relieve our fear of contemplating new ways. Sometimes it helps to have someone listen with us. In what ways might your companions on the journey into the unexpected help you go forward with confidence?

But sharing an endeavor has its downside. Deborah reminds Barak that if she goes with him, he won't get exclusive credit for the victory—and perhaps the attendant rewards will need to be shared. Our walk with God isn't exclusively for our own benefit, and the spiritual journey isn't about rewards. This walk we undertake is about living ever more fully into God's way with attendant benefits for all creation.

So how is it in your part of the body of Christ? Do you accompany one another in growth and in service? Walking with God, being the body of Christ, is a shared labor.

Ever-patient Companion, challenge us to dare to accomplish your work in this time and place. Amen.

So you think you have it all figured out? Probably each of the servants felt that way. Two servants, appreciative of the landowner's trust, wanted to give back more than they had taken in trust. The third servant entertained a more calculating thought: *I know this owner; he is shrewd, taking advantage of every opportunity.* He acts to safeguard the original investment to protect himself and the landowner. Traditional Jewish practice didn't encourage the making of money with money. So the third servant exercises fiscal prudence and traditional faithfulness.

What a surprise upon the landowner's return! The third servant has misread the situation and failed to come to the appropriate conclusion. The owner desired worthwhile use of the funds placed in trust, not merely safe return of the original sum. Two servants share the owner's joy and receive a promotion; the third is cast into outer darkness, losing even the sum he so carefully safeguarded.

We learn that there is no risk-free investment, since the road to opportunity leads through a risk-laden environment. The reward of risk taking can be astounding, as can be its failure. The reward for playing it safe, being risk-averse, is just that—no risk, safety in a particular moment but no guarantee for the future.

How is it with us, with the church, as we are entrusted with hard-won assets? Do we dare take a flyer on some unproven but needed ministry, or do we play it safe with the same approach that worked so well for our parents? If we thought less about assets and more about gifts, we could accomplish more. Gifts are to be used, not hoarded. God blesses us individually and corporately with wonderful, unique, and often unused gifts. How's our investment strategy doing for us?

Gracious God, you've granted us another week of asset-based living. May your realm of love and justice be a bit more apparent thanks to our daring. May it be so.

Power Made Perfect

NOVEMBER 17–23, 2014 • ERICA L. SCHEMPER

SCRIPTURE OVERVIEW: The universal rule of God, expressed in Christ the Shepherd-King, is a dominant theme in all this week's texts. Both Old Testament texts dwell on the nurturing, protecting role of the Shepherd-King, whose people we are. Ezekiel 34 gives the shepherd's guiding and defending role a political twist by condemning the succession of shepherd-kings who have neglected and exploited the flock. Both New Testament passages celebrate the victory of Christ: The enthroned Son of Man of Matthew 25 separates the flock, and the risen Christ of Ephesians 1 is seated by God "far above all rule and authority and power and dominion." Christ guarantees God's completed reign.

QUESTIONS AND THOUGHTS FOR REFLECTION

- Read Ezekiel 34:11-16, 20-24. When in your life have you felt like one of the weaker sheep, scattered and marginalized? When you have behaved like the fat sheep, throwing your weight around at the expense of others?
- Read Psalm 100. Reflect on the story of your own life and the lives of your spiritual forebears. What parts of the story make you want to sing?
- Read Ephesians 1:15-23. The author suggests that we inherit the power of God along with Christ. How would your actions and intentions change if you were to own fully your inheritance of God's power to transform the world?
- Read Matthew 25:31-46. Consider the reminder that all people, in their neediness, are members of Jesus' family. Commit to seeing each person you encounter as an opportunity to be nearer to Jesus.

Presbyterian (PCUSA) pastor, having served various ministries and churches in the Chicago area for a decade; now lives in the San Francisco Bay area

Royalty only comes up in my life because I'm the mother of a six-year-old girl: There's a good deal of pretending and playing princess in our house. The allure rests not so much in the power of the position as in the satin, lace, and bling on the dress-up clothes. And the only purpose of a king, as far as my daughter is concerned, is to be parent to the princess.

This coming Sunday is a feast day. Some churches call it Christ the King Sunday; others, to soften the term *King*, the Reign of Christ Sunday. The scripture passages also include images of shepherding, but even the pastoral setting is not an escape from the "theme of kings." Israel and the surrounding cultures intertwined the metaphors of shepherd and king.

On this day we do not celebrate Christ as president, with checks and balances and term limits. We celebrate Christ's sovereignty, Christ's absolute power over all of creation.

I like the idea of divine sovereignty as long as everything works to my benefit and fits with how I think the world ought to work. But passages like Ezekiel 34 make me nervous about power. The power of the shepherd-king includes the right to judge. What does it mean that God loves all of creation but, at the same time, claims the right to sort the sheep from the goats? Should this sorting frighten me? Am I a sheep or a goat?

I cling to the word images of inheritance found throughout this week's passages. The hereditary and patriarchal nature of kingship might bother my political leanings, but in my faith life, it reminds me that I need not fear the judgment of Jesus Christ, who is also brother and friend. I may struggle to make sense of God's judgment, but I struggle from the safety of the arms of one who loves me as a treasured child and heir.

Hold us close, O Lord, as we contemplate your power; remind us that your grace is big enough to conquer our fear. Amen.

O h, so small! How old is he?" asks the woman in the elevator. My husband and I stare at each other, so sleep deprived that we need a few seconds to think about it. "He's four days old." The woman looks at us like we are crazy.

The day before my son's birth, my grandmother suffered a massive stroke. I insisted that we drive forty miles the day after my son and I came home from the hospital so that she could meet him. She lived for another five weeks, her body ravaged but her mind intact. Every time I brought my son and my daughter to see her, her face glowed.

This relationship is part of the family inheritance I wanted to pass on to my children: the look of love in the eyes of the family matriarch for her children and grandchildren and great-grandchildren. No human being loves perfectly. But we catch magnificent glimpses of God's love for us even in imperfection.

When I remember the look of love on her face, I know a bit of what it means that God treasures us. We become children of God and co-inheritors with Jesus. That powerful love draws us into the glory of God's presence and the fullness of Jesus Christ. If that love powers Jesus' rule over all creation, there is nothing to fear. This power lifts us up from the lowest points in our lives. We follow Jesus through death to new life, and all of this in the face of a God who loves us immeasurably.

We are God's beloved children. The eyes of our heart are enlightened. With that in mind, return to the idea of Jesus Christ as judge. If our inheritance is the power of God's incredible love for us, there is nothing to fear.

Lord God, fill me with hope, and let me see your power in the love of those you place in my life. Amen.

Jesus of Nazareth, the King of the Jews." Pilate had this inscription placed on Jesus' cross (John 19:19). Whatever Pilate's intent—to rile the chief priests, to provide political cover for his sentence, to mock Jesus—Pilate probably doesn't realize that this label makes him a prophet.

But to call Jesus "king" while he hangs on the cross is a mysterious truth. Jesus' glory is grounded in power *and* in weakness. God's power, the writer of Ephesians reminds us, is at work in Jesus' resurrection. This power is made possible by way of weakness. The glory of victory comes after the agony of defeat. Jesus is raised to his position of prestige from having "come down" to be one of us.

We are impressed when someone with great power and position stoops to greet the ordinary people at their level. Think, for example, of the way presidential candidates make a point to eat at the hometown diner or pizza place. They come down from their place of privilege to mingle with the regular people and look good doing it.

Next month, we prepare for the arrival of Jesus as a baby. God does more than pay a visit. From the moment of his birth, Jesus lives life *with us*, experiencing the joy and pleasure of being human—as well as the pain, the mess, the frailty, the disappointment. And at the moment when he appears weakest, he will be named "King."

Lord Jesus Christ, open my heart to your reign—not by might, not by power but through the gentle work of your Spirit. Amen.

The closest equivalent I know to being part of a flock of sheep is riding public transportation. I can boil proper etiquette on the bus or subway down to one aspect: Take up only the space you need. If the bus gets crowded and you are able, stand and offer someone else a seat. Don't monopolize the spot next to you with your bag. Don't push. Don't shove. How different is it for sheep in the field?

We can easily convince ourselves that we are *not* the goats Jesus describes in Matthew 25. We're sheep; we fit right in with the rest of the flock. But sheep can harm other sheep, throwing their weight around, pushing them out of the way, leaving the weakest at the margins. What's left is a flock where some sheep grow fat, while others stray off and are left hungry and alone.

This disparity between the fat and the lean, particularly the persecution of the lean, calls God into action. God, the good shepherd, comes to the aid of the weak. The shepherd's concern is not to raise the fattest, sleekest sheep possible but to feed the entire flock on justice and bring every one safely into the fold.

Sheep fed on justice will be less concerned with grabbing the best grass at the expense of the welfare of others. These sheep will trust that the shepherd will find enough for everyone. Sheep fed on justice will not muddy the edge of the water source in a stampede. These sheep will trust that the shepherd is the source of living water.

Our trust in the good shepherd frees us from concern for ourselves. We can be comfortable in our own space; there is room for each of us in God's gracious, sovereign care. And that comfort frees us to look out for the beaten down, the bullied, the hungry, the lonely and the lost among us.

Guide us, Good Shepherd, to rich pastures and living water. Renew and refresh us, so that we may follow your way of justice. Amen.

I once worked on staff at a large, prominently placed downtown church. It was easy to find the hungry, the thirsty, and the stranger there. They came to us. They came to our charitable office for food and clothing and career assistance. They sat in our sanctuary for warmth on cold days. And on Sunday mornings, there was often someone in desperate need of a shower and a shave sitting just down the pew from an elderly matron in a fur coat. One man joined the congregation after he developed ongoing relationships with people while panhandling on the sidewalk out front each week.

In other church settings, we may have to go looking for persons in need. Many suburbs do a good job of hiding the problems of poverty and homelessness. But it's there, even in towns where we feel sure that every child goes to bed with a full tummy. Scratching the surface, we will find people who have fallen off the edge of the middle class. We will discover poverty and hunger of the spirit. We will unearth people who are sick and frightened and alone with the pain in their souls. People who need help surround us: those who need food and drink, welcome and care, concern and companionship.

The sixteenth-century saint, Teresa of Avila, wrote, "Yours are the eyes with which Christ looks with compassion on this world." And in a wonderful twist, when we look on the world with the eyes of Jesus, we see Jesus looking right back at us in the guise of those in need. We are judged not so much by our actions but by how immersed we are in the very life and being of Jesus Christ.

Lord Jesus, may I be so filled with your presence that I can't help but see and reach out to those who need your love. Amen.

Our children's minister was justifiably panicked. In spite of every effort at good policies and procedures, a third grader had left Sunday school to find her parents. But neither staff members nor the parents could find the child anywhere in the building. As news spread through the busy building, several of the homeless men in line for a bag lunch in the dining room asked to help. "We know the neighborhood better than anyone." We at the church thought we were in service to the homeless. But that day, we needed their help. Within a few minutes, the child was located, safe and sound, at a neighboring bookstore.

When Jesus tells us that he comes to us in "the least of these," it's a corrective to our tendency to hoard power. There's a danger when we help the downtrodden to turn our service into a way to make ourselves the powerful ones in the relationship. After all, aren't we the ones with the resources, the knowledge, and the ability?

Some churches have reevaluated charitable practices to make sure that the ways they help give power, control, and self-worth to those in need. For instance, instead of buying Christmas presents for needy families, the simple act of giving parents gift cards so they may tailor gifts to their children's needs creates a subtle change in the power dynamic.

Jesus is a master at turning our expectations upside down. And even here, he overturns our notions about who is in control. "Truly I tell you, just as you did it to one of the least of these who are members of my family, you did it to me." And perhaps the biggest surprise comes to those who, while immersed in the lives of helping, see nothing out of the ordinary in their actions—"Lord, when was it that we saw you?"—yet become inheritors of the kingdom.

Lord Jesus, you came to serve us. Teach us humility that serves only to glorify you. Amen.

REIGN OF CHRIST SUNDAY

When my husband accepted a job that was the sort of career-advancing position one can't refuse, we moved our young children across the country from our native Midwest to Northern California. Suddenly, we found ourselves far from our families with two little kids and an unsure future for my career. Money would be tight for the first few years. But we committed to making it work.

We discovered that our new county was packed with natural beauty. We could load the kids into the car and drive through redwood forests, over mountains, and to the Pacific coast, all within thirty miles of our new home. We often pulled the car over at a scenic overlook, and marveled, "It's so beautiful. Can you believe that we really live here?" In those moments, all the turmoil of the big move melted away, and the only thing we could do was give thanks.

The beauty of Psalm 100 is that it lays aside all other worries and grounds us in unabashed thanksgiving. There is a time and place to grapple with the mystery of God's judgment. There is also a time and place simply to enter the courts and know that God made us and loves us and keeps us safe, generation after generation.

Our lives may be full of change and turmoil. Sometimes we need to stop and take in the big picture, to look back at where we have been, to view the great span of our history with this Shepherd who will not abandon the sheep. The psalmist says God is good. Instead of entering God's courts in fear of judgment, we may enter singing about God's faithfulness and find ourselves welcomed home as beloved children, sisters and brothers of Jesus Christ.

O God, gather us into your courts. Fill us with confidence that you love us too much to let us go. Amen.

Keep Awake!

NOVEMBER 24–30, 2014 • MARTY G. BELL

SCRIPTURE OVERVIEW: Advent begins not on a note of joy but of despair. Humankind has realized that people cannot save themselves; apart from God's intervention, we are totally lost. The prayer of Advent is that Christ will soon come again to rule over God's creation. The passages from Isaiah 64 and Psalm 80 express the longing of faithful people for God to break into their isolation and to shatter the gridlock of human sin. The New Testament texts anticipate with both awe and thanksgiving the coming of "the day of our Lord Jesus Christ."

QUESTIONS AND THOUGHTS FOR REFLECTION

- Read Isaiah 64:1-9. Where have you discovered God in your life transitions?
- Read Psalm 80:1-7, 17-19. When has reading the Psalms led you to a different or perspective on a current situation?
- Read 1 Corinthians 1:3-9. Consider what the word *standard* conjures up in your mind. Does it convey to you the meaning of "ordinary" or "typical"? Or does it mean bringing your best to the task at hand? How does *your* standard enforce the attributes of grace and peace in the world?
- Read Mark 13:24-37. How often do you allow fear and doom to encroach on God's future of blessing?

Professor of Religion at Belmont University; pastor, Green's Chapel, Garrison, and Greenbrier United Methodist Churches; Nashville, Tennessee

This week's passages reflect an interesting space in the liturgical year. Yesterday the church celebrated the Reign of Christ Sunday, which announces the triumphant close of the church year with the affirmation that everything and everybody ultimately falls under the sovereignty of Christ. This coming Sunday is the first Sunday in Advent, when we begin the journey all over again, anticipating the proclamation of the mighty acts of God that find their fulcrum point in the Incarnation.

One approach to this interesting space between the Reign of Christ Sunday and the First Sunday in Advent comes in thinking about the liturgical colors for this week. From Monday through Saturday many churches will display white paraments that reflect the tone of victory proclaimed on the Reign of Christ Sunday, which began this week. However, our scripture passages are those for the First Sunday in Advent, a season of purple (or blue if you prefer). Among other reasons, purple in Advent reflects somberness related to repentance. Add to this the fact that on Thursday of this week in the United States, Americans will celebrate Thanksgiving, and we have another set of passages for that day. So, in the space of a week we're encouraged to be triumphant, thankful, and somber—quite an emotional journey to say the least.

In this liminal space between the triumphant ending and the mysterious beginning of the church year, with a national holiday that's not secular but also not a part of the worldwide Christian tradition, we have a powerful week that reflects the conflicting emotions we all feel from time to time. Remember it's human to be confused and conflicted in the seasons of life. Keep in mind that God provides deliverance and makes "the gateways."

Ever-present God, help me through the confusing emotions of life. Amen.

Yesterday I talked about this week in the church year reflecting the threshold times in our lives. Sometimes we find ourselves in transitions, which usually bring about a collision of emotions for most of us. Our passage for today reflects the agony of transition.

When we are on the boundary of one phase of our life that is giving way to another, we echo the words of our passage: "O, that you would tear open the heavens and come down, . . ." If God would just show up in dramatic fashion, we imagine our situations would all be better. We are like a small child on the first day of school saying either out loud or in his or her heart: "I want my mommy. I want my daddy." We all have security needs, and major changes feel threatening, even if the changes are for the better. I think it's healthy to express our childlike need for security, because the alternative is to repress it, which leads to greater emotional problems.

Two other ideas that present themselves in these words of lamentation reflect honest feelings but don't reflect an accurate appraisal of the situation. Both are directed toward God. First, the writer says in essence that God was angry and, as a result, the people sinned. This reminds me of one of my favorite sayings: "We don't see others as *they* are; we see others as *we* are." Sin, which primarily implies a wounded vision, keeps us stuck in the pattern of blaming others, including God. Second, in stating that nobody calls on God because God has hidden, two assumptions are made based on feelings that don't reflect reality. First, surely some still called on God—a reality that God, in another biblical story, shows Elisha when the prophet fell into similar discouragement. Second, God isn't hiding, but our emotions can make it seem that way.

God in the transitions, help me to see clearly as I try to release my fear. Amen.

Whether things start falling apart in our lives, it's natural to cry out to God. Anne Lamott in *Traveling Mercies*, says the two best prayers she knows are these: "Help me, help me, help me" and "Thank you, thank you, thank you." Psalm 80, a communal lament, in its original context referred to the disaster that befell the Northern Kingdom (Israel) when the Assyrian Empire destroyed the nation in the eighth century BCE.

Whether we are talking about personal, local, national, or international disaster, we want life to return to the way life was before catastrophe struck. In the meantime, we wait and wait, and wait some more. This psalm entered the Advent cycle of readings because it speaks to the agony of waiting for God when we feel discouraged and skewed in our thinking. We—like the psalmist—in our pain of getting what we didn't want assume that God is angry with us. We want to know when that anger will end, and we like to remind God that our humiliation and our suffering are the result of God's anger. Ah, we see the blame game at work once again.

So, if I'm correct in my interpretation, why do psalms of lament exist? The answer: They authentically and powerfully speak to our feelings. Scripture doesn't always give us right thinking, feeling, or actions. By allowing us to identify with universal human experience, scripture creates space within us to move beyond our current perspectives to find a deeper life-affirming response. For me, it's powerful to know that one of the translations for the Hebrew word that we in English render as "salvation" literally means "to create space": elbow room.

O God, the giver of space, help me work through life's catastrophes. May I remember to thank you always for your love and faithfulness to me. Amen.

Life is not fair; life is abundant." A woman I once thought that I would marry spoke these words to me. My desire for marriage with her didn't work out. Because it didn't work out, I lamented. We cry when we encounter the pains involved with living, and sometimes we find ourselves saying that life is not fair. When the relationship did not culminate in marriage and came to an end, I was tempted to blame myself, to blame her, to blame the circumstances around the situation. Nothing about the disappointment that came with the end of the relationship seemed fair. Maybe it wasn't fair. However, life was and is abundant. Endings are also beginnings.

Paul tells us that our generosity enriches us. That seems counterintuitive. How do we maintain abundance through giving away? I think it works this way: When generosity predominates in our lives, we resonate with the frequency of the goodness of creation through the Spirit and inwardly thanksgiving spontaneously becomes our modus operandi. We seek to be fair in our dealings with others; but when we focus too much on fairness rather than the fundamental abundance that exists in life, our hearts contract; we become shrill in tone; and we seek to blame.

This Thanksgiving, I'm now thankful for my terminated relationship with a woman I wanted to marry once upon a time. I learned so much from that relationship that has benefited me to this very day. Whether the end of that relationship was fair to her and/or me is not a question I entertain these days. I'm grateful for what was, for what is, and for what shall be. Life is abundant.

O God, remind me that life is not fair; life is abundant. Amen.

The apostle Paul's standard salutation in which he offers the blessing of God's grace and peace challenges us to rethink the meaning of *standard*. For many of us, the word *standard* means typical or ordinary. However, standard originally meant an emblem, such as a flag, that symbolized the highest and best attributes of a kingdom. As subjects in the kingdom of God, we claim the banner that speaks of grace and peace, attributes our world does not experience frequently enough. Many of us learned a long time ago that grace means "unmerited favor," and it does. However, it also means an arresting vision of beauty. Plotinus, an ancient Greek philosopher said, "The soul that beholds beauty becomes beautiful." From a biblical perspective, peace is not simply the absence of conflict; peace is a wholeness that integrates our lives and eliminates the divisions within. So, we are invited to accept the beauty and wholeness that is the reality of the kingdom of God.

I need the reminder that the foundational reality is that I am surrounded by beauty and wholeness. When I can live into that reality, like Paul, I can give thanks to God for others. I am not in competition with others. Like my brothers and sisters, I am enriched by life, strengthened to face whatever may come, and gifted by God to respond to others in loving exchanges. In the course of any given day we all face challenges that tempt us to see life as ugly and fractured. But that is a false vision. Don't misunderstand me. Yes, there are moments of ugliness and divisiveness in life, but those moments are not the ultimate truth. As Paul tells the Corinthians, God is faithful, and we will find strength to face those moments when we find ourselves doubting the absolute reality of grace and peace.

Gracious Creator, thank you for the beauty and wholeness that surrounds us. Amen.

I confess that the apocalyptic sections in the Gospels and elsewhere make me nervous, primarily because they have been so frequently abused down through the centuries in ways that have added to the world's mental, emotional, physical, and spiritual pain. I know this as a church historian and as a Christian who has experienced "rapture fever" firsthand. In my bathroom hangs a plaque that I bought a few years ago. It reads, "Live your life in faith, hope, and love." Unfortunately, some of the interpreters of the apocalyptic sections of the Bible have basically replaced the message of my plaque with this one: "Fear for your life in doubt, despair, and hatred."

Here is some of what I take away from our reading. Tomorrow, I'll address my biggest takeaway. First, after distressing circumstances, dramatic things happen. The passage seems to speak to the way catastrophe throws human systems into dire straits. Second, the Son of Man will return. As many of us say on a regular basis during The Great Thanksgiving of the Holy Communion liturgy: "Christ has died; Christ is risen; Christ will come again." Third, the lesson of the fig tree speaks to our need to be aware in life and not to bury our heads in the sand. Fourth, apocalyptic literature probably does not present literal facts; otherwise, verse 30 becomes problematic. Fifth, nobody, including the Son, knows when these things will happen. These things are hidden in the mind and heart of the Father.

God, may I live in faith, hope, and love. Amen.

FIRST SUNDAY OF ADVENT

Today, the First Sunday of Advent, we begin anew the journey of the church year. We may not pass "Go" and collect our two hundred dollars, but then again we are not playing Monopoly. We are living monotheism. Life finds meaning in relationship to God and to God's glorious creation. We are not trying to bankrupt others so that we can win the game. We are learning to live under this biblical mandate: Justice is the assurance for all persons of equal access to the goodness of God's creation.

For me, the biggest takeaway from this apocalyptic section of the Gospel of Mark is this: Just be awake! Not only does this apply to eschatology; this applies to life generally. We can sleep our way through life, remaining unaware of what really matters. In our negligence and indifference, we can become corrupt and corrupting. The alternative is to wake up and affirm the values of God's reign. As we enter the season of Advent today, we remember that Advent is a time of waiting and watching for the surprising work of God manifest in the Incarnation.

Athanasius, the great monk and theologian of antiquity, said, "God became human so that we might become divine." Advent reminds us to awaken to live out the image of God in our daily lives. As we begin the new church year on this first Sunday of Advent, perhaps the greatest practical value of apocalyptic literature is to remind us that life is not about business as usual. The stakes are high. What are you going to do right now with this one and only beautiful life you have?

God, awaken my spirit to live out the values of your kingdom here and now. Amen.

The One Who Changes Everything

DECEMBER 1–7, 2014 • JONATHAN C. WALLACE

SCRIPTURE OVERVIEW: Hopeful anticipation characterizes this week's texts. God's people have come to terms with their inability to save themselves. Isaiah 40 states that Jerusalem has "served her term" in bondage to sin; a new era is about to dawn. Psalm 85 continues the theme of old sins forgiven, emphasizing an urgent need for some fresh outbreak of God's initiatives. Harmonious and responsible relationships are to dominate the hearts of the people. Thoughts of righteousness and peace also pervade the passage from Second Peter. Yet the focus is clearly on Christ's Second Advent. His coming will be sudden and unannounced; the new creation will then appear. The Gospel text focuses on the earthly ministry of Jesus as John the baptizer comes to sensitize all hearts to the advent of the One promised long ago.

QUESTIONS AND THOUGHTS FOR REFLECTION

- Read Isaiah 40:1-11. God's word of comfort brings challenge as well. How are you preparing the way of the Lord?
- Read Psalm 85:1-2, 8-13. What glimpses of heaven in your daily life give you confidence in God's steadfast love?
- Read 2 Peter 3:8-15a. How are you using this time of Advent waiting to move toward more faithful living?
- Read Mark 1:1-8. What is the new thing that John the Baptizer could teach you? How will you get ready for the coming of the Christ child?

Pastor, Bethesda Presbyterian Church, Aberdeen, North Carolina

MONDAY, DECEMBER 1 ~ *Read Mark 1:1-8*

At this time every year, my kids love to go into the attic and bring down our family's nativity scene—a hand-knitted, child-friendly set of yarn figures my mother bought from a talented friend years before my kids were born. The fact that one child is in college while the others are well into their high school years has not dampened their enthusiasm in taking out and playing with these delightful and educational toys.

Every year I watch them as they unwrap each character: The baby Jesus, Mary and Joseph, the shepherds, the wise men, and all the animals. They then move the figures around until they get the scene just right. Yet every year as I look at this gentle scene, I am struck not so much by who is there as by who is missing. The fact is, I have never seen a Nativity scene, or any Christmas-themed scene, with John the Baptist in it. Not even once!

That's not how Mark sees it. The oldest Gospel does not begin with a manger. There are no stars, no shepherds, no wise men bearing gifts. It doesn't even begin in Bethlehem but in the desert, with a voice proclaiming that God is up to something new. John, echoing the voice of another wilderness prophet from centuries earlier, proclaims that God is on the move. It is time to get ready—not with decorations for our homes and offices but with a change of heart, a change of lifestyle, a change of life orientation.

Mark begins quickly and gets right to the point. He has little time for holiday niceties. As much as we treasure our scenes of heavenly peace, we run the risk of missing the point of Mark's message to us if we tarry there too long. We would do well to heed the Baptist's advice and clean up our lives a bit. After all, not just anyone is coming but the One who will change everything!

God of Advent expectation, may I not miss the point of your coming among us. Amen.

The One Who Changes Everything   397

We haven't heard John the Baptist's physical voice in two thousand years, yet in my more irreverent moods I imagine him sounding like one of those colorful parrots that some people keep as pets. One of the more fascinating characteristics of these birds is that they can actually speak. That talent is also one of their more annoying traits because they repeat the same words over and over again.

I've caught myself wondering from time to time if John knew any words other than *repent*. His message arrives right on time during the Advent season, reminding us of things we'd rather not think about during this festive season. But we don't want an honest telling of what God is up to, what is at stake, what it will cost, or how at risk we really are in the wake of this message. Yet in his time, John pierces through the uncertainty and suffering with a message that God has begun a new day. Things are going to change, and the one who comes after John will be the one who will make it all happen. This one, Jesus, will transform lives. The world as we know it will pass away. John tries to get our attention. *What* is coming and *who* is coming will make all things new and offer us a chance at the life God intended for us in the first place.

Maybe we are the parrots. *We* are the ones who keep repeating the same words, singing the same songs, and putting up the same decorations. *We* are the ones who appear to be stuck.

John presents no problem here. *We* are the problem. John brings the antidote. He reminds us that what we await is nothing less than justice being served, the poor being lifted up, and the rough places of inequity, unfairness, and selfishness being smoothed out. We want the same old thing. John is desperately trying to teach us something new.

O God, make me receptive to the newness you bring in this season to my life. Amen.

What better indicator of trouble in a relationship than the "silent treatment"? At least when we argue, we engage one another. But when we go silent—either because we don't care enough to confront the problems or because we are too angry, too hurt, or too tired to engage any further—it signals an ill-at-ease relationship. What will the other person say when he or she speaks to us again? Will there be words of hope, forgiveness, or apology?

In today's passage, God has been giving the people of Israel the silent treatment. In the first thirty-nine chapters, God lays out an overwhelming case against the people, charging them with indifference at best and downright rejection of God at worst. As a result of their infidelity to God, they lose the land and are carried off into exile. Then God goes silent. About 150 years pass between the end of chapter 39 and the first verses of chapter 40. Will the people ever hear from God again? If so, what will God say after all this time?

The first two verses of chapter 40, no doubt, contain the best news possible. After over a century of silence, God finally speaks. God speaks comfort, forgiveness, hope. The tone of the conversation totally changes. Despite all that has happened, God is willing to speak, tenderly, to the people at last. Bitterness, anger, hurt, and grief do not last. Comfort, hope, and forgiveness emerge as the conversation begins again.

What about us? Do we feel that God is giving us the silent treatment? Or is it we who are withholding our conversational intimacy with God? God speaks tenderly to God's people, offering forgiveness and hope. If it's been a long time since you've spoken to God, what will you say? If it's been a long time since you've heard God's voice, what do you think God is trying to say to you?

God, I long to hear your voice. Speak to me this day. Amen.

Have you ever read the ending of a book before you read the rest of it? Have you ever watched the last fifteen minutes of a film before seeing the rest of it? I confess to having done both. I do feel a bit like a cheater. However, when we know how a story will end, we read it from a different perspective. We can probe into and enjoy the subtleties and the nuances of the characters and the plot. Or maybe we can simply take comfort in knowing, for better or for worse, how it all works out.

The Second Letter of Peter is a small document near the back of the Bible that gets little attention. Yet, at this time of year when we focus on waiting for the fulfillment of God's promises, it offers good pastoral advice for us all. Peter reminds his troubled and confused congregation of an important fact: They already know the end of the story. God is not slow in fulfilling promises but proceeds at God's own pace. Unlike us, God is patient. The return of our Lord will come suddenly and without warning, but it will come. Because they know that God's plan will be fulfilled at the end of time, the rest of the story that is unfolding now makes a little more sense. Peter reminds them that God is in control of the future. Because that is true, they can face the difficulties that lie ahead in confidence and hope. They can busy themselves with being the people God created them to be in the first place, regardless of what the world may think of them at the moment.

The future resides in God's hands, which frees us to deal with *today*. There is no shortage of work to be done, and no shortage of love and good news to give. We have hope to share, a faith to proclaim, and compassion to spread. That will keep us busy as we await the time when righteousness truly is at home!

God of creation, may I stay busy doing your work of proclamation and compassion. I await your righteousness. Amen.

This time of year feels a lot like those long drives many of us take as a part of our family vacations. I've finally packed everything, herded the kids into the car, and gotten on the road. I relax and begin to enjoy the trip. That sense of peace does not last long, however. From the back of the car come the words that no parent wants to hear, "Are we there yet?"

Waiting is never easy, especially if you feel your very life might depend on what comes next. The community reading this epistle might fit into that category. They've heard the story. They've left their previous lives to come into community around the story of Jesus and his teachings. They've changed everything in anticipation of his return. The months turn into years, the years into decades. Where is he? When is he coming? Some have returned to their old lives.

The writer of Second Peter takes a more patient approach to his congregation than I do with my kids, but the message remains the same. The world will come to an end, and Christ will return when God decides—period. God's sense of time and perspective differs from ours, yet God is immensely patient. God wants no one left behind.

But since we cannot know God's timing, we can put the time we have to good use. We can live our lives in anticipation of history's fulfillment. We can do good, and do it well. We can let our actions and words reflect the hope that we have been given by the life, death, and resurrection of Jesus.

We have plenty left to do before the big day. Perhaps we should quit wondering where Jesus is and keep the light of love and welcome on in our hearts until he arrives. He'll get here when he gets here.

Jesus, my light of love and welcome is on. I await your salvation. Amen.

Despite the attempts of our culture to make this season a time of instant gratification in the here and now, I believe that the Advent and Christmas seasons, at their core, are a time to remember. In our families, we gather around the tree and hang ornaments that we made ourselves as children or that we bought to mark special occasions. Sometimes we bring out the photo albums and let the ghost of Christmas past have its way with us. We laugh at what we once looked like and remember those who can no longer be in our pictures in the present. What we most often do is tell stories. We do not want to forget those important times. We don't let those around us forget them either! We need those memories. We need them to remind us of who we are. We need them to strengthen the bonds of family, friendship, and community.

Most of all, we need them to remind us of what is important. That is what the singer of Psalm 85 does as he lifts his voice in worship. Before anything else is uttered, before any description of the situation is broached, the psalmist sings of what God has done for the people of Israel in the past. The psalmist reminds the people of their liberation at God's hand, of God's forgiveness, and God's unwillingness to have anger and bitterness be the last word. In order to face the present, the psalmist first calls the people to remember.

In Advent we remember the past hopes that were fulfilled and the promise made to Mary, Joseph, the shepherds, and the wise men. But we also live in the "not yet" of God's ultimate fulfillment. As the disappointments inevitably come, let us not succumb to spiritual amnesia. Above all, this season may we remember what God has done for us . . . and will do for us!

I recall your work on my behalf, O God. You have extended your graciousness to me, and I am grateful. Amen.

SUNDAY, DECEMBER 7 ~ *Read Psalm 85:8-13*

SECOND SUNDAY OF ADVENT

The Advent and Christmas seasons bring many images to our minds. We think of gentle scenes of snow or of bright stars in the sky. Some prefer to envision a crude crib and the tiny life nestled into it. Others see, and perhaps even believe in, the possibility of "peace on earth, goodwill to all people."

Psalm 85 gives us none of those things. However, Psalm 85 paints a picture; a vision; an artist's rendering, if you will, of what the kingdom of God looks like. It is a song of promise, and a reminder of what God has done for us in the past. Because of that past, we can rest confident in the future.

And what does that future look like? Verse 10 offers an image. There, the psalmist imagines the steadfast love and the faithfulness of God coming together with the people. They don't come to shake hands or to bow respectfully to one another. They come together and kiss. We can imagine the passionate kiss of lovers or the kiss of greeting of family and friends. With apologies to the movie *Casablanca*, a kiss is *not* just a kiss. A kiss is a tender, affectionate, vulnerable, and passionate expression of friendship, love, and peace. Perhaps that is why Judas's betrayal is so emotionally wrenching for us. To be betrayed with a kiss is the ultimate indignity.

But here, the vision of the future is of two people greeting each other with the most disarming expression of friendship. This peace is not simply the absence of violence. It is the presence of genuine affection and welcome.

It's not exactly greeting card material or something we will see in any Christmas play. But this image gives us a good idea of what God has in mind for us.

Jesus Christ, you come among us with disarming friendship and peace. We welcome you. Amen.

Witnesses to Grace

DECEMBER 8–14, 2014 • PAUL E. STROBLE

SCRIPTURE OVERVIEW: In Isaiah 61, the Anointed One declares a message of liberation. Justice, righteousness, and praise will blossom as new shoots of growth in the garden of the Lord. Psalm 126 remembers a time in the past when God's mercy broke forth in an unparalleled manner. The character of the community and of the individual members will be transformed. The First Thessalonians text voices a yearning for the "coming of our Lord Jesus Christ," yet the promise of the Second Advent has kindled great hope and gladness in the heart of the Christian community. The reading from the Gospel of John also raises the issue of the mood of expectancy that characterizes the period of time between promise and fulfillment.

QUESTIONS AND THOUGHTS FOR REFLECTION

- Read Isaiah 61:1-4, 8-11. What does God promise for the returning exiles? What are the short- and long-range blessings? How does Christ extend and fulfill those blessings?
- Read Psalm 126. What are the contrasting feelings of the people as they look to God's help? What kinds of sowing might we do today, during this Advent season and beyond?
- Read 1 Thessalonians 5:16-24. In this passage, what are the characteristics of Christ-followers? What does it mean to be "entirely sanctified"?
- Read John 1:6-8, 19-28. Why is it important that the Messiah be preceded by a witness? Among other aspects of Advent, how is the season important for witnessing to Christ?

Elder in the Illinois Great Rivers Conference, The United Methodist Church; freelance writer; teacher at Webster University; paulstroble.com

I enjoy finding interconnections in the Bible, not only prophecies and allusions but also themes that extend among biblical writings. One major theme is the destruction of Jerusalem in about 586 BC, the subsequent fifty-year exile of the people of Judah into Babylon, and their return to the land following the Persian conquest of Babylon. Imagine a land you love, destroyed by an invading enemy. Then that enemy is destroyed, and you can return to the land. You would have questions about God's providence, but you would also rejoice at God's blessings.

Jeremiah and Ezekiel warned that exile was God's judgment against the people's sins. But God, rich in mercy, willed to restore God's people. Isaiah 40–66 comes from those years of return to the land from exile. These writings communicate God's promises, reassurances, and images of restoration. Many of these writings, like Isaiah 61:1-4, extravagantly depict God's forthcoming blessings.

This prophet announces that he is anointed by God and empowered with God's spirit. Only one other prophet, Elisha, was anointed, so this prophet is special. And he is indeed eloquent; God's salvation and blessings are quite tangible. The oppressed, the brokenhearted, the captives and prisoners, the grief stricken and the weak—all receive the help they need. Not only that, but the ruined Israelite cities will be restored.

As years went by, the prophecies seemed unfulfilled or partially fulfilled. But Jesus quoted a portion of Isaiah 61:1-4 and announced it was fulfilled—in him (Luke 4:16-21). This Advent is a good time to ask: How does Jesus fulfill this scripture? What needs does he meet in his own time and ours? In what ways are we Christ's instruments of blessing and salvation in the world?

Lord, help us during this season to see your blessings now and to have the discernment to see your blessings as they continue to unfold. Amen.

Part of the power of leadership comes in the ability to articulate a vision that empowers people. From our vantage point, it seems that the prophet presses all the right buttons as he articulates God's future. He describes himself as adorned with God's righteousness like a fabulous outfit. We all know the feeling of getting dressed up for a nice occasion.

The prophet also assures the people of God's renewing the covenant. As Abraham had been promised many descendants, so were those who were returning from exile. In fact, their offspring will be renowned in the world and will be known as people whom God blesses and with whom God makes covenant.

The prophet assures the Israelites that the land itself will be fertile. God's righteousness will "spring up" in the world just as new growth returns to land that has been neglected and fallow. God's people were hoping for abundant crops, and they look to God for help.

The people counted on God's help as they rebuilt Jerusalem and the Temple and reestablished life and livelihood in the land. As described in Ezra and Nehemiah, the restoration wasn't as smooth and glorious as many hoped. Even by the time of Jesus, over four hundred years later, the people looked with hope toward God's future blessings.

Prophets are not always welcomed (Luke 4:24), and sometimes people feel disappointed about God's promises (Isa. 57:12; 58:2; 59:1). Perhaps for this reason the prophet speaks so confidently about God's blessings. Not only will God meet the Israelites' physical needs, but God will restore the covenant and cause righteousness, justice, and praise to grow.

Dear Lord, help us have confidence in the sureness of your blessings, even when they are delayed and life seems uncertain. Amen.

In my small church, the children's Sunday school classes met together for a devotion and a hymn or two, and then all the classes adjourned to their own rooms. In that setting, "Bringing in the Sheaves" was one of the first hymns I learned. Not being a farm kid, I didn't know what a "sheaf" was until a Sunday school teacher explained. Workers cut grain stalks by hand, tied them into sheaves (that is, bundles large enough to be carried), and stored them until they dried and could be threshed (that is, beaten to remove the grain from the stalks).

Bible commentators note that the weeping of verses 5 and 6 can be spiritual regret or sadness at life's difficulties or specifically the crisis of starvation. Biblical people couldn't run to the supermarket for bread; they had to grow their own; harvest was a life-or-death matter. Farmers could forestall hunger by eating seeds but chose instead to use them for sowing grain.

Like some of the other psalms, this one spans past and present. In verses 1-3, the psalmist reflects on the miracle of the exiles' return from Babylon. God's people have returned to their land because of God's great work. The psalmist then looks to God for another blessing: a good harvest. The evidence of God's past miracles gives confidence that God will bless the people in a more ordinary but urgent matter.

Because of that hymn, I always think of this psalm metaphorically, in terms of witnessing to Christ. The hymn refers to "sowing seeds of kindness," "sowing for the Master." There is an urgency to this kind of sowing too, no matter what the circumstances, for we are called to share Christ with others.

Dear God, what should we be sowing today, and what blessings should we expect? Amen.

This passage caused me grief when I was a young Christian. "Rejoice always, pray without ceasing, give thanks in all circumstances. . . . Do not quench the Spirit. . . . Hold fast to what is good; abstain from every form of evil." Some of these teachings seem straightforward, but I cringed at the difficulty. Am I supposed to be joyful all the time? Am I supposed to pray all the time? Am I supposed to be thankful about everything in my life, including the bad stuff? I made the mistake many Christians make when they view these qualities as matters of willpower and individual resolve for which we crank up inner fortitude and just do it.

Paul brings a different approach. God's Spirit helps us grow and upholds us when we fail. These qualities arise from relationship with God, which from our side is never perfect but which from God's side is always faithful.

Paul isn't addressing an individual here: he is addressing a church—individuals together who uphold, forgive, help, and nurture one another in a loving, forgiving fellowship. Paul describes a common life, as it were. He is not dispensing bits of advice that we're supposed to perform on our own.

Paul is also addressing an expectant church. A theme of First Thessalonians is the second coming of Jesus, about which that congregation had questions. Like the returning exiles to which Isaiah wrote, the church knew the promises of God but weren't sure how and when they would come true. Paul's teachings were gifts to an expectant congregation as they relied daily upon God's promises.

Dear God, during this season and beyond, help us love one another, pray, give thanks, and be joyful as we abide in your grace. Amen.

FRIDAY, DECEMBER 12 ~ *Read 1 Thessalonians 5:16-24*

Paul writes, "May the God of peace himself sanctify you entirely." *Sanctify* means "to make holy." Do we give much thought to holiness? Such a teaching either reminds us of our many flaws and faults or makes us think this promise is only for spiritual "athletes."

The good news is that holiness results in the growth of our character (which it partly is) *and* a receptiveness to God's blessings that lead to holiness. Although Paul often warns Christians not to fall back into sin and unrighteousness, he also stresses our current state of holiness by virtue of belonging to God and of God's power already present in our lives.

Holiness also means belonging to God. In the Isaiah passages God promises a renewed covenant, a covenant that carries with it an expectation of the people's holiness. The new covenant in Christ brings the same expectation. The New Testament also calls believers by the names of "saints" and "holy ones." We reflect God's own holiness, though in a human, imperfect way. Holiness implies purity (1 Cor. 6:9-20), love (4:13-21), and righteousness (Eph. 4:24).

So holiness comes as a gift but not without involvement on our part. God calls us to build people up rather than tearing them down; to pray for blessings for people who hurt us; to refrain from retaliating; to put away prideful feelings—a holy love.

We hear about wholistic foods and remedies. Paul's view of holiness expresses a wholistic approach: Discipleship isn't just a general feeling of spirituality but a body-spirit-soul soundness and blamelessness. God loves us, our whole selves, and hopes to fashion saints out of our imperfect elements.

Dear Lord, during this season help us to grow in your likeness and will. Amen.

A s you read today's scripture, skim the whole section of John 1:1-18. This passage contains rich ideas about God, Jesus, and the universe. But notice that within the deeply philosophical language, the author "plops" these three verses about John the Baptist. These verses seem to interrupt the flow of the section. Why are statements about John inserted here?

The Gospel writer wants to indicate right away how John the Baptist bore witness to Jesus. In case anyone wonders whether John the Baptist himself is God's light, the Gospel reminds us that as great as John was, his ministry served the purpose of alerting people to the light that was *coming* to the world, so that people might believe.

In Genesis 1 we read that God speaks Creation into being. The ancient Greeks believed that the *logos* (the Word) was God's rationality that formed the universe's orderly plan. The Gospel also affirms that God's *logos* "became flesh and dwelt among us." The word *dwelt* calls to mind the way God's presence dwelt among the Israelites in the Tabernacle (Exodus 25–40). The Gospel's first chapter brings all these ideas together.

But people might misunderstand who Jesus is. In fact, they did misunderstand! But God always sends people like Isaiah, Jeremiah, and other prophets to announce God's will and purposes. Jesus needs John to appear ahead of him and to tell people that when Jesus appears, he will indeed be the light of the world for their salvation.

John the Baptist will never appear in a manger scene, but in John's Gospel he properly belongs at the beginning of Jesus' story, as the great announcer of God's light and Word.

Dear Lord, the light is coming into the world. Give us eyes to see and witnesses to show us. Amen.

SUNDAY, DECEMBER 14 ~ *Read John 1:19-28*

THIRD SUNDAY OF ADVENT

The Swiss theologian Karl Barth (1886–1968) wrote many books. Above his desk hung a reproduction of Matthias Grünewald's painting of the Crucifixion, which Barth thought about as he wrote his theology.

The painting starkly depicts the cross's horizontal beam bent under the weight of the sins Jesus bore. Mary, Mary Magdalene, and (anachronistically) John the Baptist stand beside the cross. Barth praised John's key role in the painting. His standing position artistically draws us from his figure to the body of Christ, and John's long, pointing finger directs us to Christ's wounded, suffering body. This is John's purpose, to draw people's attention to Christ. Barth saw his own role—and our role—in the same way, as pointers to Christ. Jesus bears our sins and problems, not only straining under their weight but also bearing them in the ravages of his body.

Our scripture text reads like a guessing game, wherein we're supposed to figure out what the person is thinking about. John confesses freely that he is not the Christ. So is he Elijah? No. Is he a prophet? No. John bears witness to the one who is to come, the one who makes the impressive John seem a mere servant.

John's answer brings our week's scriptures full circle, back to those post-exilic times of Isaiah 40–66, where the prophet seeks to comfort the people with God's promises. John affirms that he is the voice (unidentified in the original Isaiah 40:3-11) who calls for the way to be made straight for the Lord. On this third Sunday of Advent, we think about the continuing lead-in to Jesus' birth and all the promises of God that become fulfilled in him.

Dear Lord, as we approach Christmas Day, show us ways we can witness to the Savior. Amen.

Witnesses to Grace   411

Living on the Edge of Promises

DECEMBER 15–21, 2014 • JOHN INDERMARK

SCRIPTURE OVERVIEW: Second Samuel 7 extols Yahweh's choice of the family of David as the extraordinary vehicle for divine salvation. God now plans to do a new and unparalleled thing in the life of humankind. Mary's song of wonder from Luke 1 serves as the psalm lection. It centers on her realization that human life will now never be the same. In the epistle reading, Paul rejoices that by the power of God the times are what they are. In the Gospel text, Gabriel announces to Mary that she will bear the "Son of God." Overwhelmed by both the holiness and the enormity of the moment, Mary nonetheless consents to the will of God as brought by God's messenger.

QUESTIONS AND THOUGHTS FOR REFLECTION

- Read 2 Samuel 7:1-11, 16. What presumptions of things you may want to "do for God" need to be tempered or transformed by what God seeks to do for or through you?
- Read Luke 1:46b-55. What has unleashed such joy toward God—and hope for God's transformation of this world—as you hear in Mary's song? What do you find most personally challenging in her words?
- Read Romans 16:25-27. Where in this season of Advent do you experience and need God's strengthening of your life? What might God be strengthening you to do?
- Read Luke 1:26-38. In what areas of life do you most need to hear and take to heart the angel's encouragement not to be afraid and "nothing will be impossible with God"? What might "let it be with me according to your word" open you and your congregation to this Advent and Christmas?

Currently visiting associate pastor, the Church of the Holy Cross, Hilo, Hawaii; writer, retired United Church of Christ minister; living in Naselle, Washington

We are almost there: "there," in the particulars of this season, being Christmas. We are but a few short days away from the promise kept of a Child born for all God's children. But in the broader vision of faith, of which Christmas is a signpost, we are also almost there: "there" being the final coming of God's promised realm. The word *Ad-vent* literally means "coming toward" and embraces both the Child-King born in a manger and the Sovereign Lord who will usher in history's end—and the new creation's beginning. We are almost there.

Do you believe that? Do you believe you live on the edge of such promises—and if so, where does your life evidence those promises?

Mary stands poised on that edge in today's verse. Promises have been offered. A choice must be made. Imagine someone standing on the edge of a high-dive platform beside a pool for the first time. A deep breath is taken. Will the step forward be taken: into the rush of air speeding by, not knowing exactly what the feel of striking water from this height will be, not sure how deep she will plunge before breaking back to the surface? "Here am I," Mary whispers, ". . . let it be with me according to your word." With that, Mary steps off into the sheer air of trust, a headlong descent—or is it ascent?—into a lifelong experience of what it means to live in trust of God's promises.

Advent bids us live on the edge of promise turning to fulfillment: not just by singing carols and reciting creeds; but rather, like Mary, by the gracious abandonment of who we are into the depth of holy possibilities of who we might yet be. "Here am I. . . . let it be with me."

Here am I, O God. What word, what promise, would you have me "let it be" this Advent? Amen.

It is easy to get things out of order. Unreal expectations for long-planned holiday gatherings can distort the actual experience of being with others. Hours spent seeking the perfect gift for those special someones can obscure the time we have to spend with them. What we would *do* for others can cause us to lose track of who we *are* to others.

Consider David. By now a man of considerable power and upward mobility, David feels sorry for God. After all, David lives in a cedar house while God dwells in a tent. Poor God.

So David resolves to fix God's "problem." The prophet Nathan initially says have at it—until God comes to Nathan at night. God informs Nathan to remind David, in essence: Let's keep things in order. God is a God of movement, so a tent will do just fine for now. David's royal decision to determine what God needs presumes too much. What David presumes he can *do* for God causes him to lose track of who he *is* to God.

Does that ever happen to you? Does all the doing and busyness of faith-works for God's sake occasionally obscure who you are to God?

Out of our feelings of self-importance (or the lack thereof), we may feel obligated to keep God happy by what we do. But God holds us in favor long before we say "yes" or "no" to all the things we can and cannot accomplish. That gracious truth also plays out in how we experience our relationships with friends and family in this season of Advent. We need to ground all the "doing for" others in the sheer joy and grace we experience simply by being in relationship with them. The "doing" is not the means, but the consequence, of relationship.

How will you put "who you are to" others and God ahead of "what you do for" others and God this season?

Have you ever had life and plans disrupted by the unexpected? Falling in love can do that. So can the onset of illness—or the receipt of a pink slip at work. Or, in the case of Mary, ordinary plans (engagement) in an ordinary place (Nazareth in Galilee) are interrupted by the extraordinary. "Greetings, favored one! The Lord is with you."

Luke informs his readers that the speaker is Gabriel but nowhere indicates that Mary knows this. For all we know, she takes him to be a stranger. In any event, she takes his words as strange. Luke describes her reaction as "perplexed." And why not? Gabriel speaks to her out of the blue with no preparation— only with an invitation to set fear aside and to take in the word that she has found favor (the word is more often translated as "grace") with God.

Consider where Mary stands in this moment and how that might relate to your place and possibilities this Advent. Longstanding plans, arranged by yourself or others, take a sudden turn to the unexpected. Life as it has been may never be the same. Initially, that fact stirs perplexity and fear. But then comes the promise: "You have found favor." The very favor that disrupts Mary promises the grace that will companion her.

We may experience the season of Advent, and indeed the whole journey of faith, in just such a way. Does the birth for which we prepare simply repeat yet another annual rerun of pious wishful thinking? Or does it take us, with Mary, to the edge of life that will never be the same? Do the fears that haunt and perplex us find antidote in the assurance of God's gracious favor for our lives, a favor that will take incarnate shape in a cooing infant?

"Do not be afraid, . . . for you have found favor with God."
How will you receive and live the gift of those words?

Now to God who is able to strengthen you." When have you last experienced God's strength in your life? In a friend's voice, in a stranger's help, in a word of scripture's assurance, or in [_____]. (You fill in the blank.)

Relying on the strength of others has become passé in some circles. Whether in the counsel to pump iron for our muscles or to inflate self-reliance unencumbered by compassion, we live in a society of changing values. Our society seemingly values more what we can do for ourselves and devalues those who cannot do for themselves. To be sure, the latter is ofttimes phrased in the pejorative "will not do for themselves"—with the presumption that we can see into the wills and hearts of others with Godlike perspective so as to levy such gospel-less assessment.

But as we have seen and will continue to see, in the lives and words of the characters who people these passages in the fourth week of Advent: We do not live unto ourselves nor by our own strength alone. For Mary, for David, and for all the rest of us who would discern what it means to live on the edge of holy promises, we come to see that reliance on God and the strength God imparts are what saves us. Such reliance saves David from the presumption that life revolves around him and what he presumes he can do, even for the likes of God. It saves Mary from the fear and perplexity that might otherwise hold her back from accepting that she is favored by God. God's strength, not our own, saves us from similar presumptions and fears in our own lives. Advent beckons us to trust that God's favor embraces and empowers us and all. For God is able to strengthen.

Strong and gracious God, may I find your strength to live with hope and grace. Amen.

Promises can be disarming. David comes armed with the plan that he will build God a house. God counters with the revelation that housework belongs to God.

Bayith, the word translated as "house" in this passage, has multifaceted meaning. While it can mean "house," as in a place or domicile, it can also mean one's household and family members—and in a broader sense, a "dynasty." The phrase "house of David" does not have in mind what can be found at a certain street address. It encapsulates the promise spoken to David in this passage—a promise that reminds the king where sovereignty ultimately resides. David's house will finally stand or fall on the grace of God's promises rather than by the edge of David's sword.

A freedom accompanies this promise of *bayith* to David. It is not the freedom of libertinism, whereby David or his successors can do whatever they please. The later prophets of Judah and Israel will excoriate succeeding kings for presuming on this promise as a sort of inoculation against regime change.

Rather, God's promise to David bestows the freedom of living by the grace of covenant. That is, David's "house" is not secured by whatever he can scheme and grasp but by what God graciously offers: "The Lord will make you a house."

What if we heard in God's promise to David the pledge of grace to establish our "houses"? What would change if we felt free from continual striving to make ourselves acceptable to God by receiving such acceptance up front? We will expend much energy in these coming days to prepare our houses for Christmas. May God's promises to David remind us that the inverse is true: The promised gift of Christmas prepares our "houses" for the coming days.

What renovations might God have in mind for your "house" in this season of Advent?

Nothing will be impossible with God." We may hear those words most every Advent. Familiarity can be a good thing—unless, as the saying goes, it breeds contempt. I doubt that many hold these particular words in contempt, though I would not be surprised if we hear them with incredulity. "Nothing will be impossible" can be a hard word to swallow when a child is killed by a drunk driver or years of working for reform in social and political life leaves us more convinced that "you can't fight city hall" than in the possibility of all good things.

Advent will soon draw to a close. A baby will be born. A manger filled with straw will once more be stowed away in the church attic until next year. Candles will be lit and then extinguished. Visits and dinners will take place, and then leavetakings for home will be made.

But where exactly will be home—in the wake of these stories and carols, in the light of this week's characters of Mary, of David, and Nathan? And most of all, where will be home for us when it comes to the God who comes to us and for us?

On a car navigation system, you can set "home" by assigning a default address. Hit the screen link to "home," and you will get your directions.

At the end of his encounter with Mary, Gabriel sets the default value for "home" for Mary—and for any of us who would dare live on the edge of God's promises this season. "Nothing will be impossible with God." God's possibilities are our home.

Do you believe that? And more important, do you hope and thus live that here and now? If so, let the word of Mary be your homing prayer:

"Here am I, the servant of the Lord; let it be with me according to your word." Amen.

SUNDAY, DECEMBER 21 ~ *Read Luke 1:46b-55*

FOURTH SUNDAY OF ADVENT

Have you ever brought so much excitement or anticipation to some promised event that you just couldn't keep from smiling, or laughing, or singing? Weddings can do that. Reunions with long-separated but much beloved friends can do that. And births can do that: lighting up our faces, unleashing voices in torrents of words that try their best to keep up with the rush of joy.

So it is that Mary, standing with Elizabeth on the edge of promises soon to unfold in coming births, launches into song. Mary's song sounds the same notes of hope and justice and compassion once sung by a barren woman named Hannah unleashed by her son, Samuel. It is thus a song deeply rooted in Israel's hymnody. But as Mary sings this song in celebration of God's saving and topsy-turvy, world-rearranging promises, she does so with such confidence that her language, grammatically speaking, is not future tense but past tense. It is as if, peering over the edge of God's promises, she sees them as already having come to pass. God "has shown strength . . . has scattered the proud . . . has brought down the powerful . . . has filled the hungry with good things." It's already happened; it's in the bank!

Now we could suggest that Mary rein it in a bit. It's plain to see that there is an appropriate way to move toward the fulfillment of those promises. But Mary's grammar of bringing future-tense hopes into past-tense assertions is the grammar of faith. It resembles the Easter hymn, "The Strife Is O'er, the Battle Done." We acknowledge the great strife and numerous battles ahead, but the hymn's lyrics, as with Mary's lyrics, understand something crucial: the trustworthiness of God's promises.

Because of that trustworthiness, like Mary, we can't help but sing!

What is your favorite carol of Christmas joy? Sing it and pray it now in celebration and hope.

Living on the Edge of Promises   419

Where Heaven and Earth Meet

DECEMBER 22–28, 2014 • JAN L. RICHARDSON

SCRIPTURE OVERVIEW: This week's passages not only announce the coming of the King but also project the nature of the divine rule. The Gospel lesson is the engaging story from Luke 2:1-20. In Isaiah 9:2-7, the new king is welcomed with all the trumpetry surrounding an important royal birth or coronation, but the text then points to the ascendancy of "justice" and "righteousness." Psalm 96 echoes that expectation, even as it looks beyond any human king to the rule of King Yahweh. Luke jolts us by its juxtaposition of the figures of King Jesus, wrapped in bands of cloth, and the Emperor Augustus, ordering the census of the people. Titus 2:11-14 celebrates not only the King who has come but him who will come again. The texts urge their readers to celebrate the coming of the King and the dawning of the kingdom, as well as to prepare for the return of One whose rule is both "already" and "not yet."

QUESTIONS AND THOUGHTS FOR REFLECTION

- Read Isaiah 9:2-7. What word of hope and freedom does God need to speak to you?
- Read Psalm 148. Where do you see Christ at work restoring creation? How do you help with that restoration?
- Read Titus 2:11-14. How will you "wait" in these remaining days of Advent?
- Read Luke 2:1-20. What will you treasure in your heart from this season of Advent and Christmas?

Artist, writer, and ordained minister in The United Methodist Church; author of such books as *In the Sanctuary of Women* and *Night Visions*; director, The Wellspring Studio, LLC; retreat leader and conference speaker, often collaborating with her husband, the singer/songwriter Garrison Doles

While we wait. In his letter to Titus, Paul captures the central theme of the Advent season: waiting, anticipating, preparing for the One who is to come. We often experience waiting as a passive and powerless state, a condition that compels us to be idle until our circumstances shift. Paul's words in his letter to Titus indicate he would find such a notion foreign. There is work to do, Paul tells us, while we wait for Christ.

For Paul, waiting means that we do not merely *bide* our time but that we *abide* in time in a godly way. Waiting provides the opportunity to put to use what we learned from Christ in his first appearing, so that we may be, as Paul describes it, "a people of [Christ's] own who are zealous for good deeds."

The zeal that Paul describes is not the same as frenzied activity; it is not the busyness that often typifies the Advent season. We may journey through these days burdened by expectations—our own or those of others—and then wonder why we arrive at December 25 disappointed and exhausted. Or we may carry losses that make the holidays so painful that we spend the season wishing it were over, and so throw ourselves into anything that will distract or numb us.

As we enter into Christmas week, we take time to ask ourselves if the way that we have spent the past days of Advent is the way we want to spend the Advent days that remain. Whatever this season has been for us, there is still time to practice the art of waiting in the way that Paul invites: to both work and to rest in the Christ whom Paul describes as "the grace of God," who imbues our waiting and who inhabits it with us.

May you know the grace of God in your waiting. In your anticipating, in your preparing, in your working, in your resting: may this day draw you closer to the Christ who is our hope.

There is a beautiful notion that comes to us from the Celtic tradition: that in the physical landscape and in the turning of the year, there are thin places. In a thin place, the veil between worlds becomes permeable. Heaven and earth meet, and we glimpse what lies at the end of all our waiting.

Many people find thin places at pilgrimage sites such as Iona. Thin places can also appear in the landscape of time, in particular days or seasons that deepen our awareness of the presence of the holy. In a thin place, God is not somehow more there than in other places and times. Rather, something about a thin place causes a veil within us to fall away, and we become more present to the God who is always present to us.

In his telling of the birth of Jesus, Luke describes a stunning space where heaven and earth meet with such power that the world will never be the same. Each Christmas, when we hear the story of Jesus' birth, we are invited to enter this thin place once again; to allow the mystery and wonder of the Incarnation to envelop us and to meet anew the God who comes to us.

We may find our eye drawn to the drama in Luke's story; when heaven and earth meet, it is indeed an occasion of glory. Yet a thin place doesn't require the presence of angels. Such a place has a quality more like the one that Luke evokes later in this passage when he tells how "Mary treasured all these words and pondered them in her heart."

What marks a thin place is not how dramatic it is but how quiet it makes us and how it invites us to pause and pay attention; how it opens our heart to the Christ who seeks to be born anew in us.

In the landscape of this day, in the terrain of these hours, may you find a thin place to ponder, a treasure to open your heart.

WEDNESDAY, DECEMBER 24 ~ *Read Isaiah 9:2-7*

CHRISTMAS EVE

In a thin place, time is not tidy. The sensation of time passing sometimes falls away entirely; distinctions among past, present, and future become blurred. In those places where heaven and earth meet, we glimpse what lies beyond the limits of chronology and touch the realm where everything comes together in fullness and is made whole.

Here on the cusp of Christmas, in the final hours of our waiting, the scripture plays with time's boundaries. It draws us deep into old, old layers of God's story as we prepare to welcome the Christ who comes again—and anew—into our midst. Today's scripture opens wide a door between the Old Testament and the New as it reaches back in time, using words from the prophet Isaiah to help us celebrate the birth of Christ. "The people who walked in darkness have seen a great light," the prophet proclaims. "For a child has been born for us . . . and he is named Wonderful Counselor, Mighty God, Everlasting Father, Prince of Peace." This text from Isaiah stands on its own as one of the most beautiful passages in the Hebrew Bible, speaking a word of hope and freedom that the people of Isaiah's time needed to hear. On this Christmas Eve, we who follow Christ can also claim this ancient text, turning toward Isaiah's words to help illuminate the Incarnation.

Millennia later, Isaiah reminds us that the longing for light is an ancient longing. The craving for freedom abides across the ages. In a world where the forces of violence, ignorance, and despair can make it difficult to perceive God's presence, we claim Isaiah's words as we welcome Christ our Light, who comes into our midst again this night.

When the night is at its darkest, may we open our eyes to the Christ who comes: Christ our Light, Christ our Peace, our God both ancient and new.

THURSDAY, DECEMBER 25 ~ *Read John 1:1-14*

CHRISTMAS DAY

No shepherds. No angels. No wise men. No Mary or Joseph. No journey to Bethlehem, no manger, no star. We could not construct a nativity set from the elements that John gives us in the prologue to his Gospel. Yet this telling of the Christmas story shimmers with poetry and mystery. In John's opening verses, we can already glimpse his penchant for thin places, for drawing our attention to the Christ in whom heaven and earth meet with such brilliance and beauty.

"In the beginning," John writes as he welcomes us into his story. With this phrase, John opens a doorway to another book that begins in the same manner. John wants us to remember the opening words of Genesis, wants to evoke that space where there once was only darkness and chaos until God spoke and, word by word, began to articulate Creation, to word the world into being.

This same God, John tells us, became the Word among us.

And this Word was life. And this Word was light.

And the darkness did not overcome it.

John gives us a tale of the Incarnation in a manner that lays it bare, that pares it down to its essence. His story is both utterly simple and rich with divine mystery. For all its simplicity, it is a story that we will, in this life, never completely understand. But on this Christmas Day, we are given a treasure, a gift beyond price: a glimpse of the thin place where heaven and earth meet in Jesus, the Christ both ancient and new, the child who will name us as children of God. "And we have seen his glory," we sing with John this day. Full of grace and truth.

May Christ the Word become flesh in you. May heaven and earth meet in you. May the light of Christ shine forth in you this day and all days; the love of Christ illuminate you this night and every night.

In his book *Anam Cara: A Book of Celtic Wisdom*, John O'Donohue shares an idea for a short story he hoped to write. At the heart of the story was the notion that in the course of our whole life, we would meet just one other person. O'Donohue's idea prompts compelling questions. If we could meet only one person, how would we prepare? What practices would we undertake in order to become ready for such an encounter?

In today's reading we meet two people who have devoted their lives to this kind of preparation. Simeon and Anna have oriented their entire beings toward waiting, to making ready for the One they knew would come. When Mary and Joseph bring the infant Jesus to Jerusalem in order to present him at the Temple, Simeon and Anna are there; Simeon, drawn by the Holy Spirit "who rested on him"; Anna, who has spent much of her life living at the Temple—a thin place in itself. Having long practiced the art of waiting, Anna and Simeon are so prepared that when they see the child whom Mary and Joseph bring, each of them recognizes Jesus. Their years of anticipation have come to an end. Waiting gives way to welcome as they greet him with blessings and with joy.

The quality of intention that Anna and Simeon bring to their waiting is much the same as O'Donohue evoked in the idea for his story. Christ calls us to this kind of anticipation. How do we prepare ourselves so that, like Anna and Simeon, we will recognize Christ when he shows up in the people who cross our path? How will we make ourselves ready to welcome him, not just at Christmas but in all the ways he will appear in the days to come?

In this and every season, may your eyes be open to see the face of Christ; your ears be open to hear the voice of Christ; your heart be open to welcome Christ; your hands be open to bless Christ in everyone you meet.

When a thin place appears in our path, it comes as an amazing gift. Whether the thin place appears in a physical landscape or in the terrain of time, as at Christmas, it assures us that God is with us, and earth is not all there is.

Yet a thin place is not meant to be a permanent dwelling. It is not a space where we can linger forever. Like the disciples who accompanied Jesus up the mountain on the day of his transfiguration, we learn that such places are for taking off our shoes in awe and wonder, not for building a home.

In today's reading, Isaiah offers a song of joy in praise of the messenger who comes to proclaim peace. We celebrate Christ as the one who comes bringing news and announcing salvation, the Christ who heals and redeems what lies in ruins. We too are meant to be messengers. God does not desire us to remain forever in the thin place that Christmas offers. Instead, God urges us to move our feet and go forth from this place. To walk into the world bearing the Word whom we have met in this season. To enter into the ruined places and announce peace.

Christmas can feel like an ending. Yet in the rhythm of the liturgical year, it not only extends for a season—twelve days, ending with Epiphany on January 6—but is a place of beginning again, of setting out anew. God draws us into the thin place of Christmas in order to send us into the world, bearing the message of what we have seen.

May this day be a day of beginnings, this season a time to enter anew into the grace of Christ who is our hope and the joy of Christ who is our peace. May you bear the good news everywhere you go, and may heaven and earth meet in you with gladness.

The Christmas story is not one of God's being born simply for my personal benefit. The Incarnation somehow transforms the world, alters the cosmos, breaks down the barriers between us. In taking on flesh, Christ draws us into relationship with the whole of creation that he is working to restore.

Psalm 148 is a hymn of praise composed for the creation, this cosmos that is our home. The psalm calls us to lift our voices not just with our other humans but also with the heavens, the sun and moon, the animals and elements, the entire natural world.

I pray this psalm often with my sisters and brothers in Saint Brigid of Kildare Monastery, a community that draws from Methodist and Benedictine traditions. It's among the psalms that we pray at Lauds, one of the morning offices in the Liturgy of the Hours. Each time we return to these words, I feel invited to pray not only with the members of the community but with all of creation: the cosmos that God both created and entered fully in the person of Christ.

The vision of wholeness we find in Psalm 148 can seem at odds with the brokenness that persists in our world. Even at Christmas—and perhaps especially now—we can find it overwhelming to see the pain that still pervades creation. We may wonder what difference the birth of Christ made. Psalm 148 offers a hymn of profound hope that we, as people of the Incarnation, need to claim: that amid the brokenness, God perpetually seeks to bring us into relationship—with God, with one another, with all that God has created. In these lines, the psalmist asks us not to ignore the pain of the world but to turn toward it with full voices, singing our way toward the restored creation that the psalm anticipates and calls forth.

May the voice of creation be one voice, the song of creation be one song in praise of the God who was, who is, and who will come again.

What God Imagines

DECEMBER 29-31, 2014 • CAROLYN WHITNEY-BROWN

SCRIPTURE OVERVIEW: This week's readings invoke praise and thanksgiving to God for God's outrageous generosity in the gift of Jesus Christ. The readings all contrast that generosity with the situation of humanity apart from God's intervention. Jeremiah 31:7–14 portrays for us a people in exile, a people for whom despair and grief seem to be the only option. The apparent eternity of winter's grasp dominates Psalm 147:12–20, with its picture of God sending "snow like wool" and "frost like ashes." Common to both of these texts is not only the assertion of human helplessness and hopelessness apart from God, but also the proclamation that God has already invaded the world and caused a new world to come into being.

QUESTIONS AND THOUGHTS FOR REFLECTION

- Read Jeremiah 31:7-14. If you could imagine a great "homecoming" of people, what would it look like? Who would be there? What would they be doing?
- Read Psalm 147:7-14. Sing to the Lord with thanksgiving. What aspects of God's creation most delight you?
- Read John 1:1-18. Imagine God as the Word, as uncreated Light, as the Life from which all life comes. Imagine God, mystical and beyond imagining. Now ask God these questions: "How do you imagine me? How do you imagine us, the human family?" Imagine how human community might appear to God.

Writer, United Church of Canada McGeachy Scholar, faculty member of St. Jerome's University at University of Waterloo; living on Vancouver Island in Canada

Jeremiah, in an unusual burst of good cheer and optimism, describes the joyous return of people long exiled—those far from home; those displaced long ago; those who are socially marginalized or who find travel difficult, who are blind or lame or with child or even in labor. God will bring them home.

It took me a long time to understand the meaning of scripture passages about straight paths. As the daughter of a geographer, I wondered what God had against topography. *Why did God want to exalt valleys and bring mountains low?*

Only later, when I lived in community with people who walk with difficulty and are often excluded from society, God's imagination seized my own. The point is that everyone can be together, in what Jeremiah calls "a great company."

Some spiritual disciplines only make sense in specific contexts. For example, when we are unemployed, we find our value and identity in our relationships and in our unpaid contributions to our community. When we are exiled, we learn to find God's presence in strangers, to meet God in any landscape on earth, and to make a home for ourselves and others wherever we are. But Jeremiah's imagery requires no self-discipline, positive thinking, or internal spiritual practices. Jeremiah describes God's initiative in gathering everyone to return home.

The unabashedly emotional scene depicts exiles who return with weeping, then with radiance, with dancing and rejoicing. There will be joy and gladness.

And God's vision doesn't stop there. God imagines for the human family living on this delicate, beautiful planet a life as abundant and effortless as a watered garden, a big homecoming party, a radiant intergenerational dance.

God, open our hearts to see the world and your people the way you see us. Amen.

The last days of the year are a curious time. As a couple of charitable businessmen pointed out to Scrooge in a book written almost 170 years ago, it is a season when abundance rejoices and want is keenly felt.

We find it difficult to acknowledge that we have enough when advertisers insist that these days after Christmas offer the best bargains of the year. Even those of us who strive to live simply feel uncertain about whether to shop for next year's supplies now, while they are half-price. It is a thick time—socially, emotionally, spiritually, materially. Our hearts find no rest.

Into this strangely unsettled time come these words of Jeremiah and the psalmist, who at God's insistence state, "My people shall be satisfied with my bounty." What a remarkable thought to ponder in our hearts on December 30.

The psalmist takes us far from post-Christmas sales, reminding us to make melody to God. Music does not buy or sell. We do not own it. Music happens in time, and we do not need to possess it. We simply rest and experience happiness through fleeting moments of melody.

The psalmist tells us to pay attention to how God covers the heavens with clouds, prepares rain for the earth, makes the grass grow on the hills, and gives animals their food. All this activity reflects God's love. God delights in those who notice, who shape their lives around the hope offered in that steadfast love. If we could decide not to crave more, there could be peace.

God, open our hearts to see and hear and delight in your bounty, to find peace in our borders and satisfaction with the finest wheat. Amen.

Whenever discouragement threatens to paralyze us, we may return to this passage over and over again. The Light shines in the darkness, and the darkness has not overcome it. "In the beginning was the Word, and the Word was with God, and the Word was God. . . . All things came into being through him." Over nearly two thousand years, John's words reach us, telling us of God's creative energy. This huge vision uses words to try to describe the Word who created everything. John goes on to explain that what has come into being through the Word is life, which is the light of all people.

It's a deep and mystical vision of God, the uncreated Word, the light and life of all things. Then, in case this concept seems too abstract, remote, or impersonal, John jumps to the heart of the Christian life: The Word became flesh and lived among us. God's own life was in this world, full of grace and truth.

Scientists speak the same language as John: All life is made possible by the original light of the sun. The gentle glow of the baby in the manger calls us to life. Jesus does not call us *out of* this world of light and darkness but joins us *in* this world, inviting us to live fully and without fear. We may find it tempting to deny the truth of our world: the painful injustices, the enormous suffering, the damage humans have done to God's exquisite creation. But the light that shines in the darkness is full of grace and truth, which go together. We need not fear or deny the truth of the world.

On the eve of this new year, John calls us back to the beginning. The Word became flesh and loved and laughed in his own historical moment. May we live fully in the time and place where God has called us.

God, open our hearts to see your divine light, to discover the fullness of grace that you see. Amen.

The Revised Common Lectionary* for 2014
Year A – Advent / Christmas Year B
(Disciplines Edition)

January 1-5

NEW YEAR'S DAY
Ecclesiastes 3:1-13
Psalm 8
Revelation 21:1-6*a*
Matthew 25:31-46

January 6

EPIPHANY
(may be used on January 5)
Isaiah 60:1-6
Psalm 72:1-7, 10-14
Ephesians 3:1-12
Matthew 2:1-12

January 6-12
BAPTISM OF THE LORD
Isaiah 42:1-9
Psalm 29
Acts 10:34-43
Matthew 3:13-17

January 13-19
Isaiah 49:1-7
Psalm 40:1-11
1 Corinthians 1:1-9
John 1:29-42

January 20-26
Isaiah 9:1-4
Psalm 27:1, 4-9
1 Corinthians 1:10-18
Matthew 4:12-23

January 27–February 2
Micah 6:1-8
Psalm 15
1 Corinthians 1:18-31
Matthew 5:1-12

February 3-9
Isaiah 58:1-12
Psalm 112:1-10
1 Corinthians 2:1-16
Matthew 5:13-20

February 10-16
Deuteronomy 30:15-20
Psalm 119:1-8
1 Corinthians 3:1-9
Matthew 5:21-37

February 17-23
Leviticus 19:1-2, 9-18
Psalm 119:33-40
1 Corinthians 3:10-11, 16-23
Matthew 5:38-48

February 24–March 2

THE TRANSFIGURATION
Exodus 24:12-18
Psalm 99
2 Peter 1:16-21
Matthew 17:1-9

March 3-9

FIRST SUNDAY IN LENT
Genesis 2:15-17; 3:1-7
Psalm 32
Romans 5:12-19
Matthew 4:1-11

March 5

ASH WEDNESDAY
Joel 2:1-2, 12-17
Psalm 51:1-17
2 Corinthians 5:20b–6:10
Matthew 6:1-6, 16-21

March 10-16

SECOND SUNDAY IN LENT
Genesis 12:1-4a
Psalm 121
Romans 4:1-5, 13-17
John 3:1-17

March 17-23

THIRD SUNDAY IN LENT
Exodus 17:1-7
Psalm 95
Romans 5:1-11
John 4:5-42

March 24-30

FOURTH SUNDAY IN LENT
1 Samuel 16:1-13
Psalm 23
Ephesians 5:8-14
John 9:1-41

March 31–April 6

FIFTH SUNDAY IN LENT
Ezekiel 37:1-14
Psalm 130
Romans 8:6-11
John 11:1-45

April 7-13

PALM SUNDAY

Liturgy of the Palms
Matthew 21:1-11
Psalm 118:1-2, 19-29

Liturgy of the Passion
Isaiah 50:4-9a
Psalm 31:9-16
Philippians 2:5-11
Matthew 26:14–27:66
    (*or* Matthew 27:11-54)

April 14-20

HOLY WEEK
Monday, April 14
Isaiah 42:1-9
Psalm 36:5-11
Hebrews 9:11-15
John 12:1-11

Tuesday, April 15
Isaiah 49:1-7
Psalm 71:1-14
1 Corinthians 1:18-31
John 12:20-36

Wednesday, April 16
Isaiah 50:4-9a
Psalm 70
Hebrews 12:1-3
John 13:21-32

Maundy Thursday, April 17
Exodus 12:1-14
Psalm 116:1-4, 12-19
1 Corinthians 11:23-26
John 13:1-17, 31b-35

Good Friday, April 18
Isaiah 52:13–53:12
Psalm 22
Hebrews 10:16-25
John 18:1–19:42

Easter Vigil, April 19
Exodus 14:10-31
Psalm 114
Isaiah 55:1-11
Romans 6:3-11
Matthew 28:1-10

Easter Day, April 20
Acts 10:34-43
Psalm 118:1-2, 14-24
Colossians 3:1-4
John 20:1-18
   (*or* Matthew 28:1-10)

April 21-27
Acts 2:14*a*, 22-32
Psalm 16
1 Peter 1:3-9
John 20:19-31

April 28–May 4
Acts 2:14*a*, 36-41
Psalm 116:1-4, 12-19
1 Peter 1:17-23
Luke 24:13-35

May 5-11
Acts 2:42-47
Psalm 23
1 Peter 2:19-25
John 10:1-10

May 12-18
Acts 7:55-60
Psalm 31:1-5, 15-16
1 Peter 2:2-10
John 14:1-14

May 19-25
Acts 17:22-31
Psalm 66:8-20
1 Peter 3:13-22
John 14:15-21

May 26–June 1
Acts 1:6-14
Psalm 68:1-10, 32-35
1 Peter 4:12-14; 5:6-11
John 17:1-11

   ASCENSION DAY–MAY 29
   (*may be used June 1*)
   Acts 1:1-11
   Psalm 47 (*or* Psalm 93)
   Ephesians 1:15-23
   Luke 24:44-53

June 2-8
PENTECOST
Psalm 104:24-34, 35*b*
Acts 2:1-21
1 Corinthians 12:3*b*-13
John 7:37–39

June 9-15
TRINITY SUNDAY
Genesis 1:1–2:4*a*
Psalm 8
2 Corinthians 13:11-13
Matthew 28:16-20

June 16-22
Genesis 21:8-21
Psalm 86:1-10, 16-17
Romans 6:1*b*-11
Matthew 10:24–39

June 23-29
Genesis 22:1-14
Psalm 13
Romans 6:12-23
Matthew 10:40-42

June 30–July 6
Genesis 24:34-38, 42-49, 58-67
Psalm 45:10-17 (*or* Psalm 72)
Romans 7:15-25*a*
Matthew 11:16-19, 25-30

July 7-13
Genesis 25:19-34
Psalm 119:105-112 (*or* Psalm 25)
Romans 8:1-11
Matthew 13:1-9, 18-23

July 14-20
Genesis 28:10-19*a*
Psalm 139:1-12, 23-24
Romans 8:12-25
Matthew 13:24-30, 36-43

July 21-27
Genesis 29:15-28
Psalm 105:1-11, 45*b*
Romans 8:26-39
Matthew 13:31-33, 44-52

July 28–August 3
Genesis 32:22-31
Psalm 17:1-7, 15
Romans 9:1-5
Matthew 14:13-21

August 4-10
Genesis 37:1-4, 12-28
Psalm 105:1-6, 16-22, 45*b*
Romans 10:5-15
Matthew 14:22-33

August 11-17
Genesis 45:1-15
Psalm 133
Romans 11:1-2*a*, 29-32
Matthew 15:10-28

August 18-24
Exodus 1:8–2:10
Psalm 124
Romans 12:1-8
Matthew 16:13-20

August 25-31
Exodus 3:1-15
Psalm 105:1-6, 23-26, 45*c*
Romans 12:9-21
Matthew 16:21-28

September 1-7
Exodus 12:1-14
Psalm 149 (*or* Psalm 148)
Romans 13:8-14
Matthew 18:15-20

September 8-14
Exodus 14:19-31
Exodus 15:1*b*-11, 20-21
Romans 14:1-12
Matthew 18:21-35

September 15-21
Exodus 16:2-15
Psalm 105:1-6, 37-45
  (*or* Psalm 78)
Philippians 1:21-30
Matthew 20:1-16

September 22-28
Exodus 17:1-7
Psalm 78:1-4, 12-16
Philippians 2:1-13
Matthew 21:23-32

September 29–October 5
Exodus 20:1-4, 7-9, 12-20
Psalm 19
Philippians 3:4*b*-14
Matthew 21:33-46

October 6-12
Exodus 32:1-14
Psalm 106:1-6, 19-23
Philippians 4:1-9
Matthew 22:1-14

October 13-19
Exodus 33:12-23
Psalm 99
1 Thessalonians 1:1-10
Matthew 22:15-22

> **October 13**
> THANKSGIVING DAY
> **Canada**
> Deuteronomy 8:7-18
> Psalm 65
> 2 Corinthians 9:6-15
> Luke 17:11-19

October 20–26
Deuteronomy 34:1-12
Psalm 90:1-6, 13-17
1 Thessalonians 2:1-8
Matthew 22:34-46

October 27–November 2
Joshua 3:7-17
Psalm 107:1-7, 33-37
1 Thessalonians 2:9-13
Matthew 23:1-12

> **November 1**
> ALL SAINTS DAY
> (*may be used November 2*)
> Revelation 7:9-17
> Psalm 34:1-10, 22
> 1 John 3:1-3
> Matthew 5:1-12

November 3–9
Joshua 24:1-3*a*, 14-25
Psalm 78:1-7
1 Thessalonians 4:13-18
Matthew 25:1-13

November 10-16
Judges 4:1-7
Psalm 123 (*or* Psalm 76)
1 Thessalonians 5:1-11
Matthew 25:14-30

November 17-23
REIGN OF CHRIST SUNDAY
Ezekiel 34:11-16, 20-24
Psalm 100
Ephesians 1:15-23
Matthew 25:31-46

November 24–30
FIRST SUNDAY OF ADVENT
Isaiah 64:1-9
Psalm 80:1-7, 17-19
1 Corinthians 1:3-9
Mark 13:24-37

> **November 27**
> THANKSGIVING DAY, USA
> Deuteronomy 8:7-18
> Psalm 65
> 2 Corinthians 9:6-15
> Luke 17:11-19

December 1-7

SECOND SUNDAY OF ADVENT
Isaiah 40:1-11
Psalm 85:1-2, 8-13
2 Peter 3:8-15*a*
Mark 1:1-8

December 8–14

THIRD SUNDAY OF ADVENT
Isaiah 61:1-4, 8-11
Psalm 126
1 Thessalonians 5:16-24
John 1:6-8, 19-28

December 15-21

FOURTH SUNDAY OF ADVENT
2 Samuel 7:1-11, 16
Luke 1:46*b*-55
Romans 16:25-27
Luke 1:26-38

December 22-28

FIRST SUNDAY AFTER
CHRISTMAS
OPTIONAL TEXTS
Isaiah 61:10–62:3
Psalm 148
Galatians 4:4-7
Luke 2:22-40

December 24
CHRISTMAS EVE
Isaiah 9:2-7
Psalm 96
Titus 2:11-14
Luke 2:1-20

December 25
CHRISTMAS DAY
Isaiah 52:7-10
Psalm 98
Hebrews 1:1-12
John 1:1-14

December 29–31
Jeremiah 31:7-14
Psalm 147:7-14
Ephesians 1:3-14
John 1:1-18

December 31
WATCH NIGHT/NEW YEAR
Ecclesiastes 3:1-13
Psalm 8
Revelation 21:1-6*a*
Matthew 25:31-46

A Guide to Daily Prayer

These prayers imply worship time with a group; feel free to adapt the plural pronouns for personal use.

"In the morning, O LORD, you hear my voice;
   in the morning I lay my requests before you
   and wait in expectation."

—Psalm 5:3

Gathering and Silence

Call to Praise and Prayer
   God said: Let there be light; and there was light.
   And God saw that the light was good.

Psalm 63:2-6
   God, my God, you I crave;
   my soul thirsts for you,
   my body aches for you
   like a dry and weary land.
      Let me gaze on you in your temple:
      a Vision of strength and glory
      Your love is better than life,
      my speech is full of praise.
      I give you a lifetime of worship,
      my hands raised in your name.
      I feast at a rich table
      my lips sing of your glory.

Prayer of Thanksgiving

We praise you with joy, loving God, for your grace is better than life itself. You have sustained us through the darkness: and you bless us with life in this new day. In the shadow of your wings we sing for joy and bless your holy name. Amen.

Scripture Reading

Silence

Prayers of the People

The Lord's Prayer (see Midday Prayer for text)

Blessing

May the light of your mercy shine brightly on all who walk in your presence today, O Lord.

MIDDAY PRAYER

"I will extol the LORD at all times;
　　God's praise will always be on my lips."
　　　　　　　　　　　　　　—Psalm 34:1

Gathering and Silence

Call to Praise and Prayer

O LORD, my Savior, teach me your ways.
　　My hope is in you all day long.

Prayer of Thanksgiving

God of mercy, we acknowledge this midday pause of refreshment as one of your many generous gifts. Look kindly upon our work this day; may it be made perfect in your time. May our purpose and prayers be pleasing to you. This we ask through Christ our Lord. Amen.

Scripture Reading

Silence

Prayers of the People

The Lord's Prayer (ecumenical text)

Our Father in heaven,
　　hallowed be your name,
　　your kingdom come,
　　your will be done,
　　on earth as in heaven.
Give us today our daily bread.
Forgive us our sins as we forgive
　　those who sin against us.

Save us from the time of trial,
   and deliver us from evil.
For the kingdom, the power, and the glory
   are yours, now and forever. Amen.

Blessing

Strong is the love embracing us, faithful the Lord from morning to night.

EVENING PRAYER

"My soul finds rest in God alone;
    my salvation comes from God."
                            —Psalm 62:1

Gathering and Silence

Call to Praise and Prayer

From the rising of the sun to its setting,
    let the name of the LORD be praised.

Psalm 134

Bless the Lord,
    all who serve in God's house,
    who stand watch
    throughout the night.

Lift up your hands
    in the holy place
    and bless the Lord.

And may God,
    the maker of earth and sky,
    bless you from Zion.

Prayer of Thanksgiving

Sovereign God, You have been our help during the day and you promise to be with us at night. Receive this prayer as a sign of our trust in you. Save us from all evil, keep us from all harm, and guide us in your way. We belong to you, Lord. Protect us by the power of your name, in Jesus Christ we pray. Amen.

Scripture Reading

Silence

Prayers of the People

The Lord's Prayer (see Midday Prayer for text)

Blessing

May your unfailing love rest upon us, O LORD,
even as we hope in you.

This Guide to Prayer was compiled from scripture and other resources by Rueben P. Job and then adapted by the Pathways Center for Spiritual Leadership while under the direction of Marjorie J. Thompson.

The Role of the Small-Group Leader

Leading a group for spiritual formation differs in many ways from teaching a class. The most obvious difference is in your basic goal as group leader. In a class, you generally want to convey particular facts or interpretations and encourage discussion of ideas. You can gauge your success at the end of a class by how well participants demonstrate some grasp of the information. In a group for spiritual formation, your goal is to enable spiritual growth in each group member. You work in partnership with the Holy Spirit, who alone brings about transformation of the heart. Here, gaining wisdom is more important than gaining knowledge, and growing in holiness is more important than either knowledge or wisdom. *Success*, if that word has any meaning in this context, will be evident over months and even years in the changed lives of group members.

Classes tend to be task-oriented in order to "cover ground." Groups for spiritual formation tend to be process-oriented. Even though group members will have done common preparation in reading and daily prayer, group reflections may move in directions you do not expect. You will need to be open to the movement of the Holy Spirit while at the same time discerning the difference between following the Spirit's lead and going off on a tangent. Such discernment requires careful, prayerful listening—a far more important skill for a small-group leader than talking.

Finally, classes tend to focus on external sources: the Bible, another book, a film, current events. In contrast, spiritual formation groups focus more on internal realities: personal faith experience in daily life and spiritual practice. Group members seek to understand and receive the graced revealing of God. When participants reflect on a scripture text, the basis for group interaction is not "What did the author intend to say to readers of that time?" but "How does this passage speak to my life or illuminate my experience?" Group reflections focus on the sharing of insights, not debate over ideas. As leader, you will model such sharing with your group. Your leadership differs substantially from that of a traditional adult class teacher. As a "participant-leader" you will read the daily meditations along with everyone else, bringing your thoughts and reflections to share with the group. You will lead by offering your honest reflections and by enabling group members to listen carefully to one another and to the Spirit in your midst.

Leading a spiritual formation group requires particular qualities. Foremost among these are patience and trust. You need patience to allow sessions to unfold as they will. Spiritual formation is a lifelong process. Identifying visible personal growth in group members over the course of the year may be difficult. It may take a while for participants to adjust to the purpose and style of formational group process. As leader, resolve to ask questions with no "right" answers in mind and to encourage group members to talk about their own experiences. Sharing your own experience rather than proclaiming abstract truths or talking about the experiences of other well-known Christians will accelerate this shift from an informational to a formational process. Trust that the Holy Spirit will indeed help group members see or hear what they really need. You may offer what you consider a great insight to which no one responds. If the group needs it, the Spirit will bring it around again at a more opportune time. Susan Muto, a modern writer on spiritual formation, often says that we need to "make space for the pace of grace." There are no shortcuts to spiritual growth. Be patient and trust the Spirit.

Listening is another critical quality for a formational group leader. This does not mean simply listening for people to say what you hope they will say so you can reinforce them. Listen for what is actually going on in participants' minds and hearts, which may differ from what you expect after reading the material yourself. While listening, jot down brief notes about themes that surface. Does sharing seem to revolve around a certain type of experience? Is a hint of direction or common understanding emerging—a clue to God's will or at least a shared sense of meaning for the group? What do you hear again and again? What action might group members take together or individually to respond to an emerging sense of call?

A group leader also needs to be accepting. Accept that group members may have spiritual perceptions quite unlike yours and that people often see common experiences in different ways. Some may be struck by an aspect that did not impress you at all, while others may be left cold by dimensions that really move you. As you model acceptance, you foster acceptance of differences within the group. Beyond this, you will need to accept lack of closure. Group meetings rarely tie up all loose ends in a neat package. Burning questions will be left hanging. You can trust the Spirit to bring resolution in time, if resolution is needed. Also be prepared to accept people's emotions along with their thoughts and experiences. Tears, fears, joy, and anger are legitimate responses during times together. One important expression of acceptance is permission-giving. Permit group members to grow and share at their own pace. Let them know in your first meeting that while you encourage full participation in every part of the process, they are free to opt out of anything that makes them feel uncomfortable. No one will be forced to share or pray without consent. "Where the Spirit of the Lord is, there is freedom" (2 Cor. 3:17).

It is important to avoid three common tendencies of small groups and their leaders:

1. *Fixing.* When someone presents a personal or theological problem, you may be tempted to find a solution or give your "priceless" advice. Problem solving generally makes

you feel better. Perhaps it makes you feel wise or helps to break the tension, but it rarely helps the other to grow. Moreover, you might prescribe the wrong "fix." If you have faced a similar problem, speak only from your own experience.

2. *Proselytizing.* You know what has brought you closer to God; naturally you would like everyone to try it. You can offer your own experience to the group, but trying to convince others to follow your path is spiritually dangerous. Here, your knowledge and wisdom come into play. Teresa of Ávila wrote that if she had to choose between a director who was spiritual and one who was learned, she would pick the learned one. The saint might be able to talk only about his or her own spiritual path. The learned one might at least recognize another person's experience from reading about it. Clarifying and celebrating someone else's experience is far more useful than urging others to follow your way.

3. *Controlling.* Many of us are accustomed to filling in silence with comment. You may be tempted to think you should have an appropriate response to whatever anyone says; that is, you may tend to dominate and control the conversation. Here again, patience and listening are essential. Do not be afraid of silence. Being comfortable with silence allows you to be a relaxed presence in the group. If you cannot bear a long silence, break it with an invitation for someone who has been quiet so far to share a thought, feeling, or question rather than with a comment of your own.